ESSENTIAL
CISA

Test Questions

Updated for the 26th
CISA Review Manual

ESSENTIAL
CISA

Test Questions

Updated for the 26th
CISA Review Manual

Phil Martin

**Nearsighted
Ninja**

Essential CISA Test Questions

ISBN: 9781720134619

About the Exam

The CISA exam is offered throughout the year, and there are no prerequisites required to take the exam. However, before the certification will be rewarded, you must have at least 5 years of experience in information system auditing, control or security. This experience must have occurred within the last 5 to 10 years.

For those not possessing the above requirements, there are several ways to fulfill the experience. For example, you may substitute 1 year of the 5 by working in information systems or in a non-IS auditing role. Another year can be filled if you have 60 hours of credit or a qualifying degree. Unfortunately, you will need at least 2 years of actual experience, possibly more.

The exam is a computer-based test exam available three times each year. It is a 4-hour exam consisting of 200 questions in multiple choice format. While ISACA does not advertise the percentage of questions you must correctly answer in order to pass, a decent estimate is between 50%-60%. This is based wholly on anecdotal evidence and may be inaccurate. But, we do know that the pass rate is around 50% - roughly half of all candidates will fail the test the first time. Successful candidates can work towards the experience requirements and apply for the certificate.

The cost for ISACA members is $575 and $760 for non-members.

An audio version of this print

book is available on audible.com!

Ordered

The first part of this book is presented in order of subject matter. The layout matches the accompanying volume *Essential CISA Exam Guide*. Questions are grouped by the chapter in which the material is encountered in the exam guide, and within each chapter, the questions are arranged in the same order as the exam guide content is presented. This should make it much easier for you to locate the subject in the exam guide book when you need a refresher. Each chapter has a Questions and an Answers section. Some answers may have additional comments to help explain why the selected answer is the correct choice.

Unfortunately, one of the side-effects of presenting material in-order is that one question can often give the answer to the next question. That is why the second part of the book is included, which presents the same questions but in a random order. Once you are comfortable with the first part of the book, move on to the second part to test your knowledge. You will more than likely be surprised at how dependent your brain has become on contextual clues from surrounding questions!

Section 1: The Process of Auditing Information Systems Domain

Chapter 1: Standards and Frameworks

Questions

1. Which process is BEST used to update an existing process to reduce costs?

    A) Balanced Scorecard

    B) Business Process Reengineering

    C) Benchmarking

    D) Root Cause Analysis

2. Which standard is BEST used to demonstrate compliance with accepted good practices?

    A) PMBOK

    B) Information Security Management Maturity Model, or ISM3

    C) ISO 20000 Series

    D) ISO 38500

3. According to ISO 25010, which attribute measures a stated level of performance over time?

    A) Efficiency

    B) Reliability

    C) Portability

    D) Functionality

4. According to ISO 25010, which attribute measures how long a product can maintain a specific level of performance under certain conditions?

    A) Portability

    B) Functionality

    C) Efficiency

    D) Reliability

5. According to ISO 25010, which attribute measures how well a product meets a set of features?

    A) Portability

    B) Functionality

    C) Reliability

    D) Efficiency

6. Which standard or process BEST allows us to develop a strategy for IT based on repeating life cycles?

    A) ISO 38500

    B) Root Cause Analysis

    C) Life Cycle Cost-Benefit Analysis

    D) PRINCE2

7. Which standard or process BEST allows us to diagnose an event to determine its origin?

    A) PRINCE2

    B) ISO 38500

    C) Root Cause Analysis

    D) Life Cycle Cost-Benefit Analysis

8. Which BEST describes an approach to creating a real-world process?

    A) Framework

    B) Standard

    C) Guideline

    D) Process

9. Which of the following is NOT a perspective used in the Balanced Scorecard?

    A) Business

    B) Process

    C) Learning

    D) Customer

10. Which framework BEST helps an organization to create clear goals and translate them into action?

    A) FEA

    B) Balanced Scorecard, or BSC

    C) Capability Maturity Model Integration, or CMMI

    D) COBIT 5

11. Which framework BEST helps an organization make improvements in an incremental and standard manner?

    A) FEA

    B) Capability Maturity Model Integration, or CMMI

    C) Balanced Scorecard, or BSC

    D) COBIT 5

12. Which framework is geared specifically to IT?

    A) Capability Maturity Model Integration, or CMMI

    B) Balanced Scorecard, or BSC

    C) COBIT 5

    D) FEA

13. Which framework is geared to governmental agencies?

    A) FEA

    B) COBIT 5

    C) Capability Maturity Model Integration, or CMMI

    D) Balanced Scorecard, or BSC

14. Which Capability Maturity Model Integration, or CMMI, layer represents a proactive approach to processes?

    A) Level 3 - Defined

    B) Level 4 – Quantitatively Managed

    C) Level 5 – Optimizing

    D) Level 2 – Managed

15. Which COBIT 5 principal defines seven enablers?

    A) Separating governance from management

    B) Enabling a holistic approach

    C) Applying a single, integrated framework

    D) Covering the enterprise end-to-end

16. What COBIT 5 process allows higher-level objectives to define what enablers should achieve?

    A) Process Assessment Model, or PAM

    B) Intrinsic Qualities

    C) Process Reference Model

    D) Goals cascade

17. What COBIT 5 approach measures how aligned data values are with the true values?

    A) Intrinsic Qualities

    B) Goals cascade

    C) Process Reference Model

    D) Process Assessment Model, or PAM

18. What COBIT 5 tool is used to capture both the current and future states?

    A) Process Assessment Model, or PAM

    B) Process Reference Model

    C) Goals cascade

    D) Intrinsic Qualities

19. Which is NOT a COBIT 5 quality subdimension?

    A) Intrinsic

    B) Security or accessibility

    C) Contextual

    D) Comprehensive

20. Which COBIT 5 intrinsic quality measures how unbiased and impartial a measurement is?

    A) Accuracy

    B) Reputation

    C) Objectivity

    D) Believability

21. Which COBIT 5 intrinsic quality measures how true and credible a value is?

    A) Accuracy

    B) Reputation

    C) Believability

    D) Objectivity

22. Which COBIT 5 intrinsic quality measures how correct or reliable a value is?

    A) Accuracy

    B) Reputation

    C) Objectivity

    D) Believability

23. Which COBIT 5 intrinsic quality measures how highly regarded the source of a value is?

    A) Accuracy

    B) Believability

    C) Reputation

    D) Objectivity

24. Which COBIT 5 contextual quality measures how applicable and helpful a value is?

    A) Interpretability

    B) Understandability

    C) Currency

    D) Relevancy

25. Which COBIT 5 contextual quality measures how easily a value is comprehended?

    A) Relevancy

    B) Currency

    C) Interpretability

    D) Understandability

26. Which COBIT 5 contextual quality measures how up-to-date a value is?

    A) Currency

    B) Understandability

    C) Relevancy

    D) Interpretability

27. Which COBIT 5 contextual quality measures how well the symbols or units for a value align?

    A) Interpretability

    B) Currency

    C) Relevancy

    D) Understandability

28. Which FEA reference model describes the information used to support all other reference models?

    A) Technical Reference Model

    B) Service Component Reference Model

    C) Business Reference Model

    D) Data Reference Model

29. Which FEA reference model describes the functions performed by the government?

    A) Business Reference Model

    B) Service Component Reference Model

    C) Data Reference Model

    D) Technical Reference Model

30. Which FEA reference model classifies services?

    A) Service Component Reference Model

    B) Technical Reference Model

    C) Business Reference Model

    D) Data Reference Model

31. Which FEA reference model describes how to build services?

    A) Service Component Reference Model

    B) Technical Reference Model

    C) Data Reference Model

    D) Business Reference Model

32. Which framework focuses on SLAs between IT and customers?

A) ISO 27000 Series

B) Risk IT Framework

C) Information Technology Infrastructure Library, or ITIL

D) The Open Group Architecture Framework, or TOGAF

33. Which framework defines the architecture development method, or ADM?

A) Risk IT Framework

B) ISO 27000 Series

C) The Open Group Architecture Framework, or TOGAF

D) Information Technology Infrastructure Library, or ITIL

34. Which framework was created by ISACA?

A) Risk IT Framework

B) ISO 27000 Series

C) The Open Group Architecture Framework, or TOGAF

D) Information Technology Infrastructure Library, or ITIL

35. Which framework is geared specifically to security?

A) Risk IT Framework

B) The Open Group Architecture Framework, or TOGAF

C) ISO 27000 Series

D) Information Technology Infrastructure Library, or ITIL

36. Which ITIL volume is responsible for creating a service?

A) Service Operations

B) Service Transition

C) Service Design

D) Service Strategy

37. Which ITIL volume aligns IT with the organization?

A) Service Transition

B) Service Operations

C) Service Design

D) Service Strategy

38. Which ITIL volume looks at stakeholder needs?

A) Service Transition

B) Service Design

C) Service Strategy

D) Service Operations

39. Which ITIL volume maintains a service?

A) Service Transition

B) Service Strategy

C) Service Design

D) Service Operations

40. Which framework improves software processes using five phases?

A) Operationally Critical Threat Asset and Vulnerability Evaluation, or OCTAVE

B) NIST SP 800-30

C) Plan-Do-Check-Act, or PDCA

D) Initiating, Diagnosing, Establishing, Acting and Learning Model, or IDEAL

41. Which framework is a well-established process to address security risk, and uses three phases?

A) NIST SP 800-30

B) Initiating, Diagnosing, Establishing, Acting and Learning Model, or IDEAL

C) Plan-Do-Check-Act, or PDCA

D) Operationally Critical Threat Asset and Vulnerability Evaluation, or OCTAVE

42. Which framework uses an agile, iterative approach to control and improve processes?

    A) NIST SP 800-30

    B) Operationally Critical Threat Asset and Vulnerability Evaluation, or OCTAVE

    C) Initiating, Diagnosing, Establishing, Acting and Learning Model, or IDEAL

    D) Plan-Do-Check-Act, or PDCA

43. Which framework provides an iterative risk assessment process that is comprised of five steps?

    A) Operationally Critical Threat Asset and Vulnerability Evaluation, or OCTAVE

    B) Initiating, Diagnosing, Establishing, Acting and Learning Model, or IDEAL

    C) Plan-Do-Check-Act, or PDCA

    D) NIST SP 800-30

44. Which of the ISO 27000 series is the one for which most businesses attain a certification?

    A) ISO 27002

    B) ISO 27003

    C) ISO 27001

    D) ISO 27004

45. Which of the ISO 27000 series provides guidance on implementing an ISMS?

    A) ISO 27001

    B) ISO 27002

    C) ISO 27003

    D) ISO 27004

46. Which ISO 27000 role provides an independent assurance to management on the effectiveness of security controls?

    A) Information security steering committee

    B) Security advisor group

    C) The auditor

    D) Information security administrator

47. Which ISO 27000 role provides physical and logical security?

    A) Information security steering committee

    B) The auditor

    C) Security advisor group

    D) Information security administrator

48. Which ISO 27000 role defines the security risk management process?

    A) Information security administrator

    B) Information security steering committee

    C) The auditor

    D) Security advisor group

49. Which ISO 27000 role drives security policies, guidelines and procedures?

    A) Information security steering committee

    B) Information security administrator

    C) The auditor

    D) Security advisor group

50. Which IT Balanced Scorecard, or IT BSC, perspective dictates how to achieve goals?

    A) Sources

    B) Measures

    C) Strategies

    D) Mission

51. Which IT Balanced Scorecard, or IT BSC, perspective defines the goals to achieve?

    A) Sources

    B) Mission

    C) Measures

    D) Strategies

52. Which TOGAF architecture domain describes the structure of management resources?

    A) Data

    B) Business

    C) Applications

    D) Technical

53. Which TOGAF architecture domain defines strategy?

    A) Data

    B) Business

    C) Applications

    D) Technical

54. Which TOGAF architecture domain provides a blueprint for systems?

    A) Applications

    B) Technical

    C) Data

    D) Business

55. Which TOGAF ADM phase creates the strategy to go from as-is to to-be?

    A) Business architecture phase

    B) Migration planning phase

    C) Opportunities and solutions phase

    D) Implementation governance phase

56. Which TOGAF ADM phase creates the roadmap?

    A) Migration planning phase

    B) Business architecture phase

    C) Opportunities and solutions phase

    D) Implementation governance phase

57. Which TOGAF ADM phase identifies the gap between as-is and to-be?

    A) Opportunities and solutions phase

    B) Business architecture phase

    C) Migration planning phase

    D) Implementation governance phase

58. Which TOGAF ADM phase checks what is being built against the original architecture?

    A) Migration planning phase

    B) Business architecture phase

    C) Implementation governance phase

    D) Opportunities and solutions phase

59. Which of the following is NOT a Zachman perspective?

    A) Business Management

    B) Architect

    C) Engineer

    D) Engineering Management

Answers

1. B	2. C
3. A	4. D
5. B	6. C
7. C	8. A
9. A	10. B
11. B	12. C
13. A	14. A
15. B	16. D
17. A	18. A
19. D	20. C
21. C	22. A
23. C	24. D
25. D	26. A
27. A	28. D
29. A	30. A
31. B	32. C
33. C	34. A
35. C	36. B
37. D	38. B
39. D	40. D
41. D	42. D
43. D	44. C
45. B	46. C
47. D	48. D
49. A	50. C
51. B	52. A
53. B	54. A
55. C	56. A
57. B	58. C
59. D	

Chapter 2: ISAAS

Questions

1. Which statement is true about the audit charter?

    A) It must be approved at the executive level

    B) It must be approved prior to the final report

    C) The audit may proceed without it being approved

    D) It must be approved at an appropriate level

2. What does ISAAS have to say about being involved in an area you are auditing?

    A) You are not allowed to audit an area in which you have been involved

    B) It is acceptable for you to remain engaged in that area as long as another member of the audit party is not involved in that area

    C) There is no conflict as long as you remain objective

    D) You must suspend work in that area during the audit

3. Which of the following statements is NOT a valid reason to not accept an engagement?

    A) It cannot be reasonably completed

    B) The scope does not allow the audit to come to a reasonable conclusion

    C) Management does not understand its obligations to provide required information

    D) A department within scope of the audit does not agree with the scope

4. Which of the following is NOT a General ISAAS standard?

    A) Ensure proper communication with management

    B) Remain independent and objective

    C) Exercise due professional care

    D) Maintain professional education and skills

5. Which is the BEST source for auditing criteria?

    A) Standards internal to the business

    B) As defined by the audit scope

    C) Well-known standards

    D) Standards a specified by ISAAS

6. What is the most important aspect of choosing a risk assessment approach?

    A) It is used consistently throughout the audit

    B) It is acceptable to all stake-holders

    C) It is based on well-known standards

    D) It reports in the same manner as other approaches used within the audit

7. Which BEST describes the term 'materiality'?

    A) How critical and sensitive the evidence is to the business

    B) If the evidence is of the same quality as system being audited

    C) How important and applicable specific evidence is to the task at-hand

    D) If the evidence can be supported by an external source

8. When using work from other experts, what is NOT true?

    A) Previous work of the expert should be examined

    B) The work should be included in the final report and not simply referenced

    C) The professional qualifications of the expert should be examined

    D) Additional test procedures may be used if the work does not provide sufficient evidence

9. According to ISAAS Reporting Standards, which of the following is NOT specified to be included in the final report?

    A) Identification of the organization

    B) Signature and date

    C) The auditor's professional qualifications

    D) Limitations in scope

10. What is NOT one of the three things an auditor should do when using an ISAAS guideline?

    A) Use it to justify a reduction of scope

    B) Use it to implement a standard

    C) If departing from a standard, justify it

    D) Use professional judgement when applying it to a specific audit

11. Which aspect of the audit charter provides both goal and scope?

    A) Responsibility

    B) Purpose

    C) Accountability

    D) Authority

12. Which aspect of the audit charter puts a limitation on what the auditor is able to carry out?

    A) Purpose

    B) Authority

    C) Accountability

    D) Responsibility

13. Which aspect of the audit charter describes how the audit will be carried out?

    A) Accountability

    B) Authority

    C) Purpose

    D) Responsibility

14. Which aspect of the audit charter determines the recipient of the final report?

    A) Authority

    B) Accountability

    C) Purpose

    D) Responsibility

15. What is NOT a follow-up activity as described by the ISAAS guidelines?

    A) Declining follow-up activities

    B) Reporting of follow-up activities

    C) Deferring follow-up activities

    D) Scheduling follow-up activities

Answers

1. D	2. A
3. D	4. A
5. C	6. A
7. C	8. B
9. C	10. A
11. B	12. B
13. D	14. B
15. A	

Chapter 3: Standards, Guidelines, Policies, Procedures, Tools and Techniques

Questions

1. Which BEST describes the relationship between a goal and a strategy?

 A) Goals and strategy are defined in parallel

 B) Strategy is the plan to reach a goal

 C) Strategy is carried out through goals

 D) A goal dictates the strategy

2. Which BEST describes an unambiguous list of steps required to accomplish a task?

 A) Procedure

 B) Standard

 C) Policy

 D) Guideline

3. Which BEST describes how to carry out a policy?

 A) Standard

 B) Guideline

 C) Procedure

 D) Strategy

4. Which BEST describes a high-level statement of what management expects?

 A) Standard

 B) Guideline

 C) Policy

 D) Procedure

5. Which BEST describes information helpful when executing procedures?

 A) Guideline

 B) Policy

 C) Strategy

 D) Standard

6. Which of the following is NOT an attribute that a good policy will exhibit?

 A) Is only a few sentences long

 B) Is part of a set that is no more than ten in number

 C) Clearly describes a strategy

 D) States only a single general mandate

7. What is NOT true about a standard?

 A) It should never change as technology changes

 B) Must not limit our technology options too much

 C) It must provide enough parameters for us to confidently state if a procedure or practice meets the requirements

 D) There are usually multiple standards for each policy

8. Which of the following are NOT something a procedure should define?

 A) Required conditions before execution

 B) What to do when the unexpected happens

 C) Recommendations on how to handle various scenarios

 D) Information displayed

Chapter 3: Standards, Guidelines, Policies, Procedures, Tools and Techniques

Answers

1. B	2. A
3. A	4. C
5. A	6. B
7. A	8. C

Chapter 4: KGI, CSF, KPI and KRI

Questions

1. Which of the following tells us if a process has achieved its goal after the fact?

    A) KPI

    B) KGI

    C) CSF

    D) KRI

2. Which of the following tells how well a process is performing relative to reaching a goal?

    A) KPI

    B) CSF

    C) KGI

    D) KRI

3. Which of the following describes something that is accompanied by a rise in risk levels?

    A) CSF

    B) KRI

    C) KGI

    D) KPI

4. Which of the following describes something that must happen if we are to reach a goal?

    A) CSF

    B) KGI

    C) KRI

    D) KPI

Answers

1. B	2. A
3. B	4. A

Chapter 5: ALE, RTO, RPO, SDO, MTO, MTD and AIW

Questions

1. Which value estimates how often within a single year we can expect a threat to occur?

    A) EF

    B) ARO

    C) ALE

    D) SLE

2. Which value estimates how much value we can expect to lose in a single year?

    A) SLE

    B) ARO

    C) ALE

    D) EF

3. Which value estimates how much we value can expect to lose during one occurrence of a threat?

    A) ARO

    B) SLE

    C) EF

    D) ALE

4. Which value estimates the percentage of an asset's value that will be destroyed during one occurrence of a threat?

    A) ALE

    B) SLE

    C) EF

    D) ARO

5. What is the formula for calculating ALE?

    A) ALE = SLE x ARO

    B) ALE = EF x ARO

    C) ALE = EF x SLE/ARO

    D) ALE = SLE/ARO

6. Which value estimates the amount of time required to getting a compromised facility back to an acceptable level of operation?

    A) MTO

    B) RTO

    C) AIW

    D) RPO

7. Which value estimates the amount of data we can stand to permanently lose in terms of time?

    A) RTO

    B) MTO

    C) RPO

    D) SDO

8. Which value defines the minimum level of capability that must be restored before normal operations can resume?

    A) MTD

    B) SDO

    C) MTO

    D) RPO

9. Which value estimates the maximum time an operation can operate in a recovery mode?

    A) AIW

    B) MTO

    C) RTO

    D) SDO

10. Which value reflects the amount of time normal operations are down before the company faces financial threats to its existence?

    A) AIW

    B) MTO

    C) RTO

    D) MTD

11. Which statement is true?

A) It is bad if RPO > RTO

B) It is bad if MTO < RTO

C) It is good if AIW < MTO

D) It is good if RTO < AIW

Answers

1. B	2. C
3. B	4. C
5. A	6. B
7. C	8. B
9. B	10. A
11. D	

Chapter 6: Risk Appetite, Tolerance and Capacity

Questions

1. Which term describes the amount of deviation form acceptable risk a business considers acceptable?

    A) Risk capacity

    B) Risk acceptance

    C) Risk tolerance

    D) Risk appetite

2. Which term describes the amount of risk a business can absorb without ceasing to exist?

    A) Risk appetite

    B) Risk acceptance

    C) Risk capacity

    D) Risk tolerance

3. Which term describes not taking action for a specific risk?

    A) Risk capacity

    B) Risk tolerance

    C) Risk acceptance

    D) Risk appetite

4. Which term describes the amount of risk a business is willing to incur?

    A) Risk appetite

    B) Risk capacity

    C) Risk acceptance

    D) Risk tolerance

5. Which statement must be true?

    A) risk appetite + risk tolerance <= risk capacity

    B) risk appetite + risk capacity >= risk tolerance

    C) risk appetite + risk capacity <= risk tolerance

    D) risk appetite + risk tolerance >= risk capacity

6. Which statement is NOT true?

    A) If there is risk associated with taking some kind of action, there is also risk associated with not taking that action.

    B) Mitigating one risk will almost always increase another risk, or perhaps even create another risk.

    C) Risk always carries a cost, whether it is controlled or not.

    D) The cost of a risk can usually be mitigated by a compensating control

Answers

1. C	2. C
3. C	4. A
5. A	6. D

Chapter 7: From Threats to Controls

Questions

1. What is the term describing the danger that a vulnerability might be exploited?

    A) Exposure

    B) Control

    C) Threat

    D) Risk

2. What is the term describing a single real-world instance of a vulnerability being exploited?

    A) Risk

    B) Threat

    C) Impact

    D) Exposure

3. What is the term describing when a vulnerability is taken advantage of by an attacker?

    A) Impact

    B) Threat

    C) Exploit

    D) Control

4. What is the term describing a weakness in a system?

    A) Vulnerability

    B) Threat

    C) Threat agent

    D) Exposure

5. What is the term describing the likelihood that a threat agent will exploit a vulnerability?

    A) Exposure

    B) Risk

    C) Threat

    D) Impact

6. What is the term describing a person or process that exploits a vulnerability?

    A) Threat

    B) Threat agent

    C) Risk

    D) Exposure

7. What is used to reduce risk?

    A) Exposure

    B) Threat Agent

    C) Risk

    D) Control

8. What does a countermeasure do?

    A) Targets a specific threat

    B) Tracks the value that a control provides

    C) Enumerates the number of times a control stops an attack

    D) Provides multiple layers of defense

9. Which is not a type of threat commonly encountered?

    A) Environmental

    B) Managerial

    C) Man-made

    D) Technical

10. Which is greatest source of man-made threats?

    A) External attackers

    B) Mistakes

    C) Employees

    D) An advanced persistent threat, or APT

11. Which is the first step in mitigating internal threats?

    A) Ensure job descriptions include security responsibilities

    B) Have employees sign an NDA

    C) Reviewing references and performing background checks

    D) Train HR personnel on secure hiring practices

12. What is a zero-day vulnerability?

A) A weakness so new that a fix is not yet available

B) A weakness that takes less than one day exploit

C) A weakness often occurring only during day-time hours

D) A weakness with so much potential damage that a fix comes out on the same day it is identified

13. What is the proper order of an APT life cycle?

A) Initial compromise, escalate privileges, establish foothold, internal reconnaissance, maintain presence, move laterally, complete the mission

B) Initial compromise, internal reconnaissance, establish foothold, escalate privileges, move laterally, maintain presence, complete the mission

C) Initial compromise, establish foothold, escalate privileges, internal reconnaissance, move laterally, maintain presence, complete the mission

D) Initial compromise, internal reconnaissance, establish foothold, move laterally, escalate privileges, maintain presence, complete the mission

14. What is NOT a typical source for APTs?

A) Intelligence agencies

B) Armed forces

C) Corporate espionage

D) Activist groups

15. What is an emerging threat?

A) A hint that something is going on based on mounting evidence

B) A threat which has struck only a handful of organizations

C) A forewarning from vendors based on anecdotal evidence from their customers

D) A threat based on new technology

16. What is a predisposing condition?

A) An existing risk which a business accepts rather than undergo mitigation

B) Risks that an insurance company will not cover

C) A scenario which may lead to rapid emergence of new vulnerabilities

D) Risks that are inherent in the industry within which a business lives

17. Which is NOT a vulnerability category?

A) Third-Party Vendors

B) Cloud computing

C) Physical access

D) Internet of Things (IoT)

18. Which is NOT something that will impact control strength?

A) If it is manual or automated

B) If it is preventative or detective

C) If it proactive or reactive

D) If it has formal or ad-hoc

19. What is the difference between a safeguard and a countermeasure?

A) A safeguard is a procedural control and a countermeasure is an administrative control

B) A safeguard is a manual control and a countermeasure is an automated control

C) A safeguard is a detective control and a countermeasure is a corrective control

D) A safeguard is a proactive control and a countermeasure is a reactive control

20. Which control category warns of attempted or successful violations of a security policy?

A) Preventative

B) Detective

C) Compensating

D) Corrective

21. Which control category provides warnings that can stop a potential compromise?

    A) Preventative

    B) Deterrent

    C) Detective

    D) Compensating

22. Which control category makes up for a weakness in another control?

    A) Deterrent

    B) Corrective

    C) Detective

    D) Compensating

23. Which control category stops attempts to violate a security policy?

    A) Deterrent

    B) Corrective

    C) Preventative

    D) Detective

24. Which control category remediates or reverses an impact after it has been felt?

    A) Detective

    B) Deterrent

    C) Corrective

    D) Preventative

25. What is NOT a term used to describe a control that oversees or reports on a process?

    A) Supportive

    B) Procedural

    C) Administrative

    D) Managerial

26. Which control method oversees or reports on a process and includes the procedures and operations of that process?

    A) Logical

    B) Physical

    C) Technical

    D) Procedural

27. Which control method always contains some type of technology?

    A) Managerial

    B) Physical

    C) Procedural

    D) Technical

28. Which control method physically restricts access to a facility or hardware?

    A) Administrative

    B) Procedural

    C) Physical

    D) Technical

29. What type of control is a policy, procedure, practice or organizational structure intentionally put in-place to reduce risk?

    A) Procedural

    B) Applicable

    C) Internal

    D) External

30. Which of the following is true?

    A) A general control will be more effective than a countermeasure

    B) A countermeasure will be more effective than a general control

    C) A countermeasure will be less effective than a general control

    D) A countermeasure will be more efficient than a general control

31. What is a valid alternative to deploying a countermeasure?

A) Adjusting the budget to offset the potential cost

B) Re-engineering a process

C) Perform an audit to justify accepting the risk

D) Increase the instances of the weak control requiring a countermeasure

32. What is the term for any unauthorized activity interfering with normal processing?

A) System exposure

B) Invalid actions

C) Technical exposure

D) Rogue activities

33. Which of the following is true?

A) Data leakage siphons information out of a computer while product leakage leaves the original copy untouched

B) Data leakage refers to information stored in a database while product leakage refers to documentation stored in other formats

C) Data leakage is restricted to internal information while product leakage includes publicly-available information

D) Data leakage occurs when digital information is stolen while product leakage occurs when marketing material is leaked

34. Which term refers to eavesdropping on telecommunications lines?

A) Wiresniffing

B) Wiretapping

C) Data inference

D) Landsniffing

Answers

1. C	2. D
3. C	4. A
5. B	6. B
7. D	8. A
9. B	10. C
11. C	12. A
13. C	14. C
15. A	16. C
17. A	18. C
19. D	20. B
21. B	22. D
23. C	24. C
25. A	26. D
27. D	28. C
29. C	30. B
31. B	32. C
33. A	34. B

Chapter 8: Risk Management

Questions

1. In general, what are the two steps for managing risk, in order?

    A) Perform a risk assessment, and then calculate the potential impact

    B) Establish purpose, and then assign responsibility

    C) Identify goals and then perform a risk assessment

    D) Identify goals, and then identify all assets and systems

2. What are three valid approaches to risk management?

    A) OCTAVE, NIST SP 800-30 and Zachman Framework

    B) Risk IT framework, NIST SP 800-30 and COBIT 5's Risk Management Process

    C) PDCA, CMMI and COBIT 5's Risk Management Process

    D) FEA, Risk IT framework and NIST SP 800-30

3. What are the five steps of ISACA's Risk IT framework, in order?

    A) Identify goals, identify assets, assess risk, mitigate risks, treat risk

    B) Identify assets, identify goals assess risk, mitigate risks, treat risk

    C) Identify goals, identify assets, assess risk, treat risk, mitigate risks

    D) Identify goals, assess risk, identify assets, mitigate risks, treat risk

4. What is residual risk?

    A) Risk that cannot be mitigated because of the business' goals

    B) Risk residing after controls have been removed due to being too costly

    C) Risk left over after all controls have been applied

    D) Risk inherent to the business' industry

5. Which of the following best represents the five steps, in order, for NIST SP 800-30?

    A) Identify threats, identify vulnerabilities, determine likelihood, determine impact, determine risk

    B) Identify threats, identify vulnerabilities, determine impact, determine likelihood, determine risk

    C) Identify vulnerabilities, identify threats, determine impact, determine likelihood, determine risk

    D) Identify vulnerabilities, identify threats, determine likelihood, determine impact, determine risk

6. Which of the following best represents the five steps, in order, for COBIT 5's Risk Management Process?

    A) Evaluation of threats, asset identification, calculation of risk, evaluation of impact, evaluation of risk and response

    B) Asset identification, evaluation of threats, evaluation of impact, calculation of risk, evaluation of risk and response

    C) Asset identification, evaluation of threats, calculation of risk, evaluation of impact, evaluation of risk and response

    D) Evaluation of threats, asset identification, evaluation of impact, calculation of risk, evaluation of risk and response

7. When accepting final residual risk, COBIT 5's Risk Management Process does NOT include which item?

    A) The approach that peer company's take

    B) Risk appetite

    C) Organizational policy

    D) Risk identification and measurement

8. At what three levels does IT risk management operate?

    A) Operational, project and strategic

    B) Operational, technical and management

    C) Strategic, technical and procedural

    D) Technical, management and procedural

9. What IT risk management level are we operating at when considering how well IT capabilities are aligned with the business strategy?

    A) Project

    B) Procedural

    C) Strategic

    D) Operational

10. What IT risk management level are we operating at when considering how IT capabilities compare to our competitors and threats posed by technological changes?

    A) Operational

    B) Procedural

    C) Project

    D) Strategic

11. What IT risk management level are we operating at when considering how risk can result in the loss of availability?

    A) Strategic

    B) Procedural

    C) Project

    D) Operational

12. What IT risk management level are we operating at when considering if we are complying with laws and regulations?

    A) Operational

    B) Project

    C) Procedural

    D) Strategic

13. What IT risk management level are we operating at when considering if efforts are too complex and measuring the likelihood of not reaching goals?

    A) Project

    B) Procedural

    C) Strategic

    D) Operational

14. Which approach to risk analysis is BEST used when we want a simple categorical approach using no calculations?

    A) Semi-qualitative

    B) Quantitative

    C) Qualitative

    D) Semi-quantitative

15. Which approach to risk analysis is BEST used when we need to interject some objectivity without requiring accuracy?

    A) Quantitative

    B) Qualitative

    C) Semi-quantitative

    D) Semi-qualitative

16. Which approach to risk analysis is BEST used when accuracy is a requirement?

    A) Semi-quantitative

    B) Qualitative

    C) Semi-qualitative

    D) Quantitative

17. When carrying out a risk analysis using a qualitative or semi-quantitative method, what are represented by the X and Y axis?

    A) Impact and Likelihood

    B) Business value and Likelihood

    C) Business value and criticality

    D) Impact and criticality

18. What are the five possible options when responding to risk?

    A) Accept, mitigate, avoid, shift, ignore

    B) Accept, diminish, avoid, transfer, disregard

    C) Accept, mitigate, avoid, transfer, ignore

    D) Accept, diminish, avoid, shift, disregard

19. Which statement is true when transferring risk?

    A) We can only transfer all risk if contracts include a right-to-audit clause

    B) We can only transfer financial responsibility

    C) Transferring risk is seldom the correct choice

    D) Transferring risk only applies to technological solutions

20. A risk assessment includes which following actions?

    A) Identification, Analysis, Evaluation

    B) Identification, Analysis, Management

    C) Analysis, Evaluation, Treatment

    D) Analysis, Evaluation, Mitigation

21. What term BEST describes the crime of using dishonest methods to take something valuable from a person or organization?

    A) Acquisition

    B) Fraud

    C) Embezzlement

    D) Theft

22. What are the three key elements in fraud?

    A) Motivation, rationalization and opportunity

    B) Reason, rationalization and opening

    C) Motivation, means and opportunity

    D) Motivation, means and opening

Answers

1. B	2. B
3. A	4. C
5. A	6. B
7. A	8. A
9. C	10. D
11. D	12. A
13. A	14. C
15. C	16. D
17. A	18. C
19. B	20. A
21. B	22. A

Chapter 9: Sampling

Questions

1. What is the BEST reason an auditor should use sampling?

    A) Many laws and regulations require this approach

    B) Sampling provides the best balance between accuracy and precision

    C) There is not enough time to look at every transaction or data point

    D) A sampling approach requires fewer authorizations

2. What term represents how close to the true value a measurement is?

    A) Precision

    B) Sample

    C) Population

    D) Accuracy

3. What term represents how many times in 100 a subset of data points represents the entire set?

    A) Confidence level

    B) Population

    C) Sample

    D) Precision

4. What term represents a subset of the entire set of data points?

    A) Confidence level

    B) Sample

    C) Precision

    D) Population

5. What term represents the entire set of data points?

    A) Population

    B) Precision

    C) Sample

    D) Accuracy

6. What term represents how close two measurements are to each other?

    A) Population

    B) Accuracy

    C) Precision

    D) Confidence level

7. When working with sampling, which one of the following statements is true?

    A) The more confident we want to be in the result, the more we will need to decrease the sample size

    B) The less confident we need to be in the result, the larger the sample size can get

    C) If the value of all data points is relatively close, then we can expect less precision, and the larger the sample size will need to be

    D) The more variable the data is, the less precision we can expect, and we therefore need to increase the sample size to get a good result

8. When working with sampling, which one of the following statements is true?

    A) The more confident we want to be in the result, the more we will need to increase the sample size

    B) The less confident we need to be in the result, the larger the sample size can get

    C) The more variable the data is, the more precision we can expect, and we therefore need to decrease the sample size to get a good result

    D) If the value of all data points is relatively close, then we can expect less precision, and the larger the sample size will need to be

9. When working with sampling, which one of the following statements is true?

A) The more confident we want to be in the result, the more we will need to decrease the sample size

B) The less confident we need to be in the result, the larger the sample size can get

C) The more variable the data is, the more precision we can expect, and we therefore need to decrease the sample size to get a good result

D) If the value of all data points is relatively close, then we can expect more precision, and the smaller the sample size will need to be

10. When working with sampling, which one of the following statements is true?

A) The more confident we want to be in the result, the more we will need to decrease the sample size

B) The less confident we need to be in the result, the smaller the sample size can get

C) If the value of all data points is relatively close, then we can expect less precision, and the larger the sample size will need to be

D) The more variable the data is, the more precision we can expect, and we therefore need to decrease the sample size to get a good result

11. When dealing with sampling, which term BEST describes how accurate the final answer is, or the chance that the answer is wrong?

A) Sample mean

B) Expected error rate

C) Level of risk

D) Tolerable error rate

12. When dealing with sampling, which term BEST describes is the percentage of samples that may be in error?

A) Sample mean

B) Level of risk

C) Tolerable error rate

D) Expected error rate

13. When dealing with sampling, which term BEST describes the average value of all samples?

A) Sample mean

B) Level of risk

C) Expected error rate

D) Tolerable error rate

14. When dealing with sampling, which term BEST describes the maximum percentage of errors our sample is allowed to have before we call it a mis-fire and do it over?

A) Sample mean

B) Expected error rate

C) Tolerable error rate

D) Level of risk

15. When dealing with sampling, which term BEST describes how far off from the average our sample set is?

A) Population standard deviation

B) Unstratified mean per unit

C) Sample standard deviation

D) Stratified mean per unit

16. When dealing with sampling, which term BEST describes the standard deviation of the entire data set?

A) Population standard deviation

B) Sample standard deviation

C) Unstratified mean per unit

D) Stratified mean per unit

17. When dealing with sampling, which term BEST describes measuring the percentage of data points in a population having a specific value?

A) Proportional sampling

B) Attribute sampling

C) Discovery sampling

D) Variable sampling

18. When dealing with sampling, which term BEST describes looking at certain attributes that match some type of criteria?

    A) Attribute sampling

    B) Discovery sampling

    C) Stop-or-go sampling

    D) Proportional sampling

19. When dealing with sampling, which term BEST describes how to prevent over-sampling?

    A) Proportional sampling

    B) Stop-or-go sampling

    C) Attribute sampling

    D) Variable sampling

20. When dealing with sampling, which term BEST describes the approach commonly used when looking for fraud or irregularities?

    A) Proportional sampling

    B) Stop-or-go sampling

    C) Attribute sampling

    D) Discovery sampling

21. When dealing with sampling, which term BEST describes looking at the total value of each data point, such as the monetary value of invoices?

    A) Stop-or-go sampling

    B) Variable sampling

    C) Proportional sampling

    D) Discovery sampling

22. When dealing with sampling, which term BEST describes a model that divides the entire population into smaller groups, and then draws samples from each group?

    A) Difference estimation

    B) Sample standard deviation

    C) Stratified mean per unit

    D) Unstratified mean per unit

23. When dealing with sampling, which term BEST describes selecting a sample set from the entire data set without dividing it into like groups?

    A) Sample standard deviation

    B) Difference estimation

    C) Unstratified mean per unit

    D) Stratified mean per unit

24. When dealing with sampling, which term BEST describes the model that estimates the variance between audited data points and what the 'books' claim?

    A) Stratified mean per unit

    B) Sample standard deviation

    C) Unstratified mean per unit

    D) Difference estimation

25. Which of the following statements is NOT true?

    A) Non-statistical sampling does not use precision to identify the sample size

    B) Non-statistical sampling does not use confidence levels to identify the sample size

    C) Non-statistical sampling decreases the likelihood that the auditor will misinterpret population data

    D) Non-statistical sampling allows the auditor to select the sampling method, the sample size and how to select the samples

Answers

1. C	2. D
3. A	4. B
5. A	6. C
7. D	8. A
9. D	10. B
11. C	12. D
13. A	14. C
15. C	16. A
17. B	18. D
19. B	20. D
21. B	22. C
23. C	24. D
25. C	

Chapter 10: IS Auditor Duties for The Process of Auditing Information System Domain

Questions

1. Which activity is NOT part of an audit?

A) Make sure that IS systems are purchased from the most cost-efficient source

B) Make sure that IS data have appropriate levels of CIA

C) Make sure that information systems follow applicable laws, regulations, contracts and industry guidelines

D) Make sure that IS operations are efficient and that targets are being reached

2. Which is the BEST method to avoid a conflict of interest within an audit?

A) Ensure that final reports are delivered to all management levels, not just the top

B) Have the members of the audit report directly to the highest level of management

C) Never use internal IT as sources of evidence

D) Use an external party to review all relevant documentation

3. What BEST describes the purpose of an audit engagement letter?

A) Provides authorization to carry out an audit

B) Lists all relevant parties to take part in an audit

C) Documents the timeline and deliverables for the audit

D) Describes a focused exercise intended for a very specific purpose and can track change requests

4. What BEST describes an audit charter?

A) Provides authorization to carry out an audit

B) A document explaining the scope, purpose and authority of an audit

C) Lists all relevant parties to take part in an audit

D) Describes a focused exercise intended for a very specific purpose and can track change requests

5. If an audit is carried out by an external party, what BEST describes what is documented in a statement of work, or SOW?

A) What is not included

B) The scope and goals

C) Escalation paths

D) Limitations of liability

6. Which statement is true regarding short-term and long-term plans?

A) Long-term goals should be revisited at least every two years

B) Long-term goals address strategic changes in the business' IT environment

C) Short-term plans cover audit goals to be covered within the next two years

D) The business should decide on a short-term or a long-term approach, but having both will simply confuse the situation

7. When approaching an audit, what BEST describes what the auditor should do first?

A) Meet with stakeholders to determine risk priorities

B) Review prior work papers

C) Identify the org structure and processes, standards, procedures and guidelines

D) Get a firm grasp on the business' mission, goals and processes

8. After carrying out a risk analysis, what is the next step an auditor should take?

    A) Set the scope and goals

    B) Create the audit strategy

    C) Assign people resources

    D) Make sure logistic issues are settled

9. When dealing with a business in a heavily-regulated industry, what are the two audit areas most affected by regulations?

    A) Legal requirements placed on the audit and the business being audited

    B) Legal requirements placed on the audit and financial IT systems being audited

    C) Legal requirements placed on the auditor's credentials and the business being audited

    D) Legal requirements placed on the auditor's credentials and financial IT systems being audited

10. Which federal law requires publicly-traded companies to use a recognized internal control framework?

    A) SOX

    B) HIPAA

    C) Basel Accords

    D) GDPR

11. Which federal law sets the minimum amount of capital for financial organizations based on the level of risk each face?

    A) Basel Accords

    B) SOX

    C) HIPAA

    D) GDPR

12. Which internal control framework is most often used by publicly-traded companies?

    A) ISO 27001

    B) COBIT 5's Risk Management Framework

    C) COSO's Internal Control – Integrated Framework

    D) RISK IT framework

13. Which of the following is NOT included with ISACA's Code of Professional Ethics?

    A) Perform duties in accordance with professional standards

    B) Escalate illegal financial practices to law enforcement officials if an organization is unwilling to correct the situation

    C) Maintain confidentiality of information obtained in the course of your activities

    D) Maintain competency and undertake only those activities which your skillset supports

14. Which BEST describes the actions to be taken if a CISA-certified auditor does not follow ISACA's Code of Professional Ethics?

    A) A formal statement may be issued requesting that organizations no longer work with the auditor

    B) A panel of peer CISA holders may be convened to assess the situation and recommend disciplinary actions

    C) The CISA certification may be revoked

    D) An investigation may be launched into the certification holder's conduct and potentially disciplinary measures

15. What is one thing that ITAF does NOT provide?

    A) Provides guidance, as well as tools and techniques

    B) Defines procedures and process

    C) Establishes standards

    D) Defines terms and concepts

16. Which BEST describes the difference between compliance and substantive testing?

A) Compliance testing proves controls are compliant, while substantive testing proves that controls can provide CIA

B) Compliance testing proves our controls match corresponding procedures, while substantive testing ensures the controls fulfill everything within the procedure

C) Compliance testing proves we have controls to carry out procedures, while substantive testing proves that those controls are working

D) Compliance testing proves we can monitor controls, while substantive testing proves we can test controls

17. Which type of audit assesses how well internal controls meet regulatory or industry requirements?

A) Compliance

B) Integrated

C) Administrative

D) Forensic

18. Which type of audit assesses the accuracy of fiscal reporting?

A) Financial

B) Compliance

C) Operational

D) Specialized

19. Which type of audit looks at how multiple controls logically function together?

A) Administrative

B) Forensic

C) Operational

D) Integrated

20. Which type of audit is a combination of both financial and operational audits?

A) Integrated

B) Operational

C) Forensic

D) Compliance

21. Which type of audit looks at how efficiently an organization carries out its primary mission?

A) Specialized

B) Administrative

C) Financial

D) Forensic

22. Which type of audit examines controls and how well they deliver CIA?

A) Financial

B) Specialized

C) Compliance

D) IS

23. Which type of audit is targeted for outsourced services?

A) Specialized

B) Administrative

C) Forensic

D) Financial

24. Which type of audit focused on the discovery, disclosure and subsequent follow-up of fraud and crimes?

A) Compliance

B) Forensic

C) IS

D) Specialized

25. Before choosing an audit methodology, what must first be completed?

A) Preaudit Planning

B) Identification of third-party contributors

C) A signed SOW

D) The definition of scope and goals

26. What BEST describes the purpose of work papers?

A) To provide authorization for the audit to proceed

B) To document progress as the audit is carried out

C) To provide a clean bridge between the audit goals and the final report

D) To document work falling outside the scope of an audit

27. What BEST describes a risk-based audit?

A) A process to reduce most risk by carrying out mitigation activities up-front

B) A type of audit in which the largest sources of risk is transferred to third-parties

C) An audit designed to identify risk caused by external sources only

D) A process to examine risk and existing controls

28. Which statement is true regarding materiality?

A) As materiality increases, the impact increases

B) Materiality is a measure of the level of risk associated with a specific control

C) Material error can often be a simple oversight

D) A material error does not fundamentally change how something is seen

29. What type of risk deals with material errors going unnoticed by the auditor?

A) Control risk

B) Detection risk

C) Audit risk

D) Inherent risk

30. What type of risk reflects material errors not being caught in time by one or more controls?

A) Control risk

B) Detection risk

C) Inherent risk

D) Audit risk

31. What reflects the risk that information used or generated by an audit will contain material error that goes unnoticed?

A) Inherent risk

B) Detection risk

C) Control risk

D) Audit risk

32. What type of risk reflects the baseline risk if no controls were in place?

A) Audit risk

B) Detection risk

C) Control risk

D) Inherent risk

33. What BEST describes overall audit risk?

A) Audit risk = control risk + detection risk - inherent risk

B) Audit risk = detection risk + inherent risk - control risk

C) Audit risk = inherent risk + control risk - detection risk

D) Audit risk = inherent risk + control risk + detection risk

34. What is the BEST way to measure risk before you encounter it?

A) Refer to previous audit findings

B) Interview all stakeholders to gauge the amount of assumed risk

C) Consult audit findings for peer businesses in the same industry

D) Take a sample of the business environment, determine risk and extrapolate

35. What is the BEST description of how to decide to treat risk or not?

A) Based on a financial evaluation of the costs to mitigate a specific risk

B) Based on how much risk a business is willing to accept without mitigation

C) The level of risk that applicable laws and regulations allow

D) Based on the effectiveness of compensating controls

36. Which represents an invalid approach to choosing a control?

A) Create one of our own design

B) Select one after work has been done to minimize risk

C) Select one from professional standards

D) Select one from industry standards

37. When can we be sure that all risk has been mitigated in a specific area?

A) When a post-audit analysis shows no remaining risk

B) Never, because it is impossible to prove all risk has been removed

C) Never – residual risk will always remain

D) Only after countermeasures have been put into place

38. Which is NOT a valid reason to perform a risk analysis?

A) To help determine audit goals

B) To mitigate selected risks

C) To evaluate the effectiveness of various controls

D) To identify areas that need attention

39. Which group BEST describes those responsible should fraud occur?

A) Management

B) Top-level executives

C) The IT department

D) The legal department

40. When considering evidence, which of the following would NOT increase the reliability?

A) Information from sources outside of the organization

B) Information previously approved by management

C) Information collected recently

D) Quantitative information instead of qualitative information

41. Which term BEST describes evidence that is both valid and relevant?

A) Fit

B) Sufficient

C) Ample

D) Competent

42. Which term BEST describes evidence for which there is an appropriate quantity?

A) Sufficient

B) Ample

C) Competent

D) Fit

43. You are auditing a financial business which has a significant risk of one person holding too much power. What audit technique is BEST suited?

A) Reviewing IS Policies and Procedures

B) Reviewing IS Documentation

C) Reviewing IS Standards

D) Review of IS Organization Structures

44. You are auditing and want to make sure that employees are executing their duties in the right manner. What audit technique is BEST suited?

    A) Reviewing IS Standards

    B) Reviewing IS Policies and Procedures

    C) Reviewing IS Documentation

    D) Review of IS Organization Structures

45. You are auditing a business and need to ensure information systems are well-documented. What audit technique is BEST suited?

    A) Reviewing IS Policies and Procedures

    B) Reviewing IS Documentation

    C) Interviewing Appropriate Personnel

    D) Observing Processes and Employee Performance

46. You are auditing a business and need to verify that a process previously audited is still valid. What audit technique is BEST suited?

    A) Reperformance

    B) Interviewing Appropriate Personnel

    C) Reviewing IS Documentation

    D) Walk-Throughs

47. You are auditing a business that will require you to run examine a process with a subject matter expert. What audit technique is BEST suited?

    A) Observing Processes and Employee Performance

    B) Reperformance

    C) Interviewing Appropriate Personnel

    D) Walk-Through

48. Which of the following subjects is an auditor NOT expected to understand when auditing information systems?

    A) Object orientation

    B) Database specifications

    C) File-layouts

    D) Various encryption algorithms

49. Which one of the following advantages is NOT associated with observing people in performance of their duties?

    A) Verifying that a person is actually carrying out their assigned duties

    B) Verifying the individual understands and follows the correct policies and procedures

    C) Ensure activities correspond with documented access rights

    D) Ensure their job descriptions align with business goals

50. When an auditor walks through each process to assess compliance and note any deviations, which control type benefits the most?

    A) Physical

    B) Technical

    C) Administrative

    D) Procedural

51. Which of the following is NOT a valid disadvantage of using the services of other auditors and experts?

    A) Regulatory and legal requirements may prohibit this activity

    B) The business is now dependent on the objectivity of the other auditors and experts

    C) The risk to the audit and potential liability may increase

    D) The final report may be leaked to competitors

52. What is a common function NOT supported by GAS?

    A) Statistical functions

    B) File reorganization

    C) Parallel processing

    D) Data selection

53. Which of the following statements is NOT true concerning CAAT?

> A) It is an audit tool geared specifically to pull electronic data from information systems
>
> B) Most CAATs do not allow downloading a copy of production data
>
> C) GAS is one category of CAAT
>
> D) It allows an auditor to act without the help of the subject

54. A control matrix is used to do identify what?

> A) The area containing the greatest number of controls
>
> B) Compensating controls
>
> C) A weak level of controls
>
> D) Strong controls

55. What is one thing not required during an exit interview?

> A) Assign individuals to close control gaps
>
> B) Ensure recommendations are realistic and cost-effective, or be prepared to negotiate
>
> C) Recommend implementation dates
>
> D) Ensure that the facts presented are accurate

56. You are presenting the audit findings with lower levels of management, who ask you to help with implementing the recommended control enhancements. What is the BEST course of action for you to take?

> A) Agree to help once upper management has accepted the findings
>
> B) Decline the offer, as being able to execute an audit does not qualify a person to implement the findings
>
> C) Decline the offer since it would call into question your objectivity
>
> D) Agree to help on the condition that upper management approves.

57. Which statement is NOT true regarding the final report of an audit?

> A) No findings should be communicated ahead of the report.
>
> B) The report should begin with an introduction listing goals, limitations to scope, and a description of the methodology used
>
> C) The report should be balanced in its findings with both negative and positive issues
>
> D) Findings should be included in separate sections of the report grouped by materiality or the intended audience

58. It has been 6 months since you delivered a final audit report for a customer, and partner of that customer has asked for a copy of the report to validate compliance. What is the BEST course of action?

> A) Get approval from the customer's senior management before providing a copy
>
> B) Agree to provide a high-level summary of the findings, but refer them to the company if they wish further details
>
> C) Provide a copy if you prefer, because as the auditor you own all rights to the information
>
> D) Decline to provide a copy and refer them to the customer

59. Which of the following is NOT a requirement for work papers?

> A) Each page must be initialed
>
> B) Each page must be individually referenced in a topical addendum
>
> C) They must be self-contained
>
> D) Each page must be dated

60. You have completed an audit and need to make sure that the findings are acted upon. What is the BEST way to do this?

A) Ensure a follow-up program is in-place by the end of the audit

B) Personally contact senior management after an applicable period and ask to see proof of follow-up

C) It is not your responsibility as an auditor to be concerned if the company does not follow up on the findings

D) Ensure the IS manager will follow-up after a specified period of time

61. What is NOT a benefit of performing a control self-assessment?

A) It forces the business to review business goals

B) It requires the IS department to review access control documentation

C) It ensures employees are aware of business risk

D) It encourages employees to take a personal interest in performing periodic reviews of controls

62. You are the sole auditor and find that the audit scope is too wide for a single person to accomplish in the given time period. Which of the following is the BEST way to overcome this risk without reducing the scope?

A) Keep detailed progress records, and when the allocated time is reached use the documentation to negotiate for additional time

B) Use a control self-assessment

C) Require management increase risk acceptance

D) Outsource the work to third-party contractors

63. What is the best way to measure success of a CSA?

A) Establish CSFs by holding a meeting with management to establish a primary goal of determining the reliability of internal controls

B) Create a baseline before the process and one after, and measure success using

C) Have stakeholders rate the success based on objective criteria

D) Once the process is complete, ask all participants to complete a self-assessment

64. Which of the following is NOT an advantage of CSA?

A) It detects risk earlier

B) It creates employees who more ware of business goals

C) It provides controls that more IT-focused

D) It develops more effective controls

65. Which of the following is NOT a disadvantage of CSA?

A) If successful, the company might mistake CSA for a real audit

B) If the company does not act on employee suggestions morale will suffer

C) It can provide a false security of remaining in compliance

D) The overhead of CSA can become just another item to get done

66. Which of the following statements is TRUE regarding the auditor's role in CSA?

A) The auditor should take full advantage of software that will move the process along faster

B) The auditor should not see themselves as simply a facilitator, but should remain in complete control of the entire process

C) CSA can decrease the auditor's role and value to a company

D) The auditor should avoid group decisions

67. Which statement BEST defines integrated auditing?

A) It combines IT, end user and management feedback to provide a holistic view of all auditing functions

B) It combines both manual and automated processing to capture evidence used for subsequent assessments

C) It combines IT, accounting and HR oversight to collect the right level of evidence for adequate auditing

D) It combines operational, financial and information system audit disciplines to assess overall internal controls

68. Which is NOT a benefit to integrated auditing?

A) Increases staff development and retention

B) Both manual and automated processes are combined

C) Employees better understand audit goals because they see how various aspects are linked together

D) A single audit provides an overview of all risk an organization faces

69. Which statement BEST defines continuous auditing?

A) Repeated auditing with a short time lapse between collection of evidence and reporting

B) Non-stop collection of evidence with short time-lapses between reports

C) Short time-lapses between evidence collection with continuous reporting based on automated triggers

D) Non-stop collection of evidence and continuous reporting with no lapses

70. Which of the following is NOT a primary driver for continuous auditing?

A) The use of software to ensure financial controls are working

B) Prevention of fraud scandals

C) Real-time financial monitoring

D) Detection of segregation of duties controls

71. What is the most common cost associated with continuous auditing?

A) Storage space requirements increase

B) Increased personnel are required to maintain the systems

C) Reporting levels go up

D) Additional hardware is required

72. What is the BEST contrast between continuous monitoring and continuous auditing?

A) Continuous monitoring an IT function, while continuous auditing is an accounting function

B) Continuous monitoring requires significant hooks to be placed into software, while continuous auditing does not directly deal with software

C) Continuous monitoring is carried out by automated IT processes, while continuous auditing requires a human to make decisions

D) Continuous monitoring creates alerts, while continuous auditing reacts to alerts

73. Which statement BEST describes continuous assurance?

A) When both continuous monitoring and continuous auditing are taking place

B) When management of the continuous monitoring and continuous auditing processes are under the same group

C) When the continuous monitoring process automatically feeds into the continuous auditing process

D) When either continuous monitoring or continuous auditing is taking place

74. Which of the following items is NOT required for continuous auditing to succeed?

A) Cost-effective controls

B) Alarms that trigger on control failures

C) A high degree of automation

D) Technically proficient auditors

75. Which term identifies the automated evaluation technique that tags transactions with a unique identifier?

    A) Integrated test facility

    B) Audit hook

    C) Snapshot

    D) SCARF/EAM

76. Which term identifies the automated evaluation technique that raises red flags when an error or irregularity is encountered?

    A) SCARF/EAM

    B) Snapshot

    C) Continuous and intermittent simulation

    D) Audit hook

77. Which term identifies the automated evaluation technique that allows a system to process real and test data simultaneously?

    A) Continuous and intermittent simulation

    B) SCARF/EAM

    C) Integrated test facility

    D) Audit hook

78. Which term identifies the automated evaluation technique that simulates the execution of each transaction?

    A) Snapshot

    B) Audit hook

    C) Continuous and intermittent simulation

    D) SCARF/EAM

79. Which term identifies the automated evaluation technique that embeds specially written audit modules into an application?

    A) Snapshot

    B) SCARF/EAM

    C) Integrated test facility

    D) Continuous and intermittent simulation

80. You are carrying out an audit in which there are too many transactions to look at. What is the BEST automated evaluation technique to use?

    A) Integrated test facility

    B) Audit Hook

    C) Continuous and intermittent simulation

    D) Snapshot

81. You are carrying out an audit in which there is a very comprehensive audit trail. What is the BEST automated evaluation technique to use?

    A) Continuous and intermittent simulation

    B) Audit Hook

    C) Snapshot

    D) Integrated test facility

82. You are carrying out an audit in which only transactions meeting certain criteria should be examined. What is the BEST automated evaluation technique to use?

    A) Continuous and intermittent simulation

    B) Audit Hook

    C) Integrated test facility

    D) Snapshot

83. You are carrying out an audit where regular processing cannot be interrupted. What is the BEST automated evaluation technique to use?

    A) Continuous and intermittent simulation

    B) Audit Hook

    C) SCARF/EM

    D) Snapshot

Answers

1. A	2. B
3. D	4. B
5. B	6. B
7. D	8. A
9. A	10. A
11. A	12. C
13. B	14. D
15. B	16. C
17. A	18. A
19. C	20. A
21. B	22. D
23. A	24. B
25. D	26. C
27. D	28. A
29. B	30. A
31. D	32. D
33. D	34. D
35. B	36. B
37. C	38. B
39. A	40. B
41. D	42. A
43. D	44. B
45. B	46. A
47. D	48. D
49. D	50. A
51. D	52. B
53. B	54. C
55. A	56. C
57. A	58. A
59. B	60. A
61. B	62. B
63. A	64. C
65. C	66. A
67. D	68. B
69. A	70. D
71. C	72. C
73. A	74. A
75. C	76. D
77. C	78. C
79. B	80. B
81. C	82. A
83. C	

Section 2: The Governance and Management of IT Domain

Chapter 11: Security Concepts
Questions

1. What term describes the prevention of unauthorized disclosure of information?

    A) Authentication

    B) Confidentiality

    C) Availability

    D) Integrity

2. What term describes the ability to protect information from improper modification?

    A) Nonrepudiation

    B) Confidentiality

    C) Integrity

    D) Authentication

3. What term describes how accessible an IT system or process is to its end users?

    A) Integrity

    B) Authentication

    C) Availability

    D) Nonrepudiation

4. What term describes proving who we claim we are?

    A) Authentication

    B) Integrity

    C) Confidentiality

    D) Nonrepudiation

5. What term describes the inability to deny having sent a message?

    A) Availability

    B) Confidentiality

    C) Authentication

    D) Nonrepudiation

6. Which BEST describes compliance?

    A) Filing the proper paperwork and credentials to ensure licenses are properly managed

    B) Measuring policies, procedures and controls to ensure they are being enacted and effective

    C) Monitoring and enforcing employee behavior such that it aligns with business goals

    D) Ensuring that applicable industrial standards are adhered to

7. What security principle segments resources so that access can be increased as-needed?

    A) Segregation of duties

    B) Access control

    C) Principle of least privilege

    D) Need-to-know

8. What security principle requires a person to have a valid need to access resources?

    A) Principle of least privilege

    B) Segregation of duties

    C) Access control

    D) Need-to-know

9. What security principle prevents a single resource from having too much power?

    A) Principle of least privilege

    B) Access control

    C) Need-to-know

    D) Segregation of duties

10. What security principle is the act of controlling access to a resource based on their identity?

    A) Segregation of duties

    B) Access control

    C) Principle of least privilege

    D) Need-to-know

11. What type of segregation of duty control restricts the ability of users to enter data along specific paths?

        A) Principle of least privilege

        B) Access to data

        C) Custody of assets

        D) Transaction authorization

12. What type of segregation of duty control identifies owners?

        A) Access to data

        B) Principle of least privilege

        C) Custody of assets

        D) Transaction authorization

13. What type of segregation of duty control can be implemented using physical, system and application controls?

        A) Access to data

        B) Transaction authorization

        C) Custody of assets

        D) Principle of least privilege

14. Which is normally implemented as file logging?

        A) Reconciliation

        B) Transaction logs

        C) Exception reporting

        D) Audit trail

15. Which contains a series of entries generated by one or more process and is focused on system activities?

        A) Reconciliation

        B) Transaction logs

        C) Exception reporting

        D) Audit trail

16. What describes the act of totaling the results of activities in multiple ways?

        A) Audit trail

        B) Exception reporting

        C) Reconciliation

        D) Transaction logs

17. What occurs when we properly handle problems encountered with normal routines?

        A) Audit trail

        B) Exception reporting

        C) Transaction logs

        D) Reconciliation

18. What describes an activity in which a user or system activity is watched, either directly or remotely?

        A) Audit trail

        B) Independent review

        C) Exception reporting

        D) Supervisory review

19. What is executed when we detect mistakes or intentional failures in following procedures?

        A) Audit trail

        B) Supervisory review

        C) Independent review

        D) Exception reporting

20. What BEST describes a compensating control?

        A) A control that accommodates the lack of efficiency in other controls

        B) A control that accommodates the lack of effectiveness in other controls

        C) A control that is applied when another control is too costly

        D) A control that makes up for weaknesses in one or more other controls

21. What term describes the impact that the loss of an asset will have?

      A) Privacy

      B) Criticality

      C) Assurance

      D) Sensitivity

22. What term describes the impact that unauthorized disclosure of an asset will have?

      A) Assurance

      B) Privacy

      C) Criticality

      D) Sensitivity

23. What term describes managing security risks by keeping vulnerabilities and threats to a level that we can live with?

      A) Assurance

      B) Criticality

      C) Privacy

      D) Sensitivity

24. What term describes being free from unauthorized intrusion or disclosure of information?

      A) Criticality

      B) Privacy

      C) Sensitivity

      D) Assurance

25. Which of the following changes would NOT directly impact privacy?

      A) A change in the CPO role

      B) New programs or changes in existing programs

      C) Updates to the change management process

      D) A change in third-parties the company does business with

Answers

1. B	2. C
3. C	4. A
5. D	6. B
7. C	8. D
9. D	10. B
11. D	12. C
13. A	14. D
15. B	16. C
17. B	18. D
19. C	20. D
21. B	22. D
23. A	24. B
25. A	

Chapter 12: Roles, Responsibilities, RACI Matrix

Questions

1. What term describes a title given to someone based on their job function?

    A) Responsibility

    B) Skill

    C) Role

    D) Informed

2. What term describes the training, expertise or experience an individual has?

    A) Skill

    B) Responsibility

    C) Role

    D) Informed

3. What term describes the activities a person should accomplish?

    A) Informed

    B) Skill

    C) Responsibility

    D) Role

4. What BEST describes the advantage of using roles?

    A) They provide an easy way to identify HR security gaps

    B) They simplify security administration

    C) They go great with turkey and dressing

    D) They allow a single individual to take on multiple responsibilities

5. What does each function in RACI stand for?

    A) Responsible, Answerable, Checked and Informed

    B) Responsible, Answerable, Consulted and Informed

    C) Responsible, Accountable, Consulted and Informed

    D) Responsible, Accountable, Checked and Informed

Answers

1. C	2. A
3. C	4. B
5. C	

Chapter 13: Human Resources, or HR

Questions

1. What is NOT true about employee bonding?

A) It protects against losses due to theft, neglect or mistakes

B) It is used only within non-federal organizations

C) It is a control used during the hiring process

D) It is not legal in some countries

2. Which of the following is NOT a recognized hiring risk?

A) Reference checks may not be carried out

B) RACI matrices may not be filled out properly

C) Contract or third-party staff may go-around the HR policies

D) An employee lack of awareness on confidentiality requirements may lead to unintentional leaks

3. Which of the following BEST describes the purpose of mandatory leave?

A) To assess how well an employee has been performing his or her job

B) To determine if a job function is actually required for continued business purposes

C) To ensure HR leave policies are being implemented

D) To detect if the employee on leave has been involved in improper or illegal activities

4. An employee is voluntarily leaving the company on good terms. Which of the following is not required under best practices?

A) Notification to appropriate staff and security personnel about the employee's status being changed to 'terminated'

B) Review of the termination interview to gather insight from the employee's perception of management

C) Arrangement of final paychecks so the employee is removed from the active payroll

D) Deletion or revocation of all assigned logon IDs and passwords

Answers

1. B	2. B
3. D	4. D

Chapter 14: Outsourcing
Questions

1. What is the BEST description of insourcing?

A) When all work is performed onsite in the IT department.

B) When the function is fully performed by the company's staff.

C) When all work being performed at a remote location in the same geographic area.

D) When the function is split between in-house and one or more outside parties.

2. What is the BEST description of outsourcing?

A) When all work being performed at a remote location in the same geographic area.

B) When all work is performed remotely in a different geographic region.

C) Having one or more outside parties perform the entire function.

D) When the function is split between in-house and one or more outside parties.

3. What is the BEST description of hybrid?

A) When all work is performed remotely in a different geographic region.

B) When all work being performed at a remote location in the same geographic area.

C) Having one or more outside parties perform the entire function.

D) When the function is split between in-house and one or more outside parties.

4. What is the BEST description of onsite?

A) When the function is fully performed by the company's staff.

B) When all work being performed at a remote location in the same geographic area.

C) When the function is split between in-house and one or more outside parties.

D) When all work is performed onsite in the IT department.

5. What is the BEST description of offsite?

A) Having one or more outside parties perform the entire function.

B) When all work being performed at a remote location in the same geographic area.

C) When all work is performed remotely in a different geographic region.

D) When the function is split between in-house and one or more outside parties.

6. What is the BEST description of nearshore?

A) When all work is performed remotely in a different geographic region.

B) When all work being performed at a remote location in the same geographic area.

C) Having one or more outside parties perform the entire function.

D) When the function is split between in-house and one or more outside parties.

7. What is the BEST description of offshore?

A) When all work is performed remotely in a different geographic region.

B) When all work being performed at a remote location in the same geographic area.

C) Having one or more outside parties perform the entire function.

D) When the function is split between in-house and one or more outside parties.

8. Which of the following is NOT an advantage of outsourcing?

A) Achieving economies of scale by reusing component software

B) Greater experience with a specific area than in-house staff

C) Better requirements and specifications

D) Liabilities are often mitigated

9. Which of the following is NOT a disadvantage of outsourcing?

    A) Loss of internal IT experience

    B) A commitment to service availability is difficult to achieve

    C) Loss or leakage of information

    D) Costs that often exceed expectations

10. Which of the following is NOT a valid way to reduce outsourcing risk?

    A) Ensure the vendor sub-contracts the most sensitive functions

    B) Contract with multiple suppliers

    C) Use short-term contracts

    D) Leverage escrows when dealing with source code

11. Which statement is NOT true concerning SLAs?

    A) An SLA can provide either penalties or bonuses in same agreement, but not both

    B) The power of an SLA kicks in when a provider fails to meet the minimum stipulations

    C) SLAs often reference external standards when defining minimum requirements

    D) A valid goal for an SLA might be a reduction in the number of help desk calls

12. Which BEST defines the term globalization?

    A) Redesigning a system so it can be used in multiple locations around the world

    B) Keeping a function in-house but physically housed in an overseas location to reduce costs

    C) Distributing a system across multiple locations to increase availability

    D) Expanding a company to operate in more than one country

13. Which of the following statements is NOT true regarding to third-party reporting?

    A) SOC 1 covers the design of provider controls

    B) SOC 3 covers the retirement disposition of provider controls

    C) SOC 2 covers the operating effectiveness of provider controls

    D) There are three SAE16 SOC reports only – SOC 1, SOC 2, and SOC 3

14. Which of the following items is NOT something that should be included in an outsourcing contract when specifying the right to audit?

    A) How auditing is allowed to be carried out

    B) What SLAs are in-place to handle incident response, and if they are documented and communicated to all involved parties

    C) The ability of the provider to sub-contract covered operations

    D) The visibility the auditor will have into the provider's internal controls that carry out CIA and preventative, detective and corrective duties

15. From an auditor's perspective, which of the following is NOT a major area of concern when moving functions to a cloud provider?

    A) The move must make sense from a business strategy viewpoint

    B) The organization must be able to accommodate this new way of doing business

    C) Billing processes must be able to accommodate the change

    D) Access control must be maintained, since employees might be able to go directly to the provider to make changes

Answers

1. B	2. C		
3. D	4. D		
5. B	6. B		
7. A	8. D		
9. B	10. A		
11. A	12. B		
13. B	14. C		
15. C			

Chapter 15: Cloud Computing

Questions

1. Which of the following is NOT an essential characteristic of cloud computing?

A) Services are accessible over a broadband network and can be used with a diverse list of client platforms

B) Cloud security controls align with corporate policies

C) It provides on-demand self-service without requiring human interaction

D) Resources are pooled and reusable so that multiple tenants can use the environment simultaneously

2. What is the BEST definition of elasticity?

A) Bandwidth can be gradually increased in response to traffic

B) Storage capabilities can increase as-needed

C) Resources can rapidly scale up or down

D) The billing model can change according to real-time use

3. What is the BEST definition for a measured service?

A) Services are available at 100% up to a pre-defined level, after which the services are maintained in a reduced capacity

B) Customer are only charged for what they use

C) A flat rate is charged to the customer unless service levels exceed the SLA threshold

D) The customer is charged based on average use across an extended time-period

4. Which definition BEST describes a private cloud?

A) The solution is privately hosted, but a select few other companies are allowed to access it

B) The solution is hosted across the Internet and is publicly accessible

C) The solution is privately hosted but connects across the public Internet into another application

D) The solution is entirely hosted inside of a company's intranet and is not accessible externally

5. Which definition BEST describes a community cloud?

A) The solution is privately hosted but connects across the public Internet into another application

B) The solution is privately hosted, but a select few other companies are allowed to access it

C) The solution is entirely hosted inside of a company's intranet and is not accessible externally

D) The solution is hosted across the Internet and is publicly accessible

6. Which definition BEST describes a public cloud?

A) The solution is entirely hosted inside of a company's intranet and is not accessible externally

B) The solution is privately hosted, but a select few other companies are allowed to access it

C) The solution is privately hosted but connects across the public Internet into another application

D) The solution is hosted across the Internet and is publicly accessible

7. Which definition BEST describes a hybrid model?

A) The solution is hosted across the Internet and is publicly accessible

B) The solution is entirely hosted inside of a company's intranet and is not accessible externally

C) The solution is privately hosted, but a select few other companies are allowed to access it

D) The solution is privately hosted but connects across the public Internet into another application

8. What does IaaS stand for?

A) Insolence as a Service

B) Infrastructure as a Service

C) Integration as a Service

D) Identity as a Service

9. What does PaaS stand for?

A) Presentation as a Service

B) Product as a Service

C) Platform as a Service

D) Policy as a Service

10. What does SaaS stand for?

A) Software as a Service

B) Security as a Service

C) Shareware as a Service

D) Solution as a Service

11. Which of the following is NOT an advantage virtualization can provide?

A) We can share the same physical memory addresses across multiple virtual machines

B) We can run different OSs or versions of an OS at the same time on the same host

C) We can easily backup a virtual machine by taking a snapshot, or image

D) We can easily clone that virtual machine by spinning up multiple copies, all running at the same time

12. Which description BEST describes a hypervisor?

A) Software that manages multiple virtual machines

B) Hardware that hosts multiple virtual machines and coordinates communication between each

C) Hardware that allows multiple virtual machines to exit simultaneously

D) Software that runs on the network to ensure virtual machines can access resources only as-needed

13. Which is NOT a major disadvantage of virtualization?

A) The host is now a single point of failure

B) It is possible for one VM to access memory belonging to another VM

C) If the hypervisor runs into performance issues, all hosted OSs suffer as well

D) Context switching of processing power between VMs is costly

14. Which of the following is NOT a recommended way to mitigate risks when using virtualization?

A) VMs should be segregated in the network just like a physical machine would be

B) A HIDS (Host IDS) should be installed on each VM as well as the hypervisor

C) Strong physical and logical access controls to the host and its management console must be applied

D) Any changes to a host must go through stringent change management processes

15. Which of the following is NOT a major advantage of cloud computing?

A) It makes it much easier to apply upgrades and patches

B) We can move capital expenditures to operational expenditures

C) It becomes easier to deploy enhancements to applications

D) We can scale resources up or down as desired, resulting in a virtually unlimited resource pool

16. Which of the following is NOT a way to mitigate risk due to cloud providers crossing international borders?

A) All assets must be encrypted prior to migration to the CSP and proper key management must be in place

B) The company should request the CSP's list of infrastructure locations and verify that regulation in those locations is aligned with the enterprise's requirements

C) The contract should stipulate that if the CSP passes data through a region not aligned with applicable regulations, the CSP will be held liable for all subsequent damages

D) Terms should be included in the contract so that assets may only be moved to those areas known to be compliant with the enterprise's own regulation

17. Which of the following is NOT a recommended method to address physical access by the CSP's staff?

A) The company should require the CSP to provide personnel details for all employees that will be accessing the company's assets

B) The CSP's disaster recovery plans should be reviewed to ensure they contain countermeasures to protect physical assets during and after a disaster

C) The company should request the CSP's physical security policy and ensure that it is aligned with the company's own security policy

D) The CSP should provide proof of independent security reviews or certification reports that meet the company's compliance requirements

18. Which of the following is NOT a recommended approach to ensure proper disposal of data when a contract expires?

A) The CSP's technical specifications and controls that wipe data and backup media should be reviewed

B) CSPs should ensure the safe disposal or destruction of any previous backups

C) A mandatory data wipe is carried out under the company's supervision

D) Only media approved by the company should be used for both backups and real-time storage

Answers

1. B		2. C	
3. B		4. D	
5. B		6. D	
7. D		8. B	
9. C		10. A	
11. A		12. A	
13. D		14. B	
15. C		16. C	
17. A		18. D	

Chapter 16: Capital Expenditures and Operational Expenditures

Questions

1. Which standard provides guidance on what software development expenses can be classified as a capital expenditure?

      A) IAS 38

      B) SOP 98-1

      C) NIST SP 800-30

      D) ISO 27001

Answers

1. A	

Chapter 17: BCP, DRP, BIA

Questions

1. What is NOT a benefit delivered through business continuity?

 A) It enables us to recover once the disaster has ended

 B) It tells us how to handle the disasters that slip through

 C) It prepares us to overcome competition by being prepared for a disaster

 D) It allows us to prevent most disasters from happening to our business

2. Which of the following is NOT something you would normally find in a DRP?

 A) How the plan links with other plans, for example an emergency response plan or crisis management plan

 B) The criteria used to decide when to activate the plan

 C) Procedures for declaring a disaster

 D) An executive succession plan

3. What is a major disadvantage of a BIA?

 A) It almost always requires an outside party

 B) It is seldom completed due to complexity

 C) Assessments tend to be worst-case

 D) Some laws prevent its use

4. What are the two perspectives that need to be addressed when defining RTO?

 A) Those who consume information, and senior management who have a broader view

 B) Day-to-day operations and strategic operations

 C) Those who create information, and those who consume it

 D) Individual contributors and management

5. What does the BCP do with RTOs?

 A) It converts the data into a scheduled mitigation plan

 B) It uses them to calculate MTO and AIW

 C) It uses them to arrive at a priority restoration order

 D) It documents them along with supporting evidence

6. Which of the following is a valid statement concerning RTO?

 A) It is acceptable for an impact loss to exceed recovery cost

 B) Near-instantaneous recovery (an RTO approaching 0) is seldom possible

 C) Shorter RTOs cost more

 D) Systems owners will lean towards longer RTOs

7. Which of the following is NOT a primary goal for a BIA?

 A) Prioritize the criticality of every business process

 B) Identify resource requirements for each critical process

 C) Estimate the amount of downtime in terms of the MTO until the business can no longer survive

 D) Finalize the decision on restoration order

8. Which of the following is NOT a step in the BIA process?

 A) Analyze the information

 B) Gather assessment material

 C) Gather final approval and record signatures

 D) Document the results and present recommendations

9. Which of the following is NOT a recognized benefit of carrying out a BIA?

A) It raises the level of awareness for response management

B) It forces the documentation of the functions analyzed

C) It prioritizes restoration activities

D) It increases the understanding around loss of a particular function

10. Which of the following is NOT a group involved in the creation of a BCP?

A) Help desk

B) Business operations

C) Information processing support

D) Support services

11. Which is the BEST definition of a negligible incident?

A) An incident that results in a negative material impact on business processes and may affect other systems, departments of customers

B) An incident that causes no significant damage

C) An incident that can have a serious material impact on the continued functioning of the business and is often proportional to the length of the incident

D) An incident that produces no negative material or financial impact

12. Which is the BEST definition of a minor incident?

A) An incident that produces no negative material or financial impact

B) An incident that can have a serious material impact on the continued functioning of the business and is often proportional to the length of the incident

C) An incident that causes no significant damage

D) An incident that results in a negative material impact on business processes and may affect other systems, departments of customers

13. Which is the BEST definition of a major incident?

A) An incident that causes no significant damage

B) An incident that results in a negative material impact on business processes and may affect other systems, departments of customers

C) An incident that produces no negative material or financial impact

D) An incident that can have a serious material impact on the continued functioning of the business and is often proportional to the length of the incident

14. Which is the BEST definition of a crisis incident?

A) An incident that produces no negative material or financial impact

B) An incident that results in a negative material impact on business processes and may affect other systems, departments of customers

C) An incident that can have a serious material impact on the continued functioning of the business and is often proportional to the length of the incident

D) An incident that causes no significant damage

15. Which of the following statements regarding incidents is NOT true?

A) A major incident can turn into a crisis based on the length of the outage

B) A crisis incident should never be assigned to an outage lasting less than 30 minutes

C) Negligible incidents do not have to be documented

D) A reasonable approach is to assign any new incident a major classification until more information can be obtained

16. Which off the following items is NOT normally contained in a BCP?

A) Continuity of operations plan

B) Business resumption plan

C) The DRP

D) Strategy resumption plan

17. Which of the following BEST describes cybersecurity insurance?

    A) Insurance that covers losses incurred as a result of a network-based attack

    B) Insurance that covers loss from dishonest or fraudulent acts by employees

    C) Insurance that reimburses lost profit as a result of an IT malfunction or security incident that causes the loss of computing resources

    D) Insurance that protects a business from losses experienced as a result of third-party claims

18. Which of the following BEST describes professional and commercial liability insurance?

    A) Insurance that reimburses lost profit as a result of an IT malfunction or security incident that causes the loss of computing resources

    B) Insurance that legally protects a business in case it commits an act, error or omission that results in a loss

    C) Insurance that reimburses the business for expenses incurred in maintaining operations at a facility that experiences damage

    D) Insurance that protects a business from losses experienced as a result of third-party claims

19. Which of the following BEST describes extra expense insurance?

    A) Insurance that reimburses the business for expenses incurred in maintaining operations at a facility that experiences damage

    B) Insurance that protects a business from losses experienced as a result of third-party claims

    C) Insurance that covers the actual cash value of papers and records that have been disclosed, or physically damaged or lost

    D) Insurance that reimburses lost profit as a result of an IT malfunction or security incident that causes the loss of computing resources

20. Which of the following BEST describes business interruption insurance?

    A) Insurance that covers the actual cash value of papers and records that have been disclosed, or physically damaged or lost

    B) Insurance that reimburses the business for expenses incurred in maintaining operations at a facility that experiences damage

    C) Insurance that covers losses incurred as a result of a cyberattack

    D) Insurance that reimburses lost profit as a result of an IT malfunction or security incident that causes the loss of computing resources

21. Which of the following BEST describes valuable papers and records insurance?

    A) Insurance that reimburses lost profit as a result of an IT malfunction or security incident that causes the loss of computing resources

    B) Insurance that covers loss from dishonest or fraudulent acts by employees and is most commonly carried by financial institutions

    C) Insurance that legally protects a business in case it commits an act, error or omission that results in a loss

    D) Insurance that covers the actual cash value of information assets that have been disclosed, or physically damaged or lost

22. Which of the following BEST describes errors and omissions insurance?

    A) Insurance that covers the actual cash value of papers and records that have been disclosed, or physically damaged or lost

    B) Insurance that reimburses the business for expenses incurred in maintaining operations at a facility that experiences damage

    C) Insurance that legally protects a business in case it commits an act, error or omission that results in a loss

    D) Insurance that covers loss from dishonest or fraudulent acts by employees and is most commonly carried by financial institutions

23. Which of the following BEST describes fidelity coverage insurance?

A) Insurance that protects a business from losses experienced as a result of third-party claims

B) Insurance that legally protects a business in case it commits an act, error or omission that results in a loss

C) Insurance that covers loss from dishonest or fraudulent acts by employees

D) Insurance that reimburses the business for expenses incurred in maintaining operations at a facility that experiences damage

24. Which statement BEST describes pandemic planning?

A) Planning for all phases of a disaster from first report to final disposition

B) Planning for disasters across all departments of a company

C) Dealing with outbreaks of infectious diseases that can impact humans

D) Accommodating scenarios in which vendors a company is dependent on are no longer available

25. Which statement BEST describes image reputation damage?

A) Repairing a portrait of the company's founder

B) The prevention of reputation erosion due to market conditions

C) Dealing with an event that will likely cause a loss of trust

D) Protecting a company's public-facing image by suppressing any knowledge of an event

26. Which statement BEST describes a black swan event?

A) A rare sighting of the 3-footed Ignoble Black Cygnus

B) An unforeseeable event that is a complete surprise and has a major impact

C) A recognized disaster of such a magnitude that if it were to occur a company would be unable to deal with the fallout, forcing it to cease operations

D) An expected and recurring instance of a risk that cannot be effectively mitigated without insurance

27. In case of a disaster, a company needs to be up and running in a backup facility within two days. Which type of recovery site is the BEST choice?

A) Duplicate site

B) Cold site

C) Warm site

D) Hot site

28. In case of a disaster, a company needs to be up and running in a backup facility within hours but operates in an area with no close recovery facilities. Which type of recovery site is the BEST choice?

A) Warm site

B) Hot site

C) Mobile site

D) Mirror site

29. A small company prioritizes cost above all else. Which type of recovery site is the BEST choice?

A) Mobile site

B) Warm site

C) Cold site

D) Duplicate site

30. Which of the following is NOT a recognized disadvantage with a reciprocal agreement?

A) The delay in transferring control between the two companies must be kept to a minimum

B) It is exceedingly difficult to create a contract that provides adequate protection

C) It is unlikely that one company can sustain usage for two companies, as normally companies cannot afford to have double their needed capacity simply sitting around until needed

D) The two companies must align on the same type of infrastructure and coordinate any changes

31. Which of the following is NOT a significant factor to consider when selecting the type of recovery site?

A) The nature of probable disruptions

B) The redundant capabilities within the primary facility

C) The location of the alternate site

D) Proximity factors of the primary facility

32. Which of the following BEST represents the relationship between RTO and alternate site cost?

A) The cost of the alternate site will remain steady until RTO nears 0

B) As RTO decreases the cost of the alternate site will increase

C) As RTO decreases the cost of the alternate site will also decrease

D) RTO has no bearing on the cost of an alternate site

33. When dealing with network continuity, which statement BEST describes redundancy?

A) Subscribing to two or more network service providers at the same time

B) Routing traffic through split or duplicate cables

C) Providing fail-over systems automatically

D) Routing information through an alternate medium such as copper cable or fiber optics

34. When dealing with network continuity, which statement BEST describes alternative routing?

A) Routing information through an alternate medium such as copper cable or fiber optics

B) Subscribing to two or more network service providers at the same time

C) Providing fail-over systems automatically

D) Routing traffic through split or duplicate cables

35. When dealing with network continuity, which statement BEST describes diverse routing?

A) Routing traffic through split or duplicate cables

B) Subscribing to two or more network service providers at the same time

C) Providing fail-over systems automatically

D) Routing information through an alternate medium such as copper cable or fiber optics

36. When dealing with network continuity, which statement BEST describes long-haul network diversity?

A) Routing traffic through split or duplicate cables

B) Routing information through an alternate medium such as copper cable or fiber optics

C) Protecting an organization from a local disaster that takes out the communications infrastructure connected directly to a facility

D) Subscribing to two or more network service providers at the same time

37. When dealing with network continuity, which statement BEST describes last-mile circuit protection?

A) Protecting an organization from a local disaster that takes out the communications infrastructure connected directly to a facility

B) Subscribing to two or more network service providers at the same time

C) Routing information through an alternate medium such as copper cable or fiber optics

D) Routing traffic through split or duplicate cables

38. Which of the following BEST describes a data storage device that is connected directly to a server or client?

A) RAID

B) DAS

C) NAS

D) RAND

39. Which of the following BEST describes a storage device that is a self-contained server?

A) RAND

B) DAS

C) NAS

D) RAID

40. Which of the following BEST describes a data storage device that writes data to multiple disks simultaneously?

A) NAS

B) RAID

C) DAS

D) RAND

41. Which definition BEST describes adaptive RAID?

A) A storage solution that switches between RAID modes depending on the configured write speed

B) A storage solution that increases available storage based on real-time needs

C) A storage solution that switches between synchronous and asynchronous mode based on the network load

D) A storage solution that allows individual hard disks to be swapped out without requiring down-time

42. Which statement is true?

A) As RTO increases, the time to recover decreases

B) High availability solutions require both a low RTO and RPO

C) A tape backup solution provides a low RPO

D) As RPO increases, data loss decreases

43. Which of the following is NOT a valid control for offsite libraries?

A) Multiple copies of backups must be maintained

B) Backups should be encrypted

C) Backup media must be physically locked up

D) Do not store backups for too long of a period

44. Which of the following is NOT a major factor that should be considered when selecting a backup method and media?

A) Select media that can be reused

B) Magnetic media is preferable over optical

C) Use a media that is sold in volume

D) Assume unexpected growth and purchase media that can hold larger amounts of data than is needed

45. Which of the following non-removable disk-based solutions BEST describes a virtual tape library?

A) Similar to host-based replication, but it is carried out at the disk array level instead of software installed on the OS

B) Software living on a server that replicates changes to another server invisibly

C) A solution that looks like a tape library but really uses a disk array for storage

D) Taking an image of a system, restoring onto a second system, and backing up this secondary environment

46. Which of the following non-removable disk-based solutions BEST describes a host-based replication?

A) A solution that looks like a tape library but really uses a disk array for storage

B) Software living on a server that replicates changes to another server invisibly

C) Similar to host-based replication, but it is carried out at the disk array level instead of software installed on the OS

D) Taking an image of a system, restoring onto a second system, and backing up this secondary environment

47. Which of the following non-removable disk-based solutions BEST describes a disk-array-based replication?

A) Taking an image of a system, restoring onto a second system, and backing up this secondary environment

B) Similar to host-based replication, but it is carried out at the disk array level instead of software installed on the OS

C) A solution that looks like a tape library but really uses a disk array for storage

D) Software living on a server that replicates changes to another server invisibly

48. Which of the following non-removable disk-based solutions BEST describes a snapshots?

A) Software living on a server that replicates changes to another server invisibly

B) Similar to host-based replication, but it is carried out at the disk array level instead of software installed on the OS

C) A solution that looks like a tape library but really uses a disk array for storage

D) Taking an image of a system, restoring onto a second system, and backing up this secondary environment

49. Which of the following is NOT a factor we should look at when selecting the frequency of backups?

A) How often the source data changes

B) The cost of backup media

C) The impact if we are unable to restore a backup

D) RTO and RPO

50. Which of the following best describes a differential backup?

A) Copies all changes within each file that has changed since the last differential or full backup

B) Copies all files and folders into a single backup set

C) Copies only the files and folders that have changes since the last incremental or full backup

D) Copies all files and folders changed since the last full backup

51. Which of the following BEST represents the grandfather-father-son rotation scheme?

A) Son is the last backup, father is the every 7th backup, and grandfather is every 30th backup

B) Son is the weekly backup, father is the last backup of the month, and grandfather is the last backup of the year

C) Son is the daily backup, father is the last backup of the week, and grandfather is the last backup of the month

D) Son is the weekly backup, father is the monthly backup, and grandfather is the annual backup

Answers

1. C	2. D
3. C	4. A
5. C	6. C
7. D	8. C
9. B	10. A
11. B	12. A
13. B	14. C
15. B	16. D
17. A	18. D
19. A	20. D
21. D	22. C
23. C	24. C
25. C	26. B
27. C	28. C
29. C	30. A
31. B	32. B
33. C	34. A
35. A	36. D
37. A	38. B
39. C	40. B
41. C	42. B
43. A	44. B
45. C	46. B
47. B	48. D
49. B	50. D
51. C	

Chapter 18: Plan Testing

Questions

1. Which of the following is NOT a checkpoint where plan testing should be carried out?

    A) According to industry standards

    B) After key changes in personnel, technology or the business environment

    C) At least once per year

    D) After major revisions

2. Which of the following is NOT a major concern that a security manager should watch for prior to each test?

    A) Final test reporting has been scheduled

    B) The business accepts the risk of testing

    C) The risk of disruption is minimized

    D) The organization has the ability to restore operation at any point during testing

3. Which of the following is NOT true regarding testing response and recovery plans?

    A) The test should be executed to the point immediately prior to declaring a disaster

    B) When a plan appears to be 100% successful, the interval between periodic testing may be increased

    C) If a plan is not tested it leaves the business with a false sense of security that it will not fail

    D) A third-party should be present to monitor and evaluate the test

4. Which of the following BEST describes a checklist review test?

    A) Team members role-playing a simulated disaster without activating the recovery site

    B) An assessment of all steps to be carried out

    C) Team members implement the plan on paper

    D) The recovery site is brought up to a state of operational readiness, but operations at the primary site continue

5. Which of the following BEST describes a structured walkthrough test?

    A) An assessment of all steps to be carried out

    B) The recovery site is brought up to a state of operational readiness, but operations at the primary site continue

    C) Team members role-playing a simulated disaster without activating the recovery site

    D) Team members implement the plan on paper

6. Which of the following BEST describes a simulation test?

    A) The recovery site is brought up to a state of operational readiness, but operations at the primary site continue

    B) Team members role-playing a simulated disaster without activating the recovery site

    C) Team members implement the plan on paper

    D) An assessment of all steps to be carried out

7. Which of the following BEST describes a parallel test?

    A) Team members implement the plan on paper

    B) The recovery site is activated, and the primary site is shut down

    C) Team members role-playing a simulated disaster without activating the recovery site

    D) The recovery site is brought up to a state of operational readiness, but operations at the primary site continue

8. Which of the following BEST describes a full interruption test?

    A) Team members role-playing a simulated disaster without activating the recovery site

    B) The recovery site is activated, and the primary site is shut down

    C) The recovery site is brought up to a state of operational readiness, but operations at the primary site continue

    D) Team members implement the plan on paper

9. Which of the five basic tests are included in the paper test category?

    A) Checklist review and structured walkthrough

    B) Simulation and parallel

    C) Parallel and full interruption

    D) Structured walkthrough and simulation

10. Which of the five basic tests are included in the preparedness test category?

    A) Simulation and parallel

    B) Parallel and full interruption

    C) Checklist review and structured walkthrough

    D) Structured walkthrough and simulation

11. What are the three phases of a test?

    A) Preparation, execution, posttest

    B) Pretest, test and posttest

    C) Pretest, execution and posttest

    D) Preparation, execution, follow-up

12. Which of the following is NOT a metric collected when testing a recovery plan?

    A) The number of people required to bring the system up to full capacity

    B) The accuracy of data entry and processing cycles at the recovery site vs. normal accuracy

    C) The amount of work performed at the backup site by people and by information systems

    D) The elapsed time for completion of each major component of the test

Answers

1. A	2. A
3. B	4. B
5. D	6. B
7. D	8. B
9. A	10. A
11. B	12. A

Chapter 19: Enterprise Architecture

Questions

1. What two states is enterprise architecture concerned with?

    A) The critical state and the stable state

    B) The current state and the desired state

    C) The draft state and the completed state

    D) The preliminary state and the final state

2. When using EA from a business perspective, what of the following BEST describes the two things it attempts to understand?

    A) The core mission and supporting processes

    B) Individual and management capabilities

    C) When to keep processes in-house, and when to outsource them

    D) The IT function and the business strategy

Answers

1. B	2. A

Chapter 20: Governance

Questions

1. Which of the following is the BEST definition for GEIT?

A) A system in which all stakeholders are part of the decision-making process, and is specific to IT

B) Providing incentives for the senior management and the board to do what is best for the company

C) The process of establishing strategy, identifying the goals to achieve that strategy, and managing risk and resources so the goals are reached

D) The system by which business corporations are directed and controlled

2. What are the three processes used with GEIT?

A) IT resource management, performance measurement and compliance management

B) HR resource management, IT performance measurement and corporate compliance management

C) Standards, performance, and compliance

D) System management, process measurement and compliance management

3. Which statement BEST describes the difference between governance and management?

A) Governance is informed, and management is responsible

B) Governance decides on the strategy, and management develops goals to meet the strategies

C) Governance is accountable, and management is responsible

D) Governance sets goals, and management reaches those goals

4. Which of the following BEST describes COBIT 5?

A) A series of standards that help an organization implement and maintain an information security program, and is the standard to which most companies are certified against

B) A specification for service management that is aligned with ITIL

C) Developed by ISACA and is intended to ensure IT goals align with business goals, resources are used properly, and that risk is being effectively managed

D) Created in the UK and provides a very hands-on and detailed framework on implementing GEIT

5. Which of the following BEST describes ISO 27001?

A) Created in the UK and provides a very hands-on and detailed framework on implementing GEIT

B) Developed by ISACA and is intended to ensure IT goals align with business goals, resources are used properly, and that risk is being effectively managed

C) A series of standards that help an organization implement and maintain an information security program, and is the standard to which most companies are certified against

D) A specification for service management that is aligned with ITIL

6. Which of the following BEST describes ITIL?

A) A process-based security model for IT

B) A specification for service management that is aligned with ITIL

C) Created in the UK and provides a very hands-on and detailed framework on implementing GEIT

D) Developed by ISACA and is intended to ensure IT goals align with business goals, resources are used properly, and that risk is being effectively managed

7. Which of the following BEST describes IT Baseline Protection Catalogs?

> A) A specification for service management that is aligned with ITIL

> B) A German collection of documents useful for detecting and addressing security weaknesses in an IT environment

> C) A process-based security model for IT

> D) Created in the UK and provides a very hands-on and detailed framework on implementing GEIT

8. Which of the following BEST describes ISM3?

> A) Created in the UK and provides a very hands-on and detailed framework on implementing GEIT

> B) A series of standards that help an organization implement and maintain an information security program, and is the standard to which most companies are certified against

> C) A process-based security model for IT

> D) A specification for service management that is aligned with ITIL

9. Which of the following BEST describes ISO/IEC 38500 Corporate governance of information technology?

> A) Created in the UK and provides a very hands-on and detailed framework on implementing GEIT

> B) Targeted for those at the highest level of an organization and provides guiding principles on the acceptable use of IT from a legal and ethical point of view

> C) A specification for service management that is aligned with ITIL

> D) A German collection of documents useful for detecting and addressing security weaknesses in an IT environment

10. Which of the following BEST describes ISO 20000?

> A) A process-based security model for IT

> B) A series of standards that help an organization implement and maintain an information security program, and is the standard to which most companies are certified against

> C) A specification for service management that is aligned with ITIL

> D) Targeted for those at the highest level of an organization and provides guiding principles on the acceptable use of IT from a legal and ethical point of view

11. Which BEST describes the difference between the IT strategy committee and the IT steering committee?

> A) The IT strategy committee is created as-needed, whereas the IT steering committee is permanently formed

> B) The IT strategy committee is made up of two executives, whereas the IT steering committee is made up of senior managers

> C) The IT strategy committee has no authority other than as advisors, whereas the IT steering committee makes all final decisions

> D) The IT strategy committee acts as an advisor to the entire board in developing the strategy, whereas the IT steering committee assists the sponsoring executive in executing the strategy

12. What are the three levels of duties for the IT steering committee?

> A) Action, delegation and transference

> B) Initiation, authority and dissolution

> C) Responsibility, authority and membership

> D) Individual, managerial and executive

13. If a company does not officially recognize a CISO role and assign it to a specific individual, what is the most LIKELY result?

A) The security auditor will ultimately lack the authority to carry out an effective audit

B) Security goals will not align with business goals

C) Security and IT functions will report up through the same management chain

D) Major security incidents will not be handled appropriately

Answers

1. A	2. A
3. D	4. C
5. C	6. C
7. B	8. C
9. B	10. C
11. D	12. C
13. B	

Chapter 21: Information Security Policy

Questions

1. Which of the following items is NOT something you would expect to find in an information security policy?

A) How risk will be assessed and managed.

B) Employee responsibilities for managing security information

C) A base list of controls to be implemented by IT

D) The importance in enabling information sharing.

2. Which of the following is a common sub-policy published as part of an information security policy?

A) New Hire Vetting Policy

B) Access Control Policy

C) Backup and Retention Policy

D) Media Disposition Policy

3. Which of the following is NOT true regarding the AUP?

A) It covers both who is a user and what the user is allowed to do

B) The Acceptable Internet Usage Policy should also exist but separately

C) The right for the company to collect logs should be included

D) It is designed to protect both the employee and organization from illegal actions

Chapter 21: Information Security Policy

Answers

1. C	2. B	
3. B		

Chapter 22: Information Technology Management Practices

Questions

1. Which of the following statements is NOT true regarding organizational change management?

A) While technology considerations are taken into account, end-user expectations are normally not part of this effort

B) It is the use of a defined and documented process to identify and apply technology improvements at either the infrastructure or application level

C) The IT department will be spearheading such initiatives

D) All levels of an organization that is affected should be involved

2. Your company's IT department is complaining that other departments are making unreasonable requests without regard for technology and support costs. What is the best way to combat this?

A) Require all requests to be approved by the accounting function

B) Give approval authority to the IT department

C) Implement a chargeback scheme

D) Require all requests to be funneled through the CTO's office

3. What is the BEST definition of performance?

A) A comparison against an external benchmark

B) Delivered value as perceived by users and stakeholders

C) How well a system works

D) How well goals are achieved based on pre-defined metrics

Answers

1. A	2. C
3. B	

Chapter 23: IT Organizational Structure Roles and Responsibilities

Questions

1. Which of the following BEST describes the systems development manager role?

A) Acts as a liaison between end users and the IT team

B) A manager or director responsible for information used to run a business

C) Plans and executes IS projects, manages the associated budget and reports progress to the appropriate management

D) Responsible for programmers and analysts who implement and maintain systems

2. Which of the following BEST describes the project manager role?

A) A manager or director responsible for information used to run a business

B) Plans and executes IS projects, manages the associated budget and reports progress to the appropriate management

C) Acts as a liaison between end users and the IT team

D) Responsible for programmers and analysts who implement and maintain systems

3. Which of the following BEST describes the end user support manager role?

A) Acts as a liaison between end users and the IT team

B) Plans and executes IS projects, manages the associated budget and reports progress to the appropriate management

C) A manager or director responsible for information used to run a business

D) Responsible for programmers and analysts who implement and maintain systems

4. Which of the following BEST describes the data owner role?

A) A manager or director responsible for information used to run a business

B) Acts as a liaison between end users and the IT team

C) Responsible for programmers and analysts who implement and maintain systems

D) Plans and executes IS projects, manages the associated budget and reports progress to the appropriate management

5. Which of the following BEST describes the data custodian role?

A) Acts as a liaison between end users and the IT team

B) Plans and executes IS projects, manages the associated budget and reports progress to the appropriate management

C) Responsible for storing and safeguarding data

D) Responsible for programmers and analysts who implement and maintain systems

6. Which of the following BEST describes the data user role?

A) Responsible for daily operations related to business services

B) Tasked with managing data and the data architecture

C) Answers technical questions and solve problems faced by internal employees

D) The actual user of data, including both internal and external users

7. Which of the following BEST describes the help desk role?

A) Answers technical questions and solve problems faced by internal employees

B) Responsible for daily operations related to business services

C) Tasked with managing data and the data architecture

D) The actual user of data, including both internal and external users

8. Which of the following BEST describes the end user role?

A) Responsible for daily operations related to business services

B) The actual user of data, including both internal and external users

C) Answers technical questions and solve problems faced by internal employees

D) Tasked with managing data and the data architecture

9. Which of the following BEST describes the data management personnel role?

A) Responsible for daily operations related to business services

B) Tasked with managing data and the data architecture

C) Answers technical questions and solve problems faced by internal employees

D) The actual user of data, including both internal and external users

10. Which of the following BEST describes the information security manager role?

A) Is normally separate from the IT department and reports up through the CISO

B) Responsible for running the data center, including managing staff

C) Responsible for maintaining multi-user computer systems including the network connecting them together

D) Defines and maintains the structure of a corporate database, and is the custodian of the company's data

11. Which of the following BEST describes the operations manager role?

A) Is normally separate from the IT department and reports up through the CISO

B) Responsible for running the data center, including managing staff

C) Responsible for maintaining multi-user computer systems including the network connecting them together

D) Defines and maintains the structure of a corporate database, and is the custodian of the company's data

12. Which of the following BEST describes the system administrator role?

A) Defines and maintains the structure of a corporate database, and is the custodian of the company's data

B) Responsible for maintaining multi-user computer systems including the network connecting them together

C) Is normally separate from the IT department and reports up through the CISO

D) Responsible for running the data center, including managing staff

13. Which of the following BEST describes the DBA role?

A) Responsible for maintaining multi-user computer systems including the network connecting them together

B) Responsible for running the data center, including managing staff

C) Defines and maintains the structure of a corporate database, and is the custodian of the company's data

D) Is normally separate from the IT department and reports up through the CISO

14. Which of the following BEST describes the control group role?

A) The process of entering information into a system manually, using a batch process or online

B) Collects and converts incoming information and ensures the proper distribution to the user community

C) Controls industrial machinery spread out over large areas

D) Controls all information stored on removable media

15. Which of the following BEST describes the media management role?

A) The process of entering information into a system manually, using a batch process or online

B) Controls all information stored on removable media

C) Collects and converts incoming information and ensures the proper distribution to the user community

D) Controls industrial machinery spread out over large areas

16. Which of the following BEST describes the data entry role?

A) Controls all information stored on removable media

B) Collects and converts incoming information and ensures the proper distribution to the user community

C) Controls industrial machinery spread out over large areas

D) The process of entering information into a system manually, using a batch process or online

17. Which of the following BEST describes the SCADA role?

A) Controls industrial machinery spread out over large areas

B) Enters information into a system manually, using a batch process or online

C) Collects and converts incoming information and ensures the proper distribution to the user community

D) Controls all information stored on removable media

18. Which of the following BEST describes the security administrator role?

A) Maintains network components such as routers, switches, firewalls and remote access

B) Carries out whatever duties are defined in the security policy

C) Develops and maintains standards for the IT group

D) Maintains the systems software, including the OS, on top of which applications sit

19. Which of the following BEST describes the quality assurance role?

A) Develops and maintains standards for the IT group

B) Carries out whatever duties are defined in the security policy

C) Maintains network components such as routers, switches, firewalls and remote access

D) Maintains the systems software, including the OS, on top of which applications sit

20. Which of the following BEST describes the Infrastructure staff role?

A) Maintains network components such as routers, switches, firewalls and remote access

B) Maintains the systems software, including the OS, on top of which applications sit

C) Develops and maintains standards for the IT group

D) Carries out whatever duties are defined in the security policy

21. Which of the following BEST describes the network administrator role?

    A) Develops and maintains standards for the IT group

    B) Maintains network components such as routers, switches, firewalls and remote access

    C) Maintains the systems software, including the OS, on top of which applications sit

    D) Carries out whatever duties are defined in the security policy

22. Which of the following BEST describes the systems analyst role?

    A) Designs systems based on user needs

    B) Evaluates potential security technologies, and establishes security policies and procedures

    C) Implements the designs created by a security architect

    D) Develops and maintains applications that eventually run in a production capacity

23. Which of the following BEST describes the security architect role?

    A) Designs systems based on user needs

    B) Implements the designs created by a security architect

    C) Evaluates potential security technologies, and establishes security policies and procedures

    D) Develops and maintains applications that eventually run in a production capacity

24. Which of the following BEST describes the system security engineer role?

    A) Implements the designs created by a security architect

    B) Designs systems based on user needs

    C) Develops and maintains applications that eventually run in a production capacity

    D) Evaluates potential security technologies, and establishes security policies and procedures

25. Which of the following BEST describes the applications staff role?

    A) Develops and maintains applications that eventually run in a production capacity

    B) Designs systems based on user needs

    C) Evaluates potential security technologies, and establishes security policies and procedures

    D) Implements the designs created by a security architect

Answers

1. D	2. B
3. A	4. A
5. C	6. D
7. A	8. A
9. B	10. A
11. B	12. B
13. C	14. B
15. B	16. D
17. A	18. B
19. A	20. B
21. B	22. A
23. C	24. A
25. A	

Chapter 24: IS Auditor Duties for the Governance and Management of IT Domain

Questions

1. Your company's IT function is not very involved with the overall business strategy. What is the BEST solution for this problem?

    A) Add the CIO or CTO to the IT strategy committee

    B) Request that the board of directors provide a top-down direction to integrate the two

    C) Create an IT steering committee chaired by a member of the board of directors who understands IT

    D) Bring in an outside party to explore options

2. What are the four BEST tools for ensuring that IT services continue to grow?

    A) Zachman, Six Sigma, TOGAF, and BSC

    B) Zachman, PAM, IDEAL and PDCA

    C) COBIT 5, TOGAF, IDEAL and BSC

    D) COBIT 5, PAM, IDEAL and CMMI

3. What is the BEST definition of opportunity cost?

    A) The potential cost of missing an opportunity due to it being outside of the organization's core expertise

    B) The cost associated with a failed attempt to invest in a new area due to a lack of in-house expertise

    C) The cost of taking advantage of an opportunity that is not within the current growth plan

    D) The cost of not being able to take advantage of an opportunity due to a lack of available resources

4. Which statement BEST describes why managing IT projects is different than managing an IT portfolio?

    A) Projects are short-term while a portfolio is long-term

    B) Projects have a definable delivery while portfolio projects interact in complex ways

    C) Portfolios simply require more management than a project

    D) Projects always require an investment, but with portfolios we must decide where to invest and where to divest

5. Which of the following tools is the BEST for managing a portfolio?

    A) PAM

    B) COBIT 5's EDM02

    C) CMMI

    D) BSC

6. Which of the following statements about auditing policies and procedures is NOT true?

    A) Policies are within audit scope and should be tested for compliance

    B) IS controls should flow from corporate policies

    C) Lower level policies must be consistent with corporate policies

    D) If an auditor discovers a policy that hinders the achievement of a business goal, it should be excluded from the final report

7. Which of the following statements about auditing the information security policy is NOT true?

    A) The review is performed by executives

    B) It should be reviewed at least once per year

    C) It should be reviewed when significant changes to the enterprise or risk levels are encountered

    D) It should have a defined owner responsible for evaluation

8. When auditing outsourcing, which of the following should the auditor be familiar with?

> A) How to obtain the report, review it and present results to management for further action
>
> B) FEA
>
> C) Management assertions and how well each address the services being provided by the service provider
>
> D) SSAE 16 reports including SOC 1, SOC 2 and SOC 3

9. When reviewing documentation, which two things should the auditor be looking for?

> A) That it was created as management authorized and intended, and is current and up-to-date
>
> B) That it is available in both hardcopy and electronic form, and exhibits the appropriate approval signatures
>
> C) That the contents align with business strategy, and proof of authority is included
>
> D) That it is referenced in a final report addendum, and all authors are noted

10. Which of the following is NOT a phase that service contracts go through?

> A) Compliance
>
> B) Bidding
>
> C) Approval
>
> D) Acceptance

11. What is NOT a basic element when reviewing the BCP?

> A) Plan testing
>
> B) Review business infrastructure
>
> C) Review the document
>
> D) Review the business continuity terms

12. When evaluating off-site storage, which of the following actions are NOT recommended?

> A) Comparing the offsite copy of the BCP to the most current version
>
> B) Physically visiting the offsite storage
>
> C) Carrying out a detailed inventory
>
> D) Turning on electronic equipment to ensure it is functioning

13. When evaluating an alternative processing facility, which of the following actions are NOT recommended?

> A) Ensure the contracted level of power and telecommunication capabilities are present
>
> B) Review any contract to ensure that all verbal promises are in writing
>
> C) Obtain a copy of the contract with the alternative processing facility's vendor
>
> D) Check the vendor's references

14. When reviewing insurance coverage, which of the following types is NOT considered to be the most important?

> A) Equipment replacement
>
> B) Errors and omissions
>
> C) Business interruption
>
> D) Media damage

Answers

1. C	2. D
3. D	4. D
5. B	6. D
7. A (The review is performed by management)	8. B (FEA is a framework and is not specific to outsourcing)
9. A	10. C (The phases are definition of requirements and service levels, bidding, selection, acceptance, maintenance and compliance)
11. B ('Review the applications covered by the plan' is the missing element)	12. D
13. A	14. B (Business continuity processing is the other important type of insurance)

Section 3: The Information Systems Acquisition, Development and Implementation Domain

Chapter 25: Project Management

Questions

1. Which of the following is NOT a prominent project management standard or organization?

    A) IPMA

    B) PMBOK

    C) PRINCE2

    D) PMPA

2. Which of the following is the BEST definition of a time context?

    A) A project's unique communication paths relative to the organization and other parallel projects

    B) The method in which a project's value is shared to stakeholders

    C) The overall project calendar that includes 'pre' and 'post' activities

    D) The intervals between components in which work is not executed

3. Which of the following is the BEST definition of a social context?

    A) The method in which a project's value is shared to stakeholders

    B) The overall project calendar that includes 'pre' and 'post' activities

    C) A project's unique communication paths relative to the organization and other parallel projects

    D) The intervals between components in which work is not executed

4. Which of the following is the BEST definition of an influence project organization?

    A) Project authority is shared between the project manager and department heads

    B) Multiple project managers share authority over the project

    C) The project manager does not have official authority to manage the project

    D) The project manager does have official authority over the project

5. Which of the following is the BEST definition of a pure project organization?

    A) Project authority is shared between the project manager and department heads

    B) Multiple project managers share authority over the project

    C) The project manager does have official authority over the project

    D) The project manager does not have official authority to manage the project

6. Which of the following is the BEST definition of a matrix project organization?

    A) The project manager does not have official authority to manage the project

    B) Multiple project managers share authority over the project

    C) The project manager does have official authority over the project

    D) Project authority is shared between the project manager and department heads

7. When starting a project, which of the following is NOT a recognized opportunity to communicate to team members?

    A) One-on-on-one meetings

    B) Project wiki standup

    C) Project start workshops

    D) Kick-off meetings

8. Of the recognized opportunities to communicate to team members at project start, which one is the preferred method?

    A) Kick-off meetings

    B) Project start workshops

    C) Project wiki standup

    D) One-on-on-one meetings

9. What does SMART stand for?

    A) Specific, maintainable, attainable, realistic and timely

    B) Specific, measurable, attainable, realistic and timely

    C) Specific, maintainable, actionable, reachable and timely

    D) Specific, measurable, actionable, realistic and timely

10. What is the BEST definition for main objective?

    A) The primary reason for a project and can always be tied directly to business success

    B) A result not directly tied to the business success, but must be achieved for ancillary reasons

    C) Results that are out of scope for the project and are not expected to be delivered

    D) A result not directly tied to the business success, but may contribute to project success

11. What is the BEST definition for additional objective?

    A) A result not directly tied to the business success, but must be achieved for ancillary reasons

    B) The primary reason for a project and can always be tied directly to business success

    C) Results that are out of scope for the project and are not expected to be delivered

    D) A result not directly tied to the business success, but may contribute to project success

12. What is the BEST definition for non-objective?

    A) A result not directly tied to the business success, but must be achieved for ancillary reasons

    B) The primary reason for a project and can always be tied directly to business success

    C) Results that are out of scope for the project and are not expected to be delivered

    D) A result not directly tied to the business success, but may contribute to project success

13. You are working on a project which produces many non-tangible results such as increasing certain skillsets in employees. Which project approach to define objectives will work best and why?

    A) WBS, since it is able to schedule the project

    B) OBS, since it simply tracks project components with relationships

    C) OBS, since it is able to schedule the project

    D) WBS, since it simply tracks project components with relationships

14. Which of the following items best represents the hierarchical nature of WBS?

    A) Schedule > WBS > Task > WP

    B) WP > Schedule > Task > WBS

    C) Task > Schedule > WP > WBS

    D) WBS > WP > Task > Schedule

15. Which of the following statements concerning WBS is NOT true?

    A) WPs can be arranged in phases

    B) Each WP must have a distinct owner

    C) WPs must contain enough detail to be able to measure performance

    D) Any WBS may represent the final deliverable

16. Which of the following statements concerning WBS is NOT true?

A) All WBS data is housed in the CMDB

B) Each WP must be unique within a WBS

C) Each WP should not exceed 10 days

D) All WPs must be detailed at the same level within a WBS

17. What dictates the total duration of a WP?

A) The total of all task durations plus slack time

B) The total of all task and sub-task durations plus slack time

C) The total of all task durations

D) The total of all task and sub-task durations

18. Which of the following BEST describes the senior management role?

A) Provides funding and defines the critical success factors and metrics that determine if the project is a success

B) Provides overall direction and represents the major stakeholders

C) Owns the project and the resulting deliverable

D) Shows commitment to the project by providing approval for the necessary resources to be successful

19. Which of the following BEST describes the project steering committee role?

A) Shows commitment to the project by providing approval for the necessary resources to be successful

B) Owns the project and the resulting deliverable

C) Provides overall direction and represents the major stakeholders

D) Provides funding and defines the critical success factors and metrics that determine if the project is a success

20. Which of the following BEST describes the project sponsor role?

A) Provides overall direction and represents the major stakeholders

B) Shows commitment to the project by providing approval for the necessary resources to be successful

C) Provides funding and defines the critical success factors and metrics that determine if the project is a success

D) Owns the project and the resulting deliverable

21. Which of the following BEST describes the user management role?

A) Shows commitment to the project by providing approval for the necessary resources to be successful

B) Owns the project and the resulting deliverable

C) Provides overall direction and represents the major stakeholders

D) Provides funding and defines the critical success factors and metrics that determine if the project is a success

22. Which of the following BEST describes the systems development management role?

A) Provides day-to-day management and leadership of the project

B) Create the core project deliverables by completing assigned tasks

C) Develops, installs and operates the requested system

D) Acts as subject matter experts for the development team

23. Which of the following BEST describes the project manager role?

A) Develops, installs and operates the requested system

B) Provides day-to-day management and leadership of the project

C) Create the core project deliverables by completing assigned tasks

D) Acts as subject matter experts for the development team

24. Which of the following BEST describes the systems development project team role?

A) Provides day-to-day management and leadership of the project

B) Create the core project deliverables by completing assigned tasks

C) Acts as subject matter experts for the development team

D) Develops, installs and operates the requested system

25. Which of the following BEST describes the user project team role?

A) Create the core project deliverables by completing assigned tasks

B) Acts as subject matter experts for the development team

C) Develops, installs and operates the requested system

D) Provides day-to-day management and leadership of the project

26. Which of the following BEST describes the security officer role?

A) Acts as subject matter experts for the development team

B) Carries out the tasks that will inform the security officer of how well the system implements proper security measures

C) Reviews results and deliverables for each phase to confirm compliance with the stated requirements

D) Ensures the deliverable provides an appropriate level of protection

27. Which of the following BEST describes the information system security engineer role?

A) Ensures the deliverable provides an appropriate level of protection

B) Carries out the tasks that will inform the security officer of how well the system implements proper security measures

C) Reviews results and deliverables for each phase to confirm compliance with the stated requirements

D) Acts as subject matter experts for the development team

28. Which of the following BEST describes the quality assurance role?

A) Ensures the deliverable provides an appropriate level of protection

B) Reviews results and deliverables for each phase to confirm compliance with the stated requirements

C) Acts as subject matter experts for the development team

D) Carries out the tasks that will inform the security officer of how well the system implements proper security measures

29. Which of the following functions below does the project steering committee NOT perform?

A) Provides qualified representatives who participate in all requirements definition, acceptance and training activities

B) Takes corrective action regarding personnel changes, budgets or schedules, changes in project objectives, and the need for redesign

C) Reviews project progress and holds emergency meetings if required

D) Coordinates and advises

30. Which of the following BEST represents the steps involved in project management?

A) Initiate, prepare, execute, close

B) Initiate, plan, execute, control

C) Initiate, prepare, execute, monitor, close

D) Initiate, plan, execute, control, close

31. Which of the following BEST represents the formula to calculate total required resources for a project?

A) Resources x Duration/Milestones

B) Resources x Duration

C) Resources/Milestones x Duration

D) (Duration x Milestones)/Resources

32. Which statement below BEST describes the 'man month' dilemma?

A) Subtracting more people does not provide an equivalent reduction in costs

B) Adding more people does not add an equivalent increase in the project timeline

C) Subtracting more people does not provide an equivalent reduction in the project timeline

D) Adding more people does not provide an equivalent boost in productivity

33. Which of the following items is NOT normally included in the PRD?

A) Who the stakeholders are

B) Who the project manager is

C) A project charter stating the objective

D) A high-level timeline

34. Which of the following items is NOT normally required for each project task?

A) Required HR resources

B) How the cost will be paid for

C) Duration

D) Required IT resources

35. Which of the following descriptions BEST describes analogous estimating?

A) The quickest estimation technique, and uses estimates from prior projects

B) Estimates the cost of each activity in the current project, and sums the results

C) Looks at previous estimates of employee hours, materials cost and technology, and uses statistics to extrapolate those estimates to our current project

D) Looks at the raw costs in a previous project and extrapolates to the current project

36. Which of the following descriptions BEST describes actual costs?

A) Looks at the raw costs in a previous project and extrapolates to the current project

B) Looks at previous estimates of employee hours, materials cost and technology, and uses statistics to extrapolate those estimates to our current project

C) Estimates the cost of each activity in the current project, and sums the results

D) The quickest estimation technique, and uses estimates from prior projects

37. Which of the following descriptions BEST describes parametric estimating?

A) Looks at previous estimates of employee hours, materials cost and technology, and uses statistics to extrapolate those estimates to our current project

B) Looks at the raw costs in a previous project and extrapolates to the current project

C) Estimates the cost of each activity in the current project, and sums the results

D) The quickest estimation technique, and uses estimates from prior projects

38. Which of the following descriptions BEST describes bottom-up estimating?

A) Looks at the raw costs in a previous project and extrapolates to the current project

B) Looks at previous estimates of employee hours, materials cost and technology, and uses statistics to extrapolate those estimates to our current project

C) The quickest estimation technique, and uses estimates from prior projects

D) Estimates the cost of each activity in the current project, and sums the results

39. When estimating software size, what are the most common methods?

A) SLOC and FPA

B) Adarac and SLOC

C) Non-FPA and FME

D) FME and EBOC

40. Which description BEST describes the critical path method?

A) Prioritizing all activities based on criticality and moving those tasks to the front of the project

B) Carrying out a detailed analysis of each task to arrive at the shortest duration and summing the results to produce the project end date

C) Finding project duration by measuring the longest path which cannot be compressed

D) Determining project duration by identifying tasks that cannot fail and adjusting the schedule around those tasks

41. Which description BEST describes slack time?

A) The time after the scheduled end of all activities and the advertised project completion date

B) The time in-between tasks that is not productive

C) The time from a task's earliest completion date and the latest completion time that does not impact the critical path

D) The amount a task's duration can be compressed if needed

42. Which of the following statements are NOT true?

A) Any path having slack time may or may not be a critical path

B) Slack time is common

C) Any path having 0 slack time is by definition a critical path

D) A critical path by definition has 0 slack time

43. What is the best definition of a forward pass?

A) Giving the project schedule to the team to finalize

B) Throwing of the ball in the direction that the offensive team is trying to move

C) Going through each task sequentially until we arrive at the shortest possible time to complete the project

D) Evaluating each task duration to arrive at a final project length

44. What is the best definition of a backward pass?

    A) Finding the completion time for each task and calculating slack time

    B) Throwing the ball to a teammate in a direction parallel to or away from the opponents' goal line

    C) Starting with the last task, iterating back through the plan to find opportunities to compress the timeline

    D) Occurs when the team hands the schedule back to the project manager for final approval

45. What is the best definition of crashing?

    A) Negotiating with stakeholders to alter scope in an effort to reduce the project delivery date

    B) An event occurring when two competing tasks consume the same resources simultaneously

    C) An event that will increase auto insurance premiums

    D) Shortening tasks by paying a premium

46. What is the best definition of relaxing?

    A) Negotiating with stakeholders to extend the project delivery date in order to relieve task conflict

    B) Removing dependencies in the critical path to shorten the project timeline

    C) Extending tasks to save on costs

    D) A beach, a hammock and a bottle of Brasserie Dupont Avec Les Bons Voeux

47. What is the best definition of resource leveling?

    A) Smoothing out resource peaks and valleys

    B) Obtaining additional resources to offset task durations that tend to spike

    C) Attempting to hire team members of the same height

    D) Assigning resources well in-advance of the project kick-off

48. What BEST describes why a Gantt chart is unique over other project presentations?

    A) It provides a visual graph of all tasks showing start and end dates, and tracks resources

    B) It is spelled with two Ts

    C) It alone provides the ability for crashing, relaxing and resource leveling

    D) It requires an advanced software package

49. You are managing a project that has a high degree of uncertainty regarding duration of each task. Which is the best project management method to use?

    A) CPM

    B) Gantt

    C) Timebox management

    D) PERT

50. You are managing a project in which a set number of resources needs to deliver in a short time. Which is the best project management method to use?

    A) Gantt

    B) CPM

    C) Timebox management

    D) PERT

51. When controlling a project, what are the three most important things should we keep an eye on?

    A) Documentation, resources and communication

    B) Communication, the critical path and risk

    C) Scope, resources and risk

    D) Scope, timeline and deliverables

52. Which is the BEST description of EVA?

    A) Tracking the tasks marked as completed relative to documented scope of the tasks

    B) Being able to take a walk in outer space

    C) Tracking how much work has been done, and how much is left to do regardless of what the schedule says

    D) Tracking the amount of work left according to the schedule

Answers

1. D	2. C
3. C	4. C
5. C	6. D
7. B	8. B
9. B	10. A
11. D	12. C
13. B	14. D
15. D (Only the top-level WBS may represent the final deliverable)	16. D (Some WPs can be lightly detailed while others can be heavily detailed as long each defines the required work, duration and cost)
17. C	18. D
19. C	20. C
21. B	22. C
23. B	24. B
25. B	26. D
27. B	28. B
29. A (This is a function of user management)	30. D
31. B	32. D
33. D (The other item to include is who is sponsoring the project)	34. A (The other items should be required non-IT resources and estimated cost)
35. A	36. A
37. A	38. D
39. A (Source lines of code (SLOC) and function point analysis (FPA) are the two most common)	40. C
41. C	42. A (Any path having slack time cannot be a critical path)
43. C	44. A
45. D	46. C
47. A	48. A
49. D (Because PERT uses three estimates per task – optimistic, most likely and worst-case – it is the best choice to use when known durations are a risk)	50. C (Timebox management is an iterative approach that favors early delivery over complete delivery, which allows the scope of each delivery to fluctuate when time and resources are set)
51. C	52. C

Chapter 26: Benefits Realization

Questions

1. Which of the following BEST represents the hierarchy in portfolio management?

    A) Portfolio > project > plan

    B) Portfolio > project > program

    C) Portfolio > plan > project

    D) Portfolio > program > project

2. Which of the following is NOT a primary goal for portfolio management?

    A) Focus on internal resources only

    B) Ensure knowledge transfer across projects

    C) Prioritize and schedule projects

    D) Optimize the results of the portfolio, but not the individual projects

3. Which of the following BEST describes a business case?

    A) Defines the problem or opportunity in a clear and concise manner

    B) Understanding the current situation as presented by both strengths and weaknesses

    C) Provides enough information to a business for it to decide if it is worth pursuing

    D) Underlies a business case by studying the problem to see if a solution is practical, meets the stated requirements and can deliver within a set budget and deadline

4. When developing a business case, which of the following BEST describes a feasibility study?

    A) Provides enough information to a business for it to decide if it is worth pursuing

    B) Understanding the current situation as presented by both strengths and weaknesses

    C) Defines the problem or opportunity in a clear and concise manner

    D) Underlies a business case by studying the problem to see if a solution is practical, meets the stated requirements and can deliver within a set budget and deadline

5. When developing a business case, which of the following BEST describes the project scope?

    A) Underlies a business case by studying the problem to see if a solution is practical, meets the stated requirements and can deliver within a set budget and deadline

    B) Defines the problem or opportunity in a clear and concise manner

    C) Understanding the current situation as presented by both strengths and weaknesses

    D) Represent both the stakeholder's needs and constraints

6. When developing a business case, which of the following BEST describes a current analysis?

    A) The recommended system or software solution that will meet the requirements

    B) Represent both the stakeholder's needs and constraints

    C) Defines the problem or opportunity in a clear and concise manner

    D) Understanding the current situation as presented by both strengths and weaknesses

7. When developing a business case, which of the following BEST describes requirements?

    A) The recommended system or software solution that will meet the requirements

    B) Provides enough information to a business for it to decide if it is worth pursuing

    C) Represents both the stakeholder's needs and constraints

    D) Defines the problem or opportunity in a clear and concise manner

8. When developing a business case, which of the following BEST describes the approach?

> A) Selecting the recommended system or software solution that will meet the requirements

> B) Deciding if the recommended approach is sufficiently cost-effective

> C) Reading the feasibility study report with all stakeholders

> D) Represent both the stakeholder's needs and constraints

9. When developing a business case, which of the following BEST describes the evaluation?

> A) Defines the problem or opportunity in a clear and concise manner

> B) Reading the feasibility study report with all stakeholders

> C) The recommended system or software solution that will meet the requirements

> D) Deciding if the recommended approach is sufficiently cost-effective

10. When developing a business case, which of the following BEST describes the review?

> A) Reading the feasibility study report with all stakeholders

> B) The recommended system or software solution that will meet the requirements

> C) Represent both the stakeholder's needs and constraints

> D) Deciding if the recommended approach is sufficiently cost-effective

11. Which statement BEST describes benefits realization?

> A) The promised benefits have been translated into business value

> B) Authorized expenses result in the value promised during the feasibility study

> C) Expenses invested in IT-related initiatives deliver the business benefits that were promised

> D) The promised benefits are completely delivered

12. What are the four steps of benefits realizations at the project level?

> A) Understand, plan, execute and close

> B) Study, plan, realize and report

> C) Understand, plan, realize and report

> D) Study, plan, execute and close

Answers

1. D	2. A (Portfolio management focuses on BOTH internal and external resources)
3. C	4. D
5. B	6. D
7. C	8. A
9. D	10. A
11. C	12. C

Chapter 27: The Software Development Life Cycle, or SDLC

Questions

1. Which of the following BEST describes a key business driver?

A) The reason behind changes within an industry

B) The primary impetus forcing a change in corporate values

C) A significant factor examined when selecting a business function

D) One of the major attributes of a business function that helps reach a company goal

2. What type of application follows the software development life cycle and attempts to collect, store and share information with users on a need-to-know basis?

A) Organization-centric applications

B) Business-focused applications

C) End-user-centric applications

D) User-acceptable applications

3. What type of application does not normally follow the software development life cycle and provides different views of data in ways that optimize performance?

A) Business-focused applications

B) End-user-centric applications

C) Organization-centric applications

D) User-acceptable applications

4. Which of the following BEST describes an ERP?

A) A fully integrated solution that covers multiple areas of business operations

B) A solution that is highly-specific to one business function

C) A fully-integrated solution that typically combines HR, manufacturing and inventory functions only

D) A solution that enables B2B communications

5. What is the primary advantage of using the V-Model SDLC?

A) As development proceeds testing becomes less granular

B) Development s split into two separate functions – testing and user acceptance

C) Development is split into two separate functions – testing and validation

D) As development proceeds testing becomes more granular

6. Which of the following is NOT a recognized risk with software development projects?

A) Risk with the selected technology

B) Risk due to time constraints

C) Risk due to suppliers

D) Risk from within the project

7. When boiling down all project management risks, what one item does it come down to?

A) The innate nature of people to be too optimistic

B) The lack of discipline in managing the software development process

C) The inability to properly estimate effort

D) The inability of management to not introduce scope creep

8. Which of the following is NOT a critical success factors (CSFs) for an SDLC project?

A) Productivity

B) Timeliness

C) Economic value

D) Customer service

9. What is a valid weakness of the Waterfall SDLC?

A) Projects are often more than 1 year in length, by which time the needed requirements have changed

B) Demonstrable functionality cannot be shown early

C) Solid documentation is seldom produced

D) Each step must be completed before starting the next

10. Which phase of the Waterfall SDLC produces an impact analysis?

A) Phase 3B

B) Phase 3A

C) Phase 1

D) Phase 2

11. Which of the following options is NOT valid when considering how to purchase software?

A) Ready-made software can be purchased that requires acceptable customization

B) Ready-made software can be purchased that does not require customization

C) The software can be outsourced and hosted by an outside vendor

D) The software can be developed by an outside vendor

12. Which phase of the Waterfall SDLC collects non-functional requirements?

A) Phase 2

B) Phase 3A

C) Phase 1

D) Phase 3B

13. In which phase of the Waterfall SDLC do we resolve conflicts between requirements and the available resources?

A) Phase 3A

B) Phase 3B

C) Phase 1

D) Phase 2

14. In which phase of the Waterfall SDLC do we identify stakeholders?

A) Phase 3B

B) Phase 3A

C) Phase 2

D) Phase 1

15. In which phase of the Waterfall SDLC do we correct conflicts between expectations and written requirements?

A) Phase 3A

B) Phase 3B

C) Phase 1

D) Phase 2

16. In which phase of the Waterfall SDLC do we create an RFP, ITT or RFI?

A) Phase 4A

B) Phase 4B

C) Phase 3B

D) Phase 3A

17. Which of the following activities is NOT covered in Phase 3A?

A) Conference room pilots

B) Request for Information

C) Entity-relationship diagrams

D) Agenda-based presentations

18. When visiting current users of a vendor's product under consideration for purchase, what is NOT an area that is a top priority?

A) What is the level of customer satisfaction regarding the vendor's commitment to provide training, support and documentation?

B) Is the vendor's deliverable dependable?

C) Is the vendor responsive to problems with its products, and do they deliver on-time?

D) Does the vendor have reliable 24x7 support?

19. In which phase of the Waterfall SDLC do we design the final solution?

    A) Phase 3A

    B) Phase 4B

    C) Phase 3B

    D) Phase 4A

20. Which of the following BEST describes a way to uniquely identify a single entity instance?

    A) A key

    B) A foreign key

    C) A relational key

    D) A primary key

21. Which of the following BEST represents one or more attributes belonging to one entity that map to another entity's primary key?

    A) A key

    B) A primary key

    C) A foreign key

    D) A relational key

22. Which of the following BEST describes a way to locate an entity based on one or more attributes?

    A) A key

    B) A foreign key

    C) A primary key

    D) A relational key

23. Which of the following BEST describes the relationships between a software baseline, a design freeze and scope creep?

    A) The software baseline describes a point in time at which no more changes are allowed to prevent scope creep until the design freeze can be implemented

    B) Design freeze represents the point at which designs are finalized, the software baseline represents core components when completed, and scope creep represents incremental changes to core components as-needed to meet the finalized designs

    C) Both software baseline and design freeze are terms describing a point in time at which no more changes are allowed to prevent scope creep

    D) All three terms deal with SDLC

24. Which of the Waterfall SLDC phases do we encounter first when purchasing software?

    A) Phase 4B

    B) Phase 3A

    C) Phase 3B

    D) Phase 4A

25. Which of the following statements is NOT true regarding Phase 4B?

    A) Since this is a phase executed for purchased software, not coding occurs

    B) If replacing an older system, this phase includes training users on the new system

    C) This phase uses the designs created in phase 3B

    D) Debugging and testing of the primary systems happens in this phase

26. Which of the following is NOT an advantage of using coding standards?

A) It minimizes disruptions when people leave and are replaced

B) It encourages modular code development

C) It requires code to align to naming patterns

D) It prevents bugs from being introduced

27. Which of the following terms refers to a block of code performing a single, dedicated function?

A) Coupled

B) Concise

C) Cohesive

D) Compounded

28. Which of the following terms refers to a block of code being dependent on other code to function?

A) Compounded

B) Cohesive

C) Concise

D) Coupled

29. Which BEST describes the main purpose of an IDE?

A) It allows programmers to write code

B) It allows project managers to manage projects with large amounts of source code

C) It allows stakeholders to track progress at the functional level

D) It allows quality managers to track defects

30. What BEST describes the capability an online programming facility gives to developers?

A) To develop programs without requiring dedicated workstations

B) To simultaneously work on the same code blocks as other developers

C) To write and test code that is stored on a server

D) To continue development efforts anywhere with a network connection

31. Which is NOT a risk when using online programming facilities?

A) Multiple software versions can result

B) An external attacker could easily access source code

C) Valid changes might be overwritten by other changes

D) Developers can bypass procedures and make unauthorized changes

32. Which of the following BEST describes a compiler?

A) Instructions that a computer can understand

B) One-step above binary code

C) Translates human-readable languages into binary code

D) The intermediate product of changing human-readable language into binary code

33. Which of the following BEST describes a compiler object code?

A) One-step above binary code

B) Instructions that a computer can understand

C) The intermediate product of changing human-readable language into binary code

D) Translates human-readable languages into binary code

34. Which of the following BEST describes a binary code?

A) Signals executed at the hardware layer

B) Codes used to represent complex instructions

C) The intermediate product of changing human-readable language into machine-readable code

D) Instructions that a computer can understand

35. Which of the following BEST describes assembly language?

A) Instructions that a computer can understand

B) The intermediate product of changing human-readable language into binary code

C) Translates human-readable languages into binary code

D) One-step above binary code

36. Which of the following languages is considered to be a 3rd generation language?

    A) COBOL

    B) Tcl

    C) Assembly

    D) FOCUS

37. Which of the following is NOT a valid category of debugging tools?

    A) Log parsing

    B) Logic path monitor

    C) Memory dump

    D) Output analyzer

38. What is the primary advantage when using a logic path monitor?

    A) It checks the results from a function and compares it to expected results

    B) It alerts us of pre-defined issues in real-time

    C) It allows us to trace after the fact the steps leading to a bug

    D) It creates a map of system memory that can be analyzed later

39. What BEST describes the two things does testing do for us?

    A) Provides proof for stakeholders that changes were implemented correctly and tells us if a change has negatively impacted other areas

    B) Validates that functions work properly and tells us if a change has negatively impacted other areas

    C) Validates that functions work properly and allows us to track changes as they are made

    D) Provides proof for stakeholders that changes were implemented correctly and allows us to track changes as they are made

40. Which of the following BEST describes a bottom-up test plan?

    A) Starts at the highest level and dives deeper in each successive pass

    B) Exercises the most recently-changed areas and tests functions dependent on those areas

    C) Starts by manipulating data elements and detecting fallout from functions

    D) Examines the smallest testable units and continues with larger units until the complete system has been tested

41. Which BEST describes unit testing?

    A) Exercises a single system

    B) Carries out exercises to ensure that two or more components communicate properly with each other

    C) Exercises the entire solution across multiple systems

    D) Exercises an individual program or module

42. Which BEST describes integration testing?

    A) Exercises an individual program or module

    B) Exercises the entire solution across multiple systems

    C) Carries out exercises to ensure that two or more components communicate properly with each other

    D) Exercises a single system

43. Which BEST describes interface testing?

    A) Carries out exercises to ensure that two or more components communicate properly with each other

    B) Exercises the entire solution across multiple systems

    C) Exercises an individual program or module

    D) Exercises a single system

44. Which BEST describes system testing?

A) Exercises an individual program or module

B) Exercises a single system

C) Carries out exercises to ensure that two or more components communicate properly with each other

D) Exercises the entire solution across multiple systems

45. Which is NOT an area that system testing is concerned with?

A) Data testing

B) Security testing

C) Recovery testing

D) Volume testing

46. Which BEST describes recovery testing?

A) Ensuring the system can return to a working state after a hardware of software failure

B) Simulating a heavy amount of traffic during peak areas

C) Incrementally increasing the size of the database until the application fails

D) Increasing the number of active users until the system fails

47. Which BEST describes security testing?

A) Increasing the number of active users until the system fails

B) Looking for a proper level of access controls

C) Incrementally increasing the size of the database until the application fails

D) Simulating a heavy amount of traffic during peak areas

48. Which BEST describes load testing?

A) Incrementally increasing the size of the database until the application fails

B) Increasing the number of active users until the system fails

C) Simulating a heavy amount of traffic during peak areas

D) Comparing the system's performance to well-defined benchmarks

49. Which BEST describes volume testing?

A) Simulating a heavy amount of traffic during peak areas

B) Increasing the number of active users until the system fails

C) Incrementally increasing the size of the database until the application fails

D) Comparing the system's performance to well-defined benchmarks

50. Which BEST describes stress testing?

A) Increasing the number of active users until the system fails

B) Incrementally increasing the size of the database until the application fails

C) Simulating a heavy amount of traffic during peak areas

D) Comparing the system's performance to well-defined benchmarks

51. Which BEST describes performance testing?

A) Comparing the system's performance to well-defined benchmarks

B) Simulating a heavy amount of traffic during peak areas

C) Increasing the number of active users until the system fails

D) Incrementally increasing the size of the database until the application fails

52. Which of the following BEST describes alpha version testing?

A) Testing an application ready for a limited rollout of an application to a very small set of end-users

B) Testing an application that has completed UAT but is not in production

C) Testing an application that is feature complete but has not yet completed UAT

D) Testing an application that is not feature complete, but is ready to undergo assumption and logic flow validations

53. Which of the following BEST describes beta version testing?

A) Testing an application ready for a limited rollout of an application to a very small set of end-users

B) Testing an application that is feature complete but has not yet completed UAT

C) Testing an application that is not feature complete, but is ready to undergo assumption and logic flow validations

D) Testing an application that has completed UAT but is not in production

54. Which of the following BEST describes pilot testing?

A) Testing an application that has completed UAT but is not in production

B) Testing an application that is not feature complete, but is ready to undergo assumption and logic flow validations

C) Testing an application that is feature complete but has not yet completed UAT

D) Testing an application ready for a limited rollout of an application to a very small set of end-users

55. Which of the following BEST describes white box testing?

A) Rerunning previous tests to ensure recent changes have not broken something that used to work

B) Testing two versions of the same application

C) Testing that answers the question 'Are we building the right product?'

D) Testing an application with full knowledge of the inner workings

56. Which of the following BEST describes function testing?

A) Rerunning previous tests to ensure recent changes have not broken something that used to work

B) Testing that answers the question 'Are we building the right product?'

C) Testing an application with full knowledge of the inner workings

D) Testing two versions of the same application

57. Which of the following BEST describes regression testing?

A) Testing an application with full knowledge of the inner workings

B) Testing two versions of the same application

C) Testing that answers the question 'Are we building the right product?'

D) Rerunning previous tests to ensure recent changes have not broken something that used to work

58. Which of the following BEST describes parallel testing?

A) Testing that answers the question 'Are we building the right product?'

B) Rerunning previous tests to ensure recent changes have not broken something that used to work

C) Testing using the same set of data to see what has broken

D) Testing an application with full knowledge of the inner workings

59. Which BEST describes sociability testing?

A) Testing an application's interface to validate integration has not been broken

B) Rerunning previous tests to determine the impact to previous versions of the same application

C) Determining the impact a new or modified application might have on other applications running in the same environment

D) Testing an application designed to integrate with social networks

60. Which statement is NOT true regarding QAT and UAT?

A) QAT and UAT normally happen in parallel

B) Both QAT and UAT are forms of final acceptance testing

C) QAT validates that the solution works as documented, while UAT validates that the end-user is happy with the result

D) QAT is carried out by IT, while UAT is carried out by end-users

61. Which of the following statements is NOT true regarding UAT?

A) The data used should represent production data as close as possible

B) The test environment should not be alterable during testing, except for changes made by the vendor

C) If production data is to be used, confidential data must be scrubbed before use

D) The accepted version must be version-controlled

62. Which of the following is NOT true regarding an integrated test facility, or ITF?

A) It is provided by an external vendor

B) It should mimic production scale and capacity

C) It is commonly used for UAT

D) Production data is seldom used for ITFs, even when scrubbed

63. Which BEST describes the difference between certification and accreditation?

A) Accreditation is carried out by an external party, while certification is an internal approval

B) Certification is carried out by an external party, while accreditation is an internal approval

C) Accreditation confirms acceptability, while certification is the acceptance of the accreditation

D) Certification confirms acceptability, while accreditation is the acceptance of the certification

64. Which of the following is NOT true concerning site acceptance testing?

A) The site is not publicly accessible during this time

B) Is happens in the production environment

C) It uses real data

D) It executes the same tests as UAT

65. Which is the BEST description of shadowing?

A) Two equally-qualified people split identical duties and slowly transition one to another position

B) A person watches what another does and asks questions, with a final hand-off on a specific date

C) Two people swap duties in increasing frequency until each is performing the other's job

D) Small portions of knowledge and responsibilities are transferred in phases

66. Which is the BEST description of relay-baton?

A) Small portions of knowledge and responsibilities are transferred in phases

B) A person watches what another does and asks questions, with a final hand-off on a specific date

C) Two equally-qualified people split identical duties and slowly transition one to another position

D) Two people swap duties in increasing frequency until each is performing the other's job

67. You are in charge of migrating from an old inventory system to a new one, but each stores color attributes in different formats. Which of the following processes will BEST help you to succeed?

    A) Data mining

    B) Data transmogrification

    C) Data porting

    D) Data migration

68. Which of the following BEST describes a module analysis?

    A) Identifying affected modules and data entities during a data migration project

    B) A list of tasks needed to deploy legacy data to production

    C) Provides adapters to connect to both the legacy and new repositories

    D) Provides translation services between two repositories

69. Which of the following BEST describes a migration screenplay?

    A) A list of tasks needed to deploy legacy data to production

    B) Identifying affected modules and data entities during a data migration project

    C) Provides adapters to connect to both the legacy and new repositories

    D) Provides translation services between two repositories

70. Which of the following BEST describes a data director?

    A) Provides adapters to connect to both the legacy and new repositories

    B) A list of tasks needed to deploy legacy data to production

    C) Provides translation services between two repositories

    D) Identifying affected modules and data entities during a data migration project

71. Which of the following BEST describes a data conversion component?

    A) Provides translation services between two repositories

    B) Provides adapters to connect to both the legacy and new repositories

    C) Identifying affected modules and data entities during a data migration project

    D) A list of tasks needed to deploy legacy data to production

72. Which of the following is NOT a true statement concerning data conversion components?

    A) A valid rollback method is to log in new, rollback in new, and reapply in old

    B) The right approach depends on transaction volume and the expected data conversion

    C) A valid rollback method is to unload from new, transfer to old, and reload old

    D) Rollback steps should be designed in from the beginning if the risk of rollback is high

73. What are the three types of changeover techniques?

    A) Delayed, variable and immediate

    B) Parallel, phased and abrupt

    C) Distinct, construed and managed

    D) Singular, multiple and variable

74. Which BEST describes the difference between a post-project review and a post-implementation review?

    A) A post-project review focuses on team performance, while a post-implementation review focuses on project performance

    B) A post-project review is held as soon as the project ends, while a post-implementation review is held at least 6 months after

    C) A post-project review focuses on how successful the project processes were, while a post-implementation review measures the value the project delivered

    D) A post-project review closes out activities, while a post-implementation review imitates maintenance mode

75. Which BEST describes the two primary needs an agile development method is meant to address?

> A) Execute before requirements are known, and react quickly to changes
>
> B) Provide reasonable timeline expectations, and keep cost overruns to a minimum
>
> C) Ensure resources are available before start, and allow for unknown requirements
>
> D) Ensure requirements are complete before start, and to provide maximum documentation

76. You are managing a project with only partial requirements but the customer needs to receive steady and incremental prototypes as work progresses. Which of the following methodologies should you use?

> A) OOSD
>
> B) Waterfall
>
> C) Scrum
>
> D) RAD

77. Which of the following statements are NOT true regarding prototyping?

> A) It keeps the traditional Waterfall methodology but in repeated iterations
>
> B) One approach is to build the entire model and then the entire system
>
> C) It does not require a trial-and-error approach
>
> D) Initial prototypes focus on screens and reports

78. What of the following is NOT a drawback of the prototyping approach?

> A) Scope-creep is a common occurrence
>
> B) Change control mechanisms are often weak
>
> C) Fundamentals such as backup and recovery methods are often left out
>
> D) The rapid pace often results in unwanted features

79. What are the four stages of RAD?

> A) Requirements collection, design, development and maintenance
>
> B) Design, development, testing and deployment
>
> C) Definition, prototyping, development and testing
>
> D) Concept definition, functional design, development and deployment

80. Which of the following statements concerning OOSD is NOT true?

> A) OOSD can be used with most SDLC methodologies
>
> B) It builds a solution by grouping data with procedures
>
> C) An object's data is called an attribute
>
> D) An object's functionality is called a method

Answers

1. D	2. A
3. B	4. A
5. A	6. B (The other risks are mistranslated requirements, from within the organization and form the external environment)
7. B	8. B (Quality is the missing CSF)
9. C	10. C
11. C (The other valid option is use software through the cloud, using a software as a service (SaaS) model)	12. A
13. D	14. C
15. D	16. D
17. C (ERDs are covered inn Phase 3B)	18. D
19. C	20. D
21. C	22. A
23. C	24. D
25. A (There is usually some custom coding required even for purchased software)	26. D (While it can reduce the number of bugs, it does not eliminate them)
27. C	28. D
29. A	30. C
31. B	32. C
33. C	34. D
35. D	36. A
37. A	38. C
39. B	40. D
41. D	42. C
43. A	44. D (While it may not make much sense, testing a single system is covered under integration or interface testing)
45. A	46. A
47. B	48. C
49. C	50. A
51. A	52. D
53. B	54. D
55. D	56. B
57. D	58. C
59. C	60. A (QAT normally completes before UAT is authorized to start)
61. B (Any change must be explicitly approved regardless of the source)	62. D
63. D	64. A (Unless this is a brand-new rollout, the site will

	almost always be live during this activity)
65. B	66. A
67. C	68. A
69. A	70. A
71. A	72. D (Rollback steps should ALWAYS be designed in regardless of the expected risk)
73. B	74. C
75. A	76. C (Waterfall requires all requirements up-front, RAD does not produce a reliable deliverable cadence and OOSD is not a development methodology. Scrum is the only viable alternative listed.)
77. C	78. D (While scope-creep often results in unnecessary features, features that were never asked for by the customer is seldom a problem)
79. D	80. A (Since OOSD is simply a programming technique, it can be used with ALL SDLC methodologies)

Chapter 28: Software Development

Questions

1. What of the following statements is NOT true regarding architectures?

    A) An n-tiered architecture has 4 or more tiers

    B) A 2-tier architecture has the client connecting directly to the database

    C) A 3-tier architecture has an intermediate layer

    D) A client-server architecture has at least one client and one server

2. Which of the following components does NOT represent mobile code?

    A) COM

    B) VBScript

    C) ActiveX

    D) JavaBeans

3. In OOSD, which of the following statements BEST describes a class?

    A) A pattern which can be instantiated

    B) The instantiation of a pattern

    C) The ability of a child instance to do something different than a parent instance would do

    D) Extending a class through another class

4. In OOSD, which of the following statements BEST describes an object?

    A) A parent class

    B) The instantiation of a class

    C) The ability of a child instance to do something different than a parent instance would do

    D) Extending a class through another class

5. In OOSD, which of the following statements BEST describes inheritance?

    A) Duplicating an object

    B) Extending a class through another class

    C) The ability of a child instance to do something different than a parent instance would do

    D) Extending the ability of one object my combining it with another

6. In OOSD, which of the following statements BEST describes polymorphism?

    A) The instantiation of a pattern

    B) Having two identical objects behave differently by changing their internal data structures

    C) Extending a class through another class

    D) The ability of a child instance to do something different than a parent instance would do

7. Which of the following BEST describes in-process client?

    A) An application that exposes parts of itself to be used by other software

    B) A service that runs across the network on a dedicated server

    C) Runs within containers hosted on another computer

    D) A component requiring some type of a host to start and execute

8. Which of the following BEST describes a stand-alone client?

    A) A service that runs across the network

    B) An application that exposes parts of itself to be used by other software

    C) A component requiring some type of a host to start and execute

    D) Runs within containers hosted on another computer

9. Which of the following BEST describes a stand-alone server?

A) A component requiring some type of a host to start and execute

B) A service that runs across the network

C) Runs within containers hosted on another computer

D) An application that exposes parts of itself to be used by other software

10. Which of the following BEST describes in-process server?

A) An application that exposes parts of itself to be used by other software

B) Runs within containers hosted on another computer

C) A component requiring some type of a host to start and execute

D) A service that runs across the network

11. Which of the following BEST describes a remote procedure call?

A) Downloading a component form a remote server that then executes locally

B) Executing a component across the network

C) The name used for functionality currently executing on a remote server

D) Sending a procedure to a remote server where it is executed

12. Which is NOT an example of a distributed object technology?

A) CORBA

B) CPR

C) DCOM

D) RMI

13. Which definition BEST describes middleware?

A) A cloud-based service that provides translation capabilities between two disparate systems

B) Hardware that negotiates between two proxies in real-time

C) Any software that provides run-time services for other components, normally accessible across the network

D) Software that intercepts encrypted web traffic and decrypts on behalf of network components

14. Which statement BEST describes SOAP?

A) A text-based protocol proprietary to the CROBA initiative

B) A web-based protocol that is self-descriptive and discoverable through the WSDL and UDDI mechanisms

C) A light-weight web protocol providing little self-description or discovery capabilities

D) A handy and delightfully pleasant cleaning agent

15. Which of the following is the BEST description of an Upper CASE tool?

A) Documents business and application requirements such as data object definitions, relationships and processes.

B) Generates program code and database schemas

C) Documents detailed designs such as screen and report layouts, editing rules and process flows

D) Produces production-ready capabilities

16. Which of the following is the BEST description of a Middle CASE tool?

A) Documents business and application requirements such as data object definitions, relationships and processes.

B) Documents detailed designs such as screen and report layouts, editing rules and process flows

C) Produces production-ready capabilities

D) Generates program code and database schemas

17. Which of the following is the BEST description of a Lower CASE tool?

A) Produces production-ready capabilities

B) Documents business and application requirements such as data object definitions, relationships and processes.

C) Documents detailed designs such as screen and report layouts, editing rules and process flows

D) Generates program code and database schemas

18. Which statement below BEST describes a 3rd generation language?

A) They are non-procedural

B) They are object-oriented

C) They replace both binary and assembly languages

D) They have one entry point and one exit point

19. Which of the statements below is NOT true regarding 4th generation languages?

A) All input is provided as parameters when invoking code

B) They often allow non-programmers to use them

C) They are non-procedural

D) They are portable

20. Which of the following is NOT a 4GL category?

A) Relational database 4GLs

B) WISE-capable generators

C) Query and report generators

D) Application generators

21. Which of the following BEST describes a 4GL query and report generator?

A) A proprietary language also running inside of a database but on an enterprise-scale server

B) A specialized language that can extract data and produce reports

C) A language that can run inside of a database on embedded devices

D) A 4GL that generates 3GL code such as COBOL or C

22. Which of the following BEST describes an embedded database 4GL?

A) A specialized language that can extract data and produce reports

B) A language that can run inside of a database on embedded devices

C) A 4GL that generates 3GL code such as COBOL or C

D) A proprietary language also running inside of a database but on an enterprise-scale server

23. Which of the following BEST describes a relational database 4GL?

A) A proprietary language also running inside of a database but on an enterprise-scale server

B) A 4GL that generates 3GL code such as COBOL or C

C) A language that can run inside of a database on embedded devices

D) A specialized language that can extract data and produce reports

24. Which of the following BEST describes a 4GL application generator?

A) A specialized language that can extract data and produce reports

B) A proprietary language also running inside of a database but on an enterprise-scale server

C) A 4GL that generates 3GL code such as COBOL or C

D) A language that can run inside of a database on embedded devices

25. You are purchasing a rather expensive software product for a vendor and want to protect yourself form risk in case the vendor goes out of business. Which of the following is the BEST course of action to take?

A) Source from two different vendors

B) Ensure language in the purchase contract includes obligations that cover such a scenario

C) Put the source code in escrow

D) Require the vendor to provide a copy of the source code at the time of purchase

Answers

1. A (An n-tiered architecture contains 3 or more tiers, so a 3-tier architecture is also called an n-tier architecture)	2. B (VBScript is a scripting language that runs inside of a browser sandbox, whereas the other options install and execute directly)
3. A	4. B
5. B	6. D
7. D	8. B
9. B	10. B
11. B	12. B (While CPR may revive a human, it is little use to computers)
13. C	14. B
15. A	16. B
17. D	18. D (4th generation languages on-procedural and often object-oriented, and while they do offer higher-level functions than binary and assembly, they don't completely replace the need for those languages (and binary code is arguably NOT a language))
19. A (3rd generation languages require input parameters, while many object-oriented 4th generation languages support object properties (or attributes) instead)	20. B
21. B	22. B
23. A	24. C
25. C	

Chapter 29: e-Commerce

Questions

1. Which of the following is NOT a common e-Commerce model?

    A) B2E

    B) B2D

    C) B2G

    D) B2C

2. Which of the following items is NOT something a company must possess to be successful in the e-Commerce space?

    A) A top-level commitment

    B) An affinity for fast-paced business transactions

    C) The ability to link legacy systems into an online presence

    D) Embrace business process reconfiguration

Chapter 29: e-Commerce

Answers

1. B (B2B is the other model)	2. B

Chapter 30: EDI
Questions

1. Which of the following BEST describes EDI?

A) The transfer of information between two systems using an intermediary format that both systems understand

B) An agreement between two entities to use an Internet-based path to share data

C) The automated synch of data across disparate networks

D) The formatting and transmission of proprietary and encrypted data

2. Which of the following is NOT a required component for an EDI system?

A) A shared standard

B) Translation software

C) A partner profile

D) Communications software

3. What are the three components required on each end of an EDI exchange?

A) Communications handler, EDI translator and an application interface

B) Communications handler, EDI interface and an application interface

C) Communications handler, EDI interface and an application system

D) Communications handler, EDI interface and EDI translator

4. Which of the following is NOT a factor for a web-based EDIT to replace traditional EDI?

A) A robust security infrastructure riding on top of the Internet

B) A reduced cost due to not having to use private networks

C) Improvements in the X.12 EDI formatting standard

D) The inability to have more than two partners share in an EDI framework

5. What is NOT a risk when using EDI?

A) Transmission mistakes can often go unnoticed for long periods of time

B) A lack of legal agreements surrounding the exchange of electronic data, increasing the uncertainty of which party is legally liable for failures

C) The lack of authentication for electronic exchange, resulting in the difficulty in knowing who is submitting data packets

D) Ensuring continuity and availability of the EDI exchange process

6. Which of the following is NOT a valid inbound transmission control?

A) Use receipt totals to verify the number and value of transactions

B) Manage change control for procedures

C) Use encryption

D) Perform edit checks prior to updating an application.

7. Which of the following is NOT a valid outbound transmission control?

A) Use check digits on control fields

B) Segregate duties for the initiation and transmission of high-risk transactions

C) Protect the trading partner profile

D) Limit the ability for employees to initiate specific EDI transactions

8. Which of the following standards is NOT based on XML?

A) XQuery

B) XSL

C) XWrap

D) XML encryption

9. What does an XML schema provide?

A) Identifies the source of the XML payload

B) A description of the accompanying XML payload

C) Retransmission requirements

D) Encryption/decryption parameters

Answers

1. A	2. C (While a partner profile is often required before data may be transmitted, it is not one of the three listed requirements for the EDI system itself)
3. C	4. D (Traditional EDI historically allows more than one partner to participate using a VAN)
5. A	6. B (Manage change control for procedures is an outbound control)
7. A (Use check digits on control fields is an inbound control)	8. C (XWrap does not exist)
9. B	

Chapter 31: Email

Questions

1. What is the primary purpose of an email gateway?

A) To provide a port-level proxy function between two email servers

B) To distribute load between multiple email servers

C) To protect an email server from attacks

D) To translate differing formats between email servers

2. Which of the following BEST describes the SMTP protocol?

A) An outgoing email protocol

B) An incoming email protocol with no security and that supports only a single client

C) An incoming email protocol designed to work with Outlook

D) An incoming email protocol that provides security and supports multiple clients

3. Which of the following BEST describes the POP protocol?

A) An incoming email protocol designed to work with Outlook

B) An incoming email protocol with no security and that supports only a single client

C) An outgoing email protocol

D) An incoming email protocol that provides security and supports multiple clients

4. Which of the following BEST describes the IMAP protocol?

A) An incoming email protocol designed to work with Outlook

B) An incoming email protocol with no security and that supports only a single client

C) An incoming email protocol that provides security and supports multiple clients

D) An outgoing email protocol

5. Which of the following BEST describes the MAPI protocol?

A) An outgoing email protocol

B) An incoming email protocol that provides security and supports multiple clients

C) An incoming email protocol designed to work with Outlook

D) An incoming email protocol with no security and that supports only a single client

6. Which of the following is NOT a common attack associated with email servers?

A) Fragging

B) DoS

C) Spear phishing

D) Phishing

7. Which of the following is NOT a primary method to improve email security?

A) Use encryption technologies

B) Educate employees on the dangers of social media attacks

C) Properly maintain the email server

D) Ensure the server meets security policies and guidelines

8. Which of the following statements is NOT true regarding a digital signature?

A) The signature cannot be forged

B) The signed message cannot be altered because it will render the signature invalid

C) The signature is authentic and encrypted

D) The signature can be reused

9. What three security guarantees does a digital signature provide?

A) Confidentiality, authentication and availability

B) Authentication, integrity and availability

C) Authentication, integrity and nonrepudiation

D) Confidentiality, authentication and integrity

Answers

1. D	2. A
3. B	4. C
5. C	6. A
7. B (While educating employees is important, it does not directly protect email security – it simply decrease the fallout after security is defeated)	8. D
9. C	

Chapter 32: Electric Money

Questions

1. Which of the following BEST describes EFT?

A) Enables payments to be made through the use of virtual transactions

B) Focuses on providing services such as mortgage loans or insurance policies

C) Allows banking customers to carry out virtually all transactions from the comfort of their home

D) Computers that physically connect with credit card readers

2. Which of the following BEST describes e-banking?

A) Computers that physically connect with credit card readers

B) Focuses on providing services such as mortgage loans or insurance policies

C) Allows banking customers to carry out virtually all transactions from the comfort of their home

D) Enables payments to be made through the use of virtual transactions

3. Which of the following BEST describes electronic finance?

A) Enables payments to be made through the use of virtual transactions

B) Focuses on providing services such as mortgage loans or insurance policies

C) Computers that physically connect with credit card readers

D) Allows banking customers to carry out virtually all transactions from the comfort of their home

4. Which of the following BEST describes POS?

A) Computers that physically connect with credit card readers

B) Focuses on providing services such as mortgage loans or insurance policies

C) Enables payments to be made through the use of virtual transactions

D) Allows banking customers to carry out virtually all transactions from the comfort of their home

5. Which of the following is NOT a common risk associated with EFT?

A) The pressure to outsource work introduces additional risk

B) Integrating legacy systems directly with Internet-facing portals

C) The non-stop transfer of physical currency to and from electronic currency introduces many opportunities for fraud

D) The rate of change is so quick that risk analysis and security reviews seldom happen

6. Which of the following is NOT a control to ensure proper board and management oversight of EFT?

A) Keep as much work in-house as possible to eliminate unneeded outsourcing risk

B) Perform comprehensive due diligence and proper management over outsourcing activities

C) Ensure that the board and management are actively engaged and have accountability for all e-banking activities

D) Establish a comprehensive security control process to eliminate gaps

7. Which of the following is not a recommended security control for ATMs?

> A) Procedures for PIN issuance and protection should exist, including delivery of PINs
>
> B) Systems should be confirmed to not stored PINs
>
> C) Access to a customer's account after a number of unsuccessful attempts should be implemented
>
> D) A reconciliation of all general ledger accounts should be executed

8. Which of the following is NOT an electronic payment method?

> A) Transfer
>
> B) Deposit
>
> C) Money
>
> D) Check

9. Which electronic payment method best protects the identity of the original sender?

> A) Electronic deposit
>
> B) Electronic check
>
> C) Electronic transfer
>
> D) Electronic money

10. Which electronic payment method is susceptible to double spending?

> A) Electronic transfer
>
> B) Electronic check
>
> C) Electronic money
>
> D) Electronic deposit

11. Which electronic payment method requires the user to be online?

> A) Electronic transfer
>
> B) Electronic deposit
>
> C) Electronic money
>
> D) Electronic check

12. Which electronic payment method does not lend itself to earning interest?

> A) Electronic check
>
> B) Electronic transfer
>
> C) Electronic money
>
> D) Electronic deposit

13. Which electronic payment method is the easiest to understand and implement?

> A) Electronic deposit
>
> B) Electronic transfer
>
> C) Electronic check
>
> D) Electronic money

Answers

1. A	2. C
3. B	4. A
5. C (The transfer of physical to electronic currency has been going on for decades)	6. A
7. B (Systems should not be allowed to store PINs in an unencrypted fashion)	8. B
9. D (Although not technically enforced, banks try to 'forget' who created a digital certificate)	10. C (Under some circumstances, a digital certificate can be redeemed more than once)
11. A (Both electronic money and checks are carried out using digital certificates which can be used offline)	12. C (Since banks forget who sent an electronic payment, no interest can be awarded)
13. B	

Chapter 33: Integrated Manufacturing System, or IMS

Questions

1. Which of the following statements BEST describes IMS?

A) Aligning multiple manufacturing solutions so that each share the same process

B) Merging complex manufacturing processes into a single solution

C) Re-engineering a manufacturing solution to maximize the sharing of resources across all processes

D) Deconstructing a complex manufacturing solution into simpler processes that can be managed separately

Answers

1. B	

Chapter 34: Industrial Control System or ICS

Questions

1. Which of the following statements BEST describes ICS?

A) The ability to monitor and alert geographically-separated industrial components

B) A system that controls industrial infrastructure components

C) The networked infrastructure shared between industrial infrastructure components

D) A system that coordinates tasks between geographically-separated industrial components

2. Which of the following is NOT a common control when dealing with ICS?

A) Use redundancy to keep availability high

B) Restrict access to the ICS network and network activity, particularly when connected to the Internet

C) Restrict physical access to the ICS network and devices such as locks, card readers and/or guards

D) Deploy security patches for zero-day exploits immediately when available, with testing completed no longer than 3 days afterward

Answers

1. B	2. D (All security patches should be tested before deployment)

Chapter 35: Artificial Intelligence, or AI

Questions

1. Which of the following statements BEST describes artificial intelligence?

A) A program that mimics a human's ability to process input and make intelligent decisions

B) A combination of hardware and software that is patterned after the human brain to detect patterns in seemingly random data

C) A combination of hardware and software that can pass the Turing Test

D) A program that distributes complex rule execution across many high-powered computers, resulting in an approximation of human thought

2. Which of the following statements BEST describes an expert system?

A) A program that accepts a large database of known facts and then derives relationships

B) A program allowing a user to specify one or more base assumptions, and then carries out an analysis of arbitrary events

C) A subset of AI that analyzes multiple disparate factual sources and aggregates a common rule set that is then applied to a single question

D) A program that allows a user to specify a small set of base conditions and then extrapolates the most likely result based on a heuristic analysis

3. In relation to an expert system, which BEST describes facts?

A) Components within a system yet to be loaded with facts or rules

B) Data that comes in from a sensor or system that is being monitored

C) Artificial intelligence to infer relationships and arrive at a decision

D) Facts expressed in one of several models

4. In relation to an expert system, which BEST describes a knowledge base?

A) Components within a system yet to be loaded with facts or rules

B) Data that comes in from a sensor or system that is being monitored

C) Facts expressed in one of several models

D) Artificial intelligence to infer relationships and arrive at a decision

5. In relation to an expert system, which BEST describes an inference engine?

A) Components within a system yet to be loaded with facts or rules

B) Facts expressed in one of several models

C) Artificial intelligence to infer relationships and arrive at a decision

D) Data that comes in from a sensor or system that is being monitored

6. In relation to an expert system, which BEST describes a shell?

A) Components within a system yet to be loaded with facts or rules

B) Artificial intelligence to infer relationships and arrive at a decision

C) Facts expressed in one of several models

D) Data that comes in from a sensor or system that is being monitored

7. In relation to an expert system, which BEST describes a decision tree?

A) Used to load facts into the knowledge base without requiring a programmer

B) A series of 'if...then' relationships

C) A graph of nodes and arcs between those nodes

D) A list of questions to ask a user until a conclusion is reached

8. In relation to an expert system, which BEST describes a rule?

A) An 'if...then' relationship

B) A list of questions to ask a user until a conclusion is reached

C) A graph of nodes and arcs between those nodes

D) Used to load facts into the knowledge base without requiring a programmer

9. In relation to an expert system, which BEST describes a semantic net?

A) A series of 'if...then' relationships

B) A list of questions to ask a user until a conclusion is reached

C) Used to load facts into the knowledge base without requiring a programmer

D) A graph of nodes and arcs between those nodes

10. In relation to an expert system, which BEST describes a knowledge interface?

A) A graph of nodes and arcs between those nodes

B) A list of questions to ask a user until a conclusion is reached

C) A series of 'if...then' relationships

D) Used to load facts into the knowledge base without requiring a programmer

11. In relation to an expert system, which BEST describes a data interface?

A) Used to load facts into the knowledge base without requiring a programmer

B) Enables the expert system to collect data from non-human sources

C) A list of questions to ask a user until a conclusion is reached

D) A graph of nodes and arcs between those nodes

Answers

1. A	2. B
3. B	4. C
5. C	6. A
7. D	8. A
9. D	10. D
11. B	

Chapter 36: Business Intelligence, or BI

Questions

1. Which of the following statements BEST describes BI?

A) It uses refined AI rules to make the best decisions for a given business

B) It is a system that harnesses the knowledge and experience of all management personnel into a single, intelligent engine

C) It employs multiple expert systems to explore the most likely business outcomes, thereby helping human management to achieve the greatest success

D) It collects massive amounts of data and uses various methods of analysis to detect trends

2. Which of the following is NOT a reason that BI is becoming more common place?

A) To meet legal and regulatory compliance

B) Increasing hardware capacity have brought BI capabilities into the mainstream

C) The drive to find new ways to beat the competition is increasing

D) Organizations are increasing in size and complexity such that massive amounts of data hide the needed answers

3. Which of the following BEST describes operational data in the data source layer of BI?

A) Data collected during normal business operations and normally held in easy-to-access databases

B) Data provided by a source external to the company

C) Data provided by systems external to the BI system

D) Data needed by end users but is not currently in an accessible format

4. Which of the following BEST describes external data in the data source layer of BI?

A) Data provided by a source external to the company

B) Data collected during normal business operations and normally held in easy-to-access databases

C) Data provided by systems external to the BI system

D) Data needed by end users but is not currently in an accessible format

5. Which of the following BEST describes non-operational in the data source layer of BI?

A) Data collected during normal business operations and normally held in easy-to-access databases

B) Data easily collected but has not yet been processed

C) Data needed by end users but is not currently in an accessible format

D) Data provided by systems external to the BI system

6. Which of the following BEST describes the data source layer of BI?

A) Provides access to the various data sources while at the same time hiding how that data is stored

B) Contains the bulk of interesting data, and is usually a relational database

C) Copies and transforms data into and out of the warehouse format and assures quality control

D) Provides access to operational, external and non-operational data

7. Which of the following BEST describes the data access layer of BI?

A) Copies and transforms data into and out of the warehouse format and assures quality control

B) Provides access to operational, external and non-operational data

C) Contains the bulk of interesting data, and is usually a relational database

D) Provides access to the various data sources while at the same time hiding how that data is stored

8. Which of the following BEST describes the data staging and quality layer of BI?

A) Contains the bulk of interesting data, and is usually a relational database

B) Provides access to operational, external and non-operational data

C) Copies and transforms data into and out of the warehouse format and assures quality control

D) Provides access to the various data sources while at the same time hiding how that data is stored

9. Which of the following BEST describes the core data warehouse layer of BI?

A) Provides access to operational, external and non-operational data

B) Provides access to the various data sources while at the same time hiding how that data is stored

C) Copies and transforms data into and out of the warehouse format and assures quality control

D) Contains the bulk of interesting data, and is usually a relational database

10. Which of the following BEST describes the data preparation layer of BI?

A) The point at which end-users interact with the system

B) Where the results of data preparation are stored

C) Contains the bulk of interesting data, and is usually a relational database

D) Contains the logic necessary to prepare data from the warehouse

11. Which of the following BEST describes the data mart layer of BI?

A) Contains the bulk of interesting data, and is usually a relational database

B) Contains the logic necessary to prepare data from the warehouse

C) The point at which end-users interact with the system

D) Where the results of data preparation are stored

12. Which of the following BEST describes the presentation access layer of BI?

A) Contains the logic necessary to prepare data from the warehouse

B) Where the results of data preparation are stored

C) Contains the bulk of interesting data, and is usually a relational database

D) The point at which end-users interact with the system

13. Which of the following BEST describes the desktop access layer of BI?

A) Contains the bulk of interesting data, and is usually a relational database

B) The point at which end-users interact with the system

C) Where the results of data preparation are stored

D) Contains the logic necessary to prepare data from the warehouse

14. Which of the following BEST describes the metadata layer of BI?

A) Data about data

B) Allows all other components to communicate using browser-based interfaces

C) Knows how to communicate between each vertical layer

D) Schedules tasks required to build, maintain and populate the warehouse

15. Which of the following BEST describes the warehouse management layer of BI?

A) Data about data

B) Knows how to communicate between each vertical layer

C) Schedules tasks required to build, maintain and populate the warehouse

D) Allows all other components to communicate using browser-based interfaces

16. Which of the following BEST describes the application messaging layer of BI?

A) Knows how to communicate between each vertical layer

B) Schedules tasks required to build, maintain and populate the warehouse

C) Data about data

D) Allows all other components to communicate using browser-based interfaces

17. Which of the following BEST describes the Internet/intranet layer of BI?

A) Data about data

B) Knows how to communicate between each vertical layer

C) Allows all other components to communicate using browser-based interfaces

D) Schedules tasks required to build, maintain and populate the warehouse

18. Which of the following descriptions BEST describes drilling up and drilling down?

A) Filtering data matching one or more attributes, and then presenting a summary of that data

B) Cross-matching a single attribute, and then sorting based on time

C) Summarizing data at a high level, and then drilling down into the detail as-needed

D) Looking back in time to see statistics as they used to be within a given time period

19. Which of the following descriptions BEST describes drilling across?

A) Filtering data matching one or more attributes, and then presenting a summary of that data

B) Looking back in time to see statistics as they used to be within a given time period

C) Summarizing data at a high level, and then drilling down into the detail as-needed

D) Cross-matching a single attribute, and then sorting based on time

20. Which of the following descriptions BEST describes a historical analysis?

A) Summarizing data at a high level, and then drilling down into the detail as-needed

B) Cross-matching a single attribute, and then sorting based on time

C) Filtering data matching one or more attributes, and then presenting a summary of that data

D) Looking back in time to see statistics as they used to be within a given time period

21. Which of the following statements BEST describes a data mart?

A) Data distributed to subsets based on time of collection

B) The results of exploring large amounts of data to find patterns and trends

C) The entire data collection prepared and indexed for real-time filtering

D) A subset of the warehouse carved off to meet a specific need

22. Which of the following statements BEST describes data mining?

A) Importing data sets not created by the business but needed to complete a proper analysis

B) Exploring large amounts of data to find patterns and trends

C) Preparing a data set for subsequent analysis by creating the proper indexing and collated attributes

D) Sifting through metadata to filter out non-legitimate data

23. What is the BEST reason that BI is designed with so many complex layers?

A) It is required when dealing with such large amounts of data

B) It allows consultants to charge the big bucks

C) It allows a business to constrain the resulting infrastructure to a small number of departments

D) It allows a business to implement BI in stages

24. In relation to BI analysis models, which is the BEST description of a context diagram?

A) Models data entities and how each relates to another

B) Allows us to deconstruct a business process

C) Outlines the major processes and external parties an organization deals with

D) Visualizes contextual relationships between entities

25. In relation to BI analysis models, which is the BEST description of an activity or swim-lane diagram?

A) Visualizes contextual relationships between entities

B) Models data entities and how each relates to another

C) Allows us to deconstruct a business process

D) Outlines the major processes and external parties an organization deals with

26. In relation to BI analysis models, which is the BEST description of an entity relationship diagram?

A) Visualizes contextual relationships between entities

B) Allows us to deconstruct a business process

C) Models data entities and how each relates to another

D) Outlines the major processes and external parties an organization deals with

Answers

1. D	2. B (While it is true that hardware has enabled BI, it is not a reason that businesses are adopting it)
3. A	4. A
5. C	6. D
7. D	8. C
9. D	10. D
11. D	12. D
13. B	14. A
15. C	16. A
17. C	18. C
19. A	20. D
21. D	22. B
23. D	24. C
25. C	26. C

Chapter 37: Decision Support System, or DSS

Questions

1. Which of the following statements BEST describes DSS?

A) A series of processes that predict likely future events based on a combination of big data analysis and trends in the organization's industry

B) A framework providing steps to reduce the possible decisions to a point at which each possibility can undergo an extensive analysis

C) An interactive system that helps in making decisions by providing decision models and data

D) A system designed to provide the top few decisions likely to result in achieving business goals by analyzing past performance

2. Which of the following is NOT a core characteristic of DSS?

A) It concentrates more on efficiency and less on effectiveness

B) It emphasizes flexibility and adaptability as the preferred method

C) It solves problems that are ambiguous and unstructured

D) It combines models and analytics with traditional databases

3. Which BEST describes the G. Gorry-M.S. Morton framework?

A) A framework that uses prototypes to evolve through each new iteration

B) A framework that focuses on generating family trees

C) A framework that employs a 2-dimensional matrix of maturity and perspectives

D) A framework that looks at how structured a process is and the level of management that watches over the process

4. Which BEST describes the Sprague-Carlson framework?

A) A framework that uses prototypes to evolve through each new iteration

B) A framework that looks at how structured a process is and the level of management that watches over the process

C) A framework that employs a 2-dimensional matrix of maturity and perspectives

D) A framework that focuses on generating family trees

5. What is the BEST description of the process a company must undergo for DSS to be successful?

A) Unfreeze, move, freeze

B) Gather, motivate, extend

C) Define, execute, solidify

D) Analyze, adapt, consolidate

6. Which group BEST describes the drivers behind DSS?

A) Decision-makers looking for more accurate information

B) IS management wanting a better approach to quantify progress

C) Executives searching for more process efficiency

D) Board members desiring to bring a higher level of accountability to executive management

7. Which of the following are NOT common risks associated with DSS?

A) A lack of support for the DSS, or it may evaporate over time

B) Users, implementers and maintainers who will tend to disappear over time

C) Users may be unable to use the prototype model

D) Nonexistent or unwilling users

8. Which of the following are NOT a common control to mitigate DSS risk?

> A) Keep the overall solution simple
>
> B) Divide the project into multiple, manageable pieces
>
> C) Focus on technical infrastructure as opposed to developing a fan-base
>
> D) Meet user needs and embed the DSS process into the company's culture

Answers

1. C	2. A
3. D	4. D
5. A	6. A
7. C (Users will be unable to specify the purpose or usage patterns in advance – that is why the prototype model is so important)	8. C (Develop a satisfactory support base in both technical infrastructure as well as a fan-base – people who are promoters of the DSS approach)

Chapter 38: Engineering

Questions

1. Which of the following BEST describes re-engineering?

A) The process of updating an existing system by extracting and reusing design and program components

B) Replacing an existing system by starting over from the original specifications

C) Developing a single system that combines all previous features or multiple systems, but delivered in a more efficient manner

D) Deconstructing two different systems and recreating a single system that provides only the required previous features

2. What BEST describes the primary goal of software re-engineering?

A) To facilitate the construction of a replacement solution that is more performant and effective

B) To create a service-oriented architecture

C) To increase efficiency by reducing overall complexity

D) To increase coupling so that common resources are shared in a more efficient manner

3. Which best describes reverse engineering?

A) Observing how a system responds to various inputs, and then documenting that behavior

B) Ensuring a system that has been re-engineered performs properly

C) Tearing down a system into its original source code and documenting how it works

D) The process of studying an application or component to see how it works, and then using that information to create a similar product

4. Which best describes decompiling?

A) Tearing down a system into its original source code and documenting how it works

B) Ensuring a system that has been re-engineered performs properly

C) Observing how a system responds to various inputs, and then documenting that behavior

D) The process of studying an application or component to see how it works, and then using that information to create a similar product

5. Which best describes black box testing?

A) The process of studying an application or component to see how it works, and then using that information to create a similar product

B) Ensuring a system that has been re-engineered performs properly

C) Observing how a system responds to various inputs, and then documenting that behavior

D) Tearing down a system into its original source code and documenting how it works

6. Which BEST describes business process re-engineering?

A) A thorough analysis and significant redesign of a business process or management system

B) Deconstructing two different processes and recreating a single process that provides only the required previous capabilities

C) Replacing an existing process by starting over from the original requirements

D) Developing a single process that combines all previous capabilities or multiple processes, but executed in a more efficient manner

7. What are the steps involved in benchmarking?

A) Define, research, observe, analyze, execute and repeat

B) Define, research, observe, analyze, adopt and improve

C) Plan, research, observe, analyze, adopt and improve

D) Plan, research, observe, analyze, execute and repeat

Answers

1. A		2. B
3. D		4. A
5. C		6. A
7. C		

Chapter 39: Other Business Applications

Questions

1. Which of the following is NOT a recommended control for a purchase accounting system?

A) Ensuring that goods ordered but not yet received are recorded

B) Ensuring that payments received are recorded and processed

C) Ensuring that payments not received are recorded

D) Ensuring that goods received but not yet invoiced are recorded

2. Which of the following is NOT an area of risk for image processing?

A) The lack of proper planning in selecting the right system

B) A redesign of workflows may not be carried out

C) Selecting the incorrect scanners

D) Insufficient storage capacity

3. Which of the following statements is false?

A) Operational CRM focuses on the customer's experience

B) Operational CRM captures data about the interaction between the customer and employees

C) CRM is the process of tracking and managing relationships with customers

D) Analytical CRM does not require operational CRM data

4. Which BEST describes the purpose of SCM?

A) To solve supply management issues by automating routing

B) To spotlight customer relationship concerns in order to increase growth

C) To provide a key metric in determining the optimum model for CRM

D) To allow all links in a chain to communicate in real-time and move to a JIT model

Answers

1. C	2. D
3. D	4. D

Chapter 40: Infrastructure

Questions

1. Which of the following is NOT a step taken when purchasing a system?

A) Review the current state

B) Install the system

C) Select vendors

D) Design the future state

2. Which of the following is NOT a fundamental criteria by which a potential vendor should be examined?

A) System reaction time

B) Turnaround time

C) Workload capacity

D) Bandwidth required

Answers

1. B (The steps are: review the current state, design the future state, write requirements, select vendors, finalize requirements, and create the POC)	2. D (The criteria are turnaround time, response time, system reaction time, throughput, workload or capacity, compatibility and utilization)

Chapter 41: Managing Change, Configuration, Patches and Releases

Questions

1. Which is the BEST definition of change management?

A) Managing change to a system so integrity is maintained

B) Managing change to electronic documents

C) Managing change to a system so reliability and security is maintained

D) Managing change to software that may impact end-users

2. Which is the BEST definition of configuration management?

A) Managing change to a system so integrity is maintained

B) Managing change to software that may impact end-users

C) Managing change to electronic documents

D) Managing change to a system so reliability and security is maintained

3. Which is the BEST definition of patch management?

A) Managing change to software that may impact end-users

B) Managing change to electronic documents

C) Managing change to a system so integrity is maintained

D) Managing change to a system so reliability and security is maintained

4. Which is the BEST definition of release management?

A) Managing change to a system so integrity is maintained

B) Managing change to software that may impact end-users

C) Managing change to electronic documents

D) Managing change to a system so reliability and security is maintained

5. What is the type of software that manages changes to software source code?

A) Change control system

B) Change management system

C) Check-in/Check-out management

D) Version control system

6. What is the BEST description of a major release?

A) A release that prevents significant downtime or impact to the customer

B) A release that addresses a small list of customer complaints

C) A release that contains small enhancements and fixes

D) A release that contains significant changes to existing functionality or the addition of new features

7. What is the BEST description of a minor release?

A) A release that prevents significant downtime or impact to the customer

B) A release that addresses a small list of customer complaints

C) A release that contains small enhancements and fixes

D) A release that contains significant changes to existing functionality or the addition of new features

8. What is the BEST description of an emergency release?

A) A release that contains small enhancements and fixes

B) A release that prevents significant downtime or impact to the customer

C) A release that addresses a small list of customer complaints

D) A release that contains significant changes to existing functionality or the addition of new features

Answers

1. A	2. C
3. D	4. B
5. D	6. D
7. C	8. B

Chapter 42: Application Controls

Questions

1. Which is NOT an example of an application control?

A) A backend server process checking incoming EDI feeds

B) Validation logic in a web form that prevents a user from submitting the form

C) A process that calculates totals for reporting every 30 minutes

D) A service that runs each hour and checks database records to ensure they align with acceptable patterns

2. Which of the following is NOT a goal for application controls?

A) Data is maintained and not lost

B) Processing results meet the expected outcome

C) Background processes execute on-time

D) Only complete, accurate and valid data is accepted

3. Which of the following statements is false concerning input controls?

A) Input controls ensure data is processed only once

B) Output from one system could easily be the input for another

C) The source of incoming data matters

D) Input controls ensure data is valid

4. Which of the following is NOT a valid authorization control?

A) A hash total

B) A unique password

C) A physical signature

D) Online access controls

5. Which of the following is NOT a valid batch total control?

A) A source document

B) The number of total documents

C) The number of total items

D) The total monetary amount

6. Which of the following is a valid batch balancing control?

A) Workstation ID

B) Online access controls

C) Computer agreement

D) Transaction logs

7. Which of the following is NOT a processing control?

A) Run-to-run totals

B) Limit checks on amount

C) Duplicate check

D) Programmed

8. Which of the following is NOT a data file control?

A) One-for-one checking

B) Prerecorded log

C) Version usage

D) Exception report

9. Which of the following is NOT an output control?

A) Output error handling

B) Report distribution

C) Parity checking

D) Verification of report receipts

Answers

1. C	2. C
3. C	4. A (A hash total is a batch control)
5. A (A source document is an authorization control)	6. C (Workstation ID and online access controls are authorization controls, and transaction logs is an input control)
7. C (A duplicate check is an input control)	8. D (An exception report check is a processing control)
9. C (Parity checking is a data file control)	

Chapter 43: IS Auditor Duties for the Information Systems Acquisition, Development and Implementation Domain

Questions

1. You are performing an audit for a system implemented 2 years ago when you were a member of IT. What is your most pressing concern?

A) Trying to remember the various aspects of the system

B) To view all opinions and test results as suspect in order to remain objective.

C) That you will not be an objective auditor because of your relationships with IT personnel

D) That you will not be an objective auditor because you were involved in implementing the system

2. When auditing a life cycle, which of the following is NOT an advantage of a V-model over an agile approach?

A) The auditor can examine all phases of the project and report directly to management on how well the progress is proceeding

B) The auditor has greater capability to help the team to course correct during each sprint

C) The auditor can become involved in the technical aspects of the project based on his skills and abilities

D) The auditor's effectiveness is much greater when there are formal procedures and guidelines identifying each phase

3. During the requirements phase, what is the most important thing an auditor can do?

A) Ensure all stakeholders are properly represented

B) Ensure security controls are designed in from the beginning

C) Ensure proper authorization has already been received to proceed with the phase

D) Ensure development or prototyping efforts do not proceed without valid requirements

4. Which of the following tasks is NOT part of an auditor's concerns when selecting and acquiring software?

A) Encourage the project team to contact current users

B) Ensure security controls have been addressed covering audit trails and password controls

C) Confirm that any contracts have been reviewed by legal representatives

D) Determine if an appropriate level of security controls have been considered before a contract is signed.

5. During the design phase of a 'buy' project, which of the following items is NOT a major focus for the auditor?

A) If a formal software change process is being used

B) If continuous online auditing if being built as part of the system

C) If the proper controls are being designed into the system

D) If different data is being used for each set of tests

6. During development of software for a 'build' project, which of the following roles can the auditor play?

A) Corrective and detective

B) Corrective and deterrent

C) Preventative and detective

D) Compensating and preventative

7. When conducting a post-implementation review, which of the following is the MOST important factor to consider?

A) At least 6 months must have elapsed since the project officially ended

B) The same processes used during the project must be used during the post-implementation review

C) All members of the project development team must still be available for this review

D) The post-implementation review auditors cannot be the same auditors who were involved with the project team during development

8. Which of the following is NOT a key metric to look for when deciding if a project has a good chance of succeeding?

A) The various parties in the project are cooperative and work together.

B) Scope creep is controlled and there is a software baseline to prevent requirements from being added into the software design.

C) Either a V-model or agile approach is used

D) Periodic review and risk analysis are performed in each project phase.

9. When auditing digital signature capabilities, which of the following is NOT an attribute to look for?

A) The signature can be verified

B) The digital signature has not expired

C) The digital signature is unique to the person using it

D) The mechanism for generating and assigning the signature is under the sole control of the person using it

10. When auditing EDI, which of the following is NOT an area that should be considered?

A) The sender should include segment count totals into the header

B) Each inbound transaction is logged on receipt

C) Edit checks identify erroneous, unusual or invalid transactions

D) Encryption is used

11. Which of the following is NOT something used to check the sender's validity when using EDI?

A) Sender's authentication credentials

B) Sending an acknowledgment transaction to the sender on message receipt

C) VAN sequential control numbers or reports

D) Control fields within an EDI message

12. Even if encrypted, which of the following data elements stored on a POS should the auditor be concerned with?

A) Card verification value numbers

B) PINs

C) Card holder name

D) Primary account number

13. Which of the following procedures does an auditor normally NOT review when auditing electronic banking?

A) Generating PINs

B) Use of devices such as a swipe reader by a consumer

C) Issuing cards and PINs

D) The software update process for devices

14. Which of the following is NOT true regarding auditing an IMS?

A) Highly integrated computer-integrated manufacturing projects require the same attention from the auditor as any ERP system might

B) Continuity planning is also a primary area that should be reviewed by the auditor

C) A BIA must be executed for the IMS apart from other systems

D) The larger the scale of integration, the more auditor attention is required

15. Which of the following is NOT an area of audit concern when reviewing ATMs?

A) Review the ability to generate exception reports from an audit trail

B) Review encryption key change management procedures

C) Examine the ATM card slot, key pad and enclosure to prevent skimming of card data and capture of PIN during entry

D) Examine the physical perimeter to ensure a well-lit area

16. When dealing with AI systems, which of the following is NOT an area an auditor should be concerned with?

A) Review source code management to ensure rule changes have been authorized

B) Review the decision logic built into the system to ensure that the expert knowledge or intelligence in the system is sound and accurate

C) Ensure that the proper level of expertise was used in developing the basic assumptions and formulas

D) Review security access over the system, specifically the knowledgebase

17. When auditing reverse engineering, which of the following statements does NOT apply?

A) The results of a decompiler can often be too convoluted to be easily understood

B) Software license agreements often contain clauses prohibiting the reverse engineering of the software

C) Decompilers are relatively new tools that depend on the use of specific computers, operating systems and programming languages

D) A change in any decompiler components may require developing or purchasing a new decompiler

18. When auditing hardware acquisitions, which of the following areas is NOT an auditor's major concern?

A) Determine if several vendors were considered and whether the comparison between them was done according to the right criteria

B) Determine whether the hardware requirements for this need were considered in the specifications

C) Determine if the selected vendor was the right choice

D) Determine if the acquisition process began with a business need

19. When auditing change management, which of the following areas is NOT an auditor's major concern?

A) Supervisory reviews are conducted

B) Access to program libraries is restricted

C) Coding standards were followed with each change

D) Change requests are approved and documented

20. When auditing software development, which of the following areas is NOT an auditor's major concern?

A) Investments in CASE tools increase both quality and speed

B) Users continue to be involved in the development process

C) Approvals are obtained for software specifications

D) Changes to the application are reflected in a version control system only

21. When auditing BPR, which of the following areas is the auditor's primary concern?

A) That a resulting risk analysis is not performed on the final solution

B) That key controls may be reengineered out of a business process

C) That controls will not be properly created in the final solution

D) That control modifications are not properly documented

22. When auditing application controls, what is NOT a duty the auditor performs?

A) Examine APIs

B) Require the proper amount of documentation to be created

C) Create a data flow diagram

D) Create a test strategy based on strengths and weaknesses

23. To avoid missing large gaps of features or capabilities, the auditor will need to review several types of documentation. Which of the following areas is NOT included?

A) Functional design specifications

B) External vendor relationship history

C) System development methodology documents

D) User manuals

24. To ensure that each phase of the SDLC is properly documented, the auditor should look for several types of documentation. Which of the following is NOT one of those types?

A) An economic breakdown showing actual vs. forecast expenses

B) A project schedule with highlighted dates for the completion of key deliverables

C) Goals describing what is to be accomplished during each phase

D) Key deliverables by phases with individuals assigned direct responsibilities for each

25. When auditing a feasibility study, which of the following is NOT something an auditor should look for?

A) A detailed discussion of each rejected alternative

B) If the need can be met with existing systems

C) If all cost justifications and benefits are stated in verifiable terms

D) A reasonable discussion of alternatives

26. When auditing requirements definition, which of the following is NOT something an auditor should look for?

A) A draft UAT specification has been provided

B) Control specifications are defined in the conceptual design

C) Project initiation and costs have been approved

D) The conceptual design specifications address the actual needs of the user

27. When auditing detailed the design and development document package, which of the following is NOT something an auditor should look for?

A) Input, processing and output controls designed into the system should be appropriate

B) Key users of the system should be generally aware of how the system will operate

C) Audit trails should be assessed to ensure traceability and accountability

D) Changes should have been discussed and approved by appropriate user management

28. When auditing the testing phase for a system acquisition, which of the following is NOT an area of focus?

A) See if internal control areas working properly

B) Make sure user requirements have been validated

C) Ensure the final implementation adheres to the design

D) Ensure the system performs as intended

29. When auditing the implementation phase, which of the following is NOT a major focus area?

A) Ensure cost/benefits forecast in the feasibility study are being measured

B) Review all system documentation and make sure that any changes resulting from the testing phase have been implemented

C) Reviewing the program schedule and parameters for kicking off the various processes

D) Check that all data conversion results are correct before placing the system into production

30. Which of the following tasks does an auditor NOT perform during a post-implementation review?

A) Look at change requests submitted after the system went live

B) Look at the error logs

C) See if the system met the original goals

D) Review defect reports that were never addressed prior to rollout

31. After a system goes live, the auditor should look at all of the following EXCPET for which one?

    A) Users are satisfied with the timeliness and costs of their requests

    B) Review internal controls to see if they are working as-designed

    C) Change control is a formal procedure

    D) Emergency change procedures are listed in the operations manual

32. When auditing source code management, the auditor should look at all of the following EXCEPT for which one?

    A) Access to source code is controlled

    B) Change and release management are streamlines as a single process with differing lines of accountability

    C) The ability to push code to production is controlled

    D) Source code is backed up, and escrow and offsite agreements are in-place if applicable

Answers

1. D	2. B (The V-model does not have sprints)
3. B	4. C
5. D (This is a focus for phase 4B, not 3B)	6. C
7. D	8. C (The SDLC methodology does not indicate failure or success, but the company's familiarity and past success with the chosen SDLC will be a good indicator)
9. B	10. A (Segment counts should be in the trailer, while batch and transaction count totals are in the header)
11. A (Traditional often EDI does not use any type of credentialed authentication)	12. A
13. D (Although this is a wise precaution, especially given recent news with Target, this is not a common area an auditor will look into)	14. C (A BIA is crucial but an IMS does not necessarily warrant a dedicated analysis)
15. D (The physical area outside of the ATM hardware is not within of the auditor's ATM responsibilities)	16. A (While reviewing source code management does fall within an auditor's description, it is not specific to AI)
17. A (While true, hard-to-understand decompiler results is not an area an auditor needs to be concerned with)	18. C (While the auditor needs to make sure the right criteria was used in making the decision, the final decision is normally not up for debate unless the process was invalid)
19. C (Coding standards should be followed, but this is not a major concern when auditing change management)	20. D (Changes to the application should be reflected in stored CASE product data as well)
21. B	22. B (While the auditor should consume any documentation, the point of this audit is not to force staff to create additional documentation)
23. B	24. A (An economic forecast is valid, but actual costs is not expected to be available at this point)

25. A (An analysis of the selection reasoning should be present, but a detailed analysis is required only for the selected alternative, not those rejected – for those a quick summary should suffice)	26. A (The UAT specifications should be thorough and complete)
27. B (Key users of the system should be interviewed to determine their understanding of how the system will operate and to assess their level of input into the design of screen formats and output reports)	28. C (The implementation phase follows the testing phase, so it is impossible to verify the final implementation at this point)
29. A (This happens in the post-implementation review)	30. D
31. B (This is carried out during the post-implementation review)	32. B (Change and release management should be aligned and respect each other, but should remain apart as processes to ensure proper SoD)

Section 4: The Information Systems Operations, Maintenance and Service Management Domain

Chapter 44: Information Systems Operations

Questions

1. Which of the following descriptions BEST describes IS management?

A) Ensures CIA, or confidentiality, integrity and availability

B) Manages resources

C) Coordinates alignment between IT execution and corporate strategy

D) Makes sure that processes run smoothly

2. Which of the following descriptions BEST describes IS operations?

A) Manages resources

B) Makes sure that processes run smoothly

C) Coordinates alignment between IT execution and corporate strategy

D) Ensures CIA, or confidentiality, integrity and availability

3. Which of the following descriptions BEST describes information security?

A) Makes sure that processes run smoothly

B) Manages resources

C) Ensures CIA, or confidentiality, integrity and availability

D) Coordinates alignment between IT execution and corporate strategy

4. Which two frameworks help to manage IS operations?

A) Zachman and Risk IT

B) ITIL and ISO 27000

C) ITIL and ISO 20000

D) BSC and Zachman

5. Which is the BEST definition of an SLA?

A) A legally-binding contract between an external provider and the internal department focused on liability mitigation

B) An agreement between a service provider and a service consumer describing responsibilities for each

C) An agreement between an IT organization and the customer detailing the service to be provided

D) A non-binding contract between two parties that expresses the optimal level of service both are striving for

6. Which of the following is NOT an area that is a focus of service-level management?

A) Customer confidence levels

B) Exception reports

C) Operator problem reports

D) Operator work schedules

7. Which of the following is NOT a major advantage of automatically scheduling jobs?

A) Jobs need to be setup only once, reducing the chances of errors

B) The reliance on error-prone human operators is reduced

C) A complete record of when each job ran and how the success is automatically maintained

D) Dependencies between jobs can be removed

8. Which of the following is the MOST important aspect of handling incidents?

A) Having good guidance on how to escalate unresolved incidents

B) Prioritizing incidents to optimize limited resources

C) Being able to quantify the impact of a given incident

D) Being able to handle multiple incidents simultaneously

9. Which of the following is NOT true regarding problem management?

> A) Its primary goal is to reduce the number or severity of incidents

> B) When escalating an issue, the documentation should reflect if the problem can wait until working hours

> C) It attempts to find root cause

> D) If we find ourselves spending too much time with problem management, then we should start focusing on handling incidents

10. To prevent an issue becoming an incident to handle, and then eventually a problem to manage, what BEST describes what we should be on the lookout for?

> A) A way to bolster security

> B) Increasing support and help desk expertise

> C) Abnormal conditions

> D) Enhanced monitoring of daily log reports

11. What is the most important first step to take to get a handle on asset management?

> A) Immediately start labeling every new asset with a unique identifier

> B) Establish checkpoints to control assets leaving and entering the facility

> C) Conduct a visual inspection of the facilities to look for weaknesses

> D) Create an inventory list of existing assets

Answers

1. B	2. B
3. C	4. C
5. C	6. A (SLAs operate based on verifiable metrics, and a 'confidence level' is not particularly helpful)
7. D (While job dependencies cannot be removed simply by automating jobs, they can be modeled so secondary jobs are not executed if the primary job fails, reducing errors)	8. B
9. D (The exact opposite is true: If we find ourselves spending too much time handling incidents, then we should look at problem management)	10. C
11. D	

Chapter 45: Hardware Architecture

Questions

1. Which of the following items is NOT contained within the CPU?

    A) ALU

    B) RAM

    C) Internal memory

    D) Control unit

2. Which of the following items is NOT a main component of the motherboard?

    A) ROM

    B) RAM

    C) CPU

    D) Power Supply

3. Which of the following BEST describes a supercomputer?

    A) Designed for individual users and use microprocessor technologies

    B) A very large, very expensive computer that represents that fastest processing available

    C) A multiprocessing system that can support thousands of users at the same time

    D) A large, general-purpose computer that is designed to share its capabilities with thousands of users at the same time

4. Which of the following BEST describes a mainframe?

    A) A very large, very expensive computer that represents that fastest processing available

    B) Designed for individual users and use microprocessor technologies

    C) A large, general-purpose computer that is designed to share its capabilities with thousands of users at the same time

    D) A multiprocessing system that can support thousands of users at the same time

5. Which of the following BEST describes a high-or-mid-range server?

    A) A multiprocessing system that can support thousands of users at the same time

    B) A large, general-purpose computer that is designed to share its capabilities with thousands of users at the same time

    C) Designed for individual users and use microprocessor technologies

    D) A very large, very expensive computer that represents that fastest processing available

6. Which of the following BEST describes an application server?

    A) A server that sits between an end-user and a resource, and makes requests to the resource on the user's behalf

    B) A server that stores data and acts as a repository for information

    C) A server that is dedicated to a single function and normally is not capable of being extended

    D) A server that hosts the software programs that networked consumers utilize

7. Which of the following BEST describes a proxy server?

    A) A server that sits between an end-user and a resource, and makes requests to the resource on the user's behalf

    B) A server that hosts the software programs that networked consumers utilize

    C) A server that stores data and acts as a repository for information

    D) A server that is dedicated to a single function and normally is not capable of being extended

8. Which of the following BEST describes a database server?

A) A server that sits between an end-user and a resource, and makes requests to the resource on the user's behalf

B) A server that hosts the software programs that networked consumers utilize

C) A server that is dedicated to a single function and normally is not capable of being extended

D) A server that stores data and acts as a repository for information

9. Which of the following BEST describes an appliance?

A) A server that hosts the software programs that networked consumers utilize

B) A server that stores data and acts as a repository for information

C) A server that sits between an end-user and a resource, and makes requests to the resource on the user's behalf

D) A server that is dedicated to a single function and normally is not capable of being extended

10. Which of the following statements is NOT true regarding USB?

A) USB 2.0 supports transfer speeds up to 480 Mbps

B) It has the ability to power small devices

C) USB 4.0 is 4 times faster than USB 3.0

D) USB 3.0 is 10 times faster than USB 2.0

11. Which of the following is NOT a common risk associated with flash drives?

A) The risk of loss of confidentiality increases with use

B) They can be used to spread viruses even when a network is not present

C) They are more prone to data corruption when used as long-term storage than other media

D) Theft is a common occurrence

12. Which of the following is NOT true regarding RFID?

A) A tag consists of both a microchip and antenna

B) An active tag has the same communication distance as a passive tag but is more reliable

C) The microchip always contains a unique identifier

D) A passive tag draws power from radiation sent from the reader

13. Which of the following is NOT a valid risk when using RFID?

A) Business process risk

B) Privacy risk

C) Integrity risk

D) Externality risk

14. Which of the following is NOT a common report used with hardware monitoring?

A) Performance report

B) Asset management report

C) Hardware error report

D) Availability report

15. Which BEST describes capacity management?

A) Watching computing and network resources so that levels match business plans

B) Ensuring that funding levels are available for required hardware purchases

C) Bringing strategy, goals and execution into alignment by setting capacity levels

D) Documenting future needs and translating into purchasing decisions

16. Which of the following metrics is NOT used for capacity management?

A) Hiring trends as provided by HR

B) Current utilization of CPU, computer storage, and network bandwidth

C) The number of active users

D) New technologies and applications becoming available

Answers

1. B	2. D
3. B	4. C
5. A	6. D
7. A	8. D
9. D	10. C (USB 4.0 does not exist at the time of this writing)
11. C (Data corruption is more common when unplugging flash drives, but it is not a factor when using as a long-term storage device)	12. B (An active tag has a greater communication distance but costs more)
13. C (Confidentiality and availability may be at risk, but risk of integrity of data is very limited as the data is relatively difficult to alter)	14. A (A utilization report is part of hardware monitoring, but it focuses on resource utilization, not performance metrics. The difference may seem like semantics, but the accepted name of the report is 'utilization report')
15. A	16. A (While this may indeed impact capacity needs, it is something that will visibly become apparent whereas the remaining metrics can remain hidden if not proactively monitored)

Chapter 46: Operating Systems

Questions

1. Which of the following is NOT a valid way in which an OS protects itself?

A) It can prevent both deliberate and accidental modifications

B) It can ensure that privileged programs cannot be interfered with by user-level programs

C) It can shut down peripherals to prevent improper access

D) It can isolate individual processes

2. Which of the following is a valid reason for an OS to isolate two processes?

A) A process should not have access to the same memory chip that the OS has access to

B) A process should not be able to communicate with other processes

C) A process should not be able to access functionality unless it has been explicitly granted authorization

D) A process should not be able to execute an instruction at the same time as another process

3. Which of the following is the BEST way to ensure an attacker cannot alter log file information in order to cover his or her tracks?

A) Protect log files with supervisory access only

B) Ensure log files are write-only

C) Log information to a separate secured server

D) Duplicate log files in two separate locations

Answers

1. C (While an OS does have such a capability as a result of a core protection mechanism, shutting down peripherals is not core function)	2. C (Process must be able to communicate to other processes, accessing memory shared on the same chip is a very common thing as long as physical memory addresses are not shared, and parallel execution is a common feature of modern OSs.)
3. C (By logging to a separate server, the attacker must own both servers to cover their tracks)	

Chapter 47: Database Management

Questions

1. What are the three subdimensions of data quality?

A) Intrinsic, secure and restricted

B) Accurate, objective and believable

C) Intrinsic, contextual and security/accessibility

D) Relevant, complete and accurate

2. What is the BEST description of accuracy?

A) True and credible

B) Correct and reliable

C) Highly regarded in terms of source or context

D) Unbiased, unprejudiced and impartial

3. What is the BEST description of objectivity?

A) Highly regarded in terms of source or context

B) True and credible

C) Correct and reliable

D) Unbiased, unprejudiced and impartial

4. What is the BEST description of believability?

A) Unbiased, unprejudiced and impartial

B) Highly regarded in terms of source or context

C) True and credible

D) Correct and reliable

5. What is the BEST description of reputation?

A) Highly regarded in terms of source or context

B) Unbiased, unprejudiced and impartial

C) True and credible

D) Correct and reliable

6. What is the BEST description of relevancy?

A) The volume

B) If it is up-to-date

C) How applicable it is

D) The breadth and depth

7. What is the BEST description of completeness?

A) How applicable it is

B) The breadth and depth

C) The volume

D) If it is up-to-date

8. What is the BEST description of currency?

A) The breadth and depth

B) If it is up-to-date

C) How applicable it is

D) The volume

9. What is the BEST description of appropriate amount?

A) The breadth and depth

B) If it is up-to-date

C) The volume

D) How applicable it is

10. What is the BEST description of concise representation?

A) If it is in the correct language and units and is clear

B) How compactly it is presented

C) How easily it is comprehended

D) If it is presented in the same format

11. What is the BEST description of consistent representation?

A) If it is in the correct language and units and is clear

B) How easily it is comprehended

C) If it is presented in the same format

D) How compactly it is presented

12. What is the BEST description of interpretability?

A) How easily it is comprehended

B) How compactly it is presented

C) If it is presented in the same format

D) If it is in the correct language and units and is clear

13. What is the BEST description of understandability?

A) How compactly it is presented

B) If it is presented in the same format

C) If it is in the correct language and units and is clear

D) How easily it is comprehended

14. What is the BEST description of ease of manipulation?

A) If it is presented in the same format

B) How compactly it is presented

C) How easy it is to apply to multiple tasks

D) If it is in the correct language and units and is clear

15. Which of the following describes the COBIT 5 data life cycle?

A) Design, implement, operate, monitor and dispose

B) Define, implement, use, monitor and dispose

C) Plan, design, build or acquire, use and operate, monitor and dispose

D) Build, use, operate, monitor and dispose

16. Which of the following BEST describes a data dictionary?

A) Provides the capability to validate and format the contents

B) Dictates attributes to be indexed

C) Describes each field's use and characteristics

D) Can be viewed or printed only

17. Which of the following BEST describes an active data dictionary?

A) Provides the capability to validate and format the contents

B) Describes each field's use and characteristics

C) Dictates attributes to be indexed

D) Can be viewed or printed only

18. Which of the following BEST describes a passive data dictionary?

A) Provides the capability to validate and format the contents

B) Can be viewed or printed only

C) Describes each field's use and characteristics

D) Dictates attributes to be indexed

19. Which of the following is NOT an advantage of using a DBMS?

A) It allows data to remain free of any dependency on an application

B) It hides the complexity of managing data so that changes are easier to implement.

C) It promotes efficiency by using transactions, which allow multiple actions to be applied at once.

D) It can reduce data duplication through the use of denormalization.

20. Which of the following BEST describes an external schema?

A) How the database sees data being stored

B) How the data is physically stored

C) How the database looks from an external viewpoint

D) How the files are arranged on a single disk

21. Which of the following BEST describes a conceptual schema?

A) How the data is physically stored

B) How the database sees data being stored

C) How the files are arranged on a single disk

D) How the database looks from an external viewpoint

22. Which of the following BEST describes an internal schema?

A) How the files are arranged on a single disk

B) How the database sees data being stored

C) How the data is physically stored

D) How the database looks from an external viewpoint

23. Which of the following is NOT a key capability that a DD/DS provides?

A) Prevents unauthorized access to metadata

B) A data definition language processor that allows an administrator to change the mappings between the external and conceptual schemas

C) Validation of any DDL command to ensure integrity of the metadata is maintained

D) Allows embedded programmatic access to data

24. Which of the following BEST describes a hierarchical database?

A) Information is stored as a container that houses both data and actions

B) All data is organized into one or more tables

C) The data is comprised of 'sets', with each set having a single owner node and one or more member nodes

D) Data is stored in a parent/child relationship

25. Which of the following BEST describes a network database?

A) All data is organized into one or more tables

B) Data is stored in a parent/child relationship

C) Information is stored as a container that houses both data and actions

D) The data is comprised of 'sets', with each set having a single owner node and one or more member nodes

26. Which of the following BEST describes a relational database?

A) All data is organized into one or more tables

B) The data is comprised of 'sets', with each set having a single owner node and one or more member nodes

C) Data is stored in a parent/child relationship

D) Is built with big data in mind

27. Which of the following BEST describes an object-oriented database?

A) Is built with big data in mind

B) Information is stored as a container that houses both data and actions

C) The data is comprised of 'sets', with each set having a single owner node and one or more member nodes

D) Data is stored in a parent/child relationship

28. Which of the following BEST describes a NoSQL database?

A) All data is organized into one or more tables

B) Data is stored in a parent/child relationship

C) Information is stored as a container that houses both data and actions

D) Is built with big data in mind

29. Which of the following BEST describes a key value NoSQL database?

A) Based on graph theory

B) Entire documents are stored as ether XML or JSON

C) Values are retrieved by specifying the column

D) All values are stored with an attribute name

30. Which of the following BEST describes a column-oriented NoSQL database?

A) Values are retrieved by specifying the column

B) Entire documents are stored as ether XML or JSON

C) Based on graph theory

D) All values are stored with an attribute name

31. Which of the following BEST describes a document-oriented NoSQL database?

> A) Values are retrieved by specifying the column
>
> B) Entire documents are stored as ether XML or JSON
>
> C) Based on graph theory
>
> D) All values are stored with an attribute name

Answers

1. C	2. B
3. D	4. C
5. A	6. C
7. B	8. B
9. C	10. B
11. C	12. D
13. D	14. C
15. C	16. C
17. A	18. B
19. D (Normalization reduces data duplication, while denormalization can increase duplication)	20. C
21. B	22. C
23. D (While a common feature of DBMSs, this capability is not provided by DD/DS)	24. D
25. D	26. A
27. B	28. D
29. D	30. A
31. B	

Chapter 48: Third-Party Software

Questions

1. Which of the following is NOT a category of utility programs?

A) Those that test a program's ability to function properly

B) Those that assess security vulnerabilities

C) Those that check data quality

D) Those that understand application systems

2. What are the three types of free licensing?

A) Public domain, limited features and shareware

B) Open source, freeware and shareware

C) Public domain, freeware and shareware

D) Open source, limited features and shareware

3. Which of the following is NOT a type of paid licensing?

A) Per seat

B) Per CPU

C) Concurrent users

D) Active users

4. Which of the following BEST describes an open source license?

A) Initially free, but requires payment at a later date to keep the software functioning or to unlock all features or benefits

B) Free, but the source code cannot be redistributed

C) The software may be used in any way the user likes without any type of payment

D) A fee is charged for each CPU core running on the computer on which the software is installed

5. Which of the following BEST describes a freeware license?

A) A fee is charged for each CPU core running on the computer on which the software is installed

B) Initially free, but requires payment at a later date to keep the software functioning or to unlock all features or benefits

C) Free, but the source code cannot be redistributed

D) The software may be used in any way the user likes without any type of payment

6. Which of the following BEST describes a shareware license?

A) Initially free, but requires payment at a later date to keep the software functioning or to unlock all features or benefits

B) Free, but the source code cannot be redistributed

C) Used when multiple end-users will be using the software

D) The software may be used in any way the user likes without any type of payment

7. Which of the following BEST describes a per CPU license?

A) Charged according to the number of login accounts

B) A fee is charged for each CPU core running on the computer on which the software is installed

C) Charged according to the number of users simultaneously using the system

D) Used when multiple end-users will be using the software

8. Which of the following BEST describes a per seat license?

A) Charged according to the number of login accounts

B) A fee is charged for each CPU core running on the computer on which the software is installed

C) Used when multiple end-users will be using the software

D) Allows unlimited use of the software throughout an entire organization

9. Which of the following BEST describes a concurrent users license?

A) A fee is charged for each CPU core running on the computer on which the software is installed

B) Used when multiple end-users will be using the software

C) Charged according to the number of users simultaneously using the system

D) Charged according to the number of login accounts

10. Which of the following BEST describes a named users license?

A) Charged according to the number of users simultaneously using the system

B) Charged according to the number of login accounts

C) Used when multiple end-users will be using the software

D) Allows unlimited use of the software throughout an entire organization

11. Which of the following BEST describes a per workstation license?

A) Allows unlimited use of the software throughout an entire organization

B) Used to install software on a single computer and allow any number of users to access it, which effectively means one user at a time.

C) Charged according to the number of login accounts

D) Used when multiple end-users will be using the software

12. Which of the following BEST describes an enterprise license?

A) Allows unlimited use of the software throughout an entire organization

B) A fee is charged for each CPU core running on the computer on which the software is installed

C) Charged according to the number of login accounts

D) Used when multiple end-users will be using the software

Answers

1. B (The remaining two are those that assist in faster program development and those that improve operational efficiency)	2. B
3. D (Per workstation, named users and enterprise are the remaining paid license types)	4. C
5. C	6. A
7. B	8. C
9. C	10. B
11. B	12. A

Chapter 49: Network Infrastructure

Questions

1. Which of the following BEST describes a dedicated circuit?

    A) A circuit that is created in real-time

    B) A symmetric telecommunications line permanently connecting two sides

    C) A circuit that is setup ahead of time

    D) A circuit that can be setup and torn down at any time based on the need

2. Which of the following BEST describes a switched circuit?

    A) A circuit that can be setup and torn down at any time based on the need

    B) A circuit that is setup ahead of time

    C) A circuit that is created in real-time

    D) A symmetric telecommunications line permanently connecting two sides

3. Which of the following BEST describes a permanent virtual circuit?

    A) A circuit that can be setup and torn down at any time based on the need

    B) A circuit that is setup ahead of time

    C) A circuit that is created in real-time

    D) A symmetric telecommunications line permanently connecting two sides

4. Which of the following BEST describes a switched virtual circuit?

    A) A symmetric telecommunications line permanently connecting two sides

    B) A circuit that is created in real-time

    C) A circuit that is setup ahead of time

    D) A circuit that can be setup and torn down at any time based on the need

5. Which of the following is NOT true regarding circuit-switching and packet switching?

    A) Circuit switching is less reliable, while packet switching implements redundancy

    B) The path for a circuit switch is defined before data is sent, while the path for a packet switch is assigned based on network conditions

    C) Circuit switching provides a constant stream rate, while packet switching can introduce additional latency

    D) Circuit switching establish a complete return path, while packet switching is one-way only

6. Which of the following statements is true regarding baseband and broadband?

    A) Baseband is more reliable than broadband

    B) Broadband is more reliable than baseband

    C) Baseband provides less throughput than broadband

    D) With baseband the entire channel is used for a single data type, but broadband supports multiple types of data simultaneously

7. Which of the following BEST describes a personal area network?

    A) Covers a limited are such as a home, office or even a campus with multiple buildings

    B) A specialized version of a LAN dedicated to storing large amounts of data

    C) Covers broad areas such as a city, region, nation or even an international link

    D) A network of personal devices such as smartphones or watches

8. Which of the following BEST describes a local area network?

    A) A network of personal devices such as smartphones or watches

    B) Covers a limited are such as a home, office or even a campus with multiple buildings

    C) A specialized version of a LAN dedicated to storing large amounts of data

    D) Covers broad areas such as a city, region, nation or even an international link

9. Which of the following BEST describes a storage area network?

    A) Covers a limited are such as a home, office or even a campus with multiple buildings

    B) A network of personal devices such as smartphones or watches

    C) A specialized version of a LAN dedicated to storing large amounts of data

    D) Covers broad areas such as a city, region, nation or even an international link

10. Which of the following BEST describes a wide area network?

    A) A network limited to a city or region, but normally offers higher data transfer rates than larger networks

    B) A specialized version of a LAN dedicated to storing large amounts of data

    C) Covers broad areas such as a city, region, nation or even an international link

    D) Covers a limited are such as a home, office or even a campus with multiple buildings

11. Which of the following BEST describes a metropolitan area network?

    A) Covers broad areas such as a city, region, nation or even an international link

    B) A network limited to a city or region, but normally offers higher data transfer rates than larger networks

    C) Covers a limited are such as a home, office or even a campus with multiple buildings

    D) A specialized version of a LAN dedicated to storing large amounts of data

12. Which of the following BEST describes interoperability?

    A) Occurs when we can connect networks using different technologies or operating at different speeds

    B) Means an organization can support a mixed network that delivers highly-integrated solutions

    C) Allows a network to scale up or to support new services

    D) Provides users with continuous, reliable and secure services

13. Which of the following BEST describes availability?

    A) Provides users with continuous, reliable and secure services

    B) Occurs when we can connect networks using different technologies or operating at different speeds

    C) Allows a network to scale up or to support new services

    D) Means an organization can support a mixed network that delivers highly-integrated solutions

14. Which of the following BEST describes flexibility?

    A) Means an organization can support a mixed network that delivers highly-integrated solutions

    B) Allows a network to scale up or to support new services

    C) Occurs when we can connect networks using different technologies or operating at different speeds

    D) Provides users with continuous, reliable and secure services

15. Which of the following BEST describes maintainability?

A) Allows a network to scale up or to support new services

B) Occurs when we can connect networks using different technologies or operating at different speeds

C) Means an organization can support a mixed network that delivers highly-integrated solutions

D) Provides users with continuous, reliable and secure services

16. At which OSI layer do protocols such as SMTP, HTTP and DNS operate?

A) Layer 6

B) Layer 5

C) Layer 4

D) Layer 7

17. At which OSI layer do standards such as TIFF, GIF and JPG operate?

A) Layer 5

B) Layer 6

C) Layer 7

D) Layer 4

18. At which OSI layer does session management occur?

A) Layer 6

B) Layer 4

C) Layer 5

D) Layer 7

19. At which OSI layer do protocols such as TCP and UDP operate?

A) Layer 3

B) Layer 4

C) Layer 5

D) Layer 6

20. At which OSI layer do protocols such as UDP and ICMP operate?

A) Layer 5

B) Layer 2

C) Layer 4

D) Layer 3

21. At which OSI layer do protocols such as Ethernet and Token Ring operate?

A) Layer 5

B) Layer 3

C) Layer 4

D) Layer 2

22. At which OSI layer are physical transmissions generated?

A) Layer 1

B) Layer 4

C) Layer 3

D) Layer 2

23. At which OSI layer do we find TCP addresses?

A) The Session layer

B) The Presentation layer

C) The Network layer

D) The Transport layer

24. At which OSI layer do we find TCP ports?

A) The Transport layer

B) The Presentation layer

C) The Network layer

D) The Session layer

25. At which OSI layer do we find HTTP browser traffic?

A) The Transport layer

B) The Presentation layer

C) The Application layer

D) The Session layer

26. Which OSI layer is broken into two sublayers?

A) The Physical layer

B) The Transport layer

C) The Network layer

D) The Data Link layer

27. Which OSI layer(s)does the TCP Application layer map to?

A) Layers 6 through 4

B) Layers 2 and 1

C) Layer 3 and 4

D) Layers 7 through 5

28. Which OSI layer(s)does the TCP Host-to-host layer map to?

A) Layer 4

B) Layer 3 and 4

C) Layer 3

D) Layers 6 through 4

29. Which OSI layer(s)does the TCP Internet layer map to?

A) Layer 4

B) Layer 3 and 4

C) Layers 2 and 1

D) Layer 3

30. Which OSI layer(s) does the TCP Network Access layer map to?

A) Layer 3

B) Layer 2

C) Layer 1

D) Layers 2 and 1

31. Which of the following is NOT true regarding network cabling?

A) Cross-talk is increased with shielded cables

B) Twisted pair cabling is more susceptible to wiretapping than fiber-optic cabling

C) Parallel runs of twisted pair should be avoided

D) The only difference between unshielded and shielded twisted pair cables is an additional sheath around the wires

32. Which is NOT true of fiber optic cabling?

A) Optical fiber is a more fragile medium and is more attractive for applications where changes are infrequent

B) Optical fiber is larger and heavier than metallic cables of the same capacity

C) Fiber is the preferred choice for high-volume, longer-distance runs

D) Fiber-optic systems have a low transmission loss as compared to twisted-pair circuits.

33. Which of the following BEST describes network topology?

A) How computers use various protocols to communicate with each other

B) How the computers communicate over the physical cabling

C) How the cables are laid out and how they are connected to each computer

D) How computers are arranged relative to each other within a network

34. Which of the following BEST describes physical topology?

A) How computers are arranged relative to each other within a network

B) How the cables are laid out and how they are connected to each computer

C) How computers use various protocols to communicate with each other

D) How the computers communicate over the physical cabling

35. Which of the following BEST describes logical topology?

A) How computers use various protocols to communicate with each other

B) How computers are arranged relative to each other within a network

C) How the cables are laid out and how they are connected to each computer

D) How the computers communicate over the physical cabling

36. Which of the following BEST describes a ring topology?

A) A single cable runs the entire length of the network, with nodes all connected directly to this backbone

B) All nodes are connected directly to a central device

C) All nodes are connected directly to each other

D) All nodes are physically connected in a ring

37. Which of the following BEST describes a bus topology?

A) All nodes are connected directly to each other

B) All nodes are physically connected in a ring

C) A single cable runs the entire length of the network, with nodes all connected directly to this backbone

D) All nodes are connected directly to a central device

38. Which of the following BEST describes a star topology?

A) All nodes are physically connected in a ring

B) All nodes are connected directly to a central device

C) All nodes are connected directly to each other

D) A single cable runs the entire length of the network, with nodes all connected directly to this backbone

39. Which of the following BEST describes a full mesh topology?

A) Any combination of token ring, bus or star topologies

B) All nodes are connected directly to a central device

C) All nodes are connected directly to each other

D) All nodes are physically connected in a ring

40. Which of the following BEST describes a partial mesh topology?

A) A single cable runs the entire length of the network, with nodes all connected directly to this backbone

B) Any combination of token ring, bus or star topologies

C) All nodes are connected directly to a central device

D) All nodes are connected directly to each other

41. Which of the following BEST describes token passing?

A) Permission to communicate is handed to each computer in-turn

B) All transmissions contain sufficient redundancy to reconstitute the original data if a collision occurs

C) Used primarily in mainframe environments where a primary station gives permission to each computer to speak

D) A computer attempts to speak and backs off if a collision is detected

42. Which of the following BEST describes CSMA?

A) Used primarily in mainframe environments where a primary station gives permission to each computer to speak

B) A computer attempts to speak and backs off if a collision is detected

C) Permission to communicate is handed to each computer in-turn

D) All transmissions contain sufficient redundancy to reconstitute the original data if a collision occurs

43. Which of the following BEST describes polling?

A) A computer attempts to speak and backs off if a collision is detected

B) Used primarily in mainframe environments where a primary station gives permission to each computer to speak

C) All transmissions contain sufficient redundancy to reconstitute the original data if a collision occurs

D) Permission to communicate is handed to each computer in-turn

44. Which of the following BEST describes a repeater?

A) A device that connects LAN segments

B) A device that simply amplifies a signal and forwards it on.

C) A device that filters traffic based on the MAC Addresses

D) A device that amplifies a signal and has multiple ports

45. Which of the following BEST describes a hub?

A) A device that simply amplifies a signal and forwards it on.

B) A device that connects LAN segments

C) A device that amplifies a signal and has multiple ports

D) A device that filters traffic based on the MAC Addresses

46. Which of the following BEST describes a hub?

A) A device that connects LAN segments

B) A device that filters traffic based on the MAC Addresses

C) A device that amplifies a signal and has multiple ports

D) A device that simply amplifies a signal and forwards it on.

47. Which of the following BEST describes a bridge?

A) A device that amplifies a signal and has multiple ports

B) A device that filters traffic based on the MAC Addresses

C) A device that connects LAN segments

D) A device that simply amplifies a signal and forwards it on.

48. Which of the following BEST describes a switch?

A) A device that amplifies a signal and has multiple ports

B) A device that simply amplifies a signal and forwards it on.

C) A device that connects LAN segments

D) A device that filters traffic based on the MAC Addresses

49. Which of the following statements is NOT true of MPLS?

A) MPLS tags are created only once per packet

B) It opens up the risk of a double-tagging attack

C) It slows down routing efficiency

D) Layer 3 and 4 devices use it

50. Which of the following statements is NOT true concerning microwave radio?

A) It requires a line-of-sight through the air, and so is susceptible to weather interference

B) It used to be largely analog, but it is almost exclusively digital for newer installations

C) One advantage is the low cost

D) If can deliver both voice and data traffic

51. Which of the following statements is NOT true concerning satellite radio?

A) It uses a transponder to send and receive data

B) It has a relatively long latency

C) It is difficult to tap into

D) It requires a line-of-sight through the air, and so is susceptible to weather interference

52. Which of the following BEST describes how data flows from a LAN to a WAN?

A) LAN > switch > CSU > DSU > switch > WAN

B) LAN > switch > DSU > CSU > switch > WAN

C) LAN > switch > DCE > DTE > switch > WAN

D) LAN > (magic happens here) > WAN

53. Which of the following statements is NOT true regarding synchronous communication?

A) It is ideal for high-volume transmissions

B) It requires a very stable connection that may be used by more than two devices

C) Both devices must agree on a start time

D) It is not as reliable as asynchronous

54. Which of the following statements is NOT true regarding asynchronous communication?

A) Each byte of data has a is surrounded by a start and stop bit

B) It is not as efficient as synchronous

C) It does not support error detection capabilities

D) It is much more forgiving when the communication path is not reliable

55. Which of the following statements is NOT true regarding a multiplexor?

A) It is used when a physical circuit has more bandwidth capabilities than required by individual signals

B) It combines multiple logical links into a single physical connection

C) It is a data link layer device

D) It divides portions of its total bandwidth and use each portion as a separate connection

56. Which of the following is NOT a valid method for multiplexing data?

A) FDM

B) TDM

C) PPP

D) ATDM

57. Which of the following is NOT a primary component of PPP?

A) LCP

B) User authentication

C) IPX

D) NCP

58. Which of the following is NOT true of PPP?

A) LCP is used to set up the communication channel

B) For each network protocol there will be a corresponding NCP

C) It implements encapsulation, but not framing, for a Point A to Point B connection

D) It encapsulates dissimilar protocols so that two different networks can communicate

59. Which of the following is NOT true of frame relay?

A) It uses packet switching for transmission

B) It is a newer technology

C) The cost to each consumer is loosely based on the amount of bandwidth needed, as opposed to the distance between the two endpoints

D) It operates at the data link layer

60. Which of the following is NOT true of ATM?

A) It is a great choice for audio and video transmission and provides QoS

B) It does not use virtual circuits so guaranteed bandwidth is not possible

C) It can be very cost-efficient because companies are billed based on the bandwidth used

D) It is a switching technology but uses cells instead of packets

61. Which of the following is NOT true of X.25?

A) It has more overhead than ATM

B) It adds error checking and correcting as well as fault tolerance

C) It is a newer WAN protocol

D) It allows many parties to use the service simultaneously, and each pays according to the amount of actual bandwidth used

62. Which of the following is NOT true of ISDN?

A) It uses circuit-switching

B) The standard has 2 types of channels – a B channel running a C Channel

C) It was the first truly digital connection for the masses to travel over copper phone lines

D) It began appearing in the late 1990s

63. Which of the following is NOT an ISDN implementation?

A) BISDN

B) PRI

C) CRI

D) BRI

64. Which of the following is NOT true of DSL?

A) It is an 'always on' connection

B) It provides rates up to 52 Mbps

C) The actual speed depends on how far from the CO the DSL modem is due to signal attenuation

D) It uses the same frequencies as ISDN

65. Which is the BEST description of DLS?

A) The first truly digital connection for the masses to travel over copper phone lines

B) Achieves higher rates because it uses all available frequencies on a UTP line

C) An older technology, it was designed to compensate by adding error checking and correcting as well as fault tolerance, resulting in a high overhead

D) A newer technology, it is a switching technology but uses cells instead of packets

66. Which is the BEST description of ISDN?

A) The first truly digital connection for the masses to travel over copper phone lines

B) Achieves higher rates because it uses all available frequencies on a UTP line

C) A newer technology, it is a switching technology but uses cells instead of packets

D) An older technology, it allowed more than one party to share in a single dedicated line across a WAN

67. Which is the BEST description of Frame Relay?

A) Achieves higher rates because it uses all available frequencies on a UTP line

B) An older technology, it allowed more than one party to share in a single dedicated line across a WAN

C) An older technology, it was designed to compensate by adding error checking and correcting as well as fault tolerance, resulting in a high overhead

D) A newer technology, it is a switching technology but uses cells instead of packets

68. Which is the BEST description of ATM?

A) A newer technology, it is a switching technology but uses cells instead of packets

B) The first truly digital connection for the masses to travel over copper phone lines

C) An older technology, it was designed to compensate by adding error checking and correcting as well as fault tolerance, resulting in a high overhead

D) An older technology, it allowed more than one party to share in a single dedicated line across a WAN

69. Which is the BEST description of X.25?

A) A newer technology, it is a switching technology but uses cells instead of packets

B) An older technology, it was designed to compensate by adding error checking and correcting as well as fault tolerance, resulting in a high overhead

C) Achieves higher rates because it uses all available frequencies on a UTP line

D) An older technology, it allowed more than one party to share in a single dedicated line across a WAN

70. Which is the BEST description of PPP?

A) It encapsulates dissimilar protocols so that two different networks can communicate

B) The first truly digital connection for the masses to travel over copper phone lines

C) A newer technology, it is a switching technology but uses cells instead of packets

D) Achieves higher rates because it uses all available frequencies on a UTP line

71. Which of the following BEST describes an ad hoc WLAN?

A) A wireless network made up of two computers talking to each other over wireless cards

B) A wireless network in which both computers are connected to an access point instead of each other

C) A wireless network in which the AP is also connected to another network

D) A frequency range within wireless traffic

72. Which of the following BEST describes a stand-alone WLAN?

A) A wireless network in which both computers are connected to an access point instead of each other

B) A wireless network in which the AP is also connected to another network

C) A wireless network made up of two computers talking to each other over wireless cards

D) A frequency range within wireless traffic

73. Which of the following BEST describes an infrastructure WLAN?

A) A wireless network in which both computers are connected to an access point instead of each other

B) A wireless network in which the AP is also connected to another network

C) A frequency range within wireless traffic

D) A wireless network made up of two computers talking to each other over wireless cards

74. Which of the following BEST describes a channel?

A) A group of devices communicating in infrastructure mode

B) A human-friendly name assigned to a group of devices communicating in infrastructure mode

C) A wireless network made up of two computers talking to each other over wireless cards

D) A frequency range within wireless traffic

75. Which of the following BEST describes a BSS?

A) A group of devices communicating in infrastructure mode

B) A human-friendly name assigned to a group of devices communicating in infrastructure mode

C) A frequency range within wireless traffic

D) A wireless network in which the AP is also connected to another network

76. Which of the following BEST describes an SSID?

A) A human-friendly name assigned to a group of devices communicating in infrastructure mode

B) A group of devices communicating in infrastructure mode

C) A wireless network made up of two computers talking to each other over wireless cards

D) A wireless network in which the AP is also connected to another network

77. Which of the following BEST describes WEP?

A) Claimed to provide protection equivalent to unsecured traffic traveling over a physical Ethernet cable

B) Only have to know the SSID and authenticate using an extremely weak protocol

C) The first real security for wireless traffic

D) Any infrastructure secured using WPA2

78. Which of the following BEST describes WEP?

A) Claimed to provide protection equivalent to unsecured traffic traveling over a physical Ethernet cable

B) Marginally better than its predecessor

C) The first real security for wireless traffic

D) Only have to know the SSID and authenticate using an extremely weak protocol

79. Which of the following BEST describes WPA?

A) Only have to know the SSID and authenticate using an extremely weak protocol

B) Claimed to provide protection equivalent to unsecured traffic traveling over a physical Ethernet cable

C) Marginally better than its predecessor

D) The first real security for wireless traffic

80. Which of the following BEST describes WPA2?

A) Claimed to provide protection equivalent to unsecured traffic traveling over a physical Ethernet cable

B) Marginally better than its predecessor

C) The first real security for wireless traffic

D) Only have to know the SSID and authenticate using an extremely weak protocol

81. Which of the following BEST describes a robust security network?

A) Marginally better than its predecessor

B) The first real security for wireless traffic

C) Any infrastructure secured using WPA2

D) Only have to know the SSID and authenticate using an extremely weak protocol

82. Which of the following BEST describes WAP?

A) The first protocol to allow devices such as smartphones to access the Internet in a limited fashion

B) The first real security for wireless traffic

C) Marginally better than its predecessor

D) Only have to know the SSID and authenticate using an extremely weak protocol

83. Which of the following is NOT true regarding honeypots?

A) Activity is not heavily logged but instead alerts network administrators to the activity

B) It is designed to get an attacker to leave more important systems alone

C) If more than one honeypot is put into place, it is called a honeynet

D) It is designed to give you time to monitor an attacker and figure what they are up to

Answers

1. B	2. A
3. B	4. B
5. D	6. D (Neither type is more reliable than the other or provides a different throughput – the difference is the type of data that can be transmitted at the same time)
7. D	8. B
9. C	10. C
11. B	12. A
13. A	14. B
15. C	16. D
17. B	18. C
19. B	20. D
21. D	22. A
23. C	24. A
25. C	26. D
27. D	28. A
29. D	30. D
31. A	32. B (Optical fiber is smaller and lighter than metallic cables of the same capacity)
33. D	34. B
35. D	36. D
37. C	38. B
39. C	40. B
41. A	42. B
43. B	44. B
45. C	46. C
47. C	48. D
49. C	50. C
51. C	52. B
53. B	54. C
55. C (It is a physical layer device)	56. C (PPP is a protocol, not a multiplexing method)
57. C (IPX is a network protocol, not a component of PPP)	58. C (It implements both encapsulation AND framing)
59. B	60. B (It uses virtual circuits so that guaranteed bandwidth is possible)
61. C (It is one of the older protocols and is not in-use much these days)	62. B (The standard has 2 types of channels – a B channel running a D Channel)
63. C (Basic rate interface, primary rate interface and broadband ISDN are the three base implementations)	64. D (It uses all available frequencies on a UTP line)

65. B	66. A
67. B	68. A
69. B	70. A
71. A	72. A
73. B	74. D
75. A	76. A
77. B	78. A
79. C	80. C
81. C	82. A
83. A (Activity IS heavily logged AND alerts network administrators to the activity)	

Chapter 50: Internet Concepts

Questions

1. Which of the following BEST describes a network access point?

A) A traffic concentration spot

B) A Java applet or small program that runs within a web server environment

C) An executable, machine-independent software program running on a web server

D) A program written in a portable, platform-independent computer language

2. Which of the following BEST describes a CGI script?

A) A Java applet or small program that runs within a web server environment

B) A traffic concentration spot

C) A program written in a portable, platform-independent computer language

D) An executable, machine-independent software program running on a web server

3. Which of the following BEST describes an applet?

A) A traffic concentration spot

B) A program written in a portable, platform-independent computer language

C) A Java applet or small program that runs within a web server environment

D) An executable, machine-independent software program running on a web server

4. Which of the following BEST describes a servlet?

A) An executable, machine-independent software program running on a web server

B) A traffic concentration spot

C) A program written in a portable, platform-independent computer language

D) A Java applet or small program that runs within a web server environment

5. Which of the following BEST describes a cookie?

A) A file that a browser stores on the local computer's hard drive

B) A marker or address that identifies a document or a specific place in a document

C) The connection between Internet users and the Internet service provider

D) Computers that do not use any type of address translation

6. Which of the following BEST describes a bookmark?

A) Computers that do not use any type of address translation

B) A file that a browser stores on the local computer's hard drive

C) A marker or address that identifies a document or a specific place in a document

D) The connection between Internet users and the Internet service provider

7. Which of the following BEST describes a direct connection?

A) Computers that do not use any type of address translation

B) The connection between Internet users and the Internet service provider

C) A file that a browser stores on the local computer's hard drive

D) A marker or address that identifies a document or a specific place in a document

8. Which of the following BEST describes an Internet link?

A) The connection between Internet users and the Internet service provider

B) A marker or address that identifies a document or a specific place in a document

C) A file that a browser stores on the local computer's hard drive

D) Computers that do not use any type of address translation

9. Which of the following BEST describes SMTP?

A) A third party that provides individuals and enterprises with access to the Internet

B) A standard terminal emulation protocol used for remote terminal connections

C) A protocol used to transfer files over a TCP/IP network

D) The standard email protocol on the Internet.

10. Which of the following BEST describes FTP?

A) The standard email protocol on the Internet.

B) A standard terminal emulation protocol used for remote terminal connections

C) A protocol used to transfer files over a TCP/IP network

D) A third party that provides individuals and enterprises with access to the Internet

11. Which of the following BEST describes ISP?

A) A third party that provides individuals and enterprises with access to the Internet

B) The standard email protocol on the Internet.

C) A protocol used to transfer files over a TCP/IP network

D) A standard terminal emulation protocol used for remote terminal connections

12. Which of the following BEST describes Telnet?

A) The standard email protocol on the Internet.

B) A protocol used to transfer files over a TCP/IP network

C) A third party that provides individuals and enterprises with access to the Internet

D) A standard terminal emulation protocol used for remote terminal connections

13. Which of the following BEST describes SSH?

A) The standard email protocol on the Internet.

B) A protocol used to transfer files over a TCP/IP network

C) A network protocol using cryptography to secure command line communication between two networked computers

D) A third party that provides individuals and enterprises with access to the Internet

Answers

1. A		2. D	
3. B		4. D	
5. A		6. C	
7. A		8. A	
9. D		10. C	
11. A		12. D	
13. C			

Chapter 51: Telecommunications

Questions

1. Which of the following is NOT a common attribute of a PBX?

A) It is computer-based and scalable to support call routing in-memory

B) It supports an operator console or switchboard for a human operator

C) It supports digital phones that can integrate both voice and data together

D) Each trunk line carries one phone line

2. Which of the following is NOT a common risk with PBXs?

A) Theft of service

B) Malware

C) Denial of service

D) Unauthorized access

3. Which of the following is NOT a unique weakness commonly encountered when dealing with PBXs?

A) DID lines

B) Voice lines can be used to send unauthorized data

C) Call-tracking logs are often not enabled

D) Lack of control over long-distance lines

4. Which of the following PBXs would NOT allow an attacker to eavesdrop on conversations?

A) Conferencing

B) Account codes

C) Auto-answer

D) Call waiting

5. Which of the following features could BEST enable an attacker to disable user tracking?

A) Silent monitoring

B) Call forwarding

C) Non-busy extensions

D) Tenanting

6. Which of the following is NOT an established method to mitigate risks for PBXs?

A) Establish control over the numbers destined for fax machines and modems

B) Block controls for long-distance phone calls to particular numbers such as cell numbers

C) Disable dedicated administrative ports

D) Configure DID lines to avoid an external party requesting a local dial tone

7. When carrying out a hardwire wiretap, which of the following activities could an attacker NOT control?

A) Send a signal to the device to turn on lights or the microphone

B) Detect which keys are being pressed

C) Listen to voice activity

D) Cause physical damage to a device

8. Which of the following is NOT a communication method used with control signals?

A) Analog voice with or without separate control signals

B) Digital voice with inclusive control signals

C) Analog voice with inclusive control signals

D) Digital voice with or without separate control signals

9. Which of the following BEST describes an attacker taking advantage of hardware conferencing?

A) Taking advantage of an undocumented feature

B) Gaining physical access to a bridge and routing all signals to a specific port

C) Listening in on voice activity by accessing the physical communication between the PBX and the end-user device

D) Listening in on the active voice channel of a line placed into maintenance mode

10. Which of the following BEST describes an attacker taking advantage of MOS?

    A) Listening in on voice activity by accessing the physical communication between the PBX and the end-user device

    B) Gaining physical access to a bridge and routing all signals to a specific port

    C) Taking advantage of an undocumented feature

    D) Listening in on the active voice channel of a line placed into maintenance mode

11. Which of the following BEST describes an attacker taking advantage of hardware wiretapping?

    A) Listening in on voice activity by accessing the physical communication between the PBX and the end-user device

    B) Gaining physical access to a bridge and routing all signals to a specific port

    C) Listening in on the active voice channel of a line placed into maintenance mode

    D) Taking advantage of an undocumented feature

12. Which of the following BEST describes an attacker taking advantage of a maintenance hook?

    A) Taking advantage of an undocumented feature

    B) Gaining physical access to a bridge and routing all signals to a specific port

    C) Listening in on the active voice channel of a line placed into maintenance mode

    D) Listening in on voice activity by accessing the physical communication between the PBX and the end-user device

13. Which of the following conditions is unlikely to cause a PBX crash?

    A) Repeated dialing of the same number

    B) Voicemail abuse

    C) Normal system shutdown procedures

    D) Physical removal of hardware or media from the PBX

14. Which of the following is NOT a recommended step to mitigate crash/restart vulnerabilities?

    A) Carry out crash/restart vulnerability tests

    B) Adjust restart procedures so they eliminate the vulnerability

    C) Alter modules to remove embedded passwords if found

    D) Use a PBX firewall

15. Which of the following are valid advantages when using VoIP?

    A) Due to the redundancy of the Internet, it is more reliable than traditional telephony

    B) Innovation proceeds at a much higher rate than does traditional telephony

    C) IP is software-based and easy to install

    D) It provides a very low cost per call

16. Which of the following are valid concerns when using VoIP?

    A) It is less reliable than traditional telephony

    B) Security concerns increase because we have to deal with voice and data

    C) Some countries ban the use of VoIP

    D) Vendors tend to be less reputable due to the low barrier of entry

Answers

1. D (It will have more than two trunk lines that terminate at the PBX; a single trunk line can carry multiple phone lines)	2. B
3. B (While it is technically possible to send data over a voice line, it would be fairly difficult to execute and slow)	4. B
5. B	6. C (Securing separate and dedicated administrative ports is recommended over disabling)
7. D	8. D
9. B	10. D
11. A	12. A
13. A	14. C (If embedded passwords are found, patch the load module to replace them. Authorized manufacturer personnel can be given the new password, if needed.)
15. A (It is actually less reliable than traditional telephony due to latency and bandwidth fluctuation)	16. D (There is little evidence that this statement is true)

Chapter 52: IS Auditor Duties for the Information Systems Operations, Maintenance and Service Management Domain

Questions

1. Which of the following statements does NOT represent an area in which an auditor will need to focus?

A) Look for an active capacity management function

B) Evaluate help desk activity to see which areas receive the most reports

C) Examining problem reports and error logs to ensure they are addressed in a timely manner

D) Review all OS configuration folders and files used to grant special privileges

2. Which of the following is NOT a step an auditor will need to carry out when reviewing software licensing?

A) Review all software contracts

B) Correlate workstation activity with actual users

C) Become familiar with the list of all standard, user and licensed software in-use

D) Scan the entire network and produce a list of all installed software

3. Which of the following is NOT an area in which an auditor should focus when auditing hardware?

A) Maintenance

B) Acquisition

C) Final disposition

D) Ensuring availability

4. When reviewing OS selection decisions, which of the following is NOT a focus area for the auditor?

A) The OS includes information system processing and control requirements

B) The OS aligns with the enterprise architecture

C) The OS is part of a comprehensive backup and restoration program

D) The OS is properly aligned with business goals

5. When auditing a database, which of the following is NOT normally included?

A) Interfaces

B) Portability

C) Design

D) The physical schema

6. When auditing network infrastructure, which of the following is NOT a primary goal?

A) Check that costs for procuring and operating a network do not exceed the benefits

B) Ensure standards are being used for selecting a network architecture

C) Ensure standards are being used for the design

D) Ensure the proper controls are being used

7. To effectively perform a network infrastructure review, which of the following is NOT something an auditor will need to identify?

A) Significant network components such as servers, routers, switches, hubs, modems, wireless devices and others

B) The network topology and design

C) Incident handling

D) Interconnected boundary networks, or where each network starts and stops

8. When performing a network infrastructure audit, which of the following logical security controls would an auditor NOT need to look for?

A) Network access change requests

B) Protocols in-use

C) Test plans

D) Unique passwords

9. Which of the following definitions BEST describes a highly distributed environment?

A) Security is under the control of individuals

B) Security is under the direction of individuals, but the overall responsibility remains with IS management

C) Security is under the direction of individuals, but adheres to the guidelines established by IS management

D) Security is under the direction of IS management, with IS management staff maintaining a close relationship with users

10. Which of the following definitions BEST describes a distributed environment?

A) Security is under the control of individuals

B) Security is under the direction of individuals, but the overall responsibility remains with IS management

C) Security is under the direction of individuals, but adheres to the guidelines established by IS management

D) Security is under the direction of IS management, with IS management staff maintaining a close relationship with users

11. Which of the following definitions BEST describes a mixed environment?

A) Security is under the direction of individuals, but the overall responsibility remains with IS management

B) Security is completely under the control of IS management

C) Security is under the direction of individuals, but adheres to the guidelines established by IS management

D) Security is under the direction of IS management, with IS management staff maintaining a close relationship with users

12. Which of the following definitions BEST describes a centralized environment?

A) Security is under the direction of individuals, but the overall responsibility remains with IS management

B) Security is under the direction of individuals, but adheres to the guidelines established by IS management

C) Security is completely under the control of IS management

D) Security is under the direction of IS management, with IS management staff maintaining a close relationship with users

13. Which of the following definitions BEST describes a highly centralized environment?

A) Security is completely under the control of IS management

B) Security is under the direction of IS management, with IS management staff maintaining a close relationship with users

C) Security is under the direction of individuals, but adheres to the guidelines established by IS management

D) Security is under the direction of individuals, but the overall responsibility remains with IS management

14. When interviewing employees responsible for network security, which of the following is NOT something the auditor needs to assess?

A) If the person is knowledgeable in how to maintain and monitor access

B) If the person is aware of the need to actively monitor logons and to account for employee changes

C) If the person is aware of the risk that must be minimized associated with physical and logical access

D) If documentation exists proving the person has been properly trained

15. When auditing IS operations and observing employees, which of the following is NOT something the auditor should note?

A) That controls have been implemented for IS management review, data integrity and security

B) That adequate supervision is present

C) A work schedule has been established and is followed

D) That controls exist to promote efficiency and to adhere to established standards and policies

16. When auditing a lights-out operation, which of the following is NOT something an auditor to validate?

A) Remote access to the master console in case of a software failure is secured

B) Routine access is properly logged

C) Contingency plans allow for the proper identification of a disaster in the unattended facility

D) Tests of the software are performed on a periodic basis, especially after changes or updates have been applied

17. Which of the following areas is NOT a focus when auditing job scheduling?

A) Re-execution of jobs is carried out properly

B) That job priorities are assigned properly

C) If each job is required

D) Exception processing logs

18. Which of the following is NOT something that an auditor would focus on when examining performance records, error log entries and help desk call logs?

A) The percentage of problems being reported outside of normal business hours

B) If a problem was encountered during processing

C) If the reasons for delays in application program processing are valid

D) If significant and recurring problems have been identified and resolved

Answers

1. B	2. B
3. C	4. C
5. D	6. D (While the proper use of controls is covered in this area, it is not a primary goal)
7. C	8. B
9. A	10. C
11. A	12. D
13. A	14. D (The point is not to prove that documentation exists, but documentation could be used to prove the other three)
15. C	16. B
17. C	18. A

Section 5: The Protection of Information Assets Domain

Chapter 53: Asset Classification

Questions

1. Which of the following statements BEST describes why asset classification is so important?

    A) So that we do not waste effort protecting resources in ways that do not help

    B) Because the DRP and BCP require assets to be classified in order to prioritize recovery and restoration activities

    C) Because it increases operational efficiencies

    D) So that we can ensure our internal assets align with business goals

2. Who is responsible for asset classification?

    A) The security manager

    B) Those who use the asset the most

    C) The asset owner

    D) Senior management

3. Which of the following is NOT an attribute used when classifying assets?

    A) The difficulty in providing security

    B) How access is granted

    C) Who is responsible for approving access

    D) How strong security controls are

Answers

| 3. A | | |
| 1. A | 2. C | |

Chapter 54: Security Awareness and Training

Questions

1. Which of the following BEST describes security training?

    A) The process of teaching security skills to security personnel

    B) The process of testing security hygiene within a department

    C) The process of spreading the need for security awareness throughout an organization

    D) The process of explaining security issues to all members of an organization

2. Which of the following BEST describes security awareness training?

    A) The process of spreading the need for security awareness throughout an organization

    B) The process of teaching security skills to security personnel

    C) The process of testing security hygiene within a department

    D) The process of explaining security issues to all members of an organization

3. Which of the following is NOT true regarding awareness training?

    A) Training materials are often administered online

    B) Posters, newsletters and screensavers are usually used to reinforce security training

    C) It extends to all third-party entities who have any level of involvement with the organization's internal processes

    D) It starts as soon as new hires have completed the onboarding process

Answers

1. A	2. D
3. D (It starts with the onboarding process, not after)	

Chapter 55: External Parties

Questions

1. When implementing authentication and authorization for external parties, which of the following is NOT an access control policy to be enforced?

A) There must be a process for revoking access rights or interrupting the connection between systems

B) An authorization process needs to exist for granting user access and privileges

C) All access that is not explicitly authorized is forbidden, also known as least-privilege

D) Each external party must have a unique identifier and passwords must be used

2. Which of the following is NOT an item that should be included with an external party contract?

A) Ownership of intellectual property, including works that are created in collaboration with the vendor

B) Assignability of the contract should be stated

C) If the vendor is allowed to subcontract work on behalf of the organization

D) How disputes will be resolved and under what legal jurisdiction the process will follow

3. Which of the following standards is the most useful in ensuring a partner stays in compliance with security controls?

A) ISO 20000

B) ISO 27001

C) ISO 27002

D) ISO 20002

Answers

1. D (Each user within an external party must have unique identifiers such as user IDs and passwords must be used)	2. B (Non-assignability of the contract should be stated)
3. B	

Chapter 56: Computer Crime

Questions

1. Which of the following is NOT a type of damage resulting from computer crime?

A) Sabotage

B) A loss of asset availability

C) Blackmail, industrial espionage and organized crime

D) Legal repercussions

2. Which of the following BEST describes a hacker or cracker?

A) Someone who is not a skilled individual, but simply uses tools created by others to break into systems

B) A skilled person who is interested in proving how smart they are by breaking into systems

C) A person who happens upon unprotected information and decides to take advantage of the situation

D) A party having an increased access but does not possess any loyalty that an employee might have

3. Which of the following BEST describes a script kiddie?

A) A person who happens upon unprotected information and decides to take advantage of the situation

B) A party having an increased access but does not possess any loyalty that an employee might have

C) Someone who is not a skilled individual, but simply uses tools created by others to break into systems

D) A skilled person who is interested in proving how smart they are by breaking into systems

4. Which of the following BEST describes a part-time and temporary personnel?

A) A skilled person who is interested in proving how smart they are by breaking into systems

B) A party having an increased access but does not possess any loyalty that an employee might have

C) Someone who is not a skilled individual, but simply uses tools created by others to break into systems

D) A person who happens upon unprotected information and decides to take advantage of the situation

5. Which of the following BEST describes an opportunist?

A) Someone who is not a skilled individual, but simply uses tools created by others to break into systems

B) A skilled person who is interested in proving how smart they are by breaking into systems

C) A party having an increased access but does not possess any loyalty that an employee might have

D) A person who happens upon unprotected information and decides to take advantage of the situation

6. Which of the following BEST describes an employee?

A) Someone who can cause significant damage and is the most common source of threats

B) Someone who is particularly dangerous due to their advanced skillset, knowledge of the company's infrastructure and has elevated access

C) A significant risk unless their credentials are deleted immediately after termination

D) Someone having authorized access into systems and have a broad range of knowledge about the inner workings

7. Which of the following BEST describes an IT employee?

A) Someone who is particularly dangerous due to their advanced skillset, knowledge of the company's infrastructure and has elevated access

B) A significant risk unless their credentials are deleted immediately after termination

C) Someone having authorized access into systems and have a broad range of knowledge about the inner workings

D) Someone who can cause significant damage and is the most common source of threats

8. Which of the following BEST describes an end user?

A) Someone having authorized access into systems and have a broad range of knowledge about the inner workings

B) Someone who is particularly dangerous due to their advanced skillset, knowledge of the company's infrastructure and has elevated access

C) A significant risk unless their credentials are deleted immediately after termination

D) Someone who can cause significant damage and is the most common source of threats

9. Which of the following BEST describes an unfavorably terminated employee?

A) Someone who can cause significant damage and is the most common source of threats

B) Someone having authorized access into systems and have a broad range of knowledge about the inner workings

C) Someone who is particularly dangerous due to their advanced skillset, knowledge of the company's infrastructure and has elevated access

D) A significant risk unless their credentials are deleted immediately after termination

10. When a computer crime is being carried out, which of the following descriptions BEST describes a target?

A) A computer being used to attack a non-computer

B) The computer being attacked when one computer attacks another

C) A computer used to trick a person into giving away confidential information

D) The computer launching an attack when one computer attacks another

11. When a computer crime is being carried out, which of the following descriptions BEST describes a subject?

A) A computer being used to attack a non-computer

B) A computer used to trick a person into giving away confidential information

C) The computer launching an attack when one computer attacks another

D) The computer being attacked when one computer attacks another

12. When a computer crime is being carried out, which of the following descriptions BEST describes a tool?

A) A computer being used to attack a non-computer

B) A computer used to trick a person into giving away confidential information

C) The computer being attacked when one computer attacks another

D) The computer launching an attack when one computer attacks another

13. When a computer crime is being carried out, which of the following descriptions BEST describes a symbol?

A) A computer used to trick a person into giving away confidential information

B) A computer being used to attack a non-computer

C) The computer being attacked when one computer attacks another

D) The computer launching an attack when one computer attacks another

14. Which of the following BEST describes the reconnaissance method of network analysis?

   A) An attack in which the names, directories, privileges, shares and policies are listed

   B) A methodical approach to identify the software and hardware running in the target's network

   C) An attack performed by a manual search in software, OSs or add-on utilities

   D) An attack that studies the communication patterns on a network to deduce information

15. Which of the following BEST describes the reconnaissance method of resource enumeration and browsing?

   A) An attack in which the names, directories, privileges, shares and policies are listed

   B) An attack performed by a manual search in software, OSs or add-on utilities

   C) An attack that studies the communication patterns on a network to deduce information

   D) A methodical approach to identify the software and hardware running in the target's network

16. Which of the following BEST describes the reconnaissance method of a browsing attack?

   A) An attack performed by a manual search in software, OSs or add-on utilities

   B) A methodical approach to identify the software and hardware running in the target's network

   C) An attack that studies the communication patterns on a network to deduce information

   D) An attack in which the names, directories, privileges, shares and policies are listed

17. Which of the following BEST describes the reconnaissance method of a traffic analysis?

   A) An attack that studies the communication patterns on a network to deduce information

   B) An attack performed by a manual search in software, OSs or add-on utilities

   C) An attack in which the names, directories, privileges, shares and policies are listed

   D) A methodical approach to identify the software and hardware running in the target's network

18. Which of the following BEST describes the reconnaissance method of a traffic analysis war chalking?

   A) The practice of driving around businesses or residential neighborhoods while scanning with a laptop computer to search for wireless networks

   B) The practice of breaking through encryption faster than keys can be changed

   C) The practice of marking a series of symbols on sidewalks and walls to indicate nearby wireless access points

   D) The practice of walking around businesses or residential neighborhoods while scanning with a small device to search for wireless networks

19. Which of the following BEST describes the reconnaissance method of a traffic analysis war driving?

   A) The practice of marking a series of symbols on sidewalks and walls to indicate nearby wireless access points

   B) The practice of walking around businesses or residential neighborhoods while scanning with a small device to search for wireless networks

   C) The practice of driving around businesses or residential neighborhoods while scanning with a laptop computer to search for wireless networks

   D) The practice of breaking through encryption faster than keys can be changed

20. Which of the following BEST describes the reconnaissance method of a traffic analysis war walking?

A) The practice of driving around businesses or residential neighborhoods while scanning with a laptop computer to search for wireless networks

B) The practice of walking around businesses or residential neighborhoods while scanning with a small device to search for wireless networks

C) The practice of marking a series of symbols on sidewalks and walls to indicate nearby wireless access points

D) The practice of breaking through encryption faster than keys can be changed

21. Which of the following BEST describes a DoS attack?

A) A DoS attack meant to bring down a service by overwhelming it with a huge amount of traffic

B) Software that waits for a specific condition to be reached and then launches an internal attack

C) An attack executed across the Internet against web applications

D) Denying consumers the use of a service or server

22. Which of the following BEST describes a flooding attack?

A) A DoS attack meant to bring down a service by overwhelming it with a huge amount of traffic

B) Denying consumers the use of a service or server

C) Software that waits for a specific condition to be reached and then launches an internal attack

D) An attack executed across the Internet against web applications

23. Which of the following BEST describes a logic bomb attack?

A) A DoS attack meant to bring down a service by overwhelming it with a huge amount of traffic

B) An attack executed across the Internet against web applications

C) Denying consumers the use of a service or server

D) Software that waits for a specific condition to be reached and then launches an internal attack

24. Which of the following BEST describes gaining access by using brute force?

A) Exploiting a small window of time between the time that a security control is applied and the time that a service is used

B) Guessing passwords to gain access to a system by simply rotating through all possible values until the system grants access

C) An attack executed across the Internet against web applications

D) Capturing legitimate packets passing by on a network, and then sending them back

25. Which of the following BEST describes gaining access by using packet replay?

A) Guessing passwords to gain access to a system by simply rotating through all possible values until the system grants access

B) Capturing legitimate packets passing by on a network, and then sending them back

C) An attack executed across the Internet against web applications

D) Exploiting a small window of time between the time that a security control is applied and the time that a service is used

26. Which of the following BEST describes gaining access by using a race condition?

A) A physical attack where an unauthorized person closely follows an authorized person through a secured gate or door

B) Guessing passwords to gain access to a system by simply rotating through all possible values until the system grants access

C) Exploiting a small window of time between the time that a security control is applied and the time that a service is used

D) Dialing random numbers until a system answers and allows a connection

27. Which of the following BEST describes gaining access by using unauthorized use from the web?

A) Dialing random numbers until a system answers and allows a connection

B) An attack executed across the Internet against web applications

C) Capturing legitimate packets passing by on a network, and then sending them back

D) A physical attack where an unauthorized person closely follows an authorized person through a secured gate or door

28. Which of the following BEST describes gaining access by using war dialing?

A) Capturing legitimate packets passing by on a network, and then sending them back

B) Guessing passwords to gain access to a system by simply rotating through all possible values until the system grants access

C) An attack executed across the Internet against web applications

D) Dialing random numbers until a system answers and allows a connection

29. Which of the following BEST describes gaining access by using piggybacking?

A) An attack executed across the Internet against web applications

B) A physical attack where an unauthorized person closely follows an authorized person through a secured gate or door

C) Guessing passwords to gain access to a system by simply rotating through all possible values until the system grants access

D) Capturing legitimate packets passing by on a network, and then sending them back

30. Which BEST describes a sequence TOC/TOU attack?

A) Occurs when an untrusted process manages to insert itself in between TOC and TOU

B) Occurs when two trusted processes get in each other's way, effectively locking them both up

C) Occurs when an untrusted and a trusted process attempt to access the same physical memory

D) Occurs when the OS and a trusted process attempt to access the same resource

31. Which BEST describes a nonatomic TOC/TOU attack?

A) Occurs when an untrusted and a trusted process attempt to access the same physical memory

B) Occurs when the OS and a trusted process attempt to access the same resource

C) Occurs when two trusted processes get in each other's way, effectively locking them both up

D) Occurs when an untrusted process manages to insert itself in between TOC and TOU

32. Which BEST describes a deadlock TOC/TOU attack?

A) Occurs when an untrusted process manages to insert itself in between TOC and TOU

B) Occurs when an untrusted and a trusted process attempt to access the same physical memory

C) Occurs when two trusted processes get in each other's way, effectively locking them both up

D) Occurs when the OS and a trusted process attempt to access the same resource

33. Which BEST describes a livelock TOC/TOU attack?

A) Occurs when two trusted processes get in each other's way, effectively locking them both up

B) Occurs when the OS and a trusted process attempt to access the same resource

C) Occurs when an untrusted and a trusted process attempt to access the same physical memory

D) Occurs when an untrusted process manages to insert itself in between TOC and TOU

34. Which BEST describes a pharming attack?

A) The act of stealing money by rounding down fractions

B) Compromising a DNS database

C) Redirecting browser traffic from a legitimate site to a bogus one

D) The act of stealing money by reducing amounts by an insignificant amount

35. Which BEST describes a DNS poisoning attack?

A) Redirecting browser traffic from a legitimate site to a bogus one

B) The act of stealing money by rounding down fractions

C) Compromising a DNS database

D) The act of stealing money by reducing amounts by an insignificant amount

36. Which BEST describes a salami attack?

A) The act of stealing money by rounding down fractions

B) The act of stealing money by reducing amounts by an insignificant amount

C) Redirecting browser traffic from a legitimate site to a bogus one

D) Compromising a DNS database

37. Which BEST describes a rounding attack?

A) Compromising a DNS database

B) The act of stealing money by rounding down fractions

C) The act of stealing money by reducing amounts by an insignificant amount

D) Redirecting browser traffic from a legitimate site to a bogus one

38. Which BEST describes eavesdropping?

A) Occurs when a computer sends packets that appear to be coming from another IP address

B) The act of modifying data without anyone noticing

C) A situation where an attacker connects to two devices and intercepts all traffic between them

D) The act of sniffing network packets as they pass by

39. Which BEST describes alteration?

A) Occurs when a computer sends packets that appear to be coming from another IP address

B) The act of sniffing network packets as they pass by

C) Occurs when the attacker waits around while a valid user or machine authenticates itself, and then assumes the authenticated identity

D) The act of modifying data without anyone noticing

40. Which BEST describes a man-in-the-middle attack?

A) A situation where an attacker connects to two devices and intercepts all traffic between them

B) The act of sniffing network packets as they pass by

C) The act of modifying data without anyone noticing

D) Occurs when the attacker waits around while a valid user or machine authenticates itself, and then assumes the authenticated identity

41. Which BEST describes masquerading?

A) The act of sniffing network packets as they pass by

B) Occurs when a computer sends packets that appear to be coming from another IP address

C) Occurs when the attacker waits around while a valid user or machine authenticates itself, and then assumes the authenticated identity

D) The act of modifying data without anyone noticing

42. Which BEST describes an IP spoofing attack?

A) A situation where an attacker connects to two devices and intercepts all traffic between them

B) The act of sniffing network packets as they pass by

C) Occurs when a computer sends packets that appear to be coming from another IP address

D) The act of modifying data without anyone noticing

43. Which BEST describes message modification?

A) Capturing a message in-transit, and modifying, delaying or deleting it

B) Malware that disguises itself as useful program such as a utility, OS patch or game

C) Bits of software code left by a programmer to allow them back in at a later date

D) Software installed onto a target computer to steal information or cause further harm

44. Which BEST describes malicious code?

A) Software installed onto a target computer to steal information or cause further harm

B) Malware that disguises itself as useful program such as a utility, OS patch or game

C) Bits of software code left by a programmer to allow them back in at a later date

D) Capturing a message in-transit, and modifying, delaying or deleting it

45. Which BEST describes a trojan horse?

A) Software installed onto a target computer to steal information or cause further harm

B) Capturing a message in-transit, and modifying, delaying or deleting it

C) Software installed onto a target computer to steal information or cause further harm

D) Bits of software code left by a programmer to allow them back in at a later date

46. Which BEST describes a trap door?

A) Bits of software code left by a programmer to allow them back in at a later date

B) Software installed onto a target computer to steal information or cause further harm

C) Capturing a message in-transit, and modifying, delaying or deleting it

D) Malware that disguises itself as useful program such as a utility, OS patch or game

47. Which BEST describes a back door?

A) Capturing a message in-transit, and modifying, delaying or deleting it

B) Bits of software code left by a programmer to allow them back in at a later date

C) Software installed onto a target computer to steal information or cause further harm

D) Malware that disguises itself as useful program such as a utility, OS patch or game

48. Which BEST describes a botnet?

A) Uses compromised computers to carry out a distributed attack

B) A compromised computer

C) A denial attack that is launched from many compromised computers

D) A collection of previously compromised computers

49. Which BEST describes a zombie?

A) A compromised computer

B) A denial attack that is launched from many compromised computers

C) Uses compromised computers to carry out a distributed attack

D) A collection of previously compromised computers

50. Which BEST describes a bot herder?

A) A collection of previously compromised computers

B) Uses compromised computers to carry out a distributed attack

C) A compromised computer

D) A denial attack that is launched from many compromised computers

51. Which BEST describes a DDoS?

A) A collection of previously compromised computers

B) Uses compromised computers to carry out a distributed attack

C) A compromised computer

D) A denial attack that is launched from many compromised computers

52. Which BEST describes malware?

A) Malicious software that can self-replicate across a network by copying itself from computer to connected computer

B) Malicious software that does not cause damage other than silently listening and collecting sensitive information to send back to the attacker

C) Malicious software that does not self-replicate or try to attach itself to other files

D) Malicious software that usually tries to get itself appended to the end of legitimate programs on a computer

53. Which BEST describes virus?

A) Malicious software that can alter its appearance to outwit scanners

B) Malicious software that does not self-replicate or try to attach itself to other files

C) Malicious software that usually tries to get itself appended to the end of legitimate programs on a computer

D) Malicious software that can self-replicate across a network by copying itself from computer to connected computer

54. Which BEST describes polymorphic virus?

A) Malicious software that can alter its appearance to outwit malware scanners

B) Malicious software that does not cause damage other than silently listening and collecting sensitive information to send back to the attacker

C) Malicious software that can self-replicate across a network by copying itself from computer to connected computer

D) Malicious software that usually tries to get itself appended to the end of legitimate programs on a computer

55. Which BEST describes worm?

A) Malicious software that can alter its appearance to outwit scanners

B) Malicious software that does not self-replicate or try to attach itself to other files

C) Malicious software that does not cause damage other than silently listening and collecting sensitive information to send back to the attacker

D) Malicious software that can self-replicate across a network by copying itself from computer to connected computer

56. Which BEST describes spyware?

A) Malicious software that does not cause damage other than silently listening and collecting sensitive information to send back to the attacker

B) Malicious software that can alter its appearance to outwit scanners

C) Malicious software that does not self-replicate or try to attach itself to other files

D) Malicious software that usually tries to get itself appended to the end of legitimate programs on a computer

57. Which of the following is NOT a type of malware?

A) Zombie

B) Virus

C) Spyware

D) Worm

58. What of the following areas of a computer is NOT targeted by malware?

A) The file directory system

B) Executable program files

C) Boot and system areas

D) In-memory page files

59. Which of the following are the five types of anti-malware technology solutions?

A) Scanners, active monitors, CRC checkers, behavior blockers and immunizers

B) Switchers, passive monitors, cyclic checkers, active blockers and immunizers

C) Switchers, active monitors, cyclic checkers, behavior blockers and destroyers

D) Scanners, passive monitors, CRC checkers, behavior blockers and destroyers

60. Which of the following statements BEST describes a scanner?

A) Examining areas of a computer looking for strings of bits that looks like malware

B) Looking for malware at the DOS and BIOS level

C) Comparing bit strings in a file against a pattern known to represent malware

D) Analyzing instructions in a file and decides if it looks like malware

61. Which of the following statements BEST describes a mask or signature?

A) Examining areas of a computer looking for strings of bits that looks like malware

B) Comparing bit strings in a file against a pattern known to represent malware

C) Looking for malware at the DOS and BIOS level

D) Analyzing instructions in a file and decides if it looks like malware

62. Which of the following statements BEST describes a heuristic scanner?

A) Examining areas of a computer looking for strings of bits that looks like malware

B) Analyzing instructions in a file and decides if it looks like malware

C) Comparing bit strings in a file against a pattern known to represent malware

D) Looking for malware at the DOS and BIOS level

63. Which of the following statements BEST describes an active monitor?

A) Looking for malware at the DOS and BIOS level

B) Examining areas of a computer looking for strings of bits that looks like malware

C) Comparing bit strings in a file against a pattern known to represent malware

D) Analyzing instructions in a file and decides if it looks like malware

64. Which of the following statements BEST describes an integrity CRC checker?

A) Mimics file by renaming themselves in the master boot record

B) Checks CRCs from previous runs against current CRCs to see if a file has changed

C) Real-time detection of malware that writes to the boot sector or master boot record, or makes changes to executables

D) Attach themselves to files in the same way that malware does

65. Which of the following statements BEST describes a behavior blocker?

A) Attach themselves to files in the same way that malware does

B) Checks CRCs from previous runs against current CRCs to see if a file has changed

C) Mimics file by renaming themselves in the master boot record

D) Real-time detection of malware that writes to the boot sector or master boot record, or makes changes to executables

66. Which of the following statements BEST describes an immunizer?

A) Real-time detection of malware that writes to the boot sector or master boot record, or makes changes to executables

B) Attach themselves to files in the same way that malware does

C) Mimics file by renaming themselves in the master boot record

D) Checks CRCs from previous runs against current CRCs to see if a file has changed

67. Which of the following statements is not true regarding how an immunizer works?

A) It can continuously watch a file it is attached to for unauthorized changes and report suspicious activity

B) It is not possible immunize a file against all known malware

C) It can pretend to be malware so that the real malware will assume a file is already infected and leave it alone

D) Once fully immunized, a computer is relatively safe from internal attacks

68. Which of the following is NOT a valid technical control to help with malware?

A) Use remote booting, such as diskless workstations

B) Use boot malware protection, such as built-in, firmware-based malware protection

C) Disallow the use of all removable media

D) Use a hardware-based password, such as 2-factor authentication

69. Which of the following is NOT true regarding anti-malware solutions?

A) If you can only choose one location to place anti-malware, use a network-based solution as it has greater coverage

B) We can place detection as traffic enters the network or installed on computers

C) Network-based protection is called a malware wall

D) The goal is to detect malware before it is able to infect a computer

70. Which of the following is NOT a protocol that a firewall-based malware solution usually supports?

A) SMTP

B) HTTP

C) IMAP

D) FTP

71. Which of the following is NOT an example of social engineering?

A) Calling someone over a phone and convincing them to give away their password

B) Dumpster diving

C) Attempting to guess the unlock code on a smartphone

D) Shoulder surfing

72. Which of the following statements BEST describes dumpster diving?

A) Repeatedly sending the same message to a particular address

B) Rummaging through trash bins to retrieve information written or printed on paper

C) Looking over someone's shoulder at a computer screen or keyboard to steal information such as passwords

D) Sending a single message to hundreds or thousands of users

73. Which of the following statements BEST describes shoulder surfing?

A) Repeatedly sending the same message to a particular address

B) Looking over someone's shoulder at a computer screen or keyboard to steal information such as passwords

C) Rummaging through trash bins to retrieve information written or printed on paper

D) Sending a single message to hundreds or thousands of users

74. Which of the following statements BEST describes email bombing?

A) Repeatedly sending the same message to a particular address

B) Rummaging through trash bins to retrieve information written or printed on paper

C) Looking over someone's shoulder at a computer screen or keyboard to steal information such as passwords

D) Sending a single message to hundreds or thousands of users

75. Which of the following statements BEST describes email spamming?

A) Repeatedly sending the same message to a particular address

B) Rummaging through trash bins to retrieve information written or printed on paper

C) Looking over someone's shoulder at a computer screen or keyboard to steal information such as passwords

D) Sending a single message to hundreds or thousands of users

76. Which of the following statements BEST describes email spoofing?

A) An email appears to come from an authoritative email address but in reality, was sent from an attacker

B) Calling someone over a phone and convincing them to give away their password

C) The use of an email to trick a person into giving away valuable information

D) The use of an email to trick a specific group of people with highly-targeted content into giving away valuable information

77. Which of the following statements BEST describes phishing?

A) An email appears to come from an authoritative email address but in reality, was sent from an attacker

B) Calling someone over a phone and convincing them to give away their password

C) The use of an email to trick a person into giving away valuable information

D) The use of an email to trick a specific group of people with highly-targeted content into giving away valuable information

78. Which of the following statements BEST describes spear phishing?

A) Calling someone over a phone and convincing them to give away their password

B) The use of an email to trick a specific group of people with highly-targeted content into giving away valuable information

C) The use of an email to trick a person into giving away valuable information

D) An email appears to come from an authoritative email address but in reality, was sent from an attacker

79. Which of the following security planning roles BEST describes a coordinator?

A) Manages individual incidents

B) Detects, investigates, contains and recovers from incidents

C) Oversees the incident response capability

D) Acts as the liaison to business process owners

80. Which of the following security planning roles BEST describes a director?

A) Oversees the incident response capability

B) Communicates to other departments such as legal, human resources, and public relations

C) Manage individual incidents

D) Detects, investigates, contains and recovers from incidents

81. Which of the following security planning roles BEST describes a managers?

A) Provides assistance based on subject matter expertise

B) Acts as the liaison to business process owners

C) Oversees the incident response capability

D) Manages individual incidents

82. Which of the following security planning roles BEST describes a security specialists?

A) Detects, investigates, contains and recovers from incidents

B) Communicates to other departments such as legal, human resources, and public relations

C) Manages individual incidents

D) Oversees the incident response capability

83. Which of the following security planning roles BEST describes a nonsecurity technical specialists?

    A) Provides assistance based on subject matter expertise

    B) Acts as the liaison to business process owners

    C) Communicates to other departments such as legal, human resources, and public relations

    D) Detects, investigates, contains and recovers from incidents

84. Which of the following security planning roles BEST describes a liaisons?

    A) Communicates to other departments such as legal, human resources, and public relations

    B) Manages individual incidents

    C) Oversees the incident response capability

    D) Provides assistance based on subject matter expertise

85. Which of the following BEST describes the steps of computer forensics?

    A) Acquire data, protect data, image, extract, ingest and normalize, interrogate, report

    B) Protect data, acquire data, image, extract, interrogate, ingest and normalize, report

    C) Protect data, image, acquire data, extract, ingest and normalize, interrogate, report

    D) Acquire data, protect data, image, extract, interrogate, ingest and normalize, report

Answers

1. B	2. B
3. C	4. B
5. D	6. A
7. A	8. A
9. D	10. B
11. C	12. A
13. A	14. B
15. A	16. A
17. A	18. C
19. C	20. B
21. D	22. A
23. D	24. B
25. B	26. C
27. B	28. D
29. B	30. A
31. D	32. C
33. A	34. C
35. C	36. B
37. B	38. D
39. D	40. A
41. C	42. C
43. A	44. A
45. A	46. A
47. B	48. D
49. A	50. B
51. D	52. D
53. D	54. A
55. B	56. A
57. A	58. D
59. A	60. A
61. B	62. B
63. A	64. B
65. D	66. B
67. D	68. C (While this might work with the most secure military facility, it is hardly a feasible step for the average organization)
69. A (A computer-based anti-malware solution is preferred, as network traffic is only one entry point for malware)	70. C
71. C	72. B
73. B	74. A
75. D	76. A
77. C	78. B
79. D	80. A
81. D	82. A
83. A	84. A
85. B	

Chapter 57: Logical Access

Questions

1. What are the three steps that logical access can be broken down into?

A) Access, identification and authentication

B) Identification, authentication and access

C) Access, authentication and authorization

D) Identification, authentication and authorization

2. Which of the following is NOT a common weakness in the identification and authentication process?

A) It requires the credentials to be stored, opening up the possibility that they could be stolen or compromised if not properly secured

B) Multi-factor authentication is seldom implemented

C) Weak authentication methods such as short or easy to guess passwords make authentication simple to overcome

D) The credentials are almost always passed over a network, and if not properly encrypted could easily be stolen by someone sniffing the network

3. When discussing paths of logical access, which of the following BEST describes a direct path?

A) Represented by physical proximity to a computer

B) Enacted by both front-end and back-end systems

C) Carried out using a local network and can be accomplished even though the user is on a different floor or even a different physical building

D) Carried out across a network, but the user is generally sitting in a location that has not been physically secured and is normally in a different city

4. When discussing paths of logical access, which of the following BEST describes a local access?

A) Enacted by both front-end and back-end systems

B) Represented by physical proximity to a computer

C) Carried out using a local network and can be accomplished even though the user is on a different floor or even a different physical building

D) Carried out across a network, but the user is generally sitting in a location that has not been physically secured and is normally in a different city

5. When discussing paths of logical access, which of the following BEST describes a remote access?

A) Carried out across a network, but the user is generally sitting in a location that has not been physically secured and is normally in a different city

B) Enacted by both front-end and back-end systems

C) Represented by physical proximity to a computer

D) Carried out using a local network and can be accomplished even though the user is on a different floor or even a different physical building

6. What BEST describes why each user should have a unique ID?

A) To avoid sharing passwords by assigning unique passwords to each user

B) To make password reset processes easier to implement

C) To better model the real world in the architecture

D) To be able to track each action back to a unique user

7. Which of the following statements about identification is NOT true?

A) Default user accounts such as Guest, Administrator or Admin should be disabled or renamed immediately on installation

B) Accounts that have not been active for a predetermined amount of time should be deactivated

C) If no activity in an active session has been detected, the user should be given a warning message

D) All IDs should follow some type of naming scheme

8. Which of the following is an example of 'something you know'?

A) A fingerprint

B) A voice print

C) A token device

D) A password

9. Which of the following is an example of 'something you have?

A) A token device

B) A fingerprint

C) A password

D) A voice print

10. Which of the following is an example of 'something you are'?

A) A passphrase

B) A token device

C) A password

D) A voice print

11. Which of the following terms does not apply to having to provide both a password and a token?

A) 2-factor authentication

B) Strong authentication

C) Bi-direction authentication

D) Multifactor authentication

12. Which of the following statements is NOT true when discussing biometric system failures?

A) The crossover error rate is the point at which FRR equals FAR

B) A type 2 error accepts an unauthorized individual

C) CER is expressed as a unitless number

D) A type 1 error rejects an authorized individual

13. Which of the following biometric terms best describes fingerprints?

A) A complete record of ridges and valley on a finger

B) Certain features of a fingerprint

C) A side camera captures the contour of the palm and fingers

D) The shape, length and width of hand and fingers

14. Which of the following biometric terms best describes a finger scan?

A) Certain features of a fingerprint

B) The shape, length and width of hand and fingers

C) A complete record of ridges and valley on a finger

D) A side camera captures the contour of the palm and fingers

15. Which of the following biometric terms best describes hand geometry?

A) A complete record of ridges and valley on a finger

B) A side camera captures the contour of the palm and fingers

C) The shape, length and width of hand and fingers

D) Certain features of a fingerprint

16. Which of the following biometric terms best describes hand topography?

    A) Certain features of a fingerprint

    B) A complete record of ridges and valley on a finger

    C) A side camera captures the contour of the palm and fingers

    D) The shape, length and width of hand and fingers

17. Which of the following biometric terms best describes a palm scan?

    A) Blood-vessel patterns on the back of an eyeball

    B) Fingerprint and the creases, ridges and grooves of the palm

    C) The colored portion surrounding the pupil

    D) Bone structure, nose ridge, eye widths, forehead size and chin shape

18. Which of the following biometric terms best describes a facial scan?

    A) Blood-vessel patterns on the back of an eyeball

    B) The colored portion surrounding the pupil

    C) Fingerprint and the creases, ridges and grooves of the palm

    D) Bone structure, nose ridge, eye widths, forehead size and chin shape

19. Which of the following biometric terms best describes a retina scan?

    A) The colored portion surrounding the pupil

    B) Fingerprint and the creases, ridges and grooves of the palm

    C) Blood-vessel patterns on the back of an eyeball

    D) Bone structure, nose ridge, eye widths, forehead size and chin shape

20. Which of the following biometric terms best describes an iris scan?

    A) The colored portion surrounding the pupil

    B) Blood-vessel patterns on the back of an eyeball

    C) Bone structure, nose ridge, eye widths, forehead size and chin shape

    D) Fingerprint and the creases, ridges and grooves of the palm

21. Which of the following biometric terms best describes signature dynamics?

    A) A complete record of ridges and valley on a finger

    B) A number of words recorded during enrollment

    C) The speed and pauses between each keypress as a password is typed

    D) The speed and movements produced when signing a name

22. Which of the following biometric terms best describes keystroke dynamics?

    A) A number of words recorded during enrollment

    B) A complete record of ridges and valley on a finger

    C) The speed and movements produced when signing a name

    D) The speed and pauses between each keypress as a password is typed

23. Which of the following biometric terms best describes a voice print?

    A) A number of words recorded during enrollment

    B) The speed and pauses between each keypress as a password is typed

    C) The speed and movements produced when signing a name

    D) A complete record of ridges and valley on a finger

24. Which represents the best response times and lowest ERR, with the best being listed first?

A) Palm, hand, iris, retina, fingerprint and voice

B) Hand, fingerprint, palm, retina, iris and voice

C) Voice, retina, palm, iris, fingerprint and hand

D) Retina, palm, iris, retina, hand, voice and fingerprint

25. What are the five rights that access rules commonly provide?

A) Create, read, update, delete and execute

B) Create, copy, update, delete and execute

C) Create, copy, move, delete and execute

D) Create, move, update, delete and execute

26. Which of the following BEST describes an access control list?

A) A matrix of users and assets with the permission residing at the intersections

B) An access method which gives the user no ability to change the level of access granted to others

C) An access method in which the user can delegate rights as-needed

D) Data that dictates the rights a user has to specific assets

27. Which of the following BEST describes discretionary access control?

A) A matrix of users and assets with the permission residing at the intersections

B) An access method in which the user can delegate rights as-needed

C) Data that dictates the rights a user has to specific assets

D) An access method which gives the user no ability to change the level of access granted to others

28. Which of the following BEST describes mandatory access control?

A) A matrix of users and assets with the permission residing at the intersections

B) An access method in which the user can delegate rights as-needed

C) Data that dictates the rights a user has to specific assets

D) An access method which gives the user no ability to change the level of access granted to others

29. Which of the following BEST describes access rules?

A) A matrix of users and assets with the permission residing at the intersections

B) An access method in which the user can delegate rights as-needed

C) Data that dictates the rights a user has to specific assets

D) An access method which gives the user no ability to change the level of access granted to others

30. Which of the following is NOT an advantage of SSO?

A) Resetting forgotten passwords becomes much easier

B) Multiple passwords are no longer required

C) It increases security for each application taking part

D) The time it takes to log into multiple applications is greatly reduced

31. Which of the following statements about SSO is NOT true?

A) It can be implemented for browsers using SAML

B) It increases reliability

C) Kerberos is one of the most common implementations

D) It often requires multiple solutions because not all Oss support it

32. Which of the following statements about logical access is NOT true?

A) Decentralized management allows each location to manage their own security

B) Centralized management implements the same rules and standards across the entire company

C) Decentralized management speeds up the resolution of issues

D) Centralized management results in controls being monitored more frequently

33. Which of the following BEST describes audit reduction tool?

A) Looks for anomalies in user or system behavior

B) Captures audit trails or logs and performs a real-time analysis on the incoming data

C) Looks for a specific sequence of events known to indicate an attack

D) Takes raw data and prepares it for a manual review by trimming out records that have no security significance

34. Which of the following BEST describes trend/variance detection tool?

A) Captures audit trails or logs and performs a real-time analysis on the incoming data

B) Looks for a specific sequence of events known to indicate an attack

C) Takes raw data and prepares it for a manual review by trimming out records that have no security significance

D) Looks for anomalies in user or system behavior

35. Which of the following BEST describes attack signature detection tool?

A) Looks for anomalies in user or system behavior

B) Looks for a specific sequence of events known to indicate an attack

C) Takes raw data and prepares it for a manual review by trimming out records that have no security significance

D) Captures audit trails or logs and performs a real-time analysis on the incoming data

36. Which of the following BEST describes security information and event management system?

A) Looks for a specific sequence of events known to indicate an attack

B) Looks for anomalies in user or system behavior

C) Takes raw data and prepares it for a manual review by trimming out records that have no security significance

D) Captures audit trails or logs and performs a real-time analysis on the incoming data

Answers

1. D	2. B
3. A	4. C
5. A	6. D
7. C (If no activity in an active session has been detected, the session should be automatically locked or logged off)	8. D
9. A	10. D
11. C	12. C (CER is expressed as a percentage)
13. A	14. A
15. C	16. C
17. B	18. D
19. C	20. A
21. D	22. D
23. A	24. A
25. A	26. A
27. B	28. D
29. C	30. C (Individual application security is not impacted)
31. B (Because SSO becomes a single point of failure, reliability is actually decreased)	32. D
33. D	34. D
35. B	36. D

Chapter 58: Remote Connectivity

Questions

1. Which of the following BEST describes a VPN concentrator?

    A) Provides direct connections for WAN links

    B) Accepts incoming connections and handles authentication and access control

    C) Supports direct modem connections

    D) Allows only VPN connections at a single point in the network

2. Which of the following BEST describes a network access server?

    A) Provides direct connections for WAN links

    B) Allows only VPN connections at a single point in the network

    C) Accepts incoming connections and handles authentication and access control

    D) Supports direct modem connections

3. Which of the following BEST describes a remote access server?

    A) Allows only VPN connections at a single point in the network

    B) Accepts incoming connections and handles authentication and access control

    C) Provides direct connections for WAN links

    D) Supports direct modem connections

4. Which of the following BEST describes a remote access VPN?

    A) Provides business partners limited access to each other's corporate network

    B) Connects telecommuters and mobile users to the enterprise WAN

    C) Connects branch offices within an enterprise WAN

    D) Provides direct connections for WAN links

5. Which of the following BEST describes an intranet VPN?

    A) Connects telecommuters and mobile users to the enterprise WAN

    B) Provides direct connections for WAN links

    C) Provides business partners limited access to each other's corporate network

    D) Connects branch offices within an enterprise WAN

6. Which of the following BEST describes an extranet VPN?

    A) Provides business partners limited access to each other's corporate network

    B) Connects branch offices within an enterprise WAN

    C) Provides direct connections for WAN links

    D) Connects telecommuters and mobile users to the enterprise WAN

Answers

1. D		2. C	
3. D		4. B	
5. D		6. A	

Chapter 59: Media Handling

Questions

1. Which of the following statements is NOT true media handling?

A) Magnetic tapes are the preferred medium for data banks

B) Encryption keys should never be stored on removable media

C) The same level of security should be applied to backups as to the originals

D) Computers holding confidential information should not be sent out for repair unless storage devices have been removed

2. Which of the following statements is NOT true media handling?

A) Media should not be transported during strong magnetic storms

B) Hard drives should be stored with Styrofoam

C) USB keys and flash drives are susceptible to strong magnetic fields

D) Tape cartridges should be stored vertically

Answers

1. A (Optical disks are the preferred medium for data banks)	2. B (Hard drives should never be stored with any packing material that can cause static, such as Styrofoam)

Chapter 60: Network Security

Questions

1. Which of the following is NOT a LAN-specific control?

A) Physically protect the CSU/DSU

B) Implement record-level locking to prevent updates by more than one user

C) Encrypt local traffic using IPSec

D) Use switches to implement port security policies as opposed to hubs or non-managed routers

2. Which of the following is NOT a client-server component that needs to be secured?

A) Database

B) Firewalls

C) LAN

D) Middleware

3. What is the BEST reason that Bluetooth s a special risk?

A) Signals can be passively intercepted and recorded

B) Discoverable mode is often left enabled

C) It has no built-in encryption

D) The Bluetooth transmitter power cannot be attenuated

4. What are the two modes in which a network can be attacked?

A) Listening and pinging

B) Passive and active

C) Quiet and noisy

D) Black box and white box

5. Which of the following is a recommended policy to combat weaknesses due to Internet connectivity?

A) All connection points to the Internet must be secured with a port-filtering firewall at a minimum

B) The classification of sensitivity and criticality must take Internet exposure into account

C) Internal networks should be divided into subnets to reduce the exposure of any one network being compromised

D) Active logging must be enabled

6. Which of the following is NOT a common concern for mobile devices?

A) Wireless networks are required

B) Mixing of business and personal data

C) Bluetooth attacks

D) Theft outside of the business walls

7. Which of the following statements BEST describes BYOD?

A) An encrypted area of a mobile device used to keep sensitive data separate from personal data

B) A system to track the location of mobile devices

C) A system to manage employee-owned devices

D) A device owned by an employee but used for work purposes

8. Which of the following statements BEST describes MDM?

A) A system to manage employee-owned devices

B) A system to track the location of mobile devices

C) A device owned by an employee but used for work purposes

D) An encrypted area of a mobile device used to keep sensitive data separate from personal data

9. Which of the following statements BEST describes a secure container?

A) A system to track the location of mobile devices

B) An encrypted area of a mobile device used to keep sensitive data separate from personal data

C) A system to manage employee-owned devices

D) A device owned by an employee but used for work purposes

10. Which of the following is NOT a risk when dealing with P2P software?

A) It increases the propagation of malware

B) It makes the computer's address well-known

C) It increases the danger of the business being held liable for copyrighted files

D) P2P software often reaches into sensitive folders and leaks information

11. Which of the following is NOT a risk when dealing with instant messaging?

A) It could allow eavesdropping

B) It becomes an entry point for viruses and malware

C) Excessive use can impact employee productivity

D) It increases internal network traffic

12. Which of the following is NOT a risk when dealing with social media?

A) It could cache information on the local computer that is deemed to be private

B) An employee may use a personal account to communicate work-related information

C) It may increase customer expectations regarding levels of customer service

D) Copyrighted material may be posted

13. Which of the following is NOT a risk when dealing with end-user computing?

A) There may be no secure mechanism to require authentication

B) It could easily increase unexpected training costs as the software is not budgeted

C) There may be no authorization implemented

D) The solution will more than likely not encrypt data

14. Which of the following BEST describes latency?

A) A measurement of the number of hops a packet requires between a source and destination

B) The delay that a message or packet will experience on its way from source to destination

C) A measurement of the maximum number of bytes possible after compression and decompression

D) A measurement of the maximum number of bytes possible through a physical medium

15. Which of the following BEST describes throughput?

A) The delay that a message or packet will experience on its way from source to destination

B) A measurement of the maximum number of bytes possible through a physical medium

C) A measurement of the number of hops a packet requires between a source and destination

D) A measurement of the maximum number of bytes possible after compression and decompression

16. Which of the following BEST describes bandwidth?

A) A measurement of the maximum number of bytes possible after compression and decompression

B) A measurement of the maximum number of bytes possible through a physical medium

C) The delay that a message or packet will experience on its way from source to destination

D) A measurement of the number of hops a packet requires between a source and destination

17. Which of the following BEST describes a response time report?

A) Tracks the availability of telecommunication lines and circuits

B) Checks for data transmission accuracy and errors

C) Provides a history of problems and their resolution

D) Identifies the time necessary for a command entered by a user at a terminal to be answered by the host system

18. Which of the following BEST describes a downtime report?

A) Provides a history of problems and their resolution

B) Tracks the availability of telecommunication lines and circuits

C) Checks for data transmission accuracy and errors

D) Identifies the time necessary for a command entered by a user at a terminal to be answered by the host system

19. Which of the following BEST describes an online monitor report?

A) Identifies the time necessary for a command entered by a user at a terminal to be answered by the host system

B) Tracks the availability of telecommunication lines and circuits

C) Provides a history of problems and their resolution

D) Checks for data transmission accuracy and errors

20. Which of the following BEST describes a help desk report?

A) Tracks the availability of telecommunication lines and circuits

B) Checks for data transmission accuracy and errors

C) Provides a history of problems and their resolution

D) Identifies the time necessary for a command entered by a user at a terminal to be answered by the host system

21. Which of the following BEST describes echo checking?

A) Operates at the data link or network level and often recommend possible solutions to issues

B) Validates that all data sent to a host is returned with no lost data

C) Monitors packets flowing along a link and produces network usage reports

D) Provides a real time display of network nodes and status

22. Which of the following BEST describes a network monitor?

A) Operates at the data link or network level and often recommend possible solutions to issues

B) A TCP/IP-based protocol that monitors and controls different variables throughout the network

C) Provides a real time display of network nodes and status

D) Validates that all data sent to a host is returned with no lost data

23. Which of the following BEST describes a network protocol analyzer?

A) Monitors packets flowing along a link and produces network usage reports

B) Validates that all data sent to a host is returned with no lost data

C) Provides a real time display of network nodes and status

D) A TCP/IP-based protocol that monitors and controls different variables throughout the network

24. Which of the following BEST describes a network analyzer?

A) Validates that all data sent to a host is returned with no lost data

B) Provides a real time display of network nodes and status

C) Monitors packets flowing along a link and produces network usage reports

D) Operates at the data link or network level and often recommend possible solutions to issues

25. Which BEST describes SNMP?

A) Monitors packets flowing along a link and produces network usage reports

B) Validates that all data sent to a host is returned with no lost data

C) A TCP/IP-based protocol that monitors and controls different variables throughout the network

D) Operates at the data link or network level and often recommend possible solutions to issues

Answers

1. A (The CSU/DSU is a WAN technology)	2. B (Firewalls are a network technology and not specific to client-server)
3. A	4. B
5. B (There are two policies recommended – the second is to implement a rule set covering who can access the Internet from within a company's network, what information should be exposed outside of the intranet, and define which networks are trusted and untrusted)	6. B
7. D	8. A
9. B	10. D (P2P itself software is generally trustworthy, but the software a person downloads using the software is not)
11. D (IM traffic is very light-weight compared to other traffic)	12. A (Social media applications will normally only cache information already publicly available)
13. B	14. B
15. B	16. A
17. D	18. B
19. D	20. C
21. B	22. C
23. A	24. D
25. C	

Chapter 61: Firewalls

Questions

1. Which of the following is NOT a function commonly performed by a firewall?

    A) Encrypting packets for VPN access

    B) Inspecting payloads for malware

    C) Block internal access to external sites

    D) Logging activity both ways

2. Which of the following is NOT a firewall category?

    A) Packet filtering

    B) Session

    C) Application

    D) Stateful inspection

3. Which of the following BEST describes a packet filtering firewall?

    A) Can only look at the IP address and port number of packets coming into and out of the intranet

    B) Focuses on the HTTP protocol

    C) Tracks all outgoing requests for a computer and ensures that external packets targeting the internal computer correspond to a previous request

    D) Runs a separate proxy server for each protocol

4. Which of the following BEST describes an application firewall?

    A) Can only look at the IP address and port number of packets coming into and out of the intranet

    B) Focuses on the HTTP protocol

    C) Tracks all outgoing requests for a computer and ensures that external packets targeting the internal computer correspond to a previous request

    D) Runs a separate proxy server for each protocol

5. Which of the following BEST describes a web application firewall?

    A) Can only look at the IP address and port number of packets coming into and out of the intranet

    B) Focuses on the HTTP protocol

    C) Runs a separate proxy server for each protocol

    D) Tracks all outgoing requests for a computer and ensures that external packets targeting the internal computer correspond to a previous request

6. Which of the following BEST describes a stateful inspection firewall?

    A) Tracks all outgoing requests for a computer and ensures that external packets targeting the internal computer correspond to a previous request

    B) Focuses on the HTTP protocol

    C) Can only look at the IP address and port number of packets coming into and out of the intranet

    D) Runs a separate proxy server for each protocol

7. Which of the following BEST describes a circuit-level firewall?

    A) An application firewall that uses only one proxy server for all traffic

    B) A computer that is physically connected to two or more different private networks by multiple network interfaces

    C) An application firewall that uses a proxy server for each protocol

    D) A computer that is physically connected to only two private networks

8. Which of the following BEST describes an application-level firewall?

    A) A computer that is physically connected to two or more different private networks by multiple network interfaces

    B) An application firewall that uses a proxy server for each protocol

    C) A computer that is physically connected to only two private networks

    D) An application firewall that uses only one proxy server for all traffic

9. Which of the following BEST describes a dual-homed firewall?

    A) An application firewall that uses a proxy server for each protocol

    B) A computer that is physically connected to only two private networks

    C) An application firewall that uses only one proxy server for all traffic

    D) A computer that is physically connected to two or more different private networks by multiple network interfaces

10. Which of the following BEST describes a screened-host firewall?

    A) A computer that is physically connected to two or more different private networks by multiple network interfaces

    B) An application firewall that uses a proxy server for each protocol

    C) A computer that is physically connected to only two private networks

    D) An application firewall that uses only one proxy server for all traffic

11. Which of the following BEST describes a screened-subnet firewall?

    A) Creates a private self-contained network between the two packet-filtering firewalls

    B) Uses two packet-filtering firewalls and an application firewall

    C) A public facing server that has been hardened against external attacks.

    D) Uses a packet-filtering firewall and a proxy server

12. Which of the following BEST describes a bastion host?

    A) Uses two packet-filtering firewalls and an application firewall

    B) A public facing server that has been hardened against external attacks.

    C) Creates a private self-contained network between the two packet-filtering firewalls

    D) Uses a packet-filtering firewall and a proxy server

13. Which of the following BEST describes a DMZ?

    A) A public facing server that has been hardened against external attacks.

    B) Uses a packet-filtering firewall and a proxy server

    C) Uses two packet-filtering firewalls and an application firewall

    D) Creates a private self-contained network between the two packet-filtering firewalls

14. Which of the following is NOT a common issue with firewalls?

    A) External firewalls may give management a false sense of security

    B) Most firewalls normally operate at lower network layers that cannot understand higher-level traffic

    C) Modems that connect directly to an ISP may circumvent firewalls entirely

    D) Firewalls are software and as a result can be easily taken over

15. Which of the following is NOT true regarding firewalls?

>A) Appliance firewalls will come already hardened

>B) Appliances and software implementations are generally equal in capabilities

>C) Appliances will perform better

>D) Software implementations will be susceptible to weaknesses in the hosting OS

Answers

1. B	2. B
3. A	4. D
5. B	6. A
7. A	8. B
9. D	10. C
11. A	12. B
13. C	14. D (While this is true, appliance firewalls have been hardened against such attacks and this risk is minimal)
15. B (Appliances are less capable than software implementations)	

Chapter 62: Intrusion Detection

Questions

1. Which of the following BEST describes an IDS?

A) Is installed on a computer and monitors all local traffic as well as network traffic

B) Is installed on a computer and monitors traffic coming into and out of the computer

C) Looks at passing traffic to see if it can detect any attach patterns or unauthorized usage

D) Monitors all network traffic

2. Which of the following BEST describes a NIDS?

A) Is installed on a computer and monitors all local traffic as well as network traffic

B) Monitors all network traffic

C) Is installed on a computer and monitors traffic coming into and out of the computer

D) Looks at passing traffic to see if it can detect any attach patterns or unauthorized usage

3. Which of the following BEST describes a HIDS?

A) Is installed on a computer and monitors traffic coming into and out of the computer

B) Looks at passing traffic to see if it can detect any attach patterns or unauthorized usage

C) Is installed on a computer and monitors all local traffic as well as network traffic

D) Monitors all network traffic

4. Which of the following is NOT an IDS component?

A) Sensor

B) Analyzer

C) User interface

D) Inference engine

5. Which of the following is NOT an IDS algorithm?

A) Neural network

B) Statistical

C) Fourier transformation

D) Signature

6. Which of the following BEST describes a signature-based IDS?

A) Uses advanced mathematics to calculate aberrant behavior based on learned patterns

B) Has the capability to learn by itself what is acceptable over time

C) Depends on pre-defined signatures to recognize an intrusion attempt

D) Must be trained to recognize normal and aberrant behavior on a given network

7. Which of the following BEST describes a statistical-based IDS?

A) Uses advanced mathematics to calculate aberrant behavior based on learned patterns

B) Depends on pre-defined signatures to recognize an intrusion attempt

C) Must be trained to recognize normal and aberrant behavior on a given network

D) Has the capability to learn by itself what is acceptable over time

8. Which of the following BEST describes a neural network IDS?

A) Depends on pre-defined signatures to recognize an intrusion attempt

B) Has the capability to learn by itself what is acceptable over time

C) Uses advanced mathematics to calculate aberrant behavior based on learned patterns

D) Must be trained to recognize normal and aberrant behavior on a given network

9. Which configuration provides the best protection?

A) A combination of the neural, statistical and signature models

B) A combination of the neural and signature models

C) A combination of the signature and statistical models

D) A combination of the neural and statistical models

10. Which of the following BEST describes an IPS?

A) Appears to be a normal environment

B) A weaponized IDS capable of aggressively defeating attacks

C) A software application that pretends to be a server vulnerable to attack

D) A real environment that can be attacked

11. Which of the following BEST describes a honeypot?

A) A software application that pretends to be a server vulnerable to attack

B) A real environment that can be attacked

C) Appears to be a normal environment

D) A weaponized IDS capable of aggressively defeating attacks

12. Which of the following BEST describes a high-interaction honeypot?

A) A real environment that can be attacked

B) A weaponized IDS capable of aggressively defeating attacks

C) Appears to be a normal environment

D) A software application that pretends to be a server vulnerable to attack

13. Which of the following BEST describes a low-interaction honeypot?

A) A real environment that can be attacked

B) A software application that pretends to be a server vulnerable to attack

C) Appears to be a normal environment

D) A weaponized IDS capable of aggressively defeating attacks

Answers

1. C	2. B
3. A	4. D (The fourth component is an administration console)
5. C (Fourier transformation is a mathematical concept, not an IDS algorithm)	6. C
7. C	8. B
9. C	10. B
11. A	12. A
13. C	

Chapter 63: Encryption

Questions

1. Which of the following is not general use for encryption?

    A) To prevent and detect both accidental and intentional alteration of data

    B) To ensure data is not intercepted or manipulated as it is transmitted across networks

    C) To enable to secure exchange of keys

    D) Verify the authenticity of a transaction of document

2. Which of the following is NOT a primary variable used with encryption systems?

    A) Key length

    B) Algorithm

    C) Input data

    D) Key

3. Why is quantum computing such an important topic?

    A) It could render all current encryption algorithms completely useless

    B) It is not compatible with asymmetric algorithms

    C) It will require all PKI infrastructure to be retooled

    D) It will do away with the need for shared keys

4. Which of the following statements is NOT true regarding digital signatures?

    A) The signature cannot be reused

    B) It provides authentication without requiring encryption

    C) Any alteration to a document renders an accompanying signature invalid

    D) The signature cannot be forged

5. Which of the following is NOT an asymmetric algorithm weakness?

    A) Key lengths must be greater than 128 bits long

    B) It is susceptible to a man-in-the-middle attack

    C) An attacker could intercept the entire message and simply replay it later with no modifications

    D) It is slower than a symmetric algorithm

6. Which of the following is the BEST description of a brute force attack?

    A) Trying random key values until one that works is found

    B) Using a single 'shared key' that both the sender and recipient know

    C) A secure email protocol that authenticates the identity of both the sender and receiver

    D) Reduces the number of required brute force attempts

7. Which of the following is the BEST description of cryptanalysis?

    A) A secure email protocol that authenticates the identity of both the sender and receiver

    B) Reduces the number of required brute force attempts

    C) Trying random key values until one that works is found

    D) Using a single 'shared key' that both the sender and recipient know

8. Which of the following is the BEST description of a symmetric scheme?

    A) Trying random key values until one that works is found

    B) Reduces the number of required brute force attempts

    C) Using a single 'shared key' that both the sender and recipient know

    D) A secure email protocol that authenticates the identity of both the sender and receiver

9. Which of the following is the BEST description of S/MIME?

> A) A secure email protocol that authenticates the identity of both the sender and receiver

> B) Reduces the number of required brute force attempts

> C) Using a single 'shared key' that both the sender and recipient know

> D) Trying random key values until one that works is found

10. Which of the following is the BEST description of hashing?

> A) The most common outdated symmetric system

> B) The most common modern symmetric system

> C) A one-way encryption that results in the same length of ciphertext regardless of the plain text

> D) Using one key for encryption and a different key for decryption

11. Which of the following is the BEST description of DES?

> A) Using one key for encryption and a different key for decryption

> B) The most common modern symmetric system

> C) The most common outdated symmetric system

> D) A one-way encryption that results in the same length of ciphertext regardless of the plain text

12. Which of the following is the BEST description of AES?

> A) A one-way encryption that results in the same length of ciphertext regardless of the plain text

> B) The most common outdated symmetric system

> C) Using one key for encryption and a different key for decryption

> D) The most common modern symmetric system

13. Which of the following is the BEST description of an asymmetric scheme?

> A) The most common modern symmetric system

> B) The most common outdated symmetric system

> C) Using one key for encryption and a different key for decryption

> D) A one-way encryption that results in the same length of ciphertext regardless of the plain text

14. Which of the following is the BEST description of CA?

> A) Confirms that you are a real person or company

> B) A list of invalid certificates

> C) Confirms that an entity is the real owner of a public key

> D) Something that tells us how a CA validates authenticity

15. Which of the following is the BEST description of RA?

> A) Something that tells us how a CA validates authenticity

> B) Confirms that an entity is the real owner of a public key

> C) A list of invalid certificates

> D) Confirms that you are a real person or company

16. Which of the following is the BEST description of CRL?

> A) Something that tells us how a CA validates authenticity

> B) Confirms that you are a real person or company

> C) A list of invalid certificates

> D) Confirms that an entity is the real owner of a public key

17. Which of the following is the BEST description of CPS?

A) Confirms that you are a real person or company

B) A list of invalid certificates

C) Confirms that an entity is the real owner of a public key

D) Something that tells us how a CA validates authenticity

18. Which of the following is the BEST description of a digital envelope?

A) The combination of an encrypted message and the secret key

B) Used to secure IP communication between two endpoints

C) An IPSec mode that only encrypts the IP payload

D) How IPSec manages keys

19. Which of the following is the BEST description of IPSec?

A) Used to secure IP communication between two endpoints

B) How IPSec manages keys

C) The combination of an encrypted message and the secret key

D) An IPSec mode that only encrypts the IP payload

20. Which of the following is the BEST description of transport mode?

A) How IPSec manages keys

B) Used to secure IP communication between two endpoints

C) The combination of an encrypted message and the secret key

D) An IPSec mode that only encrypts the IP payload

21. Which of the following is the BEST description of ISAKMP?

A) How IPSec manages keys

B) An IPSec mode that only encrypts the IP payload

C) The combination of an encrypted message and the secret key

D) Used to secure IP communication between two endpoints

22. Which of the following is the BEST description of ESP?

A) Data added to the header when using IPSec in tunnel mode

B) An IPSec mode that encrypts both the payload and header

C) The encrypted payload when using ESP

D) An IPSec session attribute that dictates various configuration options

23. Which of the following is the BEST description of tunnel mode?

A) An IPSec mode that encrypts both the payload and header

B) An IPSec session attribute that dictates various configuration options

C) The encrypted payload when using ESP

D) Data added to the header when using IPSec in tunnel mode

24. Which of the following is the BEST description of an authentication header?

A) An IPSec mode that encrypts both the payload and header

B) The encrypted payload when using ESP

C) Data added to the header when using IPSec in tunnel mode

D) An IPSec session attribute that dictates various configuration options

25. Which of the following is the BEST description of security association?

A) Data added to the header when using IPSec in tunnel mode

B) An IPSec mode that encrypts both the payload and header

C) An IPSec session attribute that dictates various configuration options

D) The encrypted payload when using ESP

Answers

1. C (Secure key exchange is a function of PKI, not basic encryption)	2. C (Input data is fed into an encryption system but is not part of one)
3. A	4. B (It can provide authentication but only by using encryption)
5. A (While longer keys provide more security, asymmetric algorithms have no limit on the key length)	6. A
7. B	8. C
9. A	10. C
11. C	12. D
13. C	14. C
15. D	16. C
17. D	18. A
19. A	20. D
21. A	22. C
23. A	24. C
25. C	

Chapter 64: Penetration Testing

Questions

1. Which of the following BEST describes an external test?

A) Requires the pen testing team to execute the simulated attack without any knowledge of the internal system, but internal staff are aware that it is happening

B) Requires the pen testing team to execute the simulated attack without any knowledge of the internal system, and internal staff are not aware that a simulated attack is being carried out

C) Executed from outside of the network's perimeter and represents an external attacker with no prior knowledge of the network

D) Executed from within the network perimeter and is designed to reveal risks from ether an internal user, or an external user that managed to get through the network perimeter

2. Which of the following BEST describes an internal test?

A) Requires the pen testing team to execute the simulated attack without any knowledge of the internal system, but internal staff are aware that it is happening

B) Requires the pen testing team to execute the simulated attack without any knowledge of the internal system, and internal staff are not aware that a simulated attack is being carried out

C) Executed from outside of the network's perimeter and represents an external attacker with no prior knowledge of the network

D) Executed from within the network perimeter and is designed to reveal risks from ether an internal user, or an external user that managed to get through the network perimeter

3. Which of the following BEST describes a blind test?

A) Carried out with the full knowledge of staff, and the pen testing team is given information about the network design

B) Requires the pen testing team to execute the simulated attack without any knowledge of the internal system, and internal staff are not aware that a simulated attack is being carried out

C) Executed from outside of the network's perimeter and represents an external attacker with no prior knowledge of the network

D) Requires the pen testing team to execute the simulated attack without any knowledge of the internal system, but internal staff are aware that it is happening

4. Which of the following BEST describes a double blind test?

A) Requires the pen testing team to execute the simulated attack without any knowledge of the internal system, and internal staff are not aware that a simulated attack is being carried out

B) Carried out with the full knowledge of staff, and the pen testing team is given information about the network design

C) Executed from within the network perimeter and is designed to reveal risks from ether an internal user, or an external user that managed to get through the network perimeter

D) Requires the pen testing team to execute the simulated attack without any knowledge of the internal system, but internal staff are aware that it is happening

5. Which of the following BEST describes a targeted test?

A) Executed from within the network perimeter and is designed to reveal risks from ether an internal user, or an external user that managed to get through the network perimeter

B) Carried out with the full knowledge of staff, and the pen testing team is given information about the network design

C) Requires the pen testing team to execute the simulated attack without any knowledge of the internal system, but internal staff are aware that it is happening

D) Requires the pen testing team to execute the simulated attack without any knowledge of the internal system, and internal staff are not aware that a simulated attack is being carried out

6. What are the phases of a penetration test?

A) planning, discovery, probing, execution and reporting

B) planning, reconnaissance, attack and reporting

C) Reconnaissance, planning, discovery, attack and reporting

D) Planning, discovery, attack and reporting

7. Which of the following is NOT a recognized risk when carrying out a penetration test?

A) Testing activities may inadvertently trigger escalation procedures that may not have been appropriately planned for

B) Miscommunication may result in some test objectives not being achieved

C) Sensitive information may be disclosed, heightening the target's exposure level

D) Internal backlash may result if the proper employees are not notified

Answers

1. C	2. D
3. D	4. A
5. B	6. D
7. D (Some penetration tests are not considered to be valid unless internal employees remain unaware)	

Chapter 65: Environmental Issues

Questions

1. Which of the following BEST describes a blackout?

A) A total failure with a complete loss of power

B) A decrease in voltage

C) A severely reduced voltage due to the failure of a power company to supply power within an acceptable range

D) An increase in voltage

2. Which of the following BEST describes a brownout?

A) A total failure with a complete loss of power

B) An increase in voltage

C) A decrease in voltage

D) A severely reduced voltage due to the failure of a power company to supply power within an acceptable range

3. Which of the following BEST describes a sag?

A) An increase in voltage

B) A severely reduced voltage due to the failure of a power company to supply power within an acceptable range

C) A decrease in voltage

D) A total failure with a complete loss of power

4. Which of the following BEST describes a spike?

A) An increase in voltage

B) A severely reduced voltage due to the failure of a power company to supply power within an acceptable range

C) A total failure with a complete loss of power

D) A decrease in voltage

5. Which of the following BEST describes a surge?

A) Measures the incoming electrical current and either increase or decrease the charge to ensure a consistent current

B) An increase in voltage

C) Mitigates short-term interruptions such as sags, spikes and surges

D) Caused by electrical storms or nearby noisy electrical equipment such as motors, fluorescent lighting or radio transmitters

6. Which of the following BEST describes EMI?

A) An increase in voltage

B) Measures the incoming electrical current and either increase or decrease the charge to ensure a consistent current

C) Caused by electrical storms or nearby noisy electrical equipment such as motors, fluorescent lighting or radio transmitters

D) Mitigates short-term interruptions such as sags, spikes and surges

7. Which of the following BEST describes a voltage regulator?

A) Measures the incoming electrical current and either increase or decrease the charge to ensure a consistent current

B) Mitigates short-term interruptions such as sags, spikes and surges

C) Caused by electrical storms or nearby noisy electrical equipment such as motors, fluorescent lighting or radio transmitters

D) An increase in voltage

8. Which of the following BEST describes a surge protector?

A) Measures the incoming electrical current and either increase or decrease the charge to ensure a consistent current

B) Mitigates short-term interruptions such as sags, spikes and surges

C) Caused by electrical storms or nearby noisy electrical equipment such as motors, fluorescent lighting or radio transmitters

D) An increase in voltage

9. Which of the following statements about water damage is NOT true?

A) When activated, the detectors should produce an audible alarm

B) Unattended equipment storage facilities should also have water detectors.

C) Water detectors in the computer room should be placed above lowered ceilings and near drain holes

D) Facilities located far above ground are susceptible to water damage

10. Which of the following statements about fire extinguishers is NOT true?

A) Hand-pull fire alarms should be placed near exit doors to ensure personnel safety

B) Smoke detectors should be installed above and below the ceiling tiles and below the raised computer room floor.

C) They should be tagged for inspection and inspected at least once every three years

D) Smoke detectors should supplement, not replace, fire suppression systems.

11. Which of the following BEST describes total flooding?

A) Fills the entire enclosed space with an extinguishing agent

B) Does not contain water in the pipes until the system is activated

C) The extinguisher sprays the agent directly on the fire

D) Can cause considerable collateral damage to equipment when activated

12. Which of the following BEST describes local application?

A) Fills the entire enclosed space with an extinguishing agent

B) Can cause considerable collateral damage to equipment when activated

C) Does not contain water in the pipes until the system is activated

D) The extinguisher sprays the agent directly on the fire

13. Which of the following BEST describes a water-based system?

A) Always has water under pressure in the pipes

B) Can cause considerable collateral damage to equipment when activated

C) The extinguisher sprays the agent directly on the fire

D) Does not contain water in the pipes until the system is activated

14. Which of the following BEST describes a dry-pipe water-based system?

A) Can cause considerable collateral damage to equipment when activated

B) Can cause considerable collateral damage to equipment when activated

C) The extinguisher sprays the agent directly on the fire

D) Always has water under pressure in the pipes

15. Which of the following BEST describes a charged water-based system?

A) Always has water under pressure in the pipes

B) Can cause considerable collateral damage to equipment when activated

C) Does not contain water in the pipes until the system is activated

D) The extinguisher sprays the agent directly on the fire

16. Which of the following BEST describes a Halon system?

A) Automated systems are only allowed in dark facilities where no people are present

B) Releases pressurized gas that removes oxygen from the air, but was discontinued in the 1990s

C) A gas that reduces the amount of oxygen available for a fire to use

D) A gas that extinguishes a fire by lowering the temperature of the components

17. Which of the following BEST describes FM-200?

A) Releases pressurized gas that removes oxygen from the air, but was discontinued in the 1990s

B) A gas that extinguishes a fire by lowering the temperature of the components

C) Automated systems are only allowed in dark facilities where no people are present

D) A gas that reduces the amount of oxygen available for a fire to use

18. Which of the following BEST describes Argonite?

A) Releases pressurized gas that removes oxygen from the air, but was discontinued in the 1990s

B) A gas that extinguishes a fire by lowering the temperature of the components

C) A gas that reduces the amount of oxygen available for a fire to use

D) Automated systems are only allowed in dark facilities where no people are present

19. Which of the following BEST describes CO2?

A) A gas that extinguishes a fire by lowering the temperature of the components

B) Releases pressurized gas that removes oxygen from the air, but was discontinued in the 1990s

C) A gas that reduces the amount of oxygen available for a fire to use

D) Automated systems are only allowed in dark facilities where no people are present

20. Which of the following NOT true regarding the placement of computer rooms?

A) Neighboring facilities must be examined to determine risk

B) The best location is on the 2nd or 3rd floor of a multi-story building

C) It should not be placed next to rooms carrying elevated risk

D) It should not be located in the basement or top floor

Answers

1. A	2. D
3. C	4. A
5. B	6. C
7. A	8. B
9. C (Water detectors in the computer room should be placed under raised floors and near drain holes)	10. C (They should be inspected at least once per year)
11. A	12. D
13. B	14. A
15. A	16. B
17. B	18. C
19. D	20. B (The best location is on the middle floors of a multi-story building)

Chapter 66: Data Leakage, or DLP

Questions

1. Which of the following BEST describes data-at-rest?

A) Applications deployed to log onto each system and look through the various data stores

B) Any information persisted to storage such as hard drives, USB drives, tape backups or in live databases

C) Information that is being manipulated by end users at their workstation

D) Any information moving around a network or being transferred between two processes

2. Which of the following BEST describes a crawler?

A) Any information moving around a network or being transferred between two processes

B) Applications deployed to log onto each system and look through the various data stores

C) Any information persisted to storage such as hard drives, USB drives, tape backups or in live databases

D) Information that is being manipulated by end users at their workstation

3. Which of the following BEST describes data-in-motion?

A) Any information moving around a network or being transferred between two processes

B) Any information persisted to storage such as hard drives, USB drives, tape backups or in live databases

C) Applications deployed to log onto each system and look through the various data stores

D) Information that is being manipulated by end users at their workstation

4. Which of the following BEST describes data-in-use?

A) Any information persisted to storage such as hard drives, USB drives, tape backups or in live databases

B) Applications deployed to log onto each system and look through the various data stores

C) Any information moving around a network or being transferred between two processes

D) Information that is being manipulated by end users at their workstation

5. Which of the following is NOT a goal for DLP?

A) To monitor and control the movement of that information as it leaves the company

B) To locate and catalog sensitive information throughout a company

C) To monitor and control the movement of that information across the internal network

D) To monitor and control the movement of that information on end-user systems

6. Which of the following is NOT a key capability that a full-fledged DLP must provide?

A) Some type of a workflow management capacity so that we can configure how incidents are handled

B) Integration with directory services allowing the DLP to map a network address to a specific user

C) The ability to control network appliance to prevent sensitive data form leaving the network

D) A backup and restore feature to preserve policies and settings

7. Which of the following is NOT a common weakness found with DFLPs?

A) A DLP might result in a large number of false positives, which can overwhelm staff and hide valid hits

B) It cannot detect sensitive information in streaming data files such as video or audio

C) DLP network modules may be improperly tuned resulting in blocking valid content or missing unauthorized content

D) It can inspect encrypted data only if it knows how to decrypt it

Answers

1. B	2. B
3. A	4. D
5. A	6. C
7. B (It cannot detect sensitive information in graphics files)	

Chapter 67: Physical Access

Questions

1. Which of the following BEST describes a bolting door lock?

    A) A lock requiring electric power

    B) A lock made of strengthened steel

    C) A lock that uses a numeric key pad or dial

    D) A lock requiring a metal key to open

2. Which of the following BEST describes a combination door lock?

    A) A lock requiring a metal key to open

    B) A lock that uses a numeric key pad or dial

    C) A lock made of strengthened steel

    D) A lock requiring electric power

3. Which of the following BEST describes a cipher lock?

    A) A lock containing a sensor that requires a magnetic card key, or a chipped card key or token to be placed against it

    B) A lock that uses human characteristics to identify an individual attempting to unlock a door

    C) A lock that uses a numeric key pad or dial

    D) A control that uses two doors, in which the person entering must close the first door before the second door may be opened

4. Which of the following BEST describes an electronic door lock?

    A) A control that uses two doors, in which the person entering must close the first door before the second door may be opened

    B) A lock that uses human characteristics to identify an individual attempting to unlock a door

    C) A lock that uses a numeric key pad or dial

    D) A lock containing a sensor that requires a magnetic card key, or a chipped card key or token to be placed against it

5. Which of the following BEST describes a biometric door lock?

    A) A lock containing a sensor that requires a magnetic card key, or a chipped card key or token to be placed against it

    B) A lock that uses a numeric key pad or dial

    C) A lock that uses human characteristics to identify an individual attempting to unlock a door

    D) A control that uses two doors, in which the person entering must close the first door before the second door may be opened

6. Which of the following BEST describes a mantrap?

    A) A control that uses two doors, in which the person entering must close the first door before the second door may be opened

    B) A lock that uses human characteristics to identify an individual attempting to unlock a door

    C) A lock containing a sensor that requires a magnetic card key, or a chipped card key or token to be placed against it

    D) A lock that uses a numeric key pad or dial

7. Which of the following BEST describes electronic logging?

    A) The act of a person signing into and out of a physical log

    B) Video cameras that capture local activity around a facility

    C) A control that uses two doors, in which the person entering must close the first door before the second door may be opened

    D) Automate logging by electronic and biometric locks

8. Which of the following BEST describes manual logging?

A) Video cameras that capture local activity around a facility

B) The act of a person signing into and out of a physical log

C) Automate logging by electronic and biometric locks

D) A control that uses two doors, in which the person entering must close the first door before the second door may be opened

9. Which of the following BEST describes CCTV?

A) The act of a person signing into and out of a physical log

B) Automate logging by electronic and biometric locks

C) Video cameras that capture local activity around a facility

D) A control that uses two doors, in which the person entering must close the first door before the second door may be opened

10. Which of the following BEST describes a deadman door?

A) Automate logging by electronic and biometric locks

B) The act of a person signing into and out of a physical log

C) Video cameras that capture local activity around a facility

D) A control that uses two doors, in which the person entering must close the first door before the second door may be opened

11. Which of the following BEST describes controlled visitor access?

A) An unauthorized person following an authorized person through a secured entry

B) A control that uses two doors, in which the person entering must close the first door before the second door may be opened

C) A control used by all incoming personnel and normally monitored by a receptionist

D) Requires that all visitors be escorted by a responsible employee

12. Which of the following BEST describes an airlock entrance?

A) Requires that all visitors be escorted by a responsible employee

B) A control that uses two doors, in which the person entering must close the first door before the second door may be opened

C) An unauthorized person following an authorized person through a secured entry

D) A control used by all incoming personnel and normally monitored by a receptionist

13. Which of the following BEST describes piggybacking?

A) A control used by all incoming personnel and normally monitored by a receptionist

B) An unauthorized person following an authorized person through a secured entry

C) Requires that all visitors be escorted by a responsible employee

D) A control that uses two doors, in which the person entering must close the first door before the second door may be opened

14. Which of the following BEST describes a controlled single entry point?

> A) Requires that all visitors be escorted by a responsible employee
>
> B) An unauthorized person following an authorized person through a secured entry
>
> C) A control used by all incoming personnel and normally monitored by a receptionist
>
> D) A control that uses two doors, in which the person entering must close the first door before the second door may be opened

Answers

1. D	2. B
3. C	4. D
5. C	6. A
7. D	8. B
9. C	10. D
11. D	12. B
13. B	14. C

Chapter 68: IS Auditor Duties for the Protection of Information Assets Domain

Questions

1. Which is the best way to ensure control monitoring is taking place?

> A) Review processes with management to ensure all monitoring aspects are covered

> B) Look for documentation that proves the correct processes are in-place

> C) Observe employees going about their daily routine

> D) Make sure the output of logs and audit hooks are in place and being validated

2. When reviewing logical access, which of the following controls is the LEAST important to an auditor?

> A) Need-to-know

> B) Segregation of duties

> C) Least-privilege

> D) Audit trails

3. Which of the following is NOT an action an auditor would execute when looking for privacy issues?

> A) Document how this information is collected, used, disclosed to the individual, and destroyed

> B) Identify legislative, regulatory and contractual requirements for privacy

> C) Identify information that is not directly associated with PII

> D) Ensure that accountability for privacy issues exists

4. Which of the following would an auditor NOT carry out when reviewing compliance with privacy policy, laws and other regulations?

> A) Validate that personal sensitive information is following that policy

> B) Update the existing privacy policy to be compliant

> C) Identify and understand applicable laws and regulations

> D) Verify that the right security measures are in place

5. Which of the following laws and regulations apply to privacy?

> A) OECD Guidelines on the Protection of Privacy and Transborder Flows of Personal Data

> B) The US-EU Safe Harbor Framework

> C) SIRS Privacy Rules for Financial Institutions

> D) The European Union Data Protection Directives

6. Which of the following transmission medium is MOST used by transborder data flow?

> A) Television links

> B) Satellites

> C) Long-range wireless transmissions

> D) Telephone lines

7. Which BEST describes the difference between computer crime and computer abuse?

> A) And abuse becomes a crime when the activity is prosecuted

> B) The jurisdiction and the court sentence

> C) Abuse calls a law into question but does not clearly violate it

> D) The geographical location

8. When dealing with network security, which is the most important area an auditor should be concerned with?

> A) Activity logs

> B) If a SEIM is in-place

> C) If the security policies align with the business strategy

> D) The ability to examine traffic in real-time

9. When looking at LAN security, which of the following areas is the LEAST important?

> A) Users or groups having privileged access rights

> B) How the business takes advantage of SSO

> C) Computer applications used on the LAN

> D) The LAN topology and network design

10. When auditing a client-server application, which of the following areas is the LEAST important for an auditor?

A) If traffic is encrypted

B) Application controls cannot be bypassed

C) Access to configuration or initialization files is kept to a minimum, and are audited

D) Passwords are always encrypted

11. Which of the following depend on the size and complexity of a PBX?

A) How long the audit will take

B) The final reports needed

C) The number of auditors required

D) Types of skills needed

12. When auditing an information security framework, which of the following areas is something an auditor will NOT focus on?

A) Logical access

B) How investigations are carried out

C) How security is tested

D) How well BRP and DCP has been taken into account

13. When auditing a security awareness training program, which of the following is likely NOT an area in which an auditor will focus?

A) Interviewing a sample of employees to determine their overall awareness

B) Performing spot checks and quizzes to how well employees respond

C) Ensuring that employee awareness is reinforced using company newsletters, visible security enforcement and reminders during staff meetings

D) Checking to see if training starts with new employee orientation

14. When reviewing data ownership, which of the following is NOT a focus area for an auditor?

A) If the data owner has authorized in writing access to data

B) A review of data classification

C) If proper ownership of data has been assigned and the data owner is aware of the assignment

D) A review of the various databases

15. When establishing a security baseline, which of the following areas is NOT an area an auditor would focus on?

A) Malware

B) Disaster recovery

C) System services

D) Inventory

16. Which of the following is NOT an area an auditor would focus on when reviewing access paths?

A) The original location of data and who can access it

B) How operating systems within the path are maintained

C) If the data owner has authorized in writing access to data

D) How input data from a user is validated

17. Which of the following techniques is not associated with testing physical security?

A) Checking to see if failed attempts result in log entries that are followed up by an administrator

B) Collecting a sample of keys and key cards and attempt to gain access beyond the point at which he or she should have been stopped

C) Attempting to physically bypass locked doors and other entry mechanisms

D) Producing a list of terminal addresses and locations and compare to actual inventory

18. Which of the following is NOT a valid technique to test password security?

    A) Look into wastebaskets

    B) Dumpster diving

    C) Trying to guess passwords on a terminal

    D) Examining the internal password table

19. Which of the following is NOT a common, legitimate feature that a programmer might use?

    A) Backdoor

    B) Special system logon IDs

    C) System exits

    D) Bypass label processing

20. When auditing computer forensics, which of the following is NOT common task for an auditor to carry out?

    A) Validating that appropriate evidence gathering technology is current and available to employees

    B) Looking to see if both process and infrastructure are in-place to provide assurance that electronic evidence will be acquired but not destroyed

    C) Checking for written protocols on how to inform appropriate parties that electronic evidence will be acquired but will not be destroyed

    D) Make sure all measures to prevent data from being altered are in-place

21. Why is it important for an auditor to review network diagrams?

    A) The absence of network diagrams indicates a lack of infrastructure management in general

    B) Network diagrams are an essential part of infrastructure planning and direction on how the network should be evaluated

    C) They will provide the necessary baseline used when interviewing employees

    D) Without this information the auditor will not be able to determine if the proper physical and logical access controls are in effect

22. Which of the following is NOT considered to be a focus area when auditing remote access?

    A) Reviewing the creation of network credentials

    B) Dialing a remote access computer from a number of authorized and unauthorized telephone lines

    C) Ensuring security controls are in-place and documented to protect information resources

    D) Identifying both known and unknown remote access points

23. Which of the following is NOT a use the auditor should look at when auditing a company's Internet presence?

    A) Personal social media use

    B) Information gathering

    C) Marketing

    D) Email

24. Which of the following is NOT something an auditor would expect to see mentioned clearly in the audit scope when evaluating penetration testing?

    A) The hosts not to be tested

    B) Acceptable testing techniques, such as social engineering, DoS or DDoS and SQL injections

    C) The precise IP addresses or ranges to be tested

    D) Expected vulnerabilities

25. Which of the following is NOT an item an auditor would look for when reviewing environmental controls?

    A) Power supply to water and smoke detectors

    B) The testing interval for fire suppression systems

    C) The most recent test dates for UPS and generators

    D) The most recent version of the DRP is available

Answers

1. D	2. D
3. C (Identify personally identifiable information, or PII, that the business processes)	4. B (The auditor would check to see if the existing privacy policy is compliant, but would not update it)
5. C (SIRS doesn't exist)	6. C
7. B	8. A
9. B	10. A
11. B	12. D
13. B	14. D
15. B	16. C
17. C	18. B
19. A (A legitimate feature is never a backdoor, which bypasses all known security and is intended to be hidden by all but the programmer)	20. A (Many companies will outsource the actual evidence gathering and will therefore have no need to maintain this type of equipment)
21. D	22. A (While network credentials are used with remote access, their creation falls under more general logical access management)
23. A (Employee social media use is a privacy concern and could negatively impact a business, but this is a topic covered under other audit areas)	24. D
25. D (Documents such as an emergency evacuation plans should be available, but a DRP is examined at a higher level than when reviewing environmental controls)	

Random

This second portion of the book presents the same questions we covered in the first part, but in a random order. You might be surprised how difficult this becomes as contextual clues between questions is no longer provided. If you want to start with this section, go right ahead. But, if you run across material for which you would like a refresher, it will be more difficult to locate that subject in the accompanying *Essential CISA Exam Guide* book.

Random Questions

1. You are auditing a business that will require you to run examine a process with a subject matter expert. What audit technique is BEST suited?

> A) Walk-Through
>
> B) Observing Processes and Employee Performance
>
> C) Reperformance
>
> D) Interviewing Appropriate Personnel

2. Which of the following BEST describes mandatory access control?

> A) Data that dictates the rights a user has to specific assets
>
> B) An access method in which the user can delegate rights as-needed
>
> C) A matrix of users and assets with the permission residing at the intersections
>
> D) An access method which gives the user no ability to change the level of access granted to others

3. Which of the following BEST describes EMI?

> A) Measures the incoming electrical current and either increase or decrease the charge to ensure a consistent current
>
> B) An increase in voltage
>
> C) Mitigates short-term interruptions such as sags, spikes and surges
>
> D) Caused by electrical storms or nearby noisy electrical equipment such as motors, fluorescent lighting or radio transmitters

4. What is the BEST description of completeness?

> A) How applicable it is
>
> B) If it is up-to-date
>
> C) The breadth and depth
>
> D) The volume

5. Which Capability Maturity Model Integration, or CMMI, layer represents a proactive approach to processes?

> A) Level 3 - Defined
>
> B) Level 4 – Quantitatively Managed
>
> C) Level 5 – Optimizing
>
> D) Level 2 – Managed

6. What is the term describing the likelihood that a threat agent will exploit a vulnerability?

> A) Exposure
>
> B) Impact
>
> C) Threat
>
> D) Risk

7. Which of the following BEST describes an open source license?

> A) The software may be used in any way the user likes without any type of payment
>
> B) A fee is charged for each CPU core running on the computer on which the software is installed
>
> C) Free, but the source code cannot be redistributed
>
> D) Initially free, but requires payment at a later date to keep the software functioning or to unlock all features or benefits

8. Which of the following BEST describes a business case?

> A) Defines the problem or opportunity in a clear and concise manner
>
> B) Understanding the current situation as presented by both strengths and weaknesses
>
> C) Provides enough information to a business for it to decide if it is worth pursuing
>
> D) Underlies a business case by studying the problem to see if a solution is practical, meets the stated requirements and can deliver within a set budget and deadline

9. According to ISAAS Reporting Standards, which of the following is NOT specified to be included in the final report?

    A) Signature and date

    B) Identification of the organization

    C) Limitations in scope

    D) The auditor's professional qualifications

10. What IT risk management level are we operating at when considering how IT capabilities compare to our competitors and threats posed by technological changes?

    A) Procedural

    B) Strategic

    C) Project

    D) Operational

11. Which BEST describes volume testing?

    A) Simulating a heavy amount of traffic during peak areas

    B) Incrementally increasing the size of the database until the application fails

    C) Increasing the number of active users until the system fails

    D) Comparing the system's performance to well-defined benchmarks

12. Which of the following BEST describes a stateful inspection firewall?

    A) Tracks all outgoing requests for a computer and ensures that external packets targeting the internal computer correspond to a previous request

    B) Runs a separate proxy server for each protocol

    C) Can only look at the IP address and port number of packets coming into and out of the intranet

    D) Focuses on the HTTP protocol

13. Which of the following BEST describes beta version testing?

    A) Testing an application that is feature complete but has not yet completed UAT

    B) Testing an application that has completed UAT but is not in production

    C) Testing an application that is not feature complete, but is ready to undergo assumption and logic flow validations

    D) Testing an application ready for a limited rollout of an application to a very small set of end-users

14. Which of the following BEST describes a network database?

    A) Information is stored as a container that houses both data and actions

    B) All data is organized into one or more tables

    C) The data is comprised of 'sets', with each set having a single owner node and one or more member nodes

    D) Data is stored in a parent/child relationship

15. Which of the following BEST describes a personal area network?

    A) A specialized version of a LAN dedicated to storing large amounts of data

    B) A network of personal devices such as smartphones or watches

    C) Covers broad areas such as a city, region, nation or even an international link

    D) Covers a limited are such as a home, office or even a campus with multiple buildings

16. Which of the following BEST describes a network monitor?

A) Provides a real time display of network nodes and status

B) Validates that all data sent to a host is returned with no lost data

C) A TCP/IP-based protocol that monitors and controls different variables throughout the network

D) Operates at the data link or network level and often recommend possible solutions to issues

17. Which of the following is NOT a common risk associated with EFT?

A) The non-stop transfer of physical currency to and from electronic currency introduces many opportunities for fraud

B) Integrating legacy systems directly with Internet-facing portals

C) The pressure to outsource work introduces additional risk

D) The rate of change is so quick that risk analysis and security reviews seldom happen

18. When auditing requirements definition, which of the following is NOT something an auditor should look for?

A) A draft UAT specification has been provided

B) The conceptual design specifications address the actual needs of the user

C) Control specifications are defined in the conceptual design

D) Project initiation and costs have been approved

19. Which of the following BEST describes the data user role?

A) The actual user of data, including both internal and external users

B) Tasked with managing data and the data architecture

C) Answers technical questions and solve problems faced by internal employees

D) Responsible for daily operations related to business services

20. Which of the following BEST describes ITIL?

A) Developed by ISACA and is intended to ensure IT goals align with business goals, resources are used properly, and that risk is being effectively managed

B) A process-based security model for IT

C) Created in the UK and provides a very hands-on and detailed framework on implementing GEIT

D) A specification for service management that is aligned with ITIL

21. Which is the BEST description of X.25?

A) Achieves higher rates because it uses all available frequencies on a UTP line

B) An older technology, it was designed to compensate by adding error checking and correcting as well as fault tolerance, resulting in a high overhead

C) A newer technology, it is a switching technology but uses cells instead of packets

D) An older technology, it allowed more than one party to share in a single dedicated line across a WAN

22. To effectively perform a network infrastructure review, which of the following is NOT something an auditor will need to identify?

A) Significant network components such as servers, routers, switches, hubs, modems, wireless devices and others

B) Incident handling

C) Interconnected boundary networks, or where each network starts and stops

D) The network topology and design

23. Which BEST describes worm?

A) Malicious software that can self-replicate across a network by copying itself from computer to connected computer

B) Malicious software that can alter its appearance to outwit scanners

C) Malicious software that does not cause damage other than silently listening and collecting sensitive information to send back to the attacker

D) Malicious software that does not self-replicate or try to attach itself to other files

24. In case of a disaster, a company needs to be up and running in a backup facility within two days. Which type of recovery site is the BEST choice?

A) Warm site

B) Duplicate site

C) Hot site

D) Cold site

25. Which of the following BEST describes an unfavorably terminated employee?

A) Someone having authorized access into systems and have a broad range of knowledge about the inner workings

B) Someone who can cause significant damage and is the most common source of threats

C) A significant risk unless their credentials are deleted immediately after termination

D) Someone who is particularly dangerous due to their advanced skillset, knowledge of the company's infrastructure and has elevated access

26. Which of the following BEST describes CO2?

A) Releases pressurized gas that removes oxygen from the air, but was discontinued in the 1990s

B) A gas that extinguishes a fire by lowering the temperature of the components

C) A gas that reduces the amount of oxygen available for a fire to use

D) Automated systems are only allowed in dark facilities where no people are present

27. What BEST describes why each user should have a unique ID?

A) To make password reset processes easier to implement

B) To avoid sharing passwords by assigning unique passwords to each user

C) To be able to track each action back to a unique user

D) To better model the real world in the architecture

28. Which of the following is NOT an electronic payment method?

A) Deposit

B) Transfer

C) Money

D) Check

29. When reviewing OS selection decisions, which of the following is NOT a focus area for the auditor?

A) The OS is part of a comprehensive backup and restoration program

B) The OS is properly aligned with business goals

C) The OS aligns with the enterprise architecture

D) The OS includes information system processing and control requirements

30. Why is it important for an auditor to review network diagrams?

A) The absence of network diagrams indicates a lack of infrastructure management in general

B) Network diagrams are an essential part of infrastructure planning and direction on how the network should be evaluated

C) Without this information the auditor will not be able to determine if the proper physical and logical access controls are in effect

D) They will provide the necessary baseline used when interviewing employees

31. Which activity is NOT part of an audit?

A) Make sure that IS operations are efficient and that targets are being reached

B) Make sure that IS data have appropriate levels of CIA

C) Make sure that IS systems are purchased from the most cost-efficient source

D) Make sure that information systems follow applicable laws, regulations, contracts and industry guidelines

32. Which of the following statements BEST describes IMS?

A) Aligning multiple manufacturing solutions so that each share the same process

B) Merging complex manufacturing processes into a single solution

C) Re-engineering a manufacturing solution to maximize the sharing of resources across all processes

D) Deconstructing a complex manufacturing solution into simpler processes that can be managed separately

33. If an audit is carried out by an external party, what BEST describes what is documented in a statement of work, or SOW?

A) Escalation paths

B) What is not included

C) The scope and goals

D) Limitations of liability

34. In general, what are the two steps for managing risk, in order?

A) Perform a risk assessment, and then calculate the potential impact

B) Identify goals, and then identify all assets and systems

C) Identify goals and then perform a risk assessment

D) Establish purpose, and then assign responsibility

35. Which type of audit assesses how well internal controls meet regulatory or industry requirements?

A) Administrative

B) Integrated

C) Forensic

D) Compliance

36. What is the term describing a person or process that exploits a vulnerability?

A) Exposure

B) Risk

C) Threat

D) Threat agent

37. What are the three levels of duties for the IT steering committee?

A) Individual, managerial and executive

B) Responsibility, authority and membership

C) Action, delegation and transference

D) Initiation, authority and dissolution

38. What is a zero-day vulnerability?

A) A weakness with so much potential damage that a fix comes out on the same day it is identified

B) A weakness that takes less than one day exploit

C) A weakness so new that a fix is not yet available

D) A weakness often occurring only during day-time hours

39. Which of the following is NOT a true statement concerning data conversion components?

A) A valid rollback method is to log in new, rollback in new, and reapply in old

B) A valid rollback method is to unload from new, transfer to old, and reload old

C) Rollback steps should be designed in from the beginning if the risk of rollback is high

D) The right approach depends on transaction volume and the expected data conversion

40. Which of the following statements BEST describes shoulder surfing?

A) Looking over someone's shoulder at a computer screen or keyboard to steal information such as passwords

B) Repeatedly sending the same message to a particular address

C) Rummaging through trash bins to retrieve information written or printed on paper

D) Sending a single message to hundreds or thousands of users

41. When approaching an audit, what BEST describes what the auditor should do first?

A) Meet with stakeholders to determine risk priorities

B) Review prior work papers

C) Identify the org structure and processes, standards, procedures and guidelines

D) Get a firm grasp on the business' mission, goals and processes

42. Which of the following is the BEST description of a symmetric scheme?

A) Trying random key values until one that works is found

B) Using a single 'shared key' that both the sender and recipient know

C) Reduces the number of required brute force attempts

D) A secure email protocol that authenticates the identity of both the sender and receiver

43. Which COBIT 5 contextual quality measures how easily a value is comprehended?

A) Interpretability

B) Relevancy

C) Currency

D) Understandability

44. Which is the BEST description of EVA?

A) Being able to take a walk in outer space

B) Tracking the amount of work left according to the schedule

C) Tracking the tasks marked as completed relative to documented scope of the tasks

D) Tracking how much work has been done, and how much is left to do regardless of what the schedule says

45. Which of the following BEST describes an active data dictionary?

A) Provides the capability to validate and format the contents

B) Dictates attributes to be indexed

C) Can be viewed or printed only

D) Describes each field's use and characteristics

46. Which framework is geared specifically to security?

A) The Open Group Architecture Framework, or TOGAF

B) Risk IT Framework

C) ISO 27000 Series

D) Information Technology Infrastructure Library, or ITIL

47. Which of the following is NOT an IDS component?

A) User interface

B) Inference engine

C) Analyzer

D) Sensor

48. When interviewing employees responsible for network security, which of the following is NOT something the auditor needs to assess?

A) If documentation exists proving the person has been properly trained

B) If the person is aware of the risk that must be minimized associated with physical and logical access

C) If the person is knowledgeable in how to maintain and monitor access

D) If the person is aware of the need to actively monitor logons and to account for employee changes

49. Who is responsible for asset classification?

A) The asset owner

B) Senior management

C) The security manager

D) Those who use the asset the most

50. Which of the five basic tests are included in the paper test category?

A) Simulation and parallel

B) Checklist review and structured walkthrough

C) Parallel and full interruption

D) Structured walkthrough and simulation

51. Which of the following BEST describes a document-oriented NoSQL database?

A) Entire documents are stored as ether XML or JSON

B) Based on graph theory

C) Values are retrieved by specifying the column

D) All values are stored with an attribute name

52. What does IaaS stand for?

A) Infrastructure as a Service

B) Insolence as a Service

C) Integration as a Service

D) Identity as a Service

53. Which of the following statements is NOT true?

A) Non-statistical sampling does not use confidence levels to identify the sample size

B) Non-statistical sampling does not use precision to identify the sample size

C) Non-statistical sampling allows the auditor to select the sampling method, the sample size and how to select the samples

D) Non-statistical sampling decreases the likelihood that the auditor will misinterpret population data

54. Which of the following is NOT an essential characteristic of cloud computing?

A) Resources are pooled and reusable so that multiple tenants can use the environment simultaneously

B) It provides on-demand self-service without requiring human interaction

C) Services are accessible over a broadband network and can be used with a diverse list of client platforms

D) Cloud security controls align with corporate policies

55. At which OSI layer do protocols such as Ethernet and Token Ring operate?

A) Layer 2

B) Layer 3

C) Layer 5

D) Layer 4

56. Which of the following is the BEST description of DES?

A) Using one key for encryption and a different key for decryption

B) The most common outdated symmetric system

C) A one-way encryption that results in the same length of ciphertext regardless of the plain text

D) The most common modern symmetric system

57. What type of segregation of duty control identifies owners?

    A) Access to data

    B) Custody of assets

    C) Principle of least privilege

    D) Transaction authorization

58. What is the BEST description of the process a company must undergo for DSS to be successful?

    A) Analyze, adapt, consolidate

    B) Define, execute, solidify

    C) Gather, motivate, extend

    D) Unfreeze, move, freeze

59. In OOSD, which of the following statements BEST describes a class?

    A) The instantiation of a pattern

    B) Extending a class through another class

    C) The ability of a child instance to do something different than a parent instance would do

    D) A pattern which can be instantiated

60. Which BEST describes the term 'materiality'?

    A) If the evidence can be supported by an external source

    B) How important and applicable specific evidence is to the task at-hand

    C) How critical and sensitive the evidence is to the business

    D) If the evidence is of the same quality as system being audited

61. What is the BEST description of objectivity?

    A) True and credible

    B) Highly regarded in terms of source or context

    C) Correct and reliable

    D) Unbiased, unprejudiced and impartial

62. Which of the following BEST describes an application firewall?

    A) Can only look at the IP address and port number of packets coming into and out of the intranet

    B) Focuses on the HTTP protocol

    C) Tracks all outgoing requests for a computer and ensures that external packets targeting the internal computer correspond to a previous request

    D) Runs a separate proxy server for each protocol

63. What security principle is the act of controlling access to a resource based on their identity?

    A) Principle of least privilege

    B) Need-to-know

    C) Access control

    D) Segregation of duties

64. In relation to an expert system, which BEST describes a decision tree?

    A) A list of questions to ask a user until a conclusion is reached

    B) A graph of nodes and arcs between those nodes

    C) Used to load facts into the knowledge base without requiring a programmer

    D) A series of 'if...then' relationships

65. Which of the following statements is NOT true media handling?

    A) Media should not be transported during strong magnetic storms

    B) USB keys and flash drives are susceptible to strong magnetic fields

    C) Tape cartridges should be stored vertically

    D) Hard drives should be stored with Styrofoam

66. Which of the following is the BEST description of transport mode?

A) An IPSec mode that only encrypts the IP payload

B) The combination of an encrypted message and the secret key

C) Used to secure IP communication between two endpoints

D) How IPSec manages keys

67. Which of the following is NOT a recommended approach to ensure proper disposal of data when a contract expires?

A) CSPs should ensure the safe disposal or destruction of any previous backups

B) The CSP's technical specifications and controls that wipe data and backup media should be reviewed

C) Only media approved by the company should be used for both backups and real-time storage

D) A mandatory data wipe is carried out under the company's supervision

68. What security principle requires a person to have a valid need to access resources?

A) Segregation of duties

B) Access control

C) Principle of least privilege

D) Need-to-know

69. Which of the following terms refers to a block of code being dependent on other code to function?

A) Cohesive

B) Compounded

C) Coupled

D) Concise

70. What is a valid weakness of the Waterfall SDLC?

A) Projects are often more than 1 year in length, by which time the needed requirements have changed

B) Each step must be completed before starting the next

C) Solid documentation is seldom produced

D) Demonstrable functionality cannot be shown early

71. Which two frameworks help to manage IS operations?

A) ITIL and ISO 20000

B) BSC and Zachman

C) ITIL and ISO 27000

D) Zachman and Risk IT

72. Which of the following items is NOT something a company must possess to be successful in the e-Commerce space?

A) The ability to link legacy systems into an online presence

B) Embrace business process reconfiguration

C) A top-level commitment

D) An affinity for fast-paced business transactions

73. Which of the following statements BEST describes a heuristic scanner?

A) Comparing bit strings in a file against a pattern known to represent malware

B) Looking for malware at the DOS and BIOS level

C) Examining areas of a computer looking for strings of bits that looks like malware

D) Analyzing instructions in a file and decides if it looks like malware

74. Which of the following BEST describes an extranet VPN?

A) Connects telecommuters and mobile users to the enterprise WAN

B) Provides business partners limited access to each other's corporate network

C) Connects branch offices within an enterprise WAN

D) Provides direct connections for WAN links

75. Which of the following PBXs would NOT allow an attacker to eavesdrop on conversations?

A) Auto-answer

B) Account codes

C) Call waiting

D) Conferencing

76. What BEST describes an audit charter?

A) A document explaining the scope, purpose and authority of an audit

B) Lists all relevant parties to take part in an audit

C) Describes a focused exercise intended for a very specific purpose and can track change requests

D) Provides authorization to carry out an audit

77. Which is the BEST definition of configuration management?

A) Managing change to software that may impact end-users

B) Managing change to a system so reliability and security is maintained

C) Managing change to electronic documents

D) Managing change to a system so integrity is maintained

78. When auditing hardware acquisitions, which of the following areas is NOT an auditor's major concern?

A) Determine if the acquisition process began with a business need

B) Determine if several vendors were considered and whether the comparison between them was done according to the right criteria

C) Determine if the selected vendor was the right choice

D) Determine whether the hardware requirements for this need were considered in the specifications

79. Which federal law requires publicly-traded companies to use a recognized internal control framework?

A) HIPAA

B) GDPR

C) SOX

D) Basel Accords

80. When auditing a feasibility study, which of the following is NOT something an auditor should look for?

A) A detailed discussion of each rejected alternative

B) If the need can be met with existing systems

C) A reasonable discussion of alternatives

D) If all cost justifications and benefits are stated in verifiable terms

81. Which of the following describes something that is accompanied by a rise in risk levels?

A) KPI

B) KGI

C) KRI

D) CSF

82. Which of the following is the BEST description of S/MIME?

A) Using a single 'shared key' that both the sender and recipient know

B) A secure email protocol that authenticates the identity of both the sender and receiver

C) Reduces the number of required brute force attempts

D) Trying random key values until one that works is found

83. Which of the following BEST describes a way to locate an entity based on one or more attributes?

A) A relational key

B) A foreign key

C) A primary key

D) A key

84. What are the three types of free licensing?

A) Open source, limited features and shareware

B) Public domain, freeware and shareware

C) Public domain, limited features and shareware

D) Open source, freeware and shareware

85. Which of the following BEST describes the quality assurance role?

A) Carries out the tasks that will inform the security officer of how well the system implements proper security measures

B) Acts as subject matter experts for the development team

C) Reviews results and deliverables for each phase to confirm compliance with the stated requirements

D) Ensures the deliverable provides an appropriate level of protection

86. In relation to BI analysis models, which is the BEST description of an entity relationship diagram?

A) Models data entities and how each relates to another

B) Outlines the major processes and external parties an organization deals with

C) Visualizes contextual relationships between entities

D) Allows us to deconstruct a business process

87. When discussing paths of logical access, which of the following BEST describes a local access?

A) Carried out across a network, but the user is generally sitting in a location that has not been physically secured and is normally in a different city

B) Enacted by both front-end and back-end systems

C) Represented by physical proximity to a computer

D) Carried out using a local network and can be accomplished even though the user is on a different floor or even a different physical building

88. What describes the act of totaling the results of activities in multiple ways?

A) Exception reporting

B) Audit trail

C) Transaction logs

D) Reconciliation

89. Which of the following BEST describes a dedicated circuit?

A) A symmetric telecommunications line permanently connecting two sides

B) A circuit that can be setup and torn down at any time based on the need

C) A circuit that is created in real-time

D) A circuit that is setup ahead of time

90. What is used to reduce risk?

A) Risk

B) Threat Agent

C) Exposure

D) Control

91. Which of the following BEST describes a column-oriented NoSQL database?

A) Entire documents are stored as ether XML or JSON

B) Values are retrieved by specifying the column

C) All values are stored with an attribute name

D) Based on graph theory

92. Which of the following statements are NOT true regarding prototyping?

A) One approach is to build the entire model and then the entire system

B) It keeps the traditional Waterfall methodology but in repeated iterations

C) Initial prototypes focus on screens and reports

D) It does not require a trial-and-error approach

93. Which of the following tells how well a process is performing relative to reaching a goal?

A) KPI

B) KGI

C) KRI

D) CSF

94. What are the steps involved in benchmarking?

A) Plan, research, observe, analyze, execute and repeat

B) Plan, research, observe, analyze, adopt and improve

C) Define, research, observe, analyze, execute and repeat

D) Define, research, observe, analyze, adopt and improve

95. What are the three types of changeover techniques?

A) Singular, multiple and variable

B) Delayed, variable and immediate

C) Parallel, phased and abrupt

D) Distinct, construed and managed

96. Which of the following BEST describes Argonite?

A) Releases pressurized gas that removes oxygen from the air, but was discontinued in the 1990s

B) Automated systems are only allowed in dark facilities where no people are present

C) A gas that reduces the amount of oxygen available for a fire to use

D) A gas that extinguishes a fire by lowering the temperature of the components

97. Which of the following BEST describes the Infrastructure staff role?

A) Maintains the systems software, including the OS, on top of which applications sit

B) Develops and maintains standards for the IT group

C) Carries out whatever duties are defined in the security policy

D) Maintains network components such as routers, switches, firewalls and remote access

98. At which OSI layer are physical transmissions generated?

A) Layer 2

B) Layer 4

C) Layer 3

D) Layer 1

99. What is the primary advantage when using a logic path monitor?

A) It creates a map of system memory that can be analyzed later

B) It checks the results from a function and compares it to expected results

C) It allows us to trace after the fact the steps leading to a bug

D) It alerts us of pre-defined issues in real-time

100. Which electronic payment method does not lend itself to earning interest?

A) Electronic money

B) Electronic transfer

C) Electronic deposit

D) Electronic check

101. Which of the following BEST describes a blackout?

A) A decrease in voltage

B) A severely reduced voltage due to the failure of a power company to supply power within an acceptable range

C) An increase in voltage

D) A total failure with a complete loss of power

102. What is the best definition of relaxing?

A) A beach, a hammock and a bottle of Brasserie Dupont Avec Les Bons Voeux

B) Removing dependencies in the critical path to shorten the project timeline

C) Extending tasks to save on costs

D) Negotiating with stakeholders to extend the project delivery date in order to relieve task conflict

103. Which statement below BEST describes a 3rd generation language?

A) They are object-oriented

B) They replace both binary and assembly languages

C) They have one entry point and one exit point

D) They are non-procedural

104. Which of the following BEST describes a 4GL application generator?

A) A 4GL that generates 3GL code such as COBOL or C

B) A specialized language that can extract data and produce reports

C) A language that can run inside of a database on embedded devices

D) A proprietary language also running inside of a database but on an enterprise-scale server

105. Which of the following BEST describes a bolting door lock?

A) A lock requiring electric power

B) A lock requiring a metal key to open

C) A lock that uses a numeric key pad or dial

D) A lock made of strengthened steel

106. What is the BEST description of relevancy?

A) The volume

B) If it is up-to-date

C) The breadth and depth

D) How applicable it is

107. Which of the following BEST represents the relationship between RTO and alternate site cost?

A) The cost of the alternate site will remain steady until RTO nears 0

B) As RTO decreases the cost of the alternate site will also decrease

C) RTO has no bearing on the cost of an alternate site

D) As RTO decreases the cost of the alternate site will increase

108. What BEST describes the primary goal of software re-engineering?

A) To create a service-oriented architecture

B) To increase efficiency by reducing overall complexity

C) To increase coupling so that common resources are shared in a more efficient manner

D) To facilitate the construction of a replacement solution that is more performant and effective

109. What IT risk management level are we operating at when considering how risk can result in the loss of availability?

A) Procedural

B) Operational

C) Strategic

D) Project

110. Which of the following is NOT a factor for a web-based EDIT to replace traditional EDI?

A) The inability to have more than two partners share in an EDI framework

B) A reduced cost due to not having to use private networks

C) A robust security infrastructure riding on top of the Internet

D) Improvements in the X.12 EDI formatting standard

111. Which of the following BEST describes logical topology?

A) How the computers communicate over the physical cabling

B) How the cables are laid out and how they are connected to each computer

C) How computers are arranged relative to each other within a network

D) How computers use various protocols to communicate with each other

112. Which BEST describes a pharming attack?

A) Compromising a DNS database

B) The act of stealing money by reducing amounts by an insignificant amount

C) Redirecting browser traffic from a legitimate site to a bogus one

D) The act of stealing money by rounding down fractions

113. Which of the following BEST describes a spike?

A) A severely reduced voltage due to the failure of a power company to supply power within an acceptable range

B) A decrease in voltage

C) A total failure with a complete loss of power

D) An increase in voltage

114. Which of the following statements is NOT true concerning satellite radio?

A) It uses a transponder to send and receive data

B) It requires a line-of-sight through the air, and so is susceptible to weather interference

C) It has a relatively long latency

D) It is difficult to tap into

115. Which of the following is the BEST description of cryptanalysis?

A) Reduces the number of required brute force attempts

B) Trying random key values until one that works is found

C) A secure email protocol that authenticates the identity of both the sender and receiver

D) Using a single 'shared key' that both the sender and recipient know

116. Which of the following describes something that must happen if we are to reach a goal?

A) KPI

B) CSF

C) KRI

D) KGI

117. What describes an activity in which a user or system activity is watched, either directly or remotely?

    A) Audit trail

    B) Independent review

    C) Exception reporting

    D) Supervisory review

118. Which of the following BEST describes the relationships between a software baseline, a design freeze and scope creep?

    A) Both software baseline and design freeze are terms describing a point in time at which no more changes are allowed to prevent scope creep

    B) The software baseline describes a point in time at which no more changes are allowed to prevent scope creep until the design freeze can be implemented

    C) Design freeze represents the point at which designs are finalized, the software baseline represents core components when completed, and scope creep represents incremental changes to core components as-needed to meet the finalized designs

    D) All three terms deal with SDLC

119. What type of control is a policy, procedure, practice or organizational structure intentionally put in-place to reduce risk?

    A) External

    B) Internal

    C) Applicable

    D) Procedural

120. Which of the following BEST describes an attacker taking advantage of a maintenance hook?

    A) Taking advantage of an undocumented feature

    B) Listening in on the active voice channel of a line placed into maintenance mode

    C) Listening in on voice activity by accessing the physical communication between the PBX and the end-user device

    D) Gaining physical access to a bridge and routing all signals to a specific port

121. What are the two perspectives that need to be addressed when defining RTO?

    A) Those who create information, and those who consume it

    B) Those who consume information, and senior management who have a broader view

    C) Individual contributors and management

    D) Day-to-day operations and strategic operations

122. Which of the following BEST describes the metadata layer of BI?

    A) Data about data

    B) Schedules tasks required to build, maintain and populate the warehouse

    C) Allows all other components to communicate using browser-based interfaces

    D) Knows how to communicate between each vertical layer

123. Which of the following BEST describes a direct connection?

    A) A marker or address that identifies a document or a specific place in a document

    B) A file that a browser stores on the local computer's hard drive

    C) Computers that do not use any type of address translation

    D) The connection between Internet users and the Internet service provider

124. When dealing with sampling, which term BEST describes selecting a sample set from the entire data set without dividing it into like groups?

    A) Stratified mean per unit

    B) Difference estimation

    C) Sample standard deviation

    D) Unstratified mean per unit

125. Which of the following is NOT a requirement for work papers?

    A) Each page must be initialed

    B) Each page must be individually referenced in a topical addendum

    C) They must be self-contained

    D) Each page must be dated

126. Which OSI layer(s)does the TCP Host-to-host layer map to?

    A) Layers 6 through 4

    B) Layer 3 and 4

    C) Layer 3

    D) Layer 4

127. When developing a business case, which of the following BEST describes the evaluation?

    A) Deciding if the recommended approach is sufficiently cost-effective

    B) Reading the feasibility study report with all stakeholders

    C) Defines the problem or opportunity in a clear and concise manner

    D) The recommended system or software solution that will meet the requirements

128. Which of the following BEST describes POS?

    A) Focuses on providing services such as mortgage loans or insurance policies

    B) Enables payments to be made through the use of virtual transactions

    C) Computers that physically connect with credit card readers

    D) Allows banking customers to carry out virtually all transactions from the comfort of their home

129. Which of the following BEST represents the formula to calculate total required resources for a project?

    A) Resources x Duration

    B) Resources x Duration/Milestones

    C) Resources/Milestones x Duration

    D) (Duration x Milestones)/Resources

130. Which of the following BEST describes the systems development project team role?

    A) Acts as subject matter experts for the development team

    B) Create the core project deliverables by completing assigned tasks

    C) Develops, installs and operates the requested system

    D) Provides day-to-day management and leadership of the project

131. Which of the following descriptions BEST describes actual costs?

    A) Estimates the cost of each activity in the current project, and sums the results

    B) Looks at the raw costs in a previous project and extrapolates to the current project

    C) Looks at previous estimates of employee hours, materials cost and technology, and uses statistics to extrapolate those estimates to our current project

    D) The quickest estimation technique, and uses estimates from prior projects

132. Which of the following BEST describes a bottom-up test plan?

A) Starts by manipulating data elements and detecting fallout from functions

B) Examines the smallest testable units and continues with larger units until the complete system has been tested

C) Exercises the most recently-changed areas and tests functions dependent on those areas

D) Starts at the highest level and dives deeper in each successive pass

133. Which is NOT an area that system testing is concerned with?

A) Security testing

B) Recovery testing

C) Volume testing

D) Data testing

134. Which of the following statements is not true regarding how an immunizer works?

A) It is not possible immunize a file against all known malware

B) It can pretend to be malware so that the real malware will assume a file is already infected and leave it alone

C) Once fully immunized, a computer is relatively safe from internal attacks

D) It can continuously watch a file it is attached to for unauthorized changes and report suspicious activity

135. When auditing software development, which of the following areas is NOT an auditor's major concern?

A) Changes to the application are reflected in a version control system only

B) Investments in CASE tools increase both quality and speed

C) Users continue to be involved in the development process

D) Approvals are obtained for software specifications

136. Which COBIT 5 contextual quality measures how well the symbols or units for a value align?

A) Understandability

B) Interpretability

C) Relevancy

D) Currency

137. Which of the following statements is NOT true regarding USB?

A) It has the ability to power small devices

B) USB 3.0 is 10 times faster than USB 2.0

C) USB 4.0 is 4 times faster than USB 3.0

D) USB 2.0 supports transfer speeds up to 480 Mbps

138. When implementing authentication and authorization for external parties, which of the following is NOT an access control policy to be enforced?

A) All access that is not explicitly authorized is forbidden, also known as least-privilege

B) Each external party must have a unique identifier and passwords must be used

C) There must be a process for revoking access rights or interrupting the connection between systems

D) An authorization process needs to exist for granting user access and privileges

139. Which of the following is an example of 'something you are'?

A) A voice print

B) A passphrase

C) A password

D) A token device

140. Which of the following statements BEST describes BI?

A) It uses refined AI rules to make the best decisions for a given business

B) It is a system that harnesses the knowledge and experience of all management personnel into a single, intelligent engine

C) It employs multiple expert systems to explore the most likely business outcomes, thereby helping human management to achieve the greatest success

D) It collects massive amounts of data and uses various methods of analysis to detect trends

141. Which of the following is NOT an ISDN implementation?

A) PRI

B) BISDN

C) CRI

D) BRI

142. Which term identifies the automated evaluation technique that embeds specially written audit modules into an application?

A) Integrated test facility

B) Snapshot

C) Continuous and intermittent simulation

D) SCARF/EAM

143. Which of the following BEST describes flexibility?

A) Provides users with continuous, reliable and secure services

B) Means an organization can support a mixed network that delivers highly-integrated solutions

C) Occurs when we can connect networks using different technologies or operating at different speeds

D) Allows a network to scale up or to support new services

144. Which of the following BEST describes a voltage regulator?

A) An increase in voltage

B) Mitigates short-term interruptions such as sags, spikes and surges

C) Caused by electrical storms or nearby noisy electrical equipment such as motors, fluorescent lighting or radio transmitters

D) Measures the incoming electrical current and either increase or decrease the charge to ensure a consistent current

145. When developing a business case, which of the following BEST describes requirements?

A) Represents both the stakeholder's needs and constraints

B) Provides enough information to a business for it to decide if it is worth pursuing

C) The recommended system or software solution that will meet the requirements

D) Defines the problem or opportunity in a clear and concise manner

146. What COBIT 5 process allows higher-level objectives to define what enablers should achieve?

A) Goals cascade

B) Process Assessment Model, or PAM

C) Intrinsic Qualities

D) Process Reference Model

147. Which term identifies the automated evaluation technique that simulates the execution of each transaction?

A) Snapshot

B) Continuous and intermittent simulation

C) Audit hook

D) SCARF/EAM

148. Which best describes black box testing?

A) The process of studying an application or component to see how it works, and then using that information to create a similar product

B) Tearing down a system into its original source code and documenting how it works

C) Ensuring a system that has been re-engineered performs properly

D) Observing how a system responds to various inputs, and then documenting that behavior

149. What is the difference between a safeguard and a countermeasure?

A) A safeguard is a manual control and a countermeasure is an automated control

B) A safeguard is a detective control and a countermeasure is a corrective control

C) A safeguard is a proactive control and a countermeasure is a reactive control

D) A safeguard is a procedural control and a countermeasure is an administrative control

150. Which of the following BEST describes the project sponsor role?

A) Owns the project and the resulting deliverable

B) Provides overall direction and represents the major stakeholders

C) Shows commitment to the project by providing approval for the necessary resources to be successful

D) Provides funding and defines the critical success factors and metrics that determine if the project is a success

151. Which of the following BEST describes a compiler object code?

A) The intermediate product of changing human-readable language into binary code

B) Translates human-readable languages into binary code

C) One-step above binary code

D) Instructions that a computer can understand

152. When auditing source code management, the auditor should look at all of the following EXCEPT for which one?

A) Source code is backed up, and escrow and offsite agreements are in-place if applicable

B) Access to source code is controlled

C) Change and release management are streamlines as a single process with differing lines of accountability

D) The ability to push code to production is controlled

153. Which term describes not taking action for a specific risk?

A) Risk appetite

B) Risk acceptance

C) Risk tolerance

D) Risk capacity

154. What term describes proving who we claim we are?

A) Authentication

B) Integrity

C) Nonrepudiation

D) Confidentiality

155. Which of the following BEST describes business interruption insurance?

A) Insurance that covers losses incurred as a result of a cyberattack

B) Insurance that reimburses lost profit as a result of an IT malfunction or security incident that causes the loss of computing resources

C) Insurance that covers the actual cash value of papers and records that have been disclosed, or physically damaged or lost

D) Insurance that reimburses the business for expenses incurred in maintaining operations at a facility that experiences damage

156. Which of the following activities is NOT covered in Phase 3A?

    A) Conference room pilots

    B) Request for Information

    C) Agenda-based presentations

    D) Entity-relationship diagrams

157. Which of the following BEST describes a dry-pipe water-based system?

    A) Can cause considerable collateral damage to equipment when activated

    B) The extinguisher sprays the agent directly on the fire

    C) Can cause considerable collateral damage to equipment when activated

    D) Always has water under pressure in the pipes

158. Which of the following BEST describes a full interruption test?

    A) The recovery site is brought up to a state of operational readiness, but operations at the primary site continue

    B) Team members implement the plan on paper

    C) Team members role-playing a simulated disaster without activating the recovery site

    D) The recovery site is activated, and the primary site is shut down

159. Which of the following BEST describes the data source layer of BI?

    A) Provides access to operational, external and non-operational data

    B) Provides access to the various data sources while at the same time hiding how that data is stored

    C) Copies and transforms data into and out of the warehouse format and assures quality control

    D) Contains the bulk of interesting data, and is usually a relational database

160. What is the BEST description of appropriate amount?

    A) The volume

    B) How applicable it is

    C) The breadth and depth

    D) If it is up-to-date

161. Which of the following BEST describes a hacker or cracker?

    A) A skilled person who is interested in proving how smart they are by breaking into systems

    B) Someone who is not a skilled individual, but simply uses tools created by others to break into systems

    C) A party having an increased access but does not possess any loyalty that an employee might have

    D) A person who happens upon unprotected information and decides to take advantage of the situation

162. Which value estimates the maximum time an operation can operate in a recovery mode?

    A) MTO

    B) AIW

    C) RTO

    D) SDO

163. Which statement is true when transferring risk?

    A) Transferring risk only applies to technological solutions

    B) We can only transfer all risk if contracts include a right-to-audit clause

    C) We can only transfer financial responsibility

    D) Transferring risk is seldom the correct choice

164. Which of the following BEST describes a hub?

A) A device that simply amplifies a signal and forwards it on.

B) A device that connects LAN segments

C) A device that filters traffic based on the MAC Addresses

D) A device that amplifies a signal and has multiple ports

165. Which electronic payment method is susceptible to double spending?

A) Electronic transfer

B) Electronic money

C) Electronic deposit

D) Electronic check

166. What is the BEST description of concise representation?

A) If it is in the correct language and units and is clear

B) If it is presented in the same format

C) How easily it is comprehended

D) How compactly it is presented

167. Which of the following BEST describes a CGI script?

A) An executable, machine-independent software program running on a web server

B) A traffic concentration spot

C) A Java applet or small program that runs within a web server environment

D) A program written in a portable, platform-independent computer language

168. Which of the following BEST describes an application-level firewall?

A) An application firewall that uses a proxy server for each protocol

B) A computer that is physically connected to only two private networks

C) A computer that is physically connected to two or more different private networks by multiple network interfaces

D) An application firewall that uses only one proxy server for all traffic

169. When accepting final residual risk, COBIT 5's Risk Management Process does NOT include which item?

A) Organizational policy

B) Risk appetite

C) Risk identification and measurement

D) The approach that peer company's take

170. What term describes a title given to someone based on their job function?

A) Role

B) Responsibility

C) Informed

D) Skill

171. From an auditor's perspective, which of the following is NOT a major area of concern when moving functions to a cloud provider?

A) The organization must be able to accommodate this new way of doing business

B) Access control must be maintained, since employees might be able to go directly to the provider to make changes

C) Billing processes must be able to accommodate the change

D) The move must make sense from a business strategy viewpoint

172. Which of the following is NOT a recommended method to address physical access by the CSP's staff?

A) The company should require the CSP to provide personnel details for all employees that will be accessing the company's assets

B) The CSP's disaster recovery plans should be reviewed to ensure they contain countermeasures to protect physical assets during and after a disaster

C) The CSP should provide proof of independent security reviews or certification reports that meet the company's compliance requirements

D) The company should request the CSP's physical security policy and ensure that it is aligned with the company's own security policy

173. Which statement is true?

A) As RTO increases, the time to recover decreases

B) A tape backup solution provides a low RPO

C) As RPO increases, data loss decreases

D) High availability solutions require both a low RTO and RPO

174. Which of the following BEST describes an electronic door lock?

A) A control that uses two doors, in which the person entering must close the first door before the second door may be opened

B) A lock that uses a numeric key pad or dial

C) A lock containing a sensor that requires a magnetic card key, or a chipped card key or token to be placed against it

D) A lock that uses human characteristics to identify an individual attempting to unlock a door

175. What type of risk reflects material errors not being caught in time by one or more controls?

A) Control risk

B) Detection risk

C) Audit risk

D) Inherent risk

176. Which of the following BEST describes external data in the data source layer of BI?

A) Data needed by end users but is not currently in an accessible format

B) Data provided by systems external to the BI system

C) Data provided by a source external to the company

D) Data collected during normal business operations and normally held in easy-to-access databases

177. Which of the following BEST describes the desktop access layer of BI?

A) The point at which end-users interact with the system

B) Contains the logic necessary to prepare data from the warehouse

C) Where the results of data preparation are stored

D) Contains the bulk of interesting data, and is usually a relational database

178. Which of the following conditions is unlikely to cause a PBX crash?

A) Voicemail abuse

B) Normal system shutdown procedures

C) Physical removal of hardware or media from the PBX

D) Repeated dialing of the same number

179. Which of the following is NOT a major concern that a security manager should watch for prior to each test?

A) The business accepts the risk of testing

B) Final test reporting has been scheduled

C) The risk of disruption is minimized

D) The organization has the ability to restore operation at any point during testing

180. Which of the following items best represents the hierarchical nature of WBS?

A) Task > Schedule > WP > WBS

B) Schedule > WBS > Task > WP

C) WP > Schedule > Task > WBS

D) WBS > WP > Task > Schedule

181. Which of the following BEST describes the reconnaissance method of a traffic analysis war walking?

A) The practice of walking around businesses or residential neighborhoods while scanning with a small device to search for wireless networks

B) The practice of breaking through encryption faster than keys can be changed

C) The practice of marking a series of symbols on sidewalks and walls to indicate nearby wireless access points

D) The practice of driving around businesses or residential neighborhoods while scanning with a laptop computer to search for wireless networks

182. Which of the following statements BEST describes a mask or signature?

A) Comparing bit strings in a file against a pattern known to represent malware

B) Analyzing instructions in a file and decides if it looks like malware

C) Looking for malware at the DOS and BIOS level

D) Examining areas of a computer looking for strings of bits that looks like malware

183. Which of the following BEST describes network topology?

A) How computers are arranged relative to each other within a network

B) How the cables are laid out and how they are connected to each computer

C) How the computers communicate over the physical cabling

D) How computers use various protocols to communicate with each other

184. In which phase of the Waterfall SDLC do we correct conflicts between expectations and written requirements?

A) Phase 3B

B) Phase 1

C) Phase 3A

D) Phase 2

185. Which of the following BEST describes attack signature detection tool?

A) Takes raw data and prepares it for a manual review by trimming out records that have no security significance

B) Looks for anomalies in user or system behavior

C) Looks for a specific sequence of events known to indicate an attack

D) Captures audit trails or logs and performs a real-time analysis on the incoming data

186. Which of the following is NOT a prominent project management standard or organization?

A) PRINCE2

B) PMBOK

C) PMPA

D) IPMA

187. Which of the following BEST describes bandwidth?

A) A measurement of the number of hops a packet requires between a source and destination

B) The delay that a message or packet will experience on its way from source to destination

C) A measurement of the maximum number of bytes possible after compression and decompression

D) A measurement of the maximum number of bytes possible through a physical medium

188. What is the BEST reason that BI is designed with so many complex layers?

A) It is required when dealing with such large amounts of data

B) It allows a business to implement BI in stages

C) It allows consultants to charge the big bucks

D) It allows a business to constrain the resulting infrastructure to a small number of departments

189. Which of the following are NOT common risks associated with DSS?

A) Users may be unable to use the prototype model

B) Nonexistent or unwilling users

C) A lack of support for the DSS, or it may evaporate over time

D) Users, implementers and maintainers who will tend to disappear over time

190. Which of the following is NOT an attribute used when classifying assets?

A) The difficulty in providing security

B) How access is granted

C) How strong security controls are

D) Who is responsible for approving access

191. Which of the following BEST describes alpha version testing?

A) Testing an application that has completed UAT but is not in production

B) Testing an application ready for a limited rollout of an application to a very small set of end-users

C) Testing an application that is feature complete but has not yet completed UAT

D) Testing an application that is not feature complete, but is ready to undergo assumption and logic flow validations

192. Which of the following BEST describes pilot testing?

A) Testing an application that is not feature complete, but is ready to undergo assumption and logic flow validations

B) Testing an application that has completed UAT but is not in production

C) Testing an application that is feature complete but has not yet completed UAT

D) Testing an application ready for a limited rollout of an application to a very small set of end-users

193. You are managing a project with only partial requirements but the customer needs to receive steady and incremental prototypes as work progresses. Which of the following methodologies should you use?

A) Scrum

B) Waterfall

C) RAD

D) OOSD

194. Which of the following BEST describes a simulation test?

A) Team members role-playing a simulated disaster without activating the recovery site

B) The recovery site is brought up to a state of operational readiness, but operations at the primary site continue

C) An assessment of all steps to be carried out

D) Team members implement the plan on paper

195. Which framework was created by ISACA?

A) ISO 27000 Series

B) Information Technology Infrastructure Library, or ITIL

C) Risk IT Framework

D) The Open Group Architecture Framework, or TOGAF

196. When developing a business case, which of the following BEST describes a current analysis?

A) Represent both the stakeholder's needs and constraints

B) Understanding the current situation as presented by both strengths and weaknesses

C) The recommended system or software solution that will meet the requirements

D) Defines the problem or opportunity in a clear and concise manner

197. During development of software for a 'build' project, which of the following roles can the auditor play?

A) Preventative and detective

B) Compensating and preventative

C) Corrective and deterrent

D) Corrective and detective

198. Which of the following BEST describes latency?

A) A measurement of the maximum number of bytes possible after compression and decompression

B) A measurement of the number of hops a packet requires between a source and destination

C) The delay that a message or packet will experience on its way from source to destination

D) A measurement of the maximum number of bytes possible through a physical medium

199. Which of the following is NOT a common control when dealing with ICS?

A) Restrict physical access to the ICS network and devices such as locks, card readers and/or guards

B) Deploy security patches for zero-day exploits immediately when available, with testing completed no longer than 3 days afterward

C) Use redundancy to keep availability high

D) Restrict access to the ICS network and network activity, particularly when connected to the Internet

200. Which of the following BEST describes data-in-use?

A) Any information moving around a network or being transferred between two processes

B) Any information persisted to storage such as hard drives, USB drives, tape backups or in live databases

C) Information that is being manipulated by end users at their workstation

D) Applications deployed to log onto each system and look through the various data stores

201. Which of the following BEST describes a packet filtering firewall?

A) Runs a separate proxy server for each protocol

B) Tracks all outgoing requests for a computer and ensures that external packets targeting the internal computer correspond to a previous request

C) Can only look at the IP address and port number of packets coming into and out of the intranet

D) Focuses on the HTTP protocol

202. What is the BEST description of offshore?

A) When the function is split between in-house and one or more outside parties.

B) Having one or more outside parties perform the entire function.

C) When all work is performed remotely in a different geographic region.

D) When all work being performed at a remote location in the same geographic area.

203. When can we be sure that all risk has been mitigated in a specific area?

A) When a post-audit analysis shows no remaining risk

B) Only after countermeasures have been put into place

C) Never – residual risk will always remain

D) Never, because it is impossible to prove all risk has been removed

204. Which of the following is NOT true of DSL?

A) It provides rates up to 52 Mbps

B) It uses the same frequencies as ISDN

C) The actual speed depends on how far from the CO the DSL modem is due to signal attenuation

D) It is an 'always on' connection

205. Which of the following is the BEST description of ESP?

A) An IPSec session attribute that dictates various configuration options

B) An IPSec mode that encrypts both the payload and header

C) Data added to the header when using IPSec in tunnel mode

D) The encrypted payload when using ESP

206. When auditing an information security framework, which of the following areas is something an auditor will NOT focus on?

A) Logical access

B) How investigations are carried out

C) How well BRP and DCP has been taken into account

D) How security is tested

207. Which framework is geared to governmental agencies?

A) FEA

B) Balanced Scorecard, or BSC

C) COBIT 5

D) Capability Maturity Model Integration, or CMMI

208. Which statement must be true?

A) risk appetite + risk tolerance >= risk capacity

B) risk appetite + risk tolerance <= risk capacity

C) risk appetite + risk capacity >= risk tolerance

D) risk appetite + risk capacity <= risk tolerance

209. Which of the following descriptions BEST describes analogous estimating?

A) Looks at the raw costs in a previous project and extrapolates to the current project

B) Estimates the cost of each activity in the current project, and sums the results

C) The quickest estimation technique, and uses estimates from prior projects

D) Looks at previous estimates of employee hours, materials cost and technology, and uses statistics to extrapolate those estimates to our current project

210. What security principle segments resources so that access can be increased as-needed?

A) Principle of least privilege

B) Access control

C) Segregation of duties

D) Need-to-know

211. When controlling a project, what are the three most important things should we keep an eye on?

A) Communication, the critical path and risk

B) Scope, resources and risk

C) Documentation, resources and communication

D) Scope, timeline and deliverables

212. Which contains a series of entries generated by one or more process and is focused on system activities?

A) Audit trail

B) Exception reporting

C) Transaction logs

D) Reconciliation

213. Which is the first step in mitigating internal threats?

A) Train HR personnel on secure hiring practices

B) Ensure job descriptions include security responsibilities

C) Have employees sign an NDA

D) Reviewing references and performing background checks

214. Which is the BEST description of ISDN?

A) An older technology, it allowed more than one party to share in a single dedicated line across a WAN

B) A newer technology, it is a switching technology but uses cells instead of packets

C) The first truly digital connection for the masses to travel over copper phone lines

D) Achieves higher rates because it uses all available frequencies on a UTP line

215. Which is NOT a valid reason to perform a risk analysis?

A) To help determine audit goals

B) To evaluate the effectiveness of various controls

C) To mitigate selected risks

D) To identify areas that need attention

216. Which of the following BEST describes COBIT 5?

A) A specification for service management that is aligned with ITIL

B) Developed by ISACA and is intended to ensure IT goals align with business goals, resources are used properly, and that risk is being effectively managed

C) Created in the UK and provides a very hands-on and detailed framework on implementing GEIT

D) A series of standards that help an organization implement and maintain an information security program, and is the standard to which most companies are certified against

217. Which of the following BEST describes a shareware license?

A) Used when multiple end-users will be using the software

B) Initially free, but requires payment at a later date to keep the software functioning or to unlock all features or benefits

C) The software may be used in any way the user likes without any type of payment

D) Free, but the source code cannot be redistributed

218. What are the three steps that logical access can be broken down into?

A) Identification, authentication and authorization

B) Access, authentication and authorization

C) Access, identification and authentication

D) Identification, authentication and access

219. Which of the following BEST describes security information and event management system?

A) Captures audit trails or logs and performs a real-time analysis on the incoming data

B) Looks for anomalies in user or system behavior

C) Looks for a specific sequence of events known to indicate an attack

D) Takes raw data and prepares it for a manual review by trimming out records that have no security significance

220. Which ISO 27000 role provides physical and logical security?

A) The auditor

B) Security advisor group

C) Information security administrator

D) Information security steering committee

221. Which of the following BEST describes a cipher lock?

A) A control that uses two doors, in which the person entering must close the first door before the second door may be opened

B) A lock containing a sensor that requires a magnetic card key, or a chipped card key or token to be placed against it

C) A lock that uses a numeric key pad or dial

D) A lock that uses human characteristics to identify an individual attempting to unlock a door

222. What BEST describes the capability an online programming facility gives to developers?

A) To simultaneously work on the same code blocks as other developers

B) To develop programs without requiring dedicated workstations

C) To continue development efforts anywhere with a network connection

D) To write and test code that is stored on a server

223. Which of the following BEST describes a BSS?

A) A wireless network in which the AP is also connected to another network

B) A frequency range within wireless traffic

C) A group of devices communicating in infrastructure mode

D) A human-friendly name assigned to a group of devices communicating in infrastructure mode

224. Which of the following statements is NOT true concerning microwave radio?

A) It used to be largely analog, but it is almost exclusively digital for newer installations

B) It requires a line-of-sight through the air, and so is susceptible to weather interference

C) One advantage is the low cost

D) If can deliver both voice and data traffic

225. Which of the following BEST describes a circuit-level firewall?

A) An application firewall that uses only one proxy server for all traffic

B) A computer that is physically connected to only two private networks

C) A computer that is physically connected to two or more different private networks by multiple network interfaces

D) An application firewall that uses a proxy server for each protocol

226. Which of the following best represents the five steps, in order, for NIST SP 800-30?

A) Identify vulnerabilities, identify threats, determine impact, determine likelihood, determine risk

B) Identify threats, identify vulnerabilities, determine likelihood, determine impact, determine risk

C) Identify vulnerabilities, identify threats, determine likelihood, determine impact, determine risk

D) Identify threats, identify vulnerabilities, determine impact, determine likelihood, determine risk

227. Which of the following statements BEST describes an expert system?

A) A program that accepts a large database of known facts and then derives relationships

B) A subset of AI that analyzes multiple disparate factual sources and aggregates a common rule set that is then applied to a single question

C) A program that allows a user to specify a small set of base conditions and then extrapolates the most likely result based on a heuristic analysis

D) A program allowing a user to specify one or more base assumptions, and then carries out an analysis of arbitrary events

228. Which of the following BEST describes an external test?

A) Executed from within the network perimeter and is designed to reveal risks from ether an internal user, or an external user that managed to get through the network perimeter

B) Requires the pen testing team to execute the simulated attack without any knowledge of the internal system, but internal staff are aware that it is happening

C) Requires the pen testing team to execute the simulated attack without any knowledge of the internal system, and internal staff are not aware that a simulated attack is being carried out

D) Executed from outside of the network's perimeter and represents an external attacker with no prior knowledge of the network

229. Which is NOT a benefit to integrated auditing?

A) Both manual and automated processes are combined

B) A single audit provides an overview of all risk an organization faces

C) Employees better understand audit goals because they see how various aspects are linked together

D) Increases staff development and retention

230. What does ISAAS have to say about being involved in an area you are auditing?

A) You are not allowed to audit an area in which you have been involved

B) There is no conflict as long as you remain objective

C) You must suspend work in that area during the audit

D) It is acceptable for you to remain engaged in that area as long as another member of the audit party is not involved in that area

231. Which aspect of the audit charter determines the recipient of the final report?

A) Purpose

B) Responsibility

C) Accountability

D) Authority

232. Which TOGAF ADM phase checks what is being built against the original architecture?

A) Opportunities and solutions phase

B) Migration planning phase

C) Business architecture phase

D) Implementation governance phase

233. Which aspect of the audit charter puts a limitation on what the auditor is able to carry out?

A) Authority

B) Purpose

C) Responsibility

D) Accountability

234. Which of the following statements BEST describes email bombing?

A) Rummaging through trash bins to retrieve information written or printed on paper

B) Looking over someone's shoulder at a computer screen or keyboard to steal information such as passwords

C) Sending a single message to hundreds or thousands of users

D) Repeatedly sending the same message to a particular address

235. Which of the following non-removable disk-based solutions BEST describes a disk-array-based replication?

A) Software living on a server that replicates changes to another server invisibly

B) Similar to host-based replication, but it is carried out at the disk array level instead of software installed on the OS

C) A solution that looks like a tape library but really uses a disk array for storage

D) Taking an image of a system, restoring onto a second system, and backing up this secondary environment

236. Which of the following statements is NOT true regarding Phase 4B?

A) This phase uses the designs created in phase 3B

B) If replacing an older system, this phase includes training users on the new system

C) Debugging and testing of the primary systems happens in this phase

D) Since this is a phase executed for purchased software, not coding occurs

237. Which BEST describes a DNS poisoning attack?

A) Compromising a DNS database

B) Redirecting browser traffic from a legitimate site to a bogus one

C) The act of stealing money by rounding down fractions

D) The act of stealing money by reducing amounts by an insignificant amount

238. Which of the following is the BEST description of a brute force attack?

A) Trying random key values until one that works is found

B) Using a single 'shared key' that both the sender and recipient know

C) Reduces the number of required brute force attempts

D) A secure email protocol that authenticates the identity of both the sender and receiver

239. Which framework provides an iterative risk assessment process that is comprised of five steps?

A) Plan-Do-Check-Act, or PDCA

B) Operationally Critical Threat Asset and Vulnerability Evaluation, or OCTAVE

C) NIST SP 800-30

D) Initiating, Diagnosing, Establishing, Acting and Learning Model, or IDEAL

240. Which value estimates how often within a single year we can expect a threat to occur?

A) SLE

B) ARO

C) ALE

D) EF

241. What are the three subdimensions of data quality?

A) Intrinsic, contextual and security/accessibility

B) Accurate, objective and believable

C) Relevant, complete and accurate

D) Intrinsic, secure and restricted

242. Which of the ISO 27000 series provides guidance on implementing an ISMS?

A) ISO 27002

B) ISO 27001

C) ISO 27004

D) ISO 27003

243. Which of the following is NOT an example of social engineering?

A) Attempting to guess the unlock code on a smartphone

B) Shoulder surfing

C) Calling someone over a phone and convincing them to give away their password

D) Dumpster diving

244. Which of the following BEST describes an IPS?

A) A weaponized IDS capable of aggressively defeating attacks

B) A real environment that can be attacked

C) A software application that pretends to be a server vulnerable to attack

D) Appears to be a normal environment

245. Which BEST describes eavesdropping?

A) Occurs when a computer sends packets that appear to be coming from another IP address

B) A situation where an attacker connects to two devices and intercepts all traffic between them

C) The act of sniffing network packets as they pass by

D) The act of modifying data without anyone noticing

246. Which of the following BEST describes a permanent virtual circuit?

A) A circuit that can be setup and torn down at any time based on the need

B) A symmetric telecommunications line permanently connecting two sides

C) A circuit that is created in real-time

D) A circuit that is setup ahead of time

247. Which of the following is NOT a key capability that a DD/DS provides?

A) A data definition language processor that allows an administrator to change the mappings between the external and conceptual schemas

B) Prevents unauthorized access to metadata

C) Allows embedded programmatic access to data

D) Validation of any DDL command to ensure integrity of the metadata is maintained

248. When dealing with network continuity, which statement BEST describes last-mile circuit protection?

A) Subscribing to two or more network service providers at the same time

B) Protecting an organization from a local disaster that takes out the communications infrastructure connected directly to a facility

C) Routing information through an alternate medium such as copper cable or fiber optics

D) Routing traffic through split or duplicate cables

249. What term describes the impact that unauthorized disclosure of an asset will have?

A) Privacy

B) Assurance

C) Sensitivity

D) Criticality

250. Which of the following BEST describes a targeted test?

A) Requires the pen testing team to execute the simulated attack without any knowledge of the internal system, but internal staff are aware that it is happening

B) Executed from within the network perimeter and is designed to reveal risks from ether an internal user, or an external user that managed to get through the network perimeter

C) Carried out with the full knowledge of staff, and the pen testing team is given information about the network design

D) Requires the pen testing team to execute the simulated attack without any knowledge of the internal system, and internal staff are not aware that a simulated attack is being carried out

251. Which of the following items is NOT normally required for each project task?

A) Required IT resources

B) How the cost will be paid for

C) Duration

D) Required HR resources

252. To prevent an issue becoming an incident to handle, and then eventually a problem to manage, what BEST describes what we should be on the lookout for?

A) Increasing support and help desk expertise

B) Enhanced monitoring of daily log reports

C) Abnormal conditions

D) A way to bolster security

253. Which of the following BEST describes assembly language?

A) Translates human-readable languages into binary code

B) The intermediate product of changing human-readable language into binary code

C) One-step above binary code

D) Instructions that a computer can understand

254. Which of the following BEST describes function testing?

A) Testing an application with full knowledge of the inner workings

B) Testing that answers the question 'Are we building the right product?'

C) Testing two versions of the same application

D) Rerunning previous tests to ensure recent changes have not broken something that used to work

255. Which of the following BEST describes a bookmark?

A) Computers that do not use any type of address translation

B) A marker or address that identifies a document or a specific place in a document

C) The connection between Internet users and the Internet service provider

D) A file that a browser stores on the local computer's hard drive

256. Which of the following BEST describes the applications staff role?

A) Develops and maintains applications that eventually run in a production capacity

B) Evaluates potential security technologies, and establishes security policies and procedures

C) Designs systems based on user needs

D) Implements the designs created by a security architect

257. Which of the following is NOT an advantage of CSA?

A) It creates employees who more ware of business goals

B) It provides controls that more IT-focused

C) It detects risk earlier

D) It develops more effective controls

258. Which of the following is NOT true regarding anti-malware solutions?

A) If you can only choose one location to place anti-malware, use a network-based solution as it has greater coverage

B) We can place detection as traffic enters the network or installed on computers

C) Network-based protection is called a malware wall

D) The goal is to detect malware before it is able to infect a computer

259. Which of the following is NOT a firewall category?

A) Stateful inspection

B) Session

C) Application

D) Packet filtering

260. Which is the BEST description of DLS?

A) Achieves higher rates because it uses all available frequencies on a UTP line

B) An older technology, it was designed to compensate by adding error checking and correcting as well as fault tolerance, resulting in a high overhead

C) A newer technology, it is a switching technology but uses cells instead of packets

D) The first truly digital connection for the masses to travel over copper phone lines

261. Which of the following is NOT a major factor that should be considered when selecting a backup method and media?

A) Select media that can be reused

B) Magnetic media is preferable over optical

C) Assume unexpected growth and purchase media that can hold larger amounts of data than is needed

D) Use a media that is sold in volume

262. Which statement BEST describes continuous assurance?

A) When both continuous monitoring and continuous auditing are taking place

B) When either continuous monitoring or continuous auditing is taking place

C) When management of the continuous monitoring and continuous auditing processes are under the same group

D) When the continuous monitoring process automatically feeds into the continuous auditing process

263. Which is NOT a major disadvantage of virtualization?

A) Context switching of processing power between VMs is costly

B) If the hypervisor runs into performance issues, all hosted OSs suffer as well

C) It is possible for one VM to access memory belonging to another VM

D) The host is now a single point of failure

264. Which of the following is NOT an attribute that a good policy will exhibit?

A) Is part of a set that is no more than ten in number

B) States only a single general mandate

C) Clearly describes a strategy

D) Is only a few sentences long

265. Which of the following statements is NOT true media handling?

A) Computers holding confidential information should not be sent out for repair unless storage devices have been removed

B) Magnetic tapes are the preferred medium for data banks

C) Encryption keys should never be stored on removable media

D) The same level of security should be applied to backups as to the originals

266. What is NOT a term used to describe a control that oversees or reports on a process?

A) Supportive

B) Procedural

C) Administrative

D) Managerial

267. Which of the following is NOT true regarding problem management?

A) If we find ourselves spending too much time with problem management, then we should start focusing on handling incidents

B) When escalating an issue, the documentation should reflect if the problem can wait until working hours

C) It attempts to find root cause

D) Its primary goal is to reduce the number or severity of incidents

268. Which of the following is the BEST description of CRL?

A) A list of invalid certificates

B) Something that tells us how a CA validates authenticity

C) Confirms that an entity is the real owner of a public key

D) Confirms that you are a real person or company

269. What COBIT 5 approach measures how aligned data values are with the true values?

A) Intrinsic Qualities

B) Goals cascade

C) Process Assessment Model, or PAM

D) Process Reference Model

270. Which off the following items is NOT normally contained in a BCP?

A) Continuity of operations plan

B) Strategy resumption plan

C) Business resumption plan

D) The DRP

271. Which control method physically restricts access to a facility or hardware?

A) Administrative

B) Procedural

C) Technical

D) Physical

272. When auditing the implementation phase, which of the following is NOT a major focus area?

A) Review all system documentation and make sure that any changes resulting from the testing phase have been implemented

B) Reviewing the program schedule and parameters for kicking off the various processes

C) Ensure cost/benefits forecast in the feasibility study are being measured

D) Check that all data conversion results are correct before placing the system into production

273. Which of the following BEST describes an appliance?

A) A server that sits between an end-user and a resource, and makes requests to the resource on the user's behalf

B) A server that is dedicated to a single function and normally is not capable of being extended

C) A server that stores data and acts as a repository for information

D) A server that hosts the software programs that networked consumers utilize

274. Which of the following laws and regulations apply to privacy?

A) The US-EU Safe Harbor Framework

B) The European Union Data Protection Directives

C) OECD Guidelines on the Protection of Privacy and Transborder Flows of Personal Data

D) SIRS Privacy Rules for Financial Institutions

275. Which control category remediates or reverses an impact after it has been felt?

A) Detective

B) Preventative

C) Deterrent

D) Corrective

276. Which of the following descriptions BEST describes parametric estimating?

A) The quickest estimation technique, and uses estimates from prior projects

B) Estimates the cost of each activity in the current project, and sums the results

C) Looks at previous estimates of employee hours, materials cost and technology, and uses statistics to extrapolate those estimates to our current project

D) Looks at the raw costs in a previous project and extrapolates to the current project

277. Which of the following BEST describes the data entry role?

A) The process of entering information into a system manually, using a batch process or online

B) Collects and converts incoming information and ensures the proper distribution to the user community

C) Controls all information stored on removable media

D) Controls industrial machinery spread out over large areas

278. What is the term describing a single real-world instance of a vulnerability being exploited?

A) Threat

B) Risk

C) Impact

D) Exposure

279. Which of the following is NOT a common e-Commerce model?

A) B2C

B) B2E

C) B2D

D) B2G

280. What is the BEST description of hybrid?

A) Having one or more outside parties perform the entire function.

B) When all work is performed remotely in a different geographic region.

C) When the function is split between in-house and one or more outside parties.

D) When all work being performed at a remote location in the same geographic area.

281. In OOSD, which of the following statements BEST describes polymorphism?

A) Extending a class through another class

B) Having two identical objects behave differently by changing their internal data structures

C) The ability of a child instance to do something different than a parent instance would do

D) The instantiation of a pattern

282. Which of the following is NOT a valid way in which an OS protects itself?

A) It can isolate individual processes

B) It can shut down peripherals to prevent improper access

C) It can prevent both deliberate and accidental modifications

D) It can ensure that privileged programs cannot be interfered with by user-level programs

283. What is the BEST description of onsite?

A) When all work is performed onsite in the IT department.

B) When all work being performed at a remote location in the same geographic area.

C) When the function is split between in-house and one or more outside parties.

D) When the function is fully performed by the company's staff.

284. Which of the following BEST describes a database server?

A) A server that hosts the software programs that networked consumers utilize

B) A server that sits between an end-user and a resource, and makes requests to the resource on the user's behalf

C) A server that is dedicated to a single function and normally is not capable of being extended

D) A server that stores data and acts as a repository for information

285. Which of the following BEST describes a robust security network?

A) Marginally better than its predecessor

B) The first real security for wireless traffic

C) Any infrastructure secured using WPA2

D) Only have to know the SSID and authenticate using an extremely weak protocol

286. Which value estimates how much we value can expect to lose during one occurrence of a threat?

A) ARO

B) SLE

C) EF

D) ALE

287. Which of the following BEST describes gaining access by using piggybacking?

A) Capturing legitimate packets passing by on a network, and then sending them back

B) An attack executed across the Internet against web applications

C) Guessing passwords to gain access to a system by simply rotating through all possible values until the system grants access

D) A physical attack where an unauthorized person closely follows an authorized person through a secured gate or door

288. Which of the following BEST describes an infrastructure WLAN?

A) A wireless network in which the AP is also connected to another network

B) A wireless network made up of two computers talking to each other over wireless cards

C) A wireless network in which both computers are connected to an access point instead of each other

D) A frequency range within wireless traffic

289. What term represents how many times in 100 a subset of data points represents the entire set?

A) Confidence level

B) Sample

C) Population

D) Precision

290. Which of the following items is NOT contained within the CPU?

A) Control unit

B) ALU

C) Internal memory

D) RAM

291. Which framework defines the architecture development method, or ADM?

A) Risk IT Framework

B) The Open Group Architecture Framework, or TOGAF

C) ISO 27000 Series

D) Information Technology Infrastructure Library, or ITIL

292. Which is not a type of threat commonly encountered?

A) Man-made

B) Technical

C) Managerial

D) Environmental

293. Which of the following is a common sub-policy published as part of an information security policy?

A) Media Disposition Policy

B) New Hire Vetting Policy

C) Backup and Retention Policy

D) Access Control Policy

294. Which of the following BEST describes data-at-rest?

A) Information that is being manipulated by end users at their workstation

B) Any information persisted to storage such as hard drives, USB drives, tape backups or in live databases

C) Any information moving around a network or being transferred between two processes

D) Applications deployed to log onto each system and look through the various data stores

295. You are the sole auditor and find that the audit scope is too wide for a single person to accomplish in the given time period. Which of the following is the BEST way to overcome this risk without reducing the scope?

A) Require management increase risk acceptance

B) Outsource the work to third-party contractors

C) Keep detailed progress records, and when the allocated time is reached use the documentation to negotiate for additional time

D) Use a control self-assessment

296. What three security guarantees does a digital signature provide?

A) Confidentiality, authentication and availability

B) Confidentiality, authentication and integrity

C) Authentication, integrity and availability

D) Authentication, integrity and nonrepudiation

297. Which of the following statements BEST describes BYOD?

A) An encrypted area of a mobile device used to keep sensitive data separate from personal data

B) A system to track the location of mobile devices

C) A device owned by an employee but used for work purposes

D) A system to manage employee-owned devices

298. Which of the following is the BEST way to ensure an attacker cannot alter log file information in order to cover his or her tracks?

A) Duplicate log files in two separate locations

B) Ensure log files are write-only

C) Protect log files with supervisory access only

D) Log information to a separate secured server

299. Which of the following BEST describes a bridge?

A) A device that connects LAN segments

B) A device that filters traffic based on the MAC Addresses

C) A device that amplifies a signal and has multiple ports

D) A device that simply amplifies a signal and forwards it on.

300. Which of the following BEST describes a combination door lock?

A) A lock requiring electric power

B) A lock made of strengthened steel

C) A lock requiring a metal key to open

D) A lock that uses a numeric key pad or dial

301. When working with sampling, which one of the following statements is true?

A) If the value of all data points is relatively close, then we can expect less precision, and the larger the sample size will need to be

B) The less confident we need to be in the result, the smaller the sample size can get

C) The more confident we want to be in the result, the more we will need to decrease the sample size

D) The more variable the data is, the more precision we can expect, and we therefore need to decrease the sample size to get a good result

302. Which of the following languages is considered to be a 3rd generation language?

A) FOCUS

B) Tcl

C) COBOL

D) Assembly

303. Which of the following metrics is NOT used for capacity management?

A) Hiring trends as provided by HR

B) Current utilization of CPU, computer storage, and network bandwidth

C) New technologies and applications becoming available

D) The number of active users

304. Which of the following BEST describes a hub?

A) A device that connects LAN segments

B) A device that amplifies a signal and has multiple ports

C) A device that simply amplifies a signal and forwards it on.

D) A device that filters traffic based on the MAC Addresses

305. What is the BEST reason that Bluetooth s a special risk?

A) Signals can be passively intercepted and recorded

B) It has no built-in encryption

C) The Bluetooth transmitter power cannot be attenuated

D) Discoverable mode is often left enabled

306. Which of the following BEST describes a water-based system?

A) Always has water under pressure in the pipes

B) The extinguisher sprays the agent directly on the fire

C) Does not contain water in the pipes until the system is activated

D) Can cause considerable collateral damage to equipment when activated

307. When working with sampling, which one of the following statements is true?

A) The more confident we want to be in the result, the more we will need to increase the sample size

B) The less confident we need to be in the result, the larger the sample size can get

C) The more variable the data is, the more precision we can expect, and we therefore need to decrease the sample size to get a good result

D) If the value of all data points is relatively close, then we can expect less precision, and the larger the sample size will need to be

308. Which of the following BEST describes IT Baseline Protection Catalogs?

A) A specification for service management that is aligned with ITIL

B) A process-based security model for IT

C) Created in the UK and provides a very hands-on and detailed framework on implementing GEIT

D) A German collection of documents useful for detecting and addressing security weaknesses in an IT environment

309. Which of the following is NOT a common weakness in the identification and authentication process?

A) It requires the credentials to be stored, opening up the possibility that they could be stolen or compromised if not properly secured

B) Weak authentication methods such as short or easy to guess passwords make authentication simple to overcome

C) Multi-factor authentication is seldom implemented

D) The credentials are almost always passed over a network, and if not properly encrypted could easily be stolen by someone sniffing the network

310. When establishing a security baseline, which of the following areas is NOT an area an auditor would focus on?

A) Malware

B) System services

C) Inventory

D) Disaster recovery

311. Which description BEST describes a hypervisor?

A) Software that manages multiple virtual machines

B) Hardware that hosts multiple virtual machines and coordinates communication between each

C) Hardware that allows multiple virtual machines to exit simultaneously

D) Software that runs on the network to ensure virtual machines can access resources only as-needed

312. Which of the statements below is NOT true regarding 4th generation languages?

A) They often allow non-programmers to use them

B) They are portable

C) All input is provided as parameters when invoking code

D) They are non-procedural

313. Which of the following BEST describes a supercomputer?

A) Designed for individual users and use microprocessor technologies

B) A very large, very expensive computer that represents that fastest processing available

C) A multiprocessing system that can support thousands of users at the same time

D) A large, general-purpose computer that is designed to share its capabilities with thousands of users at the same time

314. Which of the following BEST describes an opportunist?

A) A person who happens upon unprotected information and decides to take advantage of the situation

B) A party having an increased access but does not possess any loyalty that an employee might have

C) Someone who is not a skilled individual, but simply uses tools created by others to break into systems

D) A skilled person who is interested in proving how smart they are by breaking into systems

315. Which of the following biometric terms best describes signature dynamics?

A) A complete record of ridges and valley on a finger

B) The speed and movements produced when signing a name

C) The speed and pauses between each keypress as a password is typed

D) A number of words recorded during enrollment

316. Which of the following is NOT a common concern for mobile devices?

A) Mixing of business and personal data

B) Bluetooth attacks

C) Wireless networks are required

D) Theft outside of the business walls

317. Which statement is NOT true concerning SLAs?

A) A valid goal for an SLA might be a reduction in the number of help desk calls

B) An SLA can provide either penalties or bonuses in same agreement, but not both

C) The power of an SLA kicks in when a provider fails to meet the minimum stipulations

D) SLAs often reference external standards when defining minimum requirements

318. What is the BEST definition for a measured service?

A) Services are available at 100% up to a pre-defined level, after which the services are maintained in a reduced capacity

B) Customer are only charged for what they use

C) A flat rate is charged to the customer unless service levels exceed the SLA threshold

D) The customer is charged based on average use across an extended time-period

319. During the design phase of a 'buy' project, which of the following items is NOT a major focus for the auditor?

A) If the proper controls are being designed into the system

B) If a formal software change process is being used

C) If continuous online auditing if being built as part of the system

D) If different data is being used for each set of tests

320. Which of the following is the BEST definition for GEIT?

A) The process of establishing strategy, identifying the goals to achieve that strategy, and managing risk and resources so the goals are reached

B) Providing incentives for the senior management and the board to do what is best for the company

C) The system by which business corporations are directed and controlled

D) A system in which all stakeholders are part of the decision-making process, and is specific to IT

321. Which of the following is NOT an action an auditor would execute when looking for privacy issues?

A) Identify information that is not directly associated with PII

B) Identify legislative, regulatory and contractual requirements for privacy

C) Ensure that accountability for privacy issues exists

D) Document how this information is collected, used, disclosed to the individual, and destroyed

322. Which of the following statements is NOT true concerning CAAT?

A) It allows an auditor to act without the help of the subject

B) GAS is one category of CAAT

C) It is an audit tool geared specifically to pull electronic data from information systems

D) Most CAATs do not allow downloading a copy of production data

323. Which OSI layer(s) does the TCP Network Access layer map to?

A) Layers 2 and 1

B) Layer 3

C) Layer 2

D) Layer 1

324. Which of the following BEST describes a per workstation license?

A) Allows unlimited use of the software throughout an entire organization

B) Used to install software on a single computer and allow any number of users to access it, which effectively means one user at a time.

C) Charged according to the number of login accounts

D) Used when multiple end-users will be using the software

325. Which of the following is NOT a disadvantage of outsourcing?

A) Loss of internal IT experience

B) A commitment to service availability is difficult to achieve

C) Costs that often exceed expectations

D) Loss or leakage of information

326. If a company does not officially recognize a CISO role and assign it to a specific individual, what is the most LIKELY result?

A) The security auditor will ultimately lack the authority to carry out an effective audit

B) Security goals will not align with business goals

C) Security and IT functions will report up through the same management chain

D) Major security incidents will not be handled appropriately

327. Which of the following BEST describes a charged water-based system?

A) Can cause considerable collateral damage to equipment when activated

B) The extinguisher sprays the agent directly on the fire

C) Does not contain water in the pipes until the system is activated

D) Always has water under pressure in the pipes

328. When looking at LAN security, which of the following areas is the LEAST important?

A) Computer applications used on the LAN

B) Users or groups having privileged access rights

C) The LAN topology and network design

D) How the business takes advantage of SSO

329. What type of application does not normally follow the software development life cycle and provides different views of data in ways that optimize performance?

A) Business-focused applications

B) User-acceptable applications

C) Organization-centric applications

D) End-user-centric applications

330. Which of the following BEST describes a relational database?

A) Is built with big data in mind

B) The data is comprised of 'sets', with each set having a single owner node and one or more member nodes

C) Data is stored in a parent/child relationship

D) All data is organized into one or more tables

331. What does SaaS stand for?

A) Solution as a Service

B) Security as a Service

C) Software as a Service

D) Shareware as a Service

332. When dealing with network continuity, which statement BEST describes redundancy?

A) Subscribing to two or more network service providers at the same time

B) Routing information through an alternate medium such as copper cable or fiber optics

C) Routing traffic through split or duplicate cables

D) Providing fail-over systems automatically

333. Which of the following is NOT a category of utility programs?

A) Those that understand application systems

B) Those that check data quality

C) Those that assess security vulnerabilities

D) Those that test a program's ability to function properly

334. Which term describes the amount of deviation form acceptable risk a business considers acceptable?

A) Risk tolerance

B) Risk acceptance

C) Risk appetite

D) Risk capacity

335. Which of the following BEST describes a concurrent users license?

A) A fee is charged for each CPU core running on the computer on which the software is installed

B) Used when multiple end-users will be using the software

C) Charged according to the number of users simultaneously using the system

D) Charged according to the number of login accounts

336. Which of the following is NOT a primary variable used with encryption systems?

A) Input data

B) Key

C) Algorithm

D) Key length

337. What are the three processes used with GEIT?

A) HR resource management, IT performance measurement and corporate compliance management

B) Standards, performance, and compliance

C) System management, process measurement and compliance management

D) IT resource management, performance measurement and compliance management

338. Which of the following areas is NOT a focus when auditing job scheduling?

A) Exception processing logs

B) If each job is required

C) Re-execution of jobs is carried out properly

D) That job priorities are assigned properly

339. Which of the following statements BEST describes email spoofing?

A) The use of an email to trick a person into giving away valuable information

B) The use of an email to trick a specific group of people with highly-targeted content into giving away valuable information

C) An email appears to come from an authoritative email address but in reality, was sent from an attacker

D) Calling someone over a phone and convincing them to give away their password

340. Which of the following is NOT a use the auditor should look at when auditing a company's Internet presence?

A) Information gathering

B) Marketing

C) Email

D) Personal social media use

341. Which of the following BEST describes the warehouse management layer of BI?

A) Allows all other components to communicate using browser-based interfaces

B) Knows how to communicate between each vertical layer

C) Data about data

D) Schedules tasks required to build, maintain and populate the warehouse

342. Which of the following is NOT a common attribute of a PBX?

A) Each trunk line carries one phone line

B) It supports an operator console or switchboard for a human operator

C) It supports digital phones that can integrate both voice and data together

D) It is computer-based and scalable to support call routing in-memory

343. Which of the ISO 27000 series is the one for which most businesses attain a certification?

    A) ISO 27004

    B) ISO 27002

    C) ISO 27003

    D) ISO 27001

344. Which BEST describes performance testing?

    A) Increasing the number of active users until the system fails

    B) Simulating a heavy amount of traffic during peak areas

    C) Incrementally increasing the size of the database until the application fails

    D) Comparing the system's performance to well-defined benchmarks

345. What BEST describes the advantage of using roles?

    A) They provide an easy way to identify HR security gaps

    B) They go great with turkey and dressing

    C) They allow a single individual to take on multiple responsibilities

    D) They simplify security administration

346. Which of the following is NOT true regarding circuit-switching and packet switching?

    A) Circuit switching establish a complete return path, while packet switching is one-way only

    B) Circuit switching provides a constant stream rate, while packet switching can introduce additional latency

    C) The path for a circuit switch is defined before data is sent, while the path for a packet switch is assigned based on network conditions

    D) Circuit switching is less reliable, while packet switching implements redundancy

347. Which BEST describes a zombie?

    A) A denial attack that is launched from many compromised computers

    B) A compromised computer

    C) Uses compromised computers to carry out a distributed attack

    D) A collection of previously compromised computers

348. What are the five possible options when responding to risk?

    A) Accept, diminish, avoid, shift, disregard

    B) Accept, mitigate, avoid, transfer, ignore

    C) Accept, diminish, avoid, transfer, disregard

    D) Accept, mitigate, avoid, shift, ignore

349. What is the BEST description of nearshore?

    A) Having one or more outside parties perform the entire function.

    B) When all work is performed remotely in a different geographic region.

    C) When all work being performed at a remote location in the same geographic area.

    D) When the function is split between in-house and one or more outside parties.

350. Which value reflects the amount of time normal operations are down before the company faces financial threats to its existence?

    A) MTO

    B) AIW

    C) MTD

    D) RTO

351. Which of the following BEST describes a data storage device that writes data to multiple disks simultaneously?

    A) DAS

    B) RAID

    C) NAS

    D) RAND

352. Which of the following BEST describes a key business driver?

A) One of the major attributes of a business function that helps reach a company goal

B) The primary impetus forcing a change in corporate values

C) A significant factor examined when selecting a business function

D) The reason behind changes within an industry

353. Which IT Balanced Scorecard, or IT BSC, perspective defines the goals to achieve?

A) Sources

B) Mission

C) Strategies

D) Measures

354. What of the following is NOT a drawback of the prototyping approach?

A) Change control mechanisms are often weak

B) Scope-creep is a common occurrence

C) The rapid pace often results in unwanted features

D) Fundamentals such as backup and recovery methods are often left out

355. What is one thing that ITAF does NOT provide?

A) Defines procedures and process

B) Provides guidance, as well as tools and techniques

C) Establishes standards

D) Defines terms and concepts

356. Which term describes the amount of risk a business is willing to incur?

A) Risk capacity

B) Risk tolerance

C) Risk appetite

D) Risk acceptance

357. Which of the following is NOT a perspective used in the Balanced Scorecard?

A) Business

B) Process

C) Learning

D) Customer

358. Which COBIT 5 intrinsic quality measures how true and credible a value is?

A) Reputation

B) Believability

C) Accuracy

D) Objectivity

359. Which of the following BEST describes a full mesh topology?

A) All nodes are connected directly to each other

B) Any combination of token ring, bus or star topologies

C) All nodes are connected directly to a central device

D) All nodes are physically connected in a ring

360. Which of the following is NOT an established method to mitigate risks for PBXs?

A) Disable dedicated administrative ports

B) Establish control over the numbers destined for fax machines and modems

C) Block controls for long-distance phone calls to particular numbers such as cell numbers

D) Configure DID lines to avoid an external party requesting a local dial tone

361. Which control category provides warnings that can stop a potential compromise?

A) Detective

B) Preventative

C) Compensating

D) Deterrent

362. What is the BEST description of a minor release?

A) A release that contains small enhancements and fixes

B) A release that addresses a small list of customer complaints

C) A release that prevents significant downtime or impact to the customer

D) A release that contains significant changes to existing functionality or the addition of new features

363. Which BEST describes a man-in-the-middle attack?

A) The act of modifying data without anyone noticing

B) A situation where an attacker connects to two devices and intercepts all traffic between them

C) Occurs when the attacker waits around while a valid user or machine authenticates itself, and then assumes the authenticated identity

D) The act of sniffing network packets as they pass by

364. SNMP

A) Operates at the data link or network level and often recommend possible solutions to issues

B) Validates that all data sent to a host is returned with no lost data

C) Monitors packets flowing along a link and produces network usage reports

D) A TCP/IP-based protocol that monitors and controls different variables throughout the network

365. What IT risk management level are we operating at when considering how well IT capabilities are aligned with the business strategy?

A) Strategic

B) Procedural

C) Project

D) Operational

366. What type of segregation of duty control can be implemented using physical, system and application controls?

A) Custody of assets

B) Transaction authorization

C) Access to data

D) Principle of least privilege

367. When dealing with sampling, which term BEST describes the model that estimates the variance between audited data points and what the 'books' claim?

A) Stratified mean per unit

B) Difference estimation

C) Sample standard deviation

D) Unstratified mean per unit

368. Which value estimates the amount of data we can stand to permanently lose in terms of time?

A) RTO

B) MTO

C) RPO

D) SDO

369. Which of the following is the BEST definition of a social context?

A) A project's unique communication paths relative to the organization and other parallel projects

B) The intervals between components in which work is not executed

C) The overall project calendar that includes 'pre' and 'post' activities

D) The method in which a project's value is shared to stakeholders

370. Which of the following security planning roles BEST describes a nonsecurity technical specialists?

A) Acts as the liaison to business process owners

B) Communicates to other departments such as legal, human resources, and public relations

C) Provides assistance based on subject matter expertise

D) Detects, investigates, contains and recovers from incidents

371. Which of the following is NOT an asymmetric algorithm weakness?

A) It is slower than a symmetric algorithm

B) Key lengths must be greater than 128 bits long

C) An attacker could intercept the entire message and simply replay it later with no modifications

D) It is susceptible to a man-in-the-middle attack

372. Which of the following BEST describes security awareness training?

A) The process of teaching security skills to security personnel

B) The process of spreading the need for security awareness throughout an organization

C) The process of explaining security issues to all members of an organization

D) The process of testing security hygiene within a department

373. Which of the following BEST describes a binary code?

A) Signals executed at the hardware layer

B) Instructions that a computer can understand

C) Codes used to represent complex instructions

D) The intermediate product of changing human-readable language into machine-readable code

374. Which of the following statements BEST describes data mining?

A) Preparing a data set for subsequent analysis by creating the proper indexing and collated attributes

B) Exploring large amounts of data to find patterns and trends

C) Sifting through metadata to filter out non-legitimate data

D) Importing data sets not created by the business but needed to complete a proper analysis

375. At which OSI layer do we find TCP addresses?

A) The Session layer

B) The Network layer

C) The Transport layer

D) The Presentation layer

376. You are presenting the audit findings with lower levels of management, who ask you to help with implementing the recommended control enhancements. What is the BEST course of action for you to take?

A) Agree to help once upper management has accepted the findings

B) Decline the offer since it would call into question your objectivity

C) Decline the offer, as being able to execute an audit does not qualify a person to implement the findings

D) Agree to help on the condition that upper management approves.

377. Which of the following BEST describes a network access server?

A) Provides direct connections for WAN links

B) Allows only VPN connections at a single point in the network

C) Supports direct modem connections

D) Accepts incoming connections and handles authentication and access control

378. Which of the following statements BEST describes email spamming?

A) Repeatedly sending the same message to a particular address

B) Looking over someone's shoulder at a computer screen or keyboard to steal information such as passwords

C) Rummaging through trash bins to retrieve information written or printed on paper

D) Sending a single message to hundreds or thousands of users

379. Which of the following is NOT an area that is a focus of service-level management?

A) Operator work schedules

B) Exception reports

C) Customer confidence levels

D) Operator problem reports

380. Which of the following is NOT a function commonly performed by a firewall?

A) Block internal access to external sites

B) Encrypting packets for VPN access

C) Logging activity both ways

D) Inspecting payloads for malware

381. Which BEST describes recovery testing?

A) Increasing the number of active users until the system fails

B) Simulating a heavy amount of traffic during peak areas

C) Ensuring the system can return to a working state after a hardware of software failure

D) Incrementally increasing the size of the database until the application fails

382. Which of the following is a valid batch balancing control?

A) Transaction logs

B) Computer agreement

C) Online access controls

D) Workstation ID

383. Which of the following is NOT a 4GL category?

A) WISE-capable generators

B) Relational database 4GLs

C) Query and report generators

D) Application generators

384. Which of the following BEST describes ISO 27001?

A) Developed by ISACA and is intended to ensure IT goals align with business goals, resources are used properly, and that risk is being effectively managed

B) Created in the UK and provides a very hands-on and detailed framework on implementing GEIT

C) A series of standards that help an organization implement and maintain an information security program, and is the standard to which most companies are certified against

D) A specification for service management that is aligned with ITIL

385. What is NOT a risk when using EDI?

A) Ensuring continuity and availability of the EDI exchange process

B) The lack of authentication for electronic exchange, resulting in the difficulty in knowing who is submitting data packets

C) A lack of legal agreements surrounding the exchange of electronic data, increasing the uncertainty of which party is legally liable for failures

D) Transmission mistakes can often go unnoticed for long periods of time

386. Which of the following BEST describes a data dictionary?

A) Can be viewed or printed only

B) Describes each field's use and characteristics

C) Provides the capability to validate and format the contents

D) Dictates attributes to be indexed

387. Which of the following BEST describes a HIDS?

A) Is installed on a computer and monitors traffic coming into and out of the computer

B) Is installed on a computer and monitors all local traffic as well as network traffic

C) Monitors all network traffic

D) Looks at passing traffic to see if it can detect any attach patterns or unauthorized usage

388. When evaluating off-site storage, which of the following actions are NOT recommended?

A) Physically visiting the offsite storage

B) Turning on electronic equipment to ensure it is functioning

C) Comparing the offsite copy of the BCP to the most current version

D) Carrying out a detailed inventory

389. At which OSI layer do protocols such as SMTP, HTTP and DNS operate?

A) Layer 5

B) Layer 4

C) Layer 6

D) Layer 7

390. When reviewing data ownership, which of the following is NOT a focus area for an auditor?

A) If the data owner has authorized in writing access to data

B) A review of data classification

C) If proper ownership of data has been assigned and the data owner is aware of the assignment

D) A review of the various databases

391. Which of the following definitions BEST describes a highly distributed environment?

A) Security is under the direction of individuals, but the overall responsibility remains with IS management

B) Security is under the direction of individuals, but adheres to the guidelines established by IS management

C) Security is under the direction of IS management, with IS management staff maintaining a close relationship with users

D) Security is under the control of individuals

392. Which electronic payment method best protects the identity of the original sender?

A) Electronic transfer

B) Electronic deposit

C) Electronic money

D) Electronic check

393. Which is NOT an example of a distributed object technology?

A) CPR

B) CORBA

C) DCOM

D) RMI

394. Which of the following BEST describes controlled visitor access?

A) An unauthorized person following an authorized person through a secured entry

B) A control used by all incoming personnel and normally monitored by a receptionist

C) A control that uses two doors, in which the person entering must close the first door before the second door may be opened

D) Requires that all visitors be escorted by a responsible employee

395. When auditing a database, which of the following is NOT normally included?

    A) Design

    B) The physical schema

    C) Portability

    D) Interfaces

396. What are the five steps of ISACA's Risk IT framework, in order?

    A) Identify goals, identify assets, assess risk, mitigate risks, treat risk

    B) Identify goals, identify assets, assess risk, treat risk, mitigate risks

    C) Identify assets, identify goals assess risk, mitigate risks, treat risk

    D) Identify goals, assess risk, identify assets, mitigate risks, treat risk

397. Which of the following BEST describes a way to uniquely identify a single entity instance?

    A) A foreign key

    B) A primary key

    C) A relational key

    D) A key

398. Which of the following BEST describes the data custodian role?

    A) Acts as a liaison between end users and the IT team

    B) Plans and executes IS projects, manages the associated budget and reports progress to the appropriate management

    C) Responsible for programmers and analysts who implement and maintain systems

    D) Responsible for storing and safeguarding data

399. Which of the following BEST describes operational data in the data source layer of BI?

    A) Data needed by end users but is not currently in an accessible format

    B) Data provided by a source external to the company

    C) Data provided by systems external to the BI system

    D) Data collected during normal business operations and normally held in easy-to-access databases

400. Which of the following BEST describes the DBA role?

    A) Is normally separate from the IT department and reports up through the CISO

    B) Defines and maintains the structure of a corporate database, and is the custodian of the company's data

    C) Responsible for maintaining multi-user computer systems including the network connecting them together

    D) Responsible for running the data center, including managing staff

401. Which of the following statements is NOT a valid reason to not accept an engagement?

    A) Management does not understand its obligations to provide required information

    B) The scope does not allow the audit to come to a reasonable conclusion

    C) It cannot be reasonably completed

    D) A department within scope of the audit does not agree with the scope

402. What is a valid alternative to deploying a countermeasure?

    A) Increase the instances of the weak control requiring a countermeasure

    B) Adjusting the budget to offset the potential cost

    C) Re-engineering a process

    D) Perform an audit to justify accepting the risk

403. Which of the following is NOT a way to mitigate risk due to cloud providers crossing international borders?

A) All assets must be encrypted prior to migration to the CSP and proper key management must be in place

B) The contract should stipulate that if the CSP passes data through a region not aligned with applicable regulations, the CSP will be held liable for all subsequent damages

C) The company should request the CSP's list of infrastructure locations and verify that regulation in those locations is aligned with the enterprise's requirements

D) Terms should be included in the contract so that assets may only be moved to those areas known to be compliant with the enterprise's own regulation

404. Which of the following BEST describes an attacker taking advantage of MOS?

A) Listening in on voice activity by accessing the physical communication between the PBX and the end-user device

B) Taking advantage of an undocumented feature

C) Listening in on the active voice channel of a line placed into maintenance mode

D) Gaining physical access to a bridge and routing all signals to a specific port

405. Which standard or process BEST allows us to develop a strategy for IT based on repeating life cycles?

A) ISO 38500

B) Life Cycle Cost-Benefit Analysis

C) Root Cause Analysis

D) PRINCE2

406. Which ITIL volume is responsible for creating a service?

A) Service Design

B) Service Operations

C) Service Strategy

D) Service Transition

407. Which of the following statements BEST describes artificial intelligence?

A) A program that mimics a human's ability to process input and make intelligent decisions

B) A combination of hardware and software that is patterned after the human brain to detect patterns in seemingly random data

C) A combination of hardware and software that can pass the Turing Test

D) A program that distributes complex rule execution across many high-powered computers, resulting in an approximation of human thought

408. Which of the following is NOT a common report used with hardware monitoring?

A) Asset management report

B) Performance report

C) Availability report

D) Hardware error report

409. What is the BEST description of believability?

A) Correct and reliable

B) Highly regarded in terms of source or context

C) True and credible

D) Unbiased, unprejudiced and impartial

410. Which of the following BEST describes a neural network IDS?

A) Uses advanced mathematics to calculate aberrant behavior based on learned patterns

B) Has the capability to learn by itself what is acceptable over time

C) Must be trained to recognize normal and aberrant behavior on a given network

D) Depends on pre-defined signatures to recognize an intrusion attempt

411. Which of the following is NOT a recognized risk with software development projects?

A) Risk due to suppliers

B) Risk with the selected technology

C) Risk from within the project

D) Risk due to time constraints

412. Which of the following BEST describes the user management role?

A) Owns the project and the resulting deliverable

B) Provides funding and defines the critical success factors and metrics that determine if the project is a success

C) Provides overall direction and represents the major stakeholders

D) Shows commitment to the project by providing approval for the necessary resources to be successful

413. Which of the following tasks is NOT part of an auditor's concerns when selecting and acquiring software?

A) Encourage the project team to contact current users

B) Confirm that any contracts have been reviewed by legal representatives

C) Ensure security controls have been addressed covering audit trails and password controls

D) Determine if an appropriate level of security controls have been considered before a contract is signed.

414. Which one of the following advantages is NOT associated with observing people in performance of their duties?

A) Verifying that a person is actually carrying out their assigned duties

B) Ensure activities correspond with documented access rights

C) Verifying the individual understands and follows the correct policies and procedures

D) Ensure their job descriptions align with business goals

415. What dictates the total duration of a WP?

A) The total of all task and sub-task durations

B) The total of all task durations

C) The total of all task and sub-task durations plus slack time

D) The total of all task durations plus slack time

416. Which of the following is the BEST description of hashing?

A) A one-way encryption that results in the same length of ciphertext regardless of the plain text

B) The most common modern symmetric system

C) The most common outdated symmetric system

D) Using one key for encryption and a different key for decryption

417. Which BEST defines the term globalization?

A) Redesigning a system so it can be used in multiple locations around the world

B) Keeping a function in-house but physically housed in an overseas location to reduce costs

C) Distributing a system across multiple locations to increase availability

D) Expanding a company to operate in more than one country

418. Which of the following BEST describes a module analysis?

A) Provides adapters to connect to both the legacy and new repositories

B) A list of tasks needed to deploy legacy data to production

C) Identifying affected modules and data entities during a data migration project

D) Provides translation services between two repositories

419. Which of the following BEST describes the help desk role?

A) Tasked with managing data and the data architecture

B) The actual user of data, including both internal and external users

C) Answers technical questions and solve problems faced by internal employees

D) Responsible for daily operations related to business services

420. Which of the following BEST describes the IMAP protocol?

A) An incoming email protocol designed to work with Outlook

B) An incoming email protocol that provides security and supports multiple clients

C) An incoming email protocol with no security and that supports only a single client

D) An outgoing email protocol

421. Which of the following BEST describes throughput?

A) A measurement of the maximum number of bytes possible after compression and decompression

B) The delay that a message or packet will experience on its way from source to destination

C) A measurement of the maximum number of bytes possible through a physical medium

D) A measurement of the number of hops a packet requires between a source and destination

422. When reviewing insurance coverage, which of the following types is NOT considered to be the most important?

A) Media damage

B) Equipment replacement

C) Business interruption

D) Errors and omissions

423. Which term identifies the automated evaluation technique that allows a system to process real and test data simultaneously?

A) Continuous and intermittent simulation

B) SCARF/EAM

C) Audit hook

D) Integrated test facility

424. Which of the following is the BEST definition of a pure project organization?

A) The project manager does have official authority over the project

B) Multiple project managers share authority over the project

C) The project manager does not have official authority to manage the project

D) Project authority is shared between the project manager and department heads

425. What is the BEST description of accuracy?

A) Highly regarded in terms of source or context

B) Unbiased, unprejudiced and impartial

C) Correct and reliable

D) True and credible

426. Which of the following statements about SSO is NOT true?

A) It increases reliability

B) It can be implemented for browsers using SAML

C) It often requires multiple solutions because not all Oss support it

D) Kerberos is one of the most common implementations

427. Which framework improves software processes using five phases?

A) Initiating, Diagnosing, Establishing, Acting and Learning Model, or IDEAL

B) NIST SP 800-30

C) Plan-Do-Check-Act, or PDCA

D) Operationally Critical Threat Asset and Vulnerability Evaluation, or OCTAVE

428. What reflects the risk that information used or generated by an audit will contain material error that goes unnoticed?

A) Audit risk

B) Detection risk

C) Inherent risk

D) Control risk

429. Which type of audit is a combination of both financial and operational audits?

A) Compliance

B) Integrated

C) Operational

D) Forensic

430. Which of the following BEST describes the quality assurance role?

A) Carries out whatever duties are defined in the security policy

B) Develops and maintains standards for the IT group

C) Maintains network components such as routers, switches, firewalls and remote access

D) Maintains the systems software, including the OS, on top of which applications sit

431. When a computer crime is being carried out, which of the following descriptions BEST describes a subject?

A) A computer being used to attack a non-computer

B) The computer launching an attack when one computer attacks another

C) The computer being attacked when one computer attacks another

D) A computer used to trick a person into giving away confidential information

432. Which BEST describes the Sprague-Carlson framework?

A) A framework that employs a 2-dimensional matrix of maturity and perspectives

B) A framework that focuses on generating family trees

C) A framework that uses prototypes to evolve through each new iteration

D) A framework that looks at how structured a process is and the level of management that watches over the process

433. When auditing the testing phase for a system acquisition, which of the following is NOT an area of focus?

A) Ensure the system performs as intended

B) Make sure user requirements have been validated

C) See if internal control areas working properly

D) Ensure the final implementation adheres to the design

434. Which of the following statements is NOT true regarding asynchronous communication?

A) It does not support error detection capabilities

B) Each byte of data has a is surrounded by a start and stop bit

C) It is not as efficient as synchronous

D) It is much more forgiving when the communication path is not reliable

435. Which of the following BEST describes a signature-based IDS?

A) Must be trained to recognize normal and aberrant behavior on a given network

B) Depends on pre-defined signatures to recognize an intrusion attempt

C) Uses advanced mathematics to calculate aberrant behavior based on learned patterns

D) Has the capability to learn by itself what is acceptable over time

436. Which of the following statements BEST describes a behavior blocker?

A) Real-time detection of malware that writes to the boot sector or master boot record, or makes changes to executables

B) Attach themselves to files in the same way that malware does

C) Checks CRCs from previous runs against current CRCs to see if a file has changed

D) Mimics file by renaming themselves in the master boot record

437. Which of the following is not general use for encryption?

A) Verify the authenticity of a transaction of document

B) To prevent and detect both accidental and intentional alteration of data

C) To ensure data is not intercepted or manipulated as it is transmitted across networks

D) To enable to secure exchange of keys

438. What two states is enterprise architecture concerned with?

A) The preliminary state and the final state

B) The critical state and the stable state

C) The current state and the desired state

D) The draft state and the completed state

439. When auditing detailed the design and development document package, which of the following is NOT something an auditor should look for?

A) Changes should have been discussed and approved by appropriate user management

B) Input, processing and output controls designed into the system should be appropriate

C) Key users of the system should be generally aware of how the system will operate

D) Audit trails should be assessed to ensure traceability and accountability

440. Which of the following BEST describes the data owner role?

A) Acts as a liaison between end users and the IT team

B) Plans and executes IS projects, manages the associated budget and reports progress to the appropriate management

C) A manager or director responsible for information used to run a business

D) Responsible for programmers and analysts who implement and maintain systems

441. In relation to an expert system, which BEST describes an inference engine?

A) Facts expressed in one of several models

B) Artificial intelligence to infer relationships and arrive at a decision

C) Data that comes in from a sensor or system that is being monitored

D) Components within a system yet to be loaded with facts or rules

442. Which BEST describes spyware?

A) Malicious software that does not self-replicate or try to attach itself to other files

B) Malicious software that can alter its appearance to outwit scanners

C) Malicious software that does not cause damage other than silently listening and collecting sensitive information to send back to the attacker

D) Malicious software that usually tries to get itself appended to the end of legitimate programs on a computer

443. Which of the following is an example of 'something you know'?

A) A fingerprint

B) A voice print

C) A password

D) A token device

444. Which of the following BEST describes a named users license?

A) Charged according to the number of login accounts

B) Charged according to the number of users simultaneously using the system

C) Allows unlimited use of the software throughout an entire organization

D) Used when multiple end-users will be using the software

445. Which aspect of the audit charter provides both goal and scope?

A) Responsibility

B) Purpose

C) Authority

D) Accountability

446. Which of the following descriptions BEST describes IS operations?

A) Manages resources

B) Coordinates alignment between IT execution and corporate strategy

C) Makes sure that processes run smoothly

D) Ensures CIA, or confidentiality, integrity and availability

447. Which of the following is NOT something that an auditor would focus on when examining performance records, error log entries and help desk call logs?

A) The percentage of problems being reported outside of normal business hours

B) If a problem was encountered during processing

C) If the reasons for delays in application program processing are valid

D) If significant and recurring problems have been identified and resolved

448. Which of the following is NOT a client-server component that needs to be secured?

A) Middleware

B) Firewalls

C) Database

D) LAN

449. Which of the following BEST describes a high-or-mid-range server?

A) A multiprocessing system that can support thousands of users at the same time

B) Designed for individual users and use microprocessor technologies

C) A large, general-purpose computer that is designed to share its capabilities with thousands of users at the same time

D) A very large, very expensive computer that represents that fastest processing available

450. What security principle prevents a single resource from having too much power?

A) Access control

B) Need-to-know

C) Principle of least privilege

D) Segregation of duties

451. Which of the following BEST describes a network access point?

A) A Java applet or small program that runs within a web server environment

B) A program written in a portable, platform-independent computer language

C) A traffic concentration spot

D) An executable, machine-independent software program running on a web server

452. Which statement BEST defines continuous auditing?

A) Repeated auditing with a short time lapse between collection of evidence and reporting

B) Short time-lapses between evidence collection with continuous reporting based on automated triggers

C) Non-stop collection of evidence and continuous reporting with no lapses

D) Non-stop collection of evidence with short time-lapses between reports

453. You are performing an audit for a system implemented 2 years ago when you were a member of IT. What is your most pressing concern?

A) To view all opinions and test results as suspect in order to remain objective.

B) That you will not be an objective auditor because you were involved in implementing the system

C) That you will not be an objective auditor because of your relationships with IT personnel

D) Trying to remember the various aspects of the system

454. Which of the following is NOT true of PPP?

A) It implements encapsulation, but not framing, for a Point A to Point B connection

B) For each network protocol there will be a corresponding NCP

C) It encapsulates dissimilar protocols so that two different networks can communicate

D) LCP is used to set up the communication channel

455. Which of the following best represents the five steps, in order, for COBIT 5's Risk Management Process?

A) Evaluation of threats, asset identification, calculation of risk, evaluation of impact, evaluation of risk and response

B) Asset identification, evaluation of threats, evaluation of impact, calculation of risk, evaluation of risk and response

C) Asset identification, evaluation of threats, calculation of risk, evaluation of impact, evaluation of risk and response

D) Evaluation of threats, asset identification, evaluation of impact, calculation of risk, evaluation of risk and response

456. Which of the following BEST describes EFT?

A) Enables payments to be made through the use of virtual transactions

B) Computers that physically connect with credit card readers

C) Allows banking customers to carry out virtually all transactions from the comfort of their home

D) Focuses on providing services such as mortgage loans or insurance policies

457. Which FEA reference model describes the information used to support all other reference models?

A) Service Component Reference Model

B) Data Reference Model

C) Technical Reference Model

D) Business Reference Model

458. What occurs when we properly handle problems encountered with normal routines?

A) Reconciliation

B) Transaction logs

C) Audit trail

D) Exception reporting

459. Which FEA reference model classifies services?

    A) Service Component Reference Model

    B) Technical Reference Model

    C) Business Reference Model

    D) Data Reference Model

460. Which of the following statements BEST describes why asset classification is so important?

    A) So that we do not waste effort protecting resources in ways that do not help

    B) Because it increases operational efficiencies

    C) So that we can ensure our internal assets align with business goals

    D) Because the DRP and BCP require assets to be classified in order to prioritize recovery and restoration activities

461. When using EA from a business perspective, what of the following BEST describes the two things it attempts to understand?

    A) The IT function and the business strategy

    B) Individual and management capabilities

    C) The core mission and supporting processes

    D) When to keep processes in-house, and when to outsource them

462. Which BEST describes an IP spoofing attack?

    A) The act of modifying data without anyone noticing

    B) Occurs when a computer sends packets that appear to be coming from another IP address

    C) A situation where an attacker connects to two devices and intercepts all traffic between them

    D) The act of sniffing network packets as they pass by

463. When dealing with a business in a heavily-regulated industry, what are the two audit areas most affected by regulations?

    A) Legal requirements placed on the audit and the business being audited

    B) Legal requirements placed on the auditor's credentials and the business being audited

    C) Legal requirements placed on the auditor's credentials and financial IT systems being audited

    D) Legal requirements placed on the audit and financial IT systems being audited

464. Which of the following BEST describes a remote access server?

    A) Allows only VPN connections at a single point in the network

    B) Accepts incoming connections and handles authentication and access control

    C) Supports direct modem connections

    D) Provides direct connections for WAN links

465. Which of the following is the BEST description of a Middle CASE tool?

    A) Produces production-ready capabilities

    B) Documents detailed designs such as screen and report layouts, editing rules and process flows

    C) Documents business and application requirements such as data object definitions, relationships and processes.

    D) Generates program code and database schemas

466. Which of the following is NOT a primary component of PPP?

    A) User authentication

    B) NCP

    C) LCP

    D) IPX

467. What BEST describes a risk-based audit?

A) A type of audit in which the largest sources of risk is transferred to third-parties

B) An audit designed to identify risk caused by external sources only

C) A process to examine risk and existing controls

D) A process to reduce most risk by carrying out mitigation activities up-front

468. Of the recognized opportunities to communicate to team members at project start, which one is the preferred method?

A) Kick-off meetings

B) Project wiki standup

C) Project start workshops

D) One-on-on-one meetings

469. After carrying out a risk analysis, what is the next step an auditor should take?

A) Make sure logistic issues are settled

B) Set the scope and goals

C) Assign people resources

D) Create the audit strategy

470. Which is the BEST definition of a negligible incident?

A) An incident that can have a serious material impact on the continued functioning of the business and is often proportional to the length of the incident

B) An incident that results in a negative material impact on business processes and may affect other systems, departments of customers

C) An incident that produces no negative material or financial impact

D) An incident that causes no significant damage

471. Which of the following biometric terms best describes keystroke dynamics?

A) A number of words recorded during enrollment

B) The speed and movements produced when signing a name

C) The speed and pauses between each keypress as a password is typed

D) A complete record of ridges and valley on a finger

472. Which statement BEST describes pandemic planning?

A) Dealing with outbreaks of infectious diseases that can impact humans

B) Planning for all phases of a disaster from first report to final disposition

C) Planning for disasters across all departments of a company

D) Accommodating scenarios in which vendors a company is dependent on are no longer available

473. Which of the following BEST describes Telnet?

A) A protocol used to transfer files over a TCP/IP network

B) A third party that provides individuals and enterprises with access to the Internet

C) A standard terminal emulation protocol used for remote terminal connections

D) The standard email protocol on the Internet.

474. Which of the following is NOT true regarding network cabling?

A) Cross-talk is increased with shielded cables

B) The only difference between unshielded and shielded twisted pair cables is an additional sheath around the wires

C) Twisted pair cabling is more susceptible to wiretapping than fiber-optic cabling

D) Parallel runs of twisted pair should be avoided

475. Which of the following BEST describes a mainframe?

A) A large, general-purpose computer that is designed to share its capabilities with thousands of users at the same time

B) Designed for individual users and use microprocessor technologies

C) A very large, very expensive computer that represents that fastest processing available

D) A multiprocessing system that can support thousands of users at the same time

476. Which of the following BEST describes a statistical-based IDS?

A) Has the capability to learn by itself what is acceptable over time

B) Uses advanced mathematics to calculate aberrant behavior based on learned patterns

C) Depends on pre-defined signatures to recognize an intrusion attempt

D) Must be trained to recognize normal and aberrant behavior on a given network

477. Which is the BEST method to avoid a conflict of interest within an audit?

A) Have the members of the audit report directly to the highest level of management

B) Never use internal IT as sources of evidence

C) Ensure that final reports are delivered to all management levels, not just the top

D) Use an external party to review all relevant documentation

478. Which group BEST describes those responsible should fraud occur?

A) The IT department

B) The legal department

C) Top-level executives

D) Management

479. What is NOT a benefit delivered through business continuity?

A) It tells us how to handle the disasters that slip through

B) It enables us to recover once the disaster has ended

C) It allows us to prevent most disasters from happening to our business

D) It prepares us to overcome competition by being prepared for a disaster

480. You are carrying out an audit in which there are too many transactions to look at. What is the BEST automated evaluation technique to use?

A) Integrated test facility

B) Continuous and intermittent simulation

C) Audit Hook

D) Snapshot

481. When auditing application controls, what is NOT a duty the auditor performs?

A) Require the proper amount of documentation to be created

B) Examine APIs

C) Create a data flow diagram

D) Create a test strategy based on strengths and weaknesses

482. Which BEST describes an approach to creating a real-world process?

A) Guideline

B) Framework

C) Standard

D) Process

483. Which of the following BEST describes the data mart layer of BI?

A) Where the results of data preparation are stored

B) Contains the logic necessary to prepare data from the warehouse

C) The point at which end-users interact with the system

D) Contains the bulk of interesting data, and is usually a relational database

484. Which BEST describes the two primary needs an agile development method is meant to address?

A) Ensure requirements are complete before start, and to provide maximum documentation

B) Ensure resources are available before start, and allow for unknown requirements

C) Execute before requirements are known, and react quickly to changes

D) Provide reasonable timeline expectations, and keep cost overruns to a minimum

485. Which of the following is the BEST description of an Upper CASE tool?

A) Documents detailed designs such as screen and report layouts, editing rules and process flows

B) Documents business and application requirements such as data object definitions, relationships and processes.

C) Generates program code and database schemas

D) Produces production-ready capabilities

486. Which TOGAF ADM phase creates the roadmap?

A) Business architecture phase

B) Implementation governance phase

C) Opportunities and solutions phase

D) Migration planning phase

487. Which of the following BEST describes a dual-homed firewall?

A) A computer that is physically connected to two or more different private networks by multiple network interfaces

B) An application firewall that uses a proxy server for each protocol

C) An application firewall that uses only one proxy server for all traffic

D) A computer that is physically connected to only two private networks

488. Which of the following statements is TRUE regarding the auditor's role in CSA?

A) CSA can decrease the auditor's role and value to a company

B) The auditor should take full advantage of software that will move the process along faster

C) The auditor should not see themselves as simply a facilitator, but should remain in complete control of the entire process

D) The auditor should avoid group decisions

489. Which of the following items is NOT required for continuous auditing to succeed?

A) Alarms that trigger on control failures

B) Cost-effective controls

C) A high degree of automation

D) Technically proficient auditors

490. When auditing a security awareness training program, which of the following is likely NOT an area in which an auditor will focus?

A) Performing spot checks and quizzes to how well employees respond

B) Checking to see if training starts with new employee orientation

C) Interviewing a sample of employees to determine their overall awareness

D) Ensuring that employee awareness is reinforced using company newsletters, visible security enforcement and reminders during staff meetings

491. Which of the following BEST describes an Internet link?

A) Computers that do not use any type of address translation

B) A file that a browser stores on the local computer's hard drive

C) The connection between Internet users and the Internet service provider

D) A marker or address that identifies a document or a specific place in a document

492. Which of the following is NOT a valid technical control to help with malware?

A) Use a hardware-based password, such as 2-factor authentication

B) Use boot malware protection, such as built-in, firmware-based malware protection

C) Disallow the use of all removable media

D) Use remote booting, such as diskless workstations

493. Which BEST describes how to carry out a policy?

A) Procedure

B) Standard

C) Strategy

D) Guideline

494. When carrying out a hardwire wiretap, which of the following activities could an attacker NOT control?

A) Send a signal to the device to turn on lights or the microphone

B) Listen to voice activity

C) Detect which keys are being pressed

D) Cause physical damage to a device

495. Which of the following statements BEST describes MDM?

A) A system to manage employee-owned devices

B) An encrypted area of a mobile device used to keep sensitive data separate from personal data

C) A system to track the location of mobile devices

D) A device owned by an employee but used for work purposes

496. You are auditing a financial business which has a significant risk of one person holding too much power. What audit technique is BEST suited?

A) Reviewing IS Standards

B) Review of IS Organization Structures

C) Reviewing IS Documentation

D) Reviewing IS Policies and Procedures

497. Which BEST describes a livelock TOC/TOU attack?

A) Occurs when an untrusted and a trusted process attempt to access the same physical memory

B) Occurs when an untrusted process manages to insert itself in between TOC and TOU

C) Occurs when the OS and a trusted process attempt to access the same resource

D) Occurs when two trusted processes get in each other's way, effectively locking them both up

498. In relation to BI analysis models, which is the BEST description of an activity or swim-lane diagram?

A) Allows us to deconstruct a business process

B) Models data entities and how each relates to another

C) Outlines the major processes and external parties an organization deals with

D) Visualizes contextual relationships between entities

499. Which of the following statements is NOT true regarding digital signatures?

A) The signature cannot be forged

B) The signature cannot be reused

C) It provides authentication without requiring encryption

D) Any alteration to a document renders an accompanying signature invalid

500. Which of the following BEST describes a screened-subnet firewall?

A) Creates a private self-contained network between the two packet-filtering firewalls

B) A public facing server that has been hardened against external attacks.

C) Uses two packet-filtering firewalls and an application firewall

D) Uses a packet-filtering firewall and a proxy server

501. Which value estimates how much value we can expect to lose in a single year?

A) ALE

B) SLE

C) EF

D) ARO

502. What is the BEST definition of performance?

A) Delivered value as perceived by users and stakeholders

B) How well a system works

C) A comparison against an external benchmark

D) How well goals are achieved based on pre-defined metrics

503. Which of the following descriptions BEST describes information security?

A) Manages resources

B) Makes sure that processes run smoothly

C) Ensures CIA, or confidentiality, integrity and availability

D) Coordinates alignment between IT execution and corporate strategy

504. Which internal control framework is most often used by publicly-traded companies?

A) COSO's Internal Control – Integrated Framework

B) ISO 27001

C) RISK IT framework

D) COBIT 5's Risk Management Framework

505. Which of the following is NOT a type of malware?

A) Worm

B) Virus

C) Spyware

D) Zombie

506. Which of the following statements BEST describes an integrity CRC checker?

A) Attach themselves to files in the same way that malware does

B) Checks CRCs from previous runs against current CRCs to see if a file has changed

C) Mimics file by renaming themselves in the master boot record

D) Real-time detection of malware that writes to the boot sector or master boot record, or makes changes to executables

507. Which of the following is NOT a Zachman perspective?

A) Engineering Management

B) Engineer

C) Architect

D) Business Management

508. Which is NOT a risk when using online programming facilities?

A) An external attacker could easily access source code

B) Developers can bypass procedures and make unauthorized changes

C) Multiple software versions can result

D) Valid changes might be overwritten by other changes

509. Which of the following is NOT true regarding auditing an IMS?

A) Continuity planning is also a primary area that should be reviewed by the auditor

B) A BIA must be executed for the IMS apart from other systems

C) The larger the scale of integration, the more auditor attention is required

D) Highly integrated computer-integrated manufacturing projects require the same attention from the auditor as any ERP system might

510. What type of risk reflects the baseline risk if no controls were in place?

A) Control risk

B) Detection risk

C) Inherent risk

D) Audit risk

511. Which of the following is NOT a factor we should look at when selecting the frequency of backups?

A) The impact if we are unable to restore a backup

B) RTO and RPO

C) How often the source data changes

D) The cost of backup media

512. Which of the following BEST describes e-banking?

A) Allows banking customers to carry out virtually all transactions from the comfort of their home

B) Enables payments to be made through the use of virtual transactions

C) Computers that physically connect with credit card readers

D) Focuses on providing services such as mortgage loans or insurance policies

513. What term BEST describes the crime of using dishonest methods to take something valuable from a person or organization?

A) Theft

B) Acquisition

C) Fraud

D) Embezzlement

514. Which of the following is NOT a primary goal for a BIA?

A) Finalize the decision on restoration order

B) Identify resource requirements for each critical process

C) Estimate the amount of downtime in terms of the MTO until the business can no longer survive

D) Prioritize the criticality of every business process

515. What is the BEST definition for main objective?

A) The primary reason for a project and can always be tied directly to business success

B) A result not directly tied to the business success, but must be achieved for ancillary reasons

C) Results that are out of scope for the project and are not expected to be delivered

D) A result not directly tied to the business success, but may contribute to project success

516. Which of the following BEST describes a web application firewall?

A) Tracks all outgoing requests for a computer and ensures that external packets targeting the internal computer correspond to a previous request

B) Runs a separate proxy server for each protocol

C) Focuses on the HTTP protocol

D) Can only look at the IP address and port number of packets coming into and out of the intranet

517. In relation to an expert system, which BEST describes a shell?

A) Components within a system yet to be loaded with facts or rules

B) Artificial intelligence to infer relationships and arrive at a decision

C) Data that comes in from a sensor or system that is being monitored

D) Facts expressed in one of several models

518. Which of the following BEST describes the reconnaissance method of network analysis?

A) A methodical approach to identify the software and hardware running in the target's network

B) An attack performed by a manual search in software, OSs or add-on utilities

C) An attack in which the names, directories, privileges, shares and policies are listed

D) An attack that studies the communication patterns on a network to deduce information

519. Which of the following biometric terms best describes fingerprints?

A) The shape, length and width of hand and fingers

B) Certain features of a fingerprint

C) A complete record of ridges and valley on a finger

D) A side camera captures the contour of the palm and fingers

520. A risk assessment includes which following actions?

A) Identification, Analysis, Management

B) Identification, Analysis, Evaluation

C) Analysis, Evaluation, Treatment

D) Analysis, Evaluation, Mitigation

521. Which of the following BEST describes the data preparation layer of BI?

A) Contains the logic necessary to prepare data from the warehouse

B) The point at which end-users interact with the system

C) Contains the bulk of interesting data, and is usually a relational database

D) Where the results of data preparation are stored

522. Which of the following BEST describes CSMA?

A) A computer attempts to speak and backs off if a collision is detected

B) All transmissions contain sufficient redundancy to reconstitute the original data if a collision occurs

C) Permission to communicate is handed to each computer in-turn

D) Used primarily in mainframe environments where a primary station gives permission to each computer to speak

523. Which COBIT 5 intrinsic quality measures how unbiased and impartial a measurement is?

A) Reputation

B) Accuracy

C) Objectivity

D) Believability

524. When working with sampling, which one of the following statements is true?

A) If the value of all data points is relatively close, then we can expect more precision, and the smaller the sample size will need to be

B) The more variable the data is, the more precision we can expect, and we therefore need to decrease the sample size to get a good result

C) The less confident we need to be in the result, the larger the sample size can get

D) The more confident we want to be in the result, the more we will need to decrease the sample size

525. Which of the following is NOT true regarding the AUP?

A) It covers both who is a user and what the user is allowed to do

B) The Acceptable Internet Usage Policy should also exist but separately

C) It is designed to protect both the employee and organization from illegal actions

D) The right for the company to collect logs should be included

526. Which BEST describes malware?

A) Malicious software that usually tries to get itself appended to the end of legitimate programs on a computer

B) Malicious software that does not cause damage other than silently listening and collecting sensitive information to send back to the attacker

C) Malicious software that does not self-replicate or try to attach itself to other files

D) Malicious software that can self-replicate across a network by copying itself from computer to connected computer

527. Which of the following BEST describes a switch?

A) A device that filters traffic based on the MAC Addresses

B) A device that connects LAN segments

C) A device that simply amplifies a signal and forwards it on.

D) A device that amplifies a signal and has multiple ports

528. What is NOT a benefit of performing a control self-assessment?

A) It forces the business to review business goals

B) It encourages employees to take a personal interest in performing periodic reviews of controls

C) It requires the IS department to review access control documentation

D) It ensures employees are aware of business risk

529. Which statement is NOT true regarding QAT and UAT?

A) QAT is carried out by IT, while UAT is carried out by end-users

B) QAT validates that the solution works as documented, while UAT validates that the end-user is happy with the result

C) QAT and UAT normally happen in parallel

D) Both QAT and UAT are forms of final acceptance testing

530. Which approach to risk analysis is BEST used when accuracy is a requirement?

A) Semi-quantitative

B) Quantitative

C) Semi-qualitative

D) Qualitative

531. Which of the following BEST describes a hierarchical database?

A) All data is organized into one or more tables

B) Data is stored in a parent/child relationship

C) Information is stored as a container that houses both data and actions

D) The data is comprised of 'sets', with each set having a single owner node and one or more member nodes

532. Which of the following statements BEST describes dumpster diving?

A) Repeatedly sending the same message to a particular address

B) Sending a single message to hundreds or thousands of users

C) Rummaging through trash bins to retrieve information written or printed on paper

D) Looking over someone's shoulder at a computer screen or keyboard to steal information such as passwords

533. Which statement is NOT true regarding the final report of an audit?

A) The report should be balanced in its findings with both negative and positive issues

B) The report should begin with an introduction listing goals, limitations to scope, and a description of the methodology used

C) No findings should be communicated ahead of the report.

D) Findings should be included in separate sections of the report grouped by materiality or the intended audience

534. You have completed an audit and need to make sure that the findings are acted upon. What is the BEST way to do this?

A) It is not your responsibility as an auditor to be concerned if the company does not follow up on the findings

B) Personally contact senior management after an applicable period and ask to see proof of follow-up

C) Ensure the IS manager will follow-up after a specified period of time

D) Ensure a follow-up program is in-place by the end of the audit

535. Which of the following is a recommended policy to combat weaknesses due to Internet connectivity?

A) The classification of sensitivity and criticality must take Internet exposure into account

B) Active logging must be enabled

C) Internal networks should be divided into subnets to reduce the exposure of any one network being compromised

D) All connection points to the Internet must be secured with a port-filtering firewall at a minimum

536. Which of the following BEST describes a conceptual schema?

A) How the database looks from an external viewpoint

B) How the data is physically stored

C) How the database sees data being stored

D) How the files are arranged on a single disk

537. Which of the following BEST describes a NoSQL database?

A) All data is organized into one or more tables

B) Data is stored in a parent/child relationship

C) Is built with big data in mind

D) Information is stored as a container that houses both data and actions

538. Which of the following BEST describes a remote access VPN?

A) Connects branch offices within an enterprise WAN

B) Provides business partners limited access to each other's corporate network

C) Connects telecommuters and mobile users to the enterprise WAN

D) Provides direct connections for WAN links

539. Which of the following BEST describes the Internet/intranet layer of BI?

A) Schedules tasks required to build, maintain and populate the warehouse

B) Allows all other components to communicate using browser-based interfaces

C) Data about data

D) Knows how to communicate between each vertical layer

540. Which of the following is NOT a step taken when purchasing a system?

A) Review the current state

B) Design the future state

C) Select vendors

D) Install the system

541. Which of the following biometric terms best describes a facial scan?

A) Blood-vessel patterns on the back of an eyeball

B) The colored portion surrounding the pupil

C) Bone structure, nose ridge, eye widths, forehead size and chin shape

D) Fingerprint and the creases, ridges and grooves of the palm

542. Which of the following is NOT a goal for DLP?

A) To monitor and control the movement of that information on end-user systems

B) To monitor and control the movement of that information as it leaves the company

C) To locate and catalog sensitive information throughout a company

D) To monitor and control the movement of that information across the internal network

543. When developing a business case, which of the following BEST describes the approach?

A) Represent both the stakeholder's needs and constraints

B) Selecting the recommended system or software solution that will meet the requirements

C) Deciding if the recommended approach is sufficiently cost-effective

D) Reading the feasibility study report with all stakeholders

544. Which of the following is the BEST description of RA?

A) Confirms that you are a real person or company

B) Confirms that an entity is the real owner of a public key

C) A list of invalid certificates

D) Something that tells us how a CA validates authenticity

545. You are carrying out an audit in which only transactions meeting certain criteria should be examined. What is the BEST automated evaluation technique to use?

A) Continuous and intermittent simulation

B) Snapshot

C) Audit Hook

D) Integrated test facility

546. Which of the following is NOT something an auditor would expect to see mentioned clearly in the audit scope when evaluating penetration testing?

> A) The precise IP addresses or ranges to be tested
>
> B) Expected vulnerabilities
>
> C) Acceptable testing techniques, such as social engineering, DoS or DDoS and SQL injections
>
> D) The hosts not to be tested

547. What IT risk management level are we operating at when considering if efforts are too complex and measuring the likelihood of not reaching goals?

> A) Procedural
>
> B) Project
>
> C) Strategic
>
> D) Operational

548. Which of the following BEST describes the project manager role?

> A) Acts as subject matter experts for the development team
>
> B) Develops, installs and operates the requested system
>
> C) Create the core project deliverables by completing assigned tasks
>
> D) Provides day-to-day management and leadership of the project

549. Which BEST describes a salami attack?

> A) Redirecting browser traffic from a legitimate site to a bogus one
>
> B) The act of stealing money by reducing amounts by an insignificant amount
>
> C) The act of stealing money by rounding down fractions
>
> D) Compromising a DNS database

550. Which of the following is NOT a key metric to look for when deciding if a project has a good chance of succeeding?

> A) Either a V-model or agile approach is used
>
> B) The various parties in the project are cooperative and work together.
>
> C) Periodic review and risk analysis are performed in each project phase.
>
> D) Scope creep is controlled and there is a software baseline to prevent requirements from being added into the software design.

551. Which of the following BEST describes a bastion host?

> A) A public facing server that has been hardened against external attacks.
>
> B) Uses two packet-filtering firewalls and an application firewall
>
> C) Creates a private self-contained network between the two packet-filtering firewalls
>
> D) Uses a packet-filtering firewall and a proxy server

552. Which IT Balanced Scorecard, or IT BSC, perspective dictates how to achieve goals?

> A) Mission
>
> B) Strategies
>
> C) Sources
>
> D) Measures

553. Which definition BEST describes adaptive RAID?

> A) A storage solution that switches between RAID modes depending on the configured write speed
>
> B) A storage solution that allows individual hard disks to be swapped out without requiring down-time
>
> C) A storage solution that increases available storage based on real-time needs
>
> D) A storage solution that switches between synchronous and asynchronous mode based on the network load

554. When reviewing documentation, which two things should the auditor be looking for?

A) That it is available in both hardcopy and electronic form, and exhibits the appropriate approval signatures

B) That it was created as management authorized and intended, and is current and up-to-date

C) That the contents align with business strategy, and proof of authority is included

D) That it is referenced in a final report addendum, and all authors are noted

555. Which of the following is NOT a recommended control for a purchase accounting system?

A) Ensuring that goods received but not yet invoiced are recorded

B) Ensuring that payments received are recorded and processed

C) Ensuring that payments not received are recorded

D) Ensuring that goods ordered but not yet received are recorded

556. Which of the following is NOT a common risk with PBXs?

A) Malware

B) Theft of service

C) Denial of service

D) Unauthorized access

557. Which of the following BEST describes a storage area network?

A) Covers broad areas such as a city, region, nation or even an international link

B) Covers a limited are such as a home, office or even a campus with multiple buildings

C) A network of personal devices such as smartphones or watches

D) A specialized version of a LAN dedicated to storing large amounts of data

558. At which OSI layer do standards such as TIFF, GIF and JPG operate?

A) Layer 6

B) Layer 4

C) Layer 5

D) Layer 7

559. Which of the following BEST describes an internal schema?

A) How the database looks from an external viewpoint

B) How the database sees data being stored

C) How the data is physically stored

D) How the files are arranged on a single disk

560. Which of the following statements BEST describes an active monitor?

A) Examining areas of a computer looking for strings of bits that looks like malware

B) Analyzing instructions in a file and decides if it looks like malware

C) Comparing bit strings in a file against a pattern known to represent malware

D) Looking for malware at the DOS and BIOS level

561. When dealing with sampling, which term BEST describes a model that divides the entire population into smaller groups, and then draws samples from each group?

A) Stratified mean per unit

B) Difference estimation

C) Sample standard deviation

D) Unstratified mean per unit

562. Which of the following statements BEST describes an immunizer?

A) Attach themselves to files in the same way that malware does

B) Real-time detection of malware that writes to the boot sector or master boot record, or makes changes to executables

C) Checks CRCs from previous runs against current CRCs to see if a file has changed

D) Mimics file by renaming themselves in the master boot record

563. Which statement BEST describes SOAP?

A) A light-weight web protocol providing little self-description or discovery capabilities

B) A handy and delightfully pleasant cleaning agent

C) A web-based protocol that is self-descriptive and discoverable through the WSDL and UDDI mechanisms

D) A text-based protocol proprietary to the CROBA initiative

564. Which of the following BEST describes a surge?

A) An increase in voltage

B) Mitigates short-term interruptions such as sags, spikes and surges

C) Measures the incoming electrical current and either increase or decrease the charge to ensure a consistent current

D) Caused by electrical storms or nearby noisy electrical equipment such as motors, fluorescent lighting or radio transmitters

565. Which of the following tasks does an auditor NOT perform during a post-implementation review?

A) Look at change requests submitted after the system went live

B) See if the system met the original goals

C) Review defect reports that were never addressed prior to rollout

D) Look at the error logs

566. Which of the following BEST describes the system security engineer role?

A) Evaluates potential security technologies, and establishes security policies and procedures

B) Designs systems based on user needs

C) Implements the designs created by a security architect

D) Develops and maintains applications that eventually run in a production capacity

567. Which of the following biometric terms best describes a voice print?

A) The speed and pauses between each keypress as a password is typed

B) A number of words recorded during enrollment

C) A complete record of ridges and valley on a finger

D) The speed and movements produced when signing a name

568. You are managing a project that has a high degree of uncertainty regarding duration of each task. Which is the best project management method to use?

A) PERT

B) Gantt

C) CPM

D) Timebox management

569. Which of the following is NOT a protocol that a firewall-based malware solution usually supports?

A) SMTP

B) IMAP

C) FTP

D) HTTP

570. According to ISO 25010, which attribute measures how long a product can maintain a specific level of performance under certain conditions?

A) Portability

B) Efficiency

C) Reliability

D) Functionality

571. What are the three phases of a test?

A) Pretest, execution and posttest

B) Preparation, execution, posttest

C) Preparation, execution, follow-up

D) Pretest, test and posttest

572. Which of the following statements concerning WBS is NOT true?

A) WPs can be arranged in phases

B) WPs must contain enough detail to be able to measure performance

C) Each WP must have a distinct owner

D) Any WBS may represent the final deliverable

573. Which of the following BEST describes the SCADA role?

A) Controls all information stored on removable media

B) Enters information into a system manually, using a batch process or online

C) Controls industrial machinery spread out over large areas

D) Collects and converts incoming information and ensures the proper distribution to the user community

574. Which of the following BEST describes SMTP?

A) A protocol used to transfer files over a TCP/IP network

B) A third party that provides individuals and enterprises with access to the Internet

C) A standard terminal emulation protocol used for remote terminal connections

D) The standard email protocol on the Internet.

575. Which of the following transmission medium is MOST used by transborder data flow?

A) Television links

B) Long-range wireless transmissions

C) Satellites

D) Telephone lines

576. Which control category stops attempts to violate a security policy?

A) Corrective

B) Detective

C) Preventative

D) Deterrent

577. Which statement BEST defines integrated auditing?

A) It combines IT, accounting and HR oversight to collect the right level of evidence for adequate auditing

B) It combines both manual and automated processing to capture evidence used for subsequent assessments

C) It combines operational, financial and information system audit disciplines to assess overall internal controls

D) It combines IT, end user and management feedback to provide a holistic view of all auditing functions

578. When auditing reverse engineering, which of the following statements does NOT apply?

A) Software license agreements often contain clauses prohibiting the reverse engineering of the software

B) A change in any decompiler components may require developing or purchasing a new decompiler

C) The results of a decompiler can often be too convoluted to be easily understood

D) Decompilers are relatively new tools that depend on the use of specific computers, operating systems and programming languages

579. Which of the following biometric terms best describes a finger scan?

A) Certain features of a fingerprint

B) A side camera captures the contour of the palm and fingers

C) A complete record of ridges and valley on a finger

D) The shape, length and width of hand and fingers

580. Which of the following BEST describes trend/variance detection tool?

A) Takes raw data and prepares it for a manual review by trimming out records that have no security significance

B) Captures audit trails or logs and performs a real-time analysis on the incoming data

C) Looks for anomalies in user or system behavior

D) Looks for a specific sequence of events known to indicate an attack

581. Which framework uses an agile, iterative approach to control and improve processes?

A) Plan-Do-Check-Act, or PDCA

B) Initiating, Diagnosing, Establishing, Acting and Learning Model, or IDEAL

C) Operationally Critical Threat Asset and Vulnerability Evaluation, or OCTAVE

D) NIST SP 800-30

582. Which of the following is true?

A) Data leakage siphons information out of a computer while product leakage leaves the original copy untouched

B) Data leakage occurs when digital information is stolen while product leakage occurs when marketing material is leaked

C) Data leakage refers to information stored in a database while product leakage refers to documentation stored in other formats

D) Data leakage is restricted to internal information while product leakage includes publicly-available information

583. What is the BEST description of offsite?

A) When the function is split between in-house and one or more outside parties.

B) When all work is performed remotely in a different geographic region.

C) When all work being performed at a remote location in the same geographic area.

D) Having one or more outside parties perform the entire function.

584. Which of the following BEST describes gaining access by using unauthorized use from the web?

A) Capturing legitimate packets passing by on a network, and then sending them back

B) A physical attack where an unauthorized person closely follows an authorized person through a secured gate or door

C) An attack executed across the Internet against web applications

D) Dialing random numbers until a system answers and allows a connection

585. Which of the following BEST describes discretionary access control?

A) An access method which gives the user no ability to change the level of access granted to others

B) A matrix of users and assets with the permission residing at the intersections

C) Data that dictates the rights a user has to specific assets

D) An access method in which the user can delegate rights as-needed

586. Which of the following procedures does an auditor normally NOT review when auditing electronic banking?

A) Issuing cards and PINs

B) The software update process for devices

C) Use of devices such as a swipe reader by a consumer

D) Generating PINs

587. Which of the following is NOT a unique weakness commonly encountered when dealing with PBXs?

A) Call-tracking logs are often not enabled

B) DID lines

C) Voice lines can be used to send unauthorized data

D) Lack of control over long-distance lines

588. Which of the following BEST describes a stand-alone server?

A) Runs within containers hosted on another computer

B) A service that runs across the network

C) A component requiring some type of a host to start and execute

D) An application that exposes parts of itself to be used by other software

589. Which represents the best response times and lowest ERR, with the best being listed first?

A) Retina, palm, iris, retina, hand, voice and fingerprint

B) Voice, retina, palm, iris, fingerprint and hand

C) Palm, hand, iris, retina, fingerprint and voice

D) Hand, fingerprint, palm, retina, iris and voice

590. Which BEST describes information helpful when executing procedures?

A) Strategy

B) Policy

C) Standard

D) Guideline

591. Which of the following statements BEST describes a secure container?

A) An encrypted area of a mobile device used to keep sensitive data separate from personal data

B) A system to manage employee-owned devices

C) A device owned by an employee but used for work purposes

D) A system to track the location of mobile devices

592. Which BEST describes sociability testing?

A) Determining the impact a new or modified application might have on other applications running in the same environment

B) Testing an application designed to integrate with social networks

C) Rerunning previous tests to determine the impact to previous versions of the same application

D) Testing an application's interface to validate integration has not been broken

593. Which of the following is NOT something used to check the sender's validity when using EDI?

A) Sender's authentication credentials

B) VAN sequential control numbers or reports

C) Sending an acknowledgment transaction to the sender on message receipt

D) Control fields within an EDI message

594. Which of the following statements about water damage is NOT true?

A) Facilities located far above ground are susceptible to water damage

B) When activated, the detectors should produce an audible alarm

C) Water detectors in the computer room should be placed above lowered ceilings and near drain holes

D) Unattended equipment storage facilities should also have water detectors.

595. Which of the following BEST describes an online monitor report?

A) Identifies the time necessary for a command entered by a user at a terminal to be answered by the host system

B) Provides a history of problems and their resolution

C) Tracks the availability of telecommunication lines and circuits

D) Checks for data transmission accuracy and errors

596. You are carrying out an audit where regular processing cannot be interrupted. What is the BEST automated evaluation technique to use?

A) Continuous and intermittent simulation

B) Audit Hook

C) Snapshot

D) SCARF/EM

597. What is the term describing a weakness in a system?

A) Exposure

B) Threat agent

C) Vulnerability

D) Threat

598. When considering evidence, which of the following would NOT increase the reliability?

A) Information previously approved by management

B) Information collected recently

C) Information from sources outside of the organization

D) Quantitative information instead of qualitative information

599. Which of the following BEST describes the control group role?

A) Collects and converts incoming information and ensures the proper distribution to the user community

B) The process of entering information into a system manually, using a batch process or online

C) Controls all information stored on removable media

D) Controls industrial machinery spread out over large areas

600. Which of the following is NOT a significant factor to consider when selecting the type of recovery site?

A) The redundant capabilities within the primary facility

B) Proximity factors of the primary facility

C) The location of the alternate site

D) The nature of probable disruptions

601. Which of the following NOT true regarding the placement of computer rooms?

A) It should not be placed next to rooms carrying elevated risk

B) The best location is on the 2nd or 3rd floor of a multi-story building

C) It should not be located in the basement or top floor

D) Neighboring facilities must be examined to determine risk

602. What is the BEST way to measure risk before you encounter it?

A) Consult audit findings for peer businesses in the same industry

B) Refer to previous audit findings

C) Take a sample of the business environment, determine risk and extrapolate

D) Interview all stakeholders to gauge the amount of assumed risk

603. Which of the following BEST describes a mantrap?

A) A lock containing a sensor that requires a magnetic card key, or a chipped card key or token to be placed against it

B) A lock that uses human characteristics to identify an individual attempting to unlock a door

C) A control that uses two doors, in which the person entering must close the first door before the second door may be opened

D) A lock that uses a numeric key pad or dial

604. Which of the following are NOT something a procedure should define?

A) Information displayed

B) Recommendations on how to handle various scenarios

C) Required conditions before execution

D) What to do when the unexpected happens

605. Which of the following biometric terms best describes a palm scan?

A) Blood-vessel patterns on the back of an eyeball

B) Fingerprint and the creases, ridges and grooves of the palm

C) The colored portion surrounding the pupil

D) Bone structure, nose ridge, eye widths, forehead size and chin shape

606. Which of the following BEST describes a parallel test?

A) Team members implement the plan on paper

B) The recovery site is activated, and the primary site is shut down

C) Team members role-playing a simulated disaster without activating the recovery site

D) The recovery site is brought up to a state of operational readiness, but operations at the primary site continue

607. Which of the following features could BEST enable an attacker to disable user tracking?

A) Non-busy extensions

B) Silent monitoring

C) Call forwarding

D) Tenanting

608. Which of the following BEST describes a flooding attack?

A) A DoS attack meant to bring down a service by overwhelming it with a huge amount of traffic

B) Software that waits for a specific condition to be reached and then launches an internal attack

C) Denying consumers the use of a service or server

D) An attack executed across the Internet against web applications

609. Which of the following is NOT a valid disadvantage of using the services of other auditors and experts?

A) The business is now dependent on the objectivity of the other auditors and experts

B) Regulatory and legal requirements may prohibit this activity

C) The final report may be leaked to competitors

D) The risk to the audit and potential liability may increase

610. Which of the following security planning roles BEST describes a liaisons?

A) Provides assistance based on subject matter expertise

B) Manages individual incidents

C) Oversees the incident response capability

D) Communicates to other departments such as legal, human resources, and public relations

611. What are the four BEST tools for ensuring that IT services continue to grow?

A) COBIT 5, TOGAF, IDEAL and BSC

B) COBIT 5, PAM, IDEAL and CMMI

C) Zachman, PAM, IDEAL and PDCA

D) Zachman, Six Sigma, TOGAF, and BSC

612. Which control method oversees or reports on a process and includes the procedures and operations of that process?

    A) Logical

    B) Technical

    C) Procedural

    D) Physical

613. Which of the following BEST describes fidelity coverage insurance?

    A) Insurance that covers loss from dishonest or fraudulent acts by employees

    B) Insurance that legally protects a business in case it commits an act, error or omission that results in a loss

    C) Insurance that reimburses the business for expenses incurred in maintaining operations at a facility that experiences damage

    D) Insurance that protects a business from losses experienced as a result of third-party claims

614. Which of the following BEST describes professional and commercial liability insurance?

    A) Insurance that reimburses the business for expenses incurred in maintaining operations at a facility that experiences damage

    B) Insurance that protects a business from losses experienced as a result of third-party claims

    C) Insurance that legally protects a business in case it commits an act, error or omission that results in a loss

    D) Insurance that reimburses lost profit as a result of an IT malfunction or security incident that causes the loss of computing resources

615. Which description BEST describes slack time?

    A) The time from a task's earliest completion date and the latest completion time that does not impact the critical path

    B) The amount a task's duration can be compressed if needed

    C) The time after the scheduled end of all activities and the advertised project completion date

    D) The time in-between tasks that is not productive

616. Which statement BEST describes benefits realization?

    A) The promised benefits have been translated into business value

    B) Expenses invested in IT-related initiatives deliver the business benefits that were promised

    C) The promised benefits are completely delivered

    D) Authorized expenses result in the value promised during the feasibility study

617. What is the term describing the danger that a vulnerability might be exploited?

    A) Control

    B) Exposure

    C) Threat

    D) Risk

618. What is the BEST description of how to decide to treat risk or not?

    A) Based on how much risk a business is willing to accept without mitigation

    B) Based on the effectiveness of compensating controls

    C) Based on a financial evaluation of the costs to mitigate a specific risk

    D) The level of risk that applicable laws and regulations allow

619. Which of the following is NOT a common weakness found with DFLPs?

A) A DLP might result in a large number of false positives, which can overwhelm staff and hide valid hits

B) It cannot detect sensitive information in streaming data files such as video or audio

C) It can inspect encrypted data only if it knows how to decrypt it

D) DLP network modules may be improperly tuned resulting in blocking valid content or missing unauthorized content

620. Which represents an invalid approach to choosing a control?

A) Select one from professional standards

B) Select one from industry standards

C) Create one of our own design

D) Select one after work has been done to minimize risk

621. Which of the following is NOT an output control?

A) Verification of report receipts

B) Report distribution

C) Output error handling

D) Parity checking

622. Which of the following BEST describes WEP?

A) Only have to know the SSID and authenticate using an extremely weak protocol

B) Any infrastructure secured using WPA2

C) The first real security for wireless traffic

D) Claimed to provide protection equivalent to unsecured traffic traveling over a physical Ethernet cable

623. Which of the following BEST describes the reconnaissance method of a traffic analysis war driving?

A) The practice of marking a series of symbols on sidewalks and walls to indicate nearby wireless access points

B) The practice of driving around businesses or residential neighborhoods while scanning with a laptop computer to search for wireless networks

C) The practice of walking around businesses or residential neighborhoods while scanning with a small device to search for wireless networks

D) The practice of breaking through encryption faster than keys can be changed

624. Which type of audit looks at how efficiently an organization carries out its primary mission?

A) Administrative

B) Specialized

C) Forensic

D) Financial

625. Which of the following describes the COBIT 5 data life cycle?

A) Plan, design, build or acquire, use and operate, monitor and dispose

B) Build, use, operate, monitor and dispose

C) Design, implement, operate, monitor and dispose

D) Define, implement, use, monitor and dispose

626. Which approach to risk analysis is BEST used when we want a simple categorical approach using no calculations?

A) Semi-quantitative

B) Semi-qualitative

C) Quantitative

D) Qualitative

627. Which of the following biometric terms best describes hand geometry?

A) A side camera captures the contour of the palm and fingers

B) The shape, length and width of hand and fingers

C) Certain features of a fingerprint

D) A complete record of ridges and valley on a finger

628. What are the two modes in which a network can be attacked?

A) Passive and active

B) Listening and pinging

C) Quiet and noisy

D) Black box and white box

629. Which OSI layer is broken into two sublayers?

A) The Data Link layer

B) The Transport layer

C) The Network layer

D) The Physical layer

630. Which of the following statements is true regarding baseband and broadband?

A) Baseband is more reliable than broadband

B) Baseband provides less throughput than broadband

C) With baseband the entire channel is used for a single data type, but broadband supports multiple types of data simultaneously

D) Broadband is more reliable than baseband

631. Which of the following BEST describes an attacker taking advantage of hardware wiretapping?

A) Listening in on the active voice channel of a line placed into maintenance mode

B) Taking advantage of an undocumented feature

C) Gaining physical access to a bridge and routing all signals to a specific port

D) Listening in on voice activity by accessing the physical communication between the PBX and the end-user device

632. What is the best definition of a backward pass?

A) Finding the completion time for each task and calculating slack time

B) Starting with the last task, iterating back through the plan to find opportunities to compress the timeline

C) Occurs when the team hands the schedule back to the project manager for final approval

D) Throwing the ball to a teammate in a direction parallel to or away from the opponents' goal line

633. Which BEST describes alteration?

A) Occurs when the attacker waits around while a valid user or machine authenticates itself, and then assumes the authenticated identity

B) The act of sniffing network packets as they pass by

C) Occurs when a computer sends packets that appear to be coming from another IP address

D) The act of modifying data without anyone noticing

634. Which of the following BEST describes a VPN concentrator?

A) Supports direct modem connections

B) Provides direct connections for WAN links

C) Accepts incoming connections and handles authentication and access control

D) Allows only VPN connections at a single point in the network

635. Which of the following BEST describes electronic logging?

A) A control that uses two doors, in which the person entering must close the first door before the second door may be opened

B) The act of a person signing into and out of a physical log

C) Automate logging by electronic and biometric locks

D) Video cameras that capture local activity around a facility

636. What term describes how accessible an IT system or process is to its end users?

A) Nonrepudiation

B) Authentication

C) Availability

D) Integrity

637. Which of the five basic tests are included in the preparedness test category?

A) Parallel and full interruption

B) Structured walkthrough and simulation

C) Checklist review and structured walkthrough

D) Simulation and parallel

638. Even if encrypted, which of the following data elements stored on a POS should the auditor be concerned with?

A) Card verification value numbers

B) Primary account number

C) Card holder name

D) PINs

639. Which of the following BEST describes ISP?

A) A protocol used to transfer files over a TCP/IP network

B) A standard terminal emulation protocol used for remote terminal connections

C) The standard email protocol on the Internet.

D) A third party that provides individuals and enterprises with access to the Internet

640. Which of the following non-removable disk-based solutions BEST describes a virtual tape library?

A) Software living on a server that replicates changes to another server invisibly

B) Taking an image of a system, restoring onto a second system, and backing up this secondary environment

C) A solution that looks like a tape library but really uses a disk array for storage

D) Similar to host-based replication, but it is carried out at the disk array level instead of software installed on the OS

641. What is the BEST description of ease of manipulation?

A) How compactly it is presented

B) How easy it is to apply to multiple tasks

C) If it is in the correct language and units and is clear

D) If it is presented in the same format

642. Which of the following is the BEST description of an asymmetric scheme?

A) Using one key for encryption and a different key for decryption

B) The most common outdated symmetric system

C) The most common modern symmetric system

D) A one-way encryption that results in the same length of ciphertext regardless of the plain text

643. Which of the following statements is NOT true regarding organizational change management?

A) It is the use of a defined and documented process to identify and apply technology improvements at either the infrastructure or application level

B) All levels of an organization that is affected should be involved

C) While technology considerations are taken into account, end-user expectations are normally not part of this effort

D) The IT department will be spearheading such initiatives

644. Which of the following definitions BEST describes a highly centralized environment?

A) Security is under the direction of IS management, with IS management staff maintaining a close relationship with users

B) Security is under the direction of individuals, but adheres to the guidelines established by IS management

C) Security is completely under the control of IS management

D) Security is under the direction of individuals, but the overall responsibility remains with IS management

645. When a computer crime is being carried out, which of the following descriptions BEST describes a symbol?

A) The computer being attacked when one computer attacks another

B) The computer launching an attack when one computer attacks another

C) A computer being used to attack a non-computer

D) A computer used to trick a person into giving away confidential information

646. According to ISO 25010, which attribute measures how well a product meets a set of features?

A) Reliability

B) Functionality

C) Efficiency

D) Portability

647. Which of the following BEST describes an ad hoc WLAN?

A) A wireless network in which the AP is also connected to another network

B) A wireless network made up of two computers talking to each other over wireless cards

C) A frequency range within wireless traffic

D) A wireless network in which both computers are connected to an access point instead of each other

648. Why is quantum computing such an important topic?

A) It is not compatible with asymmetric algorithms

B) It will do away with the need for shared keys

C) It could render all current encryption algorithms completely useless

D) It will require all PKI infrastructure to be retooled

649. Which of the following BEST describes a per CPU license?

A) Used when multiple end-users will be using the software

B) Charged according to the number of login accounts

C) A fee is charged for each CPU core running on the computer on which the software is installed

D) Charged according to the number of users simultaneously using the system

650. When dealing with network continuity, which statement BEST describes long-haul network diversity?

A) Subscribing to two or more network service providers at the same time

B) Routing traffic through split or duplicate cables

C) Routing information through an alternate medium such as copper cable or fiber optics

D) Protecting an organization from a local disaster that takes out the communications infrastructure connected directly to a facility

651. Which of the following BEST describes the systems analyst role?

A) Designs systems based on user needs

B) Evaluates potential security technologies, and establishes security policies and procedures

C) Develops and maintains applications that eventually run in a production capacity

D) Implements the designs created by a security architect

652. Which of the following BEST describes the project steering committee role?

A) Provides overall direction and represents the major stakeholders

B) Provides funding and defines the critical success factors and metrics that determine if the project is a success

C) Shows commitment to the project by providing approval for the necessary resources to be successful

D) Owns the project and the resulting deliverable

653. Which of the following BEST describes EDI?

A) The automated synch of data across disparate networks

B) An agreement between two entities to use an Internet-based path to share data

C) The formatting and transmission of proprietary and encrypted data

D) The transfer of information between two systems using an intermediary format that both systems understand

654. Which of the following statements is NOT true regarding to third-party reporting?

A) SOC 2 covers the operating effectiveness of provider controls

B) SOC 3 covers the retirement disposition of provider controls

C) SOC 1 covers the design of provider controls

D) There are three SAE16 SOC reports only – SOC 1, SOC 2, and SOC 3

655. Which group BEST describes the drivers behind DSS?

A) Board members desiring to bring a higher level of accountability to executive management

B) IS management wanting a better approach to quantify progress

C) Decision-makers looking for more accurate information

D) Executives searching for more process efficiency

656. Which of the following are valid advantages when using VoIP?

A) Innovation proceeds at a much higher rate than does traditional telephony

B) Due to the redundancy of the Internet, it is more reliable than traditional telephony

C) It provides a very low cost per call

D) IP is software-based and easy to install

657. Which BEST describes the difference between a post-project review and a post-implementation review?

A) A post-project review focuses on how successful the project processes were, while a post-implementation review measures the value the project delivered

B) A post-project review focuses on team performance, while a post-implementation review focuses on project performance

C) A post-project review closes out activities, while a post-implementation review imitates maintenance mode

D) A post-project review is held as soon as the project ends, while a post-implementation review is held at least 6 months after

658. Which of the following is NOT a major advantage of automatically scheduling jobs?

A) A complete record of when each job ran and how the success is automatically maintained

B) The reliance on error-prone human operators is reduced

C) Jobs need to be setup only once, reducing the chances of errors

D) Dependencies between jobs can be removed

659. Which of the following BEST describes the data management personnel role?

A) Answers technical questions and solve problems faced by internal employees

B) Responsible for daily operations related to business services

C) The actual user of data, including both internal and external users

D) Tasked with managing data and the data architecture

660. In which phase of the Waterfall SDLC do we create an RFP, ITT or RFI?

A) Phase 4A

B) Phase 4B

C) Phase 3A

D) Phase 3B

661. Which of the following is NOT a phase that service contracts go through?

A) Acceptance

B) Compliance

C) Bidding

D) Approval

662. What is the primary purpose of an email gateway?

A) To translate differing formats between email servers

B) To provide a port-level proxy function between two email servers

C) To protect an email server from attacks

D) To distribute load between multiple email servers

663. Which standard provides guidance on what software development expenses can be classified as a capital expenditure?

A) ISO 27001

B) NIST SP 800-30

C) IAS 38

D) SOP 98-1

664. Which of the following is NOT a control to ensure proper board and management oversight of EFT?

A) Ensure that the board and management are actively engaged and have accountability for all e-banking activities

B) Establish a comprehensive security control process to eliminate gaps

C) Perform comprehensive due diligence and proper management over outsourcing activities

D) Keep as much work in-house as possible to eliminate unneeded outsourcing risk

665. Which of the following is NOT a LAN-specific control?

A) Encrypt local traffic using IPSec

B) Implement record-level locking to prevent updates by more than one user

C) Physically protect the CSU/DSU

D) Use switches to implement port security policies as opposed to hubs or non-managed routers

666. What term represents the entire set of data points?

A) Precision

B) Sample

C) Accuracy

D) Population

667. When auditing computer forensics, which of the following is NOT common task for an auditor to carry out?

A) Looking to see if both process and infrastructure are in-place to provide assurance that electronic evidence will be acquired but not destroyed

B) Checking for written protocols on how to inform appropriate parties that electronic evidence will be acquired but will not be destroyed

C) Make sure all measures to prevent data from being altered are in-place

D) Validating that appropriate evidence gathering technology is current and available to employees

668. When dealing with sampling, which term BEST describes looking at the total value of each data point, such as the monetary value of invoices?

A) Proportional sampling

B) Discovery sampling

C) Variable sampling

D) Stop-or-go sampling

669. Which framework BEST helps an organization to create clear goals and translate them into action?

A) COBIT 5

B) Balanced Scorecard, or BSC

C) FEA

D) Capability Maturity Model Integration, or CMMI

670. When a computer crime is being carried out, which of the following descriptions BEST describes a tool?

A) A computer used to trick a person into giving away confidential information

B) A computer being used to attack a non-computer

C) The computer launching an attack when one computer attacks another

D) The computer being attacked when one computer attacks another

671. Which of the following is NOT considered to be a focus area when auditing remote access?

A) Identifying both known and unknown remote access points

B) Reviewing the creation of network credentials

C) Dialing a remote access computer from a number of authorized and unauthorized telephone lines

D) Ensuring security controls are in-place and documented to protect information resources

672. Which of the following BEST describes a structured walkthrough test?

A) Team members implement the plan on paper

B) Team members role-playing a simulated disaster without activating the recovery site

C) An assessment of all steps to be carried out

D) The recovery site is brought up to a state of operational readiness, but operations at the primary site continue

673. Which of the following is NOT a common risk associated with flash drives?

A) The risk of loss of confidentiality increases with use

B) They are more prone to data corruption when used as long-term storage than other media

C) They can be used to spread viruses even when a network is not present

D) Theft is a common occurrence

674. Which control method always contains some type of technology?

A) Procedural

B) Managerial

C) Physical

D) Technical

675. Which of the following BEST describes parallel testing?

A) Testing using the same set of data to see what has broken

B) Testing that answers the question 'Are we building the right product?'

C) Testing an application with full knowledge of the inner workings

D) Rerunning previous tests to ensure recent changes have not broken something that used to work

676. Which of the following tells us if a process has achieved its goal after the fact?

A) KPI

B) KRI

C) KGI

D) CSF

677. Which of the following is a valid statement concerning RTO?

A) Shorter RTOs cost more

B) Near-instantaneous recovery (an RTO approaching 0) is seldom possible

C) Systems owners will lean towards longer RTOs

D) It is acceptable for an impact loss to exceed recovery cost

678. Which of the following BEST describes WAP?

A) The first real security for wireless traffic

B) Marginally better than its predecessor

C) Only have to know the SSID and authenticate using an extremely weak protocol

D) The first protocol to allow devices such as smartphones to access the Internet in a limited fashion

679. Which of the following BEST describes security training?

A) The process of teaching security skills to security personnel

B) The process of spreading the need for security awareness throughout an organization

C) The process of testing security hygiene within a department

D) The process of explaining security issues to all members of an organization

680. What term represents a subset of the entire set of data points?

A) Precision

B) Sample

C) Confidence level

D) Population

681. What term describes the impact that the loss of an asset will have?

A) Sensitivity

B) Assurance

C) Criticality

D) Privacy

682. What term represents how close to the true value a measurement is?

A) Accuracy

B) Population

C) Sample

D) Precision

683. Which description BEST describes the critical path method?

A) Carrying out a detailed analysis of each task to arrive at the shortest duration and summing the results to produce the project end date

B) Prioritizing all activities based on criticality and moving those tasks to the front of the project

C) Determining project duration by identifying tasks that cannot fail and adjusting the schedule around those tasks

D) Finding project duration by measuring the longest path which cannot be compressed

684. Which aspect of the audit charter describes how the audit will be carried out?

A) Responsibility

B) Authority

C) Accountability

D) Purpose

685. Which of the following non-removable disk-based solutions BEST describes a snapshots?

A) Software living on a server that replicates changes to another server invisibly

B) Taking an image of a system, restoring onto a second system, and backing up this secondary environment

C) Similar to host-based replication, but it is carried out at the disk array level instead of software installed on the OS

D) A solution that looks like a tape library but really uses a disk array for storage

686. Which of the following items is NOT normally included in the PRD?

A) Who the stakeholders are

B) A high-level timeline

C) Who the project manager is

D) A project charter stating the objective

687. Which of the following BEST describes the network administrator role?

A) Maintains the systems software, including the OS, on top of which applications sit

B) Develops and maintains standards for the IT group

C) Maintains network components such as routers, switches, firewalls and remote access

D) Carries out whatever duties are defined in the security policy

688. Which FEA reference model describes the functions performed by the government?

A) Service Component Reference Model

B) Technical Reference Model

C) Business Reference Model

D) Data Reference Model

689. What is the BEST description of outsourcing?

A) When the function is split between in-house and one or more outside parties.

B) When all work is performed remotely in a different geographic region.

C) Having one or more outside parties perform the entire function.

D) When all work being performed at a remote location in the same geographic area.

690. At which OSI layer does session management occur?

A) Layer 7

B) Layer 4

C) Layer 5

D) Layer 6

691. Which BEST describes a high-level statement of what management expects?

A) Guideline

B) Procedure

C) Standard

D) Policy

692. When dealing with sampling, which term BEST describes how far off from the average our sample set is?

A) Unstratified mean per unit

B) Population standard deviation

C) Sample standard deviation

D) Stratified mean per unit

693. Which of the following BEST describes the reconnaissance method of a traffic analysis war chalking?

A) The practice of driving around businesses or residential neighborhoods while scanning with a laptop computer to search for wireless networks

B) The practice of walking around businesses or residential neighborhoods while scanning with a small device to search for wireless networks

C) The practice of marking a series of symbols on sidewalks and walls to indicate nearby wireless access points

D) The practice of breaking through encryption faster than keys can be changed

694. When using work from other experts, what is NOT true?

A) Previous work of the expert should be examined

B) The work should be included in the final report and not simply referenced

C) Additional test procedures may be used if the work does not provide sufficient evidence

D) The professional qualifications of the expert should be examined

695. What is the formula for calculating ALE?

A) ALE = EF x SLE/ARO

B) ALE = SLE x ARO

C) ALE = SLE/ARO

D) ALE = EF x ARO

696. Which term describes the amount of risk a business can absorb without ceasing to exist?

A) Risk capacity

B) Risk tolerance

C) Risk appetite

D) Risk acceptance

697. Which term BEST describes evidence that is both valid and relevant?

A) Fit

B) Ample

C) Competent

D) Sufficient

698. Which is the BEST definition of a minor incident?

A) An incident that can have a serious material impact on the continued functioning of the business and is often proportional to the length of the incident

B) An incident that results in a negative material impact on business processes and may affect other systems, departments of customers

C) An incident that causes no significant damage

D) An incident that produces no negative material or financial impact

699. When developing a business case, which of the following BEST describes the project scope?

A) Represent both the stakeholder's needs and constraints

B) Underlies a business case by studying the problem to see if a solution is practical, meets the stated requirements and can deliver within a set budget and deadline

C) Understanding the current situation as presented by both strengths and weaknesses

D) Defines the problem or opportunity in a clear and concise manner

700. Which of the following BEST describes the security administrator role?

A) Maintains network components such as routers, switches, firewalls and remote access

B) Carries out whatever duties are defined in the security policy

C) Maintains the systems software, including the OS, on top of which applications sit

D) Develops and maintains standards for the IT group

701. Which of the following BEST describes the systems development management role?

A) Provides day-to-day management and leadership of the project

B) Acts as subject matter experts for the development team

C) Develops, installs and operates the requested system

D) Create the core project deliverables by completing assigned tasks

702. When dealing with network continuity, which statement BEST describes diverse routing?

A) Providing fail-over systems automatically

B) Routing information through an alternate medium such as copper cable or fiber optics

C) Routing traffic through split or duplicate cables

D) Subscribing to two or more network service providers at the same time

703. Which of the following statements is NOT true of MPLS?

A) It slows down routing efficiency

B) It opens up the risk of a double-tagging attack

C) Layer 3 and 4 devices use it

D) MPLS tags are created only once per packet

704. Which OSI layer(s)does the TCP Internet layer map to?

A) Layer 4

B) Layer 3 and 4

C) Layers 2 and 1

D) Layer 3

705. Which of the following BEST describes the information security manager role?

A) Responsible for running the data center, including managing staff

B) Responsible for maintaining multi-user computer systems including the network connecting them together

C) Is normally separate from the IT department and reports up through the CISO

D) Defines and maintains the structure of a corporate database, and is the custodian of the company's data

706. Your company's IT department is complaining that other departments are making unreasonable requests without regard for technology and support costs. What is the best way to combat this?

A) Require all requests to be funneled through the CTO's office

B) Implement a chargeback scheme

C) Require all requests to be approved by the accounting function

D) Give approval authority to the IT department

707. Which of the following BEST describes a freeware license?

A) A fee is charged for each CPU core running on the computer on which the software is installed

B) Free, but the source code cannot be redistributed

C) Initially free, but requires payment at a later date to keep the software functioning or to unlock all features or benefits

D) The software may be used in any way the user likes without any type of payment

708. Which of the following is NOT an area in which an auditor should focus when auditing hardware?

A) Ensuring availability

B) Final disposition

C) Maintenance

D) Acquisition

709. To avoid missing large gaps of features or capabilities, the auditor will need to review several types of documentation. Which of the following areas is NOT included?

A) System development methodology documents

B) External vendor relationship history

C) User manuals

D) Functional design specifications

710. Which of the following BEST describes a per seat license?

A) Charged according to the number of login accounts

B) Allows unlimited use of the software throughout an entire organization

C) Used when multiple end-users will be using the software

D) A fee is charged for each CPU core running on the computer on which the software is installed

711. Which of the following would an auditor NOT carry out when reviewing compliance with privacy policy, laws and other regulations?

A) Update the existing privacy policy to be compliant

B) Verify that the right security measures are in place

C) Identify and understand applicable laws and regulations

D) Validate that personal sensitive information is following that policy

712. Which of the following BEST describes an intranet VPN?

A) Provides business partners limited access to each other's corporate network

B) Connects telecommuters and mobile users to the enterprise WAN

C) Connects branch offices within an enterprise WAN

D) Provides direct connections for WAN links

713. Which of the following is NOT true of X.25?

A) It adds error checking and correcting as well as fault tolerance

B) It has more overhead than ATM

C) It allows many parties to use the service simultaneously, and each pays according to the amount of actual bandwidth used

D) It is a newer WAN protocol

714. Which of the following best describes a differential backup?

A) Copies all files and folders changed since the last full backup

B) Copies all changes within each file that has changed since the last differential or full backup

C) Copies only the files and folders that have changes since the last incremental or full backup

D) Copies all files and folders into a single backup set

715. Which BEST describes a rounding attack?

A) Redirecting browser traffic from a legitimate site to a bogus one

B) Compromising a DNS database

C) The act of stealing money by rounding down fractions

D) The act of stealing money by reducing amounts by an insignificant amount

716. Which of the following is NOT a recognized risk when carrying out a penetration test?

A) Sensitive information may be disclosed, heightening the target's exposure level

B) Miscommunication may result in some test objectives not being achieved

C) Internal backlash may result if the proper employees are not notified

D) Testing activities may inadvertently trigger escalation procedures that may not have been appropriately planned for

717. Which of the following is NOT an advantage of using coding standards?

A) It requires code to align to naming patterns

B) It prevents bugs from being introduced

C) It encourages modular code development

D) It minimizes disruptions when people leave and are replaced

718. You are in charge of migrating from an old inventory system to a new one, but each stores color attributes in different formats. Which of the following processes will BEST help you to succeed?

A) Data mining

B) Data porting

C) Data migration

D) Data transmogrification

719. Which of the following descriptions BEST describes a historical analysis?

A) Looking back in time to see statistics as they used to be within a given time period

B) Filtering data matching one or more attributes, and then presenting a summary of that data

C) Summarizing data at a high level, and then drilling down into the detail as-needed

D) Cross-matching a single attribute, and then sorting based on time

720. Which of the following biometric terms best describes an iris scan?

A) The colored portion surrounding the pupil

B) Bone structure, nose ridge, eye widths, forehead size and chin shape

C) Fingerprint and the creases, ridges and grooves of the palm

D) Blood-vessel patterns on the back of an eyeball

721. What is one thing not required during an exit interview?

A) Ensure that the facts presented are accurate

B) Ensure recommendations are realistic and cost-effective, or be prepared to negotiate

C) Recommend implementation dates

D) Assign individuals to close control gaps

722. You are managing a project in which a set number of resources needs to deliver in a short time. Which is the best project management method to use?

A) PERT

B) Gantt

C) CPM

D) Timebox management

723. What is the BEST description of consistent representation?

A) How compactly it is presented

B) If it is presented in the same format

C) If it is in the correct language and units and is clear

D) How easily it is comprehended

724. Which of the following is NOT true regarding an integrated test facility, or ITF?

A) It is provided by an external vendor

B) It should mimic production scale and capacity

C) It is commonly used for UAT

D) Production data is seldom used for ITFs, even when scrubbed

725. What does SMART stand for?

A) Specific, maintainable, actionable, reachable and timely

B) Specific, measurable, attainable, realistic and timely

C) Specific, measurable, actionable, realistic and timely

D) Specific, maintainable, attainable, realistic and timely

726. You are auditing a business and need to verify that a process previously audited is still valid. What audit technique is BEST suited?

A) Walk-Throughs

B) Interviewing Appropriate Personnel

C) Reviewing IS Documentation

D) Reperformance

727. Which of the following BEST describes a response time report?

A) Tracks the availability of telecommunication lines and circuits

B) Checks for data transmission accuracy and errors

C) Identifies the time necessary for a command entered by a user at a terminal to be answered by the host system

D) Provides a history of problems and their resolution

728. Which of the following BEST describes an object-oriented database?

A) Information is stored as a container that houses both data and actions

B) Is built with big data in mind

C) The data is comprised of 'sets', with each set having a single owner node and one or more member nodes

D) Data is stored in a parent/child relationship

729. Which term BEST describes evidence for which there is an appropriate quantity?

A) Ample

B) Competent

C) Sufficient

D) Fit

730. Which is the BEST description of shadowing?

A) Small portions of knowledge and responsibilities are transferred in phases

B) Two equally-qualified people split identical duties and slowly transition one to another position

C) A person watches what another does and asks questions, with a final hand-off on a specific date

D) Two people swap duties in increasing frequency until each is performing the other's job

731. What of the following statements is NOT true regarding architectures?

A) A client-server architecture has at least one client and one server

B) A 2-tier architecture has the client connecting directly to the database

C) An n-tiered architecture has 4 or more tiers

D) A 3-tier architecture has an intermediate layer

732. Which of the following is NOT a valid outbound transmission control?

A) Protect the trading partner profile

B) Limit the ability for employees to initiate specific EDI transactions

C) Segregate duties for the initiation and transmission of high-risk transactions

D) Use check digits on control fields

733. Which of the following is NOT a critical success factors (CSFs) for an SDLC project?

A) Customer service

B) Economic value

C) Productivity

D) Timeliness

734. Which of the following is NOT true regarding honeypots?

A) It is designed to get an attacker to leave more important systems alone

B) It is designed to give you time to monitor an attacker and figure what they are up to

C) Activity is not heavily logged but instead alerts network administrators to the activity

D) If more than one honeypot is put into place, it is called a honeynet

735. When performing a network infrastructure audit, which of the following logical security controls would an auditor NOT need to look for?

A) Network access change requests

B) Test plans

C) Protocols in-use

D) Unique passwords

736. Which of the following BEST describes gaining access by using war dialing?

A) Dialing random numbers until a system answers and allows a connection

B) Capturing legitimate packets passing by on a network, and then sending them back

C) An attack executed across the Internet against web applications

D) Guessing passwords to gain access to a system by simply rotating through all possible values until the system grants access

737. What is the best way to measure success of a CSA?

A) Once the process is complete, ask all participants to complete a self-assessment

B) Create a baseline before the process and one after, and measure success using

C) Establish CSFs by holding a meeting with management to establish a primary goal of determining the reliability of internal controls

D) Have stakeholders rate the success based on objective criteria

738. Which of the following statements about fire extinguishers is NOT true?

A) Smoke detectors should supplement, not replace, fire suppression systems.

B) Hand-pull fire alarms should be placed near exit doors to ensure personnel safety

C) They should be tagged for inspection and inspected at least once every three years

D) Smoke detectors should be installed above and below the ceiling tiles and below the raised computer room floor.

739. At which OSI layer do protocols such as TCP and UDP operate?

A) Layer 5

B) Layer 4

C) Layer 3

D) Layer 6

740. Which of the following is NOT a common issue with firewalls?

A) Most firewalls normally operate at lower network layers that cannot understand higher-level traffic

B) Modems that connect directly to an ISP may circumvent firewalls entirely

C) Firewalls are software and as a result can be easily taken over

D) External firewalls may give management a false sense of security

741. What BEST describes a compensating control?

A) A control that accommodates the lack of efficiency in other controls

B) A control that is applied when another control is too costly

C) A control that makes up for weaknesses in one or more other controls

D) A control that accommodates the lack of effectiveness in other controls

742. Which of the following terms refers to a block of code performing a single, dedicated function?

A) Compounded

B) Coupled

C) Cohesive

D) Concise

743. When dealing with sampling, which term BEST describes how accurate the final answer is, or the chance that the answer is wrong?

A) Expected error rate

B) Sample mean

C) Level of risk

D) Tolerable error rate

744. Which COBIT 5 intrinsic quality measures how correct or reliable a value is?

A) Accuracy

B) Objectivity

C) Believability

D) Reputation

745. Which of the following is NOT a common attack associated with email servers?

A) Spear phishing

B) Phishing

C) Fragging

D) DoS

746. Which of the following BEST describes gaining access by using a race condition?

A) Guessing passwords to gain access to a system by simply rotating through all possible values until the system grants access

B) Exploiting a small window of time between the time that a security control is applied and the time that a service is used

C) A physical attack where an unauthorized person closely follows an authorized person through a secured gate or door

D) Dialing random numbers until a system answers and allows a connection

747. Which of the following BEST describes the application messaging layer of BI?

A) Allows all other components to communicate using browser-based interfaces

B) Data about data

C) Schedules tasks required to build, maintain and populate the warehouse

D) Knows how to communicate between each vertical layer

748. Which of the following statements is NOT true regarding a multiplexor?

A) It combines multiple logical links into a single physical connection

B) It divides portions of its total bandwidth and use each portion as a separate connection

C) It is used when a physical circuit has more bandwidth capabilities than required by individual signals

D) It is a data link layer device

749. Which of the following BEST describes a brownout?

A) A decrease in voltage

B) A severely reduced voltage due to the failure of a power company to supply power within an acceptable range

C) An increase in voltage

D) A total failure with a complete loss of power

750. Which of the following BEST describes WPA?

A) Claimed to provide protection equivalent to unsecured traffic traveling over a physical Ethernet cable

B) The first real security for wireless traffic

C) Marginally better than its predecessor

D) Only have to know the SSID and authenticate using an extremely weak protocol

751. Which of the following BEST describes a wide area network?

A) A network limited to a city or region, but normally offers higher data transfer rates than larger networks

B) Covers a limited are such as a home, office or even a campus with multiple buildings

C) Covers broad areas such as a city, region, nation or even an international link

D) A specialized version of a LAN dedicated to storing large amounts of data

752. Which of the following is NOT a recognized disadvantage with a reciprocal agreement?

A) The delay in transferring control between the two companies must be kept to a minimum

B) It is exceedingly difficult to create a contract that provides adequate protection

C) The two companies must align on the same type of infrastructure and coordinate any changes

D) It is unlikely that one company can sustain usage for two companies, as normally companies cannot afford to have double their needed capacity simply sitting around until needed

753. Which standard is BEST used to demonstrate compliance with accepted good practices?

A) Information Security Management Maturity Model, or ISM3

B) PMBOK

C) ISO 20000 Series

D) ISO 38500

754. Which of the following BEST describes regression testing?

A) Rerunning previous tests to ensure recent changes have not broken something that used to work

B) Testing two versions of the same application

C) Testing an application with full knowledge of the inner workings

D) Testing that answers the question 'Are we building the right product?'

755. When conducting a post-implementation review, which of the following is the MOST important factor to consider?

A) The post-implementation review auditors cannot be the same auditors who were involved with the project team during development

B) All members of the project development team must still be available for this review

C) The same processes used during the project must be used during the post-implementation review

D) At least 6 months must have elapsed since the project officially ended

756. Which of the following BEST describes a controlled single entry point?

A) A control that uses two doors, in which the person entering must close the first door before the second door may be opened

B) Requires that all visitors be escorted by a responsible employee

C) An unauthorized person following an authorized person through a secured entry

D) A control used by all incoming personnel and normally monitored by a receptionist

757. Which type of audit assesses the accuracy of fiscal reporting?

A) Operational

B) Specialized

C) Financial

D) Compliance

758. Which of the following BEST describes the data staging and quality layer of BI?

A) Contains the bulk of interesting data, and is usually a relational database

B) Provides access to operational, external and non-operational data

C) Provides access to the various data sources while at the same time hiding how that data is stored

D) Copies and transforms data into and out of the warehouse format and assures quality control

759. Which of the following BEST describes a storage device that is a self-contained server?

A) RAND

B) RAID

C) DAS

D) NAS

760. When reviewing logical access, which of the following controls is the LEAST important to an auditor?

A) Audit trails

B) Segregation of duties

C) Need-to-know

D) Least-privilege

761. Which BEST describes a nonatomic TOC/TOU attack?

A) Occurs when an untrusted process manages to insert itself in between TOC and TOU

B) Occurs when two trusted processes get in each other's way, effectively locking them both up

C) Occurs when the OS and a trusted process attempt to access the same resource

D) Occurs when an untrusted and a trusted process attempt to access the same physical memory

762. In relation to an expert system, which BEST describes a rule?

A) A graph of nodes and arcs between those nodes

B) A list of questions to ask a user until a conclusion is reached

C) An 'if...then' relationship

D) Used to load facts into the knowledge base without requiring a programmer

763. Which of the following BEST describes a low-interaction honeypot?

A) A software application that pretends to be a server vulnerable to attack

B) A weaponized IDS capable of aggressively defeating attacks

C) A real environment that can be attacked

D) Appears to be a normal environment

764. Which statement BEST describes why managing IT projects is different than managing an IT portfolio?

A) Portfolios simply require more management than a project

B) Projects have a definable delivery while portfolio projects interact in complex ways

C) Projects always require an investment, but with portfolios we must decide where to invest and where to divest

D) Projects are short-term while a portfolio is long-term

765. During the requirements phase, what is the most important thing an auditor can do?

A) Ensure development or prototyping efforts do not proceed without valid requirements

B) Ensure proper authorization has already been received to proceed with the phase

C) Ensure security controls are designed in from the beginning

D) Ensure all stakeholders are properly represented

766. Which of the following is the BEST description of IPSec?

A) How IPSec manages keys

B) The combination of an encrypted message and the secret key

C) Used to secure IP communication between two endpoints

D) An IPSec mode that only encrypts the IP payload

767. Which statement is true?

A) It is bad if MTO < RTO

B) It is good if RTO < AIW

C) It is bad if RPO > RTO

D) It is good if AIW < MTO

768. Which BEST describes load testing?

A) Simulating a heavy amount of traffic during peak areas

B) Increasing the number of active users until the system fails

C) Comparing the system's performance to well-defined benchmarks

D) Incrementally increasing the size of the database until the application fails

769. Which framework is a well-established process to address security risk, and uses three phases?

A) Operationally Critical Threat Asset and Vulnerability Evaluation, or OCTAVE

B) Plan-Do-Check-Act, or PDCA

C) Initiating, Diagnosing, Establishing, Acting and Learning Model, or IDEAL

D) NIST SP 800-30

770. Which BEST describes integration testing?

A) Exercises an individual program or module

B) Exercises a single system

C) Exercises the entire solution across multiple systems

D) Carries out exercises to ensure that two or more components communicate properly with each other

771. Which of the following BEST describes the user project team role?

A) Develops, installs and operates the requested system

B) Provides day-to-day management and leadership of the project

C) Acts as subject matter experts for the development team

D) Create the core project deliverables by completing assigned tasks

772. Which statement BEST describes a black swan event?

A) An expected and recurring instance of a risk that cannot be effectively mitigated without insurance

B) A rare sighting of the 3-footed Ignoble Black Cygnus

C) An unforeseeable event that is a complete surprise and has a major impact

D) A recognized disaster of such a magnitude that if it were to occur a company would be unable to deal with the fallout, forcing it to cease operations

773. Which of the following BEST describes polling?

A) All transmissions contain sufficient redundancy to reconstitute the original data if a collision occurs

B) Used primarily in mainframe environments where a primary station gives permission to each computer to speak

C) Permission to communicate is handed to each computer in-turn

D) A computer attempts to speak and backs off if a collision is detected

774. What are the four steps of benefits realizations at the project level?

A) Understand, plan, execute and close

B) Understand, plan, realize and report

C) Study, plan, execute and close

D) Study, plan, realize and report

775. Which of the following BEST describes an employee?

A) Someone having authorized access into systems and have a broad range of knowledge about the inner workings

B) A significant risk unless their credentials are deleted immediately after termination

C) Someone who can cause significant damage and is the most common source of threats

D) Someone who is particularly dangerous due to their advanced skillset, knowledge of the company's infrastructure and has elevated access

776. Which of the following BEST describes local application?

A) Does not contain water in the pipes until the system is activated

B) Fills the entire enclosed space with an extinguishing agent

C) Can cause considerable collateral damage to equipment when activated

D) The extinguisher sprays the agent directly on the fire

777. You are carrying out an audit in which there is a very comprehensive audit trail. What is the BEST automated evaluation technique to use?

A) Audit Hook

B) Snapshot

C) Continuous and intermittent simulation

D) Integrated test facility

778. When estimating software size, what are the most common methods?

A) Non-FPA and FME

B) Adarac and SLOC

C) SLOC and FPA

D) FME and EBOC

779. When dealing with sampling, which term BEST describes how to prevent over-sampling?

A) Proportional sampling

B) Stop-or-go sampling

C) Variable sampling

D) Attribute sampling

780. What BEST describes the purpose of work papers?

A) To provide authorization for the audit to proceed

B) To provide a clean bridge between the audit goals and the final report

C) To document work falling outside the scope of an audit

D) To document progress as the audit is carried out

781. What is the BEST description of insourcing?

A) When all work is performed onsite in the IT department.

B) When the function is split between in-house and one or more outside parties.

C) When the function is fully performed by the company's staff.

D) When all work being performed at a remote location in the same geographic area.

782. In relation to an expert system, which BEST describes a semantic net?

A) A graph of nodes and arcs between those nodes

B) A list of questions to ask a user until a conclusion is reached

C) A series of 'if...then' relationships

D) Used to load facts into the knowledge base without requiring a programmer

783. When dealing with sampling, which term BEST describes the approach commonly used when looking for fraud or irregularities?

A) Proportional sampling

B) Discovery sampling

C) Stop-or-go sampling

D) Attribute sampling

784. What is the most common cost associated with continuous auditing?

A) Storage space requirements increase

B) Additional hardware is required

C) Increased personnel are required to maintain the systems

D) Reporting levels go up

785. When developing a business case, which of the following BEST describes a feasibility study?

A) Provides enough information to a business for it to decide if it is worth pursuing

B) Defines the problem or opportunity in a clear and concise manner

C) Underlies a business case by studying the problem to see if a solution is practical, meets the stated requirements and can deliver within a set budget and deadline

D) Understanding the current situation as presented by both strengths and weaknesses

786. Which BEST describes the main purpose of an IDE?

A) It allows programmers to write code

B) It allows project managers to manage projects with large amounts of source code

C) It allows quality managers to track defects

D) It allows stakeholders to track progress at the functional level

787. Which is NOT a vulnerability category?

A) Internet of Things (IoT)

B) Cloud computing

C) Physical access

D) Third-Party Vendors

788. What are the four stages of RAD?

A) Requirements collection, design, development and maintenance

B) Concept definition, functional design, development and deployment

C) Design, development, testing and deployment

D) Definition, prototyping, development and testing

789. Which of the following BEST describes the reconnaissance method of a traffic analysis?

A) An attack performed by a manual search in software, OSs or add-on utilities

B) A methodical approach to identify the software and hardware running in the target's network

C) An attack that studies the communication patterns on a network to deduce information

D) An attack in which the names, directories, privileges, shares and policies are listed

790. Which of the following BEST describes a switched virtual circuit?

A) A symmetric telecommunications line permanently connecting two sides

B) A circuit that is created in real-time

C) A circuit that is setup ahead of time

D) A circuit that can be setup and torn down at any time based on the need

791. Which of the following BEST describes total flooding?

A) Fills the entire enclosed space with an extinguishing agent

B) Can cause considerable collateral damage to equipment when activated

C) The extinguisher sprays the agent directly on the fire

D) Does not contain water in the pipes until the system is activated

792. Which of the following BEST describes WEP?

A) Marginally better than its predecessor

B) Claimed to provide protection equivalent to unsecured traffic traveling over a physical Ethernet cable

C) The first real security for wireless traffic

D) Only have to know the SSID and authenticate using an extremely weak protocol

793. Which of the following statements are NOT true?

A) Any path having 0 slack time is by definition a critical path

B) Any path having slack time may or may not be a critical path

C) A critical path by definition has 0 slack time

D) Slack time is common

794. What term describes managing security risks by keeping vulnerabilities and threats to a level that we can live with?

A) Assurance

B) Privacy

C) Criticality

D) Sensitivity

795. Which BEST describes a sequence TOC/TOU attack?

A) Occurs when an untrusted and a trusted process attempt to access the same physical memory

B) Occurs when two trusted processes get in each other's way, effectively locking them both up

C) Occurs when the OS and a trusted process attempt to access the same resource

D) Occurs when an untrusted process manages to insert itself in between TOC and TOU

796. Which of the following is NOT true regarding firewalls?

A) Appliances will perform better

B) Software implementations will be susceptible to weaknesses in the hosting OS

C) Appliance firewalls will come already hardened

D) Appliances and software implementations are generally equal in capabilities

797. What term describes being free from unauthorized intrusion or disclosure of information?

A) Sensitivity

B) Privacy

C) Assurance

D) Criticality

798. Which BEST describes stress testing?

A) Simulating a heavy amount of traffic during peak areas

B) Comparing the system's performance to well-defined benchmarks

C) Increasing the number of active users until the system fails

D) Incrementally increasing the size of the database until the application fails

799. What is NOT a follow-up activity as described by the ISAAS guidelines?

A) Reporting of follow-up activities

B) Declining follow-up activities

C) Deferring follow-up activities

D) Scheduling follow-up activities

800. When discussing paths of logical access, which of the following BEST describes a direct path?

A) Carried out across a network, but the user is generally sitting in a location that has not been physically secured and is normally in a different city

B) Enacted by both front-end and back-end systems

C) Carried out using a local network and can be accomplished even though the user is on a different floor or even a different physical building

D) Represented by physical proximity to a computer

801. Which of the following techniques is not associated with testing physical security?

A) Attempting to physically bypass locked doors and other entry mechanisms

B) Collecting a sample of keys and key cards and attempt to gain access beyond the point at which he or she should have been stopped

C) Checking to see if failed attempts result in log entries that are followed up by an administrator

D) Producing a list of terminal addresses and locations and compare to actual inventory

802. In which phase of the Waterfall SDLC do we resolve conflicts between requirements and the available resources?

A) Phase 2

B) Phase 3B

C) Phase 1

D) Phase 3A

803. In which phase of the Waterfall SDLC do we design the final solution?

A) Phase 3A

B) Phase 4B

C) Phase 3B

D) Phase 4A

804. Which of the following is NOT a fundamental criteria by which a potential vendor should be examined?

A) Bandwidth required

B) Turnaround time

C) Workload capacity

D) System reaction time

805. When boiling down all project management risks, what one item does it come down to?

A) The inability of management to not introduce scope creep

B) The inability to properly estimate effort

C) The innate nature of people to be too optimistic

D) The lack of discipline in managing the software development process

806. Which of the following BEST describes the project manager role?

A) A manager or director responsible for information used to run a business

B) Acts as a liaison between end users and the IT team

C) Plans and executes IS projects, manages the associated budget and reports progress to the appropriate management

D) Responsible for programmers and analysts who implement and maintain systems

807. What is NOT true about a standard?

A) Must not limit our technology options too much

B) There are usually multiple standards for each policy

C) It should never change as technology changes

D) It must provide enough parameters for us to confidently state if a procedure or practice meets the requirements

808. Which of the following statements about auditing policies and procedures is NOT true?

A) IS controls should flow from corporate policies

B) Lower level policies must be consistent with corporate policies

C) If an auditor discovers a policy that hinders the achievement of a business goal, it should be excluded from the final report

D) Policies are within audit scope and should be tested for compliance

809. Which definition BEST describes middleware?

A) Hardware that negotiates between two proxies in real-time

B) Any software that provides run-time services for other components, normally accessible across the network

C) Software that intercepts encrypted web traffic and decrypts on behalf of network components

D) A cloud-based service that provides translation capabilities between two disparate systems

810. Which TOGAF architecture domain defines strategy?

A) Data

B) Technical

C) Business

D) Applications

811. What is the BEST definition for additional objective?

A) The primary reason for a project and can always be tied directly to business success

B) A result not directly tied to the business success, but may contribute to project success

C) Results that are out of scope for the project and are not expected to be delivered

D) A result not directly tied to the business success, but must be achieved for ancillary reasons

812. Which is the BEST definition of release management?

A) Managing change to a system so reliability and security is maintained

B) Managing change to software that may impact end-users

C) Managing change to a system so integrity is maintained

D) Managing change to electronic documents

813. Which BEST describes a botnet?

A) A compromised computer

B) Uses compromised computers to carry out a distributed attack

C) A denial attack that is launched from many compromised computers

D) A collection of previously compromised computers

814. Which of the following BEST describes an applet?

A) A traffic concentration spot

B) An executable, machine-independent software program running on a web server

C) A Java applet or small program that runs within a web server environment

D) A program written in a portable, platform-independent computer language

815. Which of the following BEST describes a DoS attack?

A) Software that waits for a specific condition to be reached and then launches an internal attack

B) Denying consumers the use of a service or server

C) A DoS attack meant to bring down a service by overwhelming it with a huge amount of traffic

D) An attack executed across the Internet against web applications

816. Which of the following BEST describes an SSID?

A) A group of devices communicating in infrastructure mode

B) A wireless network made up of two computers talking to each other over wireless cards

C) A human-friendly name assigned to a group of devices communicating in infrastructure mode

D) A wireless network in which the AP is also connected to another network

817. Which of the following BEST describes maintainability?

A) Provides users with continuous, reliable and secure services

B) Allows a network to scale up or to support new services

C) Occurs when we can connect networks using different technologies or operating at different speeds

D) Means an organization can support a mixed network that delivers highly-integrated solutions

818. When developing a business case, which of the following BEST describes the review?

A) Represent both the stakeholder's needs and constraints

B) Reading the feasibility study report with all stakeholders

C) Deciding if the recommended approach is sufficiently cost-effective

D) The recommended system or software solution that will meet the requirements

819. Which is NOT true of fiber optic cabling?

A) Fiber-optic systems have a low transmission loss as compared to twisted-pair circuits.

B) Optical fiber is larger and heavier than metallic cables of the same capacity

C) Fiber is the preferred choice for high-volume, longer-distance runs

D) Optical fiber is a more fragile medium and is more attractive for applications where changes are infrequent

820. Which of the following BEST describes an enterprise license?

A) Used when multiple end-users will be using the software

B) Allows unlimited use of the software throughout an entire organization

C) Charged according to the number of login accounts

D) A fee is charged for each CPU core running on the computer on which the software is installed

821. Which BEST describes virus?

A) Malicious software that usually tries to get itself appended to the end of legitimate programs on a computer

B) Malicious software that can self-replicate across a network by copying itself from computer to connected computer

C) Malicious software that does not self-replicate or try to attach itself to other files

D) Malicious software that can alter its appearance to outwit scanners

822. Which of the following BEST describes a downtime report?

A) Checks for data transmission accuracy and errors

B) Tracks the availability of telecommunication lines and circuits

C) Identifies the time necessary for a command entered by a user at a terminal to be answered by the host system

D) Provides a history of problems and their resolution

823. Which of the following BEST describes an IT employee?

A) Someone having authorized access into systems and have a broad range of knowledge about the inner workings

B) Someone who can cause significant damage and is the most common source of threats

C) A significant risk unless their credentials are deleted immediately after termination

D) Someone who is particularly dangerous due to their advanced skillset, knowledge of the company's infrastructure and has elevated access

824. Which is the BEST definition of a major incident?

A) An incident that can have a serious material impact on the continued functioning of the business and is often proportional to the length of the incident

B) An incident that produces no negative material or financial impact

C) An incident that causes no significant damage

D) An incident that results in a negative material impact on business processes and may affect other systems, departments of customers

825. Which of the following is NOT an advantage of using a DBMS?

A) It can reduce data duplication through the use of denormalization.

B) It allows data to remain free of any dependency on an application

C) It promotes efficiency by using transactions, which allow multiple actions to be applied at once.

D) It hides the complexity of managing data so that changes are easier to implement.

826. Which of the following statements about identification is NOT true?

A) All IDs should follow some type of naming scheme

B) Accounts that have not been active for a predetermined amount of time should be deactivated

C) Default user accounts such as Guest, Administrator or Admin should be disabled or renamed immediately on installation

D) If no activity in an active session has been detected, the user should be given a warning message

827. Which of the following BEST describes a star topology?

A) All nodes are connected directly to a central device

B) A single cable runs the entire length of the network, with nodes all connected directly to this backbone

C) All nodes are connected directly to each other

D) All nodes are physically connected in a ring

828. What is residual risk?

A) Risk inherent to the business' industry

B) Risk left over after all controls have been applied

C) Risk that cannot be mitigated because of the business' goals

D) Risk residing after controls have been removed due to being too costly

829. Which ITIL volume maintains a service?

A) Service Design

B) Service Operations

C) Service Transition

D) Service Strategy

830. Which of the following is NOT a data file control?

A) Exception report

B) Prerecorded log

C) Version usage

D) One-for-one checking

831. After a system goes live, the auditor should look at all of the following EXCPET for which one?

A) Review internal controls to see if they are working as-designed

B) Users are satisfied with the timeliness and costs of their requests

C) Emergency change procedures are listed in the operations manual

D) Change control is a formal procedure

832. Which of the following is NOT something you would normally find in a DRP?

A) An executive succession plan

B) Procedures for declaring a disaster

C) How the plan links with other plans, for example an emergency response plan or crisis management plan

D) The criteria used to decide when to activate the plan

833. Which of the following statements is false concerning input controls?

A) The source of incoming data matters

B) Output from one system could easily be the input for another

C) Input controls ensure data is valid

D) Input controls ensure data is processed only once

834. Which of the following is NOT a common, legitimate feature that a programmer might use?

A) Special system logon IDs

B) System exits

C) Bypass label processing

D) Backdoor

835. What term describes the training, expertise or experience an individual has?

A) Responsibility

B) Role

C) Informed

D) Skill

836. Which of the following is the BEST description of a Lower CASE tool?

A) Documents detailed designs such as screen and report layouts, editing rules and process flows

B) Generates program code and database schemas

C) Documents business and application requirements such as data object definitions, relationships and processes.

D) Produces production-ready capabilities

837. Which of the following BEST describes a channel?

A) A human-friendly name assigned to a group of devices communicating in infrastructure mode

B) A group of devices communicating in infrastructure mode

C) A wireless network made up of two computers talking to each other over wireless cards

D) A frequency range within wireless traffic

838. Which of the following BEST describes an embedded database 4GL?

A) A proprietary language also running inside of a database but on an enterprise-scale server

B) A language that can run inside of a database on embedded devices

C) A specialized language that can extract data and produce reports

D) A 4GL that generates 3GL code such as COBOL or C

839. Which ISO 27000 role defines the security risk management process?

A) Information security steering committee

B) The auditor

C) Security advisor group

D) Information security administrator

840. Which of the following BEST describes a data storage device that is connected directly to a server or client?

A) DAS

B) RAND

C) NAS

D) RAID

841. Which statement BEST describes the difference between governance and management?

A) Governance is accountable, and management is responsible

B) Governance is informed, and management is responsible

C) Governance decides on the strategy, and management develops goals to meet the strategies

D) Governance sets goals, and management reaches those goals

842. Which of the following BEST describes electronic finance?

A) Allows banking customers to carry out virtually all transactions from the comfort of their home

B) Focuses on providing services such as mortgage loans or insurance policies

C) Enables payments to be made through the use of virtual transactions

D) Computers that physically connect with credit card readers

843. Which of the following BEST describes a part-time and temporary personnel?

A) A party having an increased access but does not possess any loyalty that an employee might have

B) Someone who is not a skilled individual, but simply uses tools created by others to break into systems

C) A skilled person who is interested in proving how smart they are by breaking into systems

D) A person who happens upon unprotected information and decides to take advantage of the situation

844. Which of the following is NOT a communication method used with control signals?

A) Digital voice with or without separate control signals

B) Analog voice with or without separate control signals

C) Digital voice with inclusive control signals

D) Analog voice with inclusive control signals

845. Which of the following options is NOT valid when considering how to purchase software?

A) Ready-made software can be purchased that does not require customization

B) Ready-made software can be purchased that requires acceptable customization

C) The software can be outsourced and hosted by an outside vendor

D) The software can be developed by an outside vendor

846. Which of the following BEST describes a remote procedure call?

A) The name used for functionality currently executing on a remote server

B) Sending a procedure to a remote server where it is executed

C) Executing a component across the network

D) Downloading a component form a remote server that then executes locally

847. What is the BEST description of currency?

A) The breadth and depth

B) How applicable it is

C) The volume

D) If it is up-to-date

848. Which COBIT 5 contextual quality measures how applicable and helpful a value is?

A) Interpretability

B) Relevancy

C) Currency

D) Understandability

849. What does the BCP do with RTOs?

A) It uses them to arrive at a priority restoration order

B) It uses them to calculate MTO and AIW

C) It converts the data into a scheduled mitigation plan

D) It documents them along with supporting evidence

850. Which of the following BEST describes an ERP?

A) A fully-integrated solution that typically combines HR, manufacturing and inventory functions only

B) A solution that enables B2B communications

C) A fully integrated solution that covers multiple areas of business operations

D) A solution that is highly-specific to one business function

851. Which of the following descriptions BEST describes drilling across?

A) Cross-matching a single attribute, and then sorting based on time

B) Looking back in time to see statistics as they used to be within a given time period

C) Filtering data matching one or more attributes, and then presenting a summary of that data

D) Summarizing data at a high level, and then drilling down into the detail as-needed

852. Which of the following BEST describes a switched circuit?

A) A symmetric telecommunications line permanently connecting two sides

B) A circuit that is created in real-time

C) A circuit that can be setup and torn down at any time based on the need

D) A circuit that is setup ahead of time

853. Which of the following statements BEST describes phishing?

A) The use of an email to trick a person into giving away valuable information

B) An email appears to come from an authoritative email address but in reality, was sent from an attacker

C) The use of an email to trick a specific group of people with highly-targeted content into giving away valuable information

D) Calling someone over a phone and convincing them to give away their password

854. Which TOGAF architecture domain describes the structure of management resources?

A) Technical

B) Business

C) Data

D) Applications

855. Which value estimates the percentage of an asset's value that will be destroyed during one occurrence of a threat?

A) EF

B) SLE

C) ARO

D) ALE

856. Which of the following is the BEST description of CA?

A) Confirms that an entity is the real owner of a public key

B) Confirms that you are a real person or company

C) A list of invalid certificates

D) Something that tells us how a CA validates authenticity

857. Which of the following is NOT included with ISACA's Code of Professional Ethics?

A) Maintain confidentiality of information obtained in the course of your activities

B) Maintain competency and undertake only those activities which your skillset supports

C) Perform duties in accordance with professional standards

D) Escalate illegal financial practices to law enforcement officials if an organization is unwilling to correct the situation

858. When dealing with sampling, which term BEST describes measuring the percentage of data points in a population having a specific value?

A) Attribute sampling

B) Discovery sampling

C) Variable sampling

D) Proportional sampling

859. Which of the following standards is the most useful in ensuring a partner stays in compliance with security controls?

A) ISO 20000

B) ISO 27001

C) ISO 20002

D) ISO 27002

860. In relation to BI analysis models, which is the BEST description of a context diagram?

A) Allows us to deconstruct a business process

B) Models data entities and how each relates to another

C) Visualizes contextual relationships between entities

D) Outlines the major processes and external parties an organization deals with

861. Which of the following is NOT a major advantage of cloud computing?

A) We can scale resources up or down as desired, resulting in a virtually unlimited resource pool

B) We can move capital expenditures to operational expenditures

C) It becomes easier to deploy enhancements to applications

D) It makes it much easier to apply upgrades and patches

862. Which is the BEST description of Frame Relay?

A) Achieves higher rates because it uses all available frequencies on a UTP line

B) An older technology, it was designed to compensate by adding error checking and correcting as well as fault tolerance, resulting in a high overhead

C) A newer technology, it is a switching technology but uses cells instead of packets

D) An older technology, it allowed more than one party to share in a single dedicated line across a WAN

863. At what three levels does IT risk management operate?

A) Strategic, technical and procedural

B) Operational, project and strategic

C) Technical, management and procedural

D) Operational, technical and management

864. Which of the following statements BEST describes ICS?

A) A system that coordinates tasks between geographically-separated industrial components

B) The ability to monitor and alert geographically-separated industrial components

C) A system that controls industrial infrastructure components

D) The networked infrastructure shared between industrial infrastructure components

865. What are the three components required on each end of an EDI exchange?

A) Communications handler, EDI interface and an application interface

B) Communications handler, EDI interface and an application system

C) Communications handler, EDI translator and an application interface

D) Communications handler, EDI interface and EDI translator

866. Which of the following statements BEST describes a scanner?

A) Analyzing instructions in a file and decides if it looks like malware

B) Comparing bit strings in a file against a pattern known to represent malware

C) Looking for malware at the DOS and BIOS level

D) Examining areas of a computer looking for strings of bits that looks like malware

867. What are the three key elements in fraud?

A) Reason, rationalization and opening

B) Motivation, means and opening

C) Motivation, rationalization and opportunity

D) Motivation, means and opportunity

868. Which of the following BEST describes a data conversion component?

A) Identifying affected modules and data entities during a data migration project

B) Provides translation services between two repositories

C) Provides adapters to connect to both the legacy and new repositories

D) A list of tasks needed to deploy legacy data to production

869. Which of the following BEST describes a checklist review test?

A) The recovery site is brought up to a state of operational readiness, but operations at the primary site continue

B) Team members role-playing a simulated disaster without activating the recovery site

C) An assessment of all steps to be carried out

D) Team members implement the plan on paper

870. What is the type of software that manages changes to software source code?

A) Check-in/Check-out management

B) Change management system

C) Version control system

D) Change control system

871. Which of the following BEST describes a repeater?

A) A device that connects LAN segments

B) A device that simply amplifies a signal and forwards it on.

C) A device that amplifies a signal and has multiple ports

D) A device that filters traffic based on the MAC Addresses

872. Which COBIT 5 principal defines seven enablers?

A) Enabling a holistic approach

B) Covering the enterprise end-to-end

C) Separating governance from management

D) Applying a single, integrated framework

873. What term describes the ability to protect information from improper modification?

A) Nonrepudiation

B) Authentication

C) Integrity

D) Confidentiality

874. Which BEST describes a DDoS?

A) A collection of previously compromised computers

B) Uses compromised computers to carry out a distributed attack

C) A denial attack that is launched from many compromised computers

D) A compromised computer

875. Which statement is true about the audit charter?

A) It must be approved at the executive level

B) The audit may proceed without it being approved

C) It must be approved at an appropriate level

D) It must be approved prior to the final report

876. Which standard or process BEST allows us to diagnose an event to determine its origin?

A) PRINCE2

B) ISO 38500

C) Life Cycle Cost-Benefit Analysis

D) Root Cause Analysis

877. Which of the following BEST describes a local area network?

A) A network of personal devices such as smartphones or watches

B) Covers a limited are such as a home, office or even a campus with multiple buildings

C) Covers broad areas such as a city, region, nation or even an international link

D) A specialized version of a LAN dedicated to storing large amounts of data

878. Which of the following BEST describes a Halon system?

A) A gas that extinguishes a fire by lowering the temperature of the components

B) Releases pressurized gas that removes oxygen from the air, but was discontinued in the 1990s

C) A gas that reduces the amount of oxygen available for a fire to use

D) Automated systems are only allowed in dark facilities where no people are present

879. Which of the following BEST describes the senior management role?

A) Shows commitment to the project by providing approval for the necessary resources to be successful

B) Owns the project and the resulting deliverable

C) Provides funding and defines the critical success factors and metrics that determine if the project is a success

D) Provides overall direction and represents the major stakeholders

880. What does each function in RACI stand for?

A) Responsible, Accountable, Checked and Informed

B) Responsible, Answerable, Checked and Informed

C) Responsible, Answerable, Consulted and Informed

D) Responsible, Accountable, Consulted and Informed

881. Which BEST describes the difference between the IT strategy committee and the IT steering committee?

A) The IT strategy committee has no authority other than as advisors, whereas the IT steering committee makes all final decisions

B) The IT strategy committee is created as-needed, whereas the IT steering committee is permanently formed

C) The IT strategy committee is made up of two executives, whereas the IT steering committee is made up of senior managers

D) The IT strategy committee acts as an advisor to the entire board in developing the strategy, whereas the IT steering committee assists the sponsoring executive in executing the strategy

882. Which of the following BEST describes an access control list?

A) An access method in which the user can delegate rights as-needed

B) A matrix of users and assets with the permission residing at the intersections

C) An access method which gives the user no ability to change the level of access granted to others

D) Data that dictates the rights a user has to specific assets

883. In relation to an expert system, which BEST describes a data interface?

A) A graph of nodes and arcs between those nodes

B) Used to load facts into the knowledge base without requiring a programmer

C) Enables the expert system to collect data from non-human sources

D) A list of questions to ask a user until a conclusion is reached

884. Which of the following BEST describes an end user?

A) Someone who is particularly dangerous due to their advanced skillset, knowledge of the company's infrastructure and has elevated access

B) Someone who can cause significant damage and is the most common source of threats

C) A significant risk unless their credentials are deleted immediately after termination

D) Someone having authorized access into systems and have a broad range of knowledge about the inner workings

885. Which of the following is NOT a valid technique to test password security?

A) Examining the internal password table

B) Dumpster diving

C) Trying to guess passwords on a terminal

D) Look into wastebaskets

886. Which of the following BEST describes an attacker taking advantage of hardware conferencing?

A) Taking advantage of an undocumented feature

B) Listening in on the active voice channel of a line placed into maintenance mode

C) Gaining physical access to a bridge and routing all signals to a specific port

D) Listening in on voice activity by accessing the physical communication between the PBX and the end-user device

887. Which of the following is NOT a risk when dealing with instant messaging?

A) It becomes an entry point for viruses and malware

B) Excessive use can impact employee productivity

C) It increases internal network traffic

D) It could allow eavesdropping

888. Which of the following is NOT a valid batch total control?

A) The total monetary amount

B) The number of total documents

C) A source document

D) The number of total items

889. Which of the following is NOT true of frame relay?

A) It operates at the data link layer

B) It is a newer technology

C) The cost to each consumer is loosely based on the amount of bandwidth needed, as opposed to the distance between the two endpoints

D) It uses packet switching for transmission

890. Which statement is NOT true?

A) The cost of a risk can usually be mitigated by a compensating control

B) Risk always carries a cost, whether it is controlled or not.

C) If there is risk associated with taking some kind of action, there is also risk associated with not taking that action.

D) Mitigating one risk will almost always increase another risk, or perhaps even create another risk.

891. Which of the following BEST describes an IDS?

A) Is installed on a computer and monitors all local traffic as well as network traffic

B) Is installed on a computer and monitors traffic coming into and out of the computer

C) Monitors all network traffic

D) Looks at passing traffic to see if it can detect any attach patterns or unauthorized usage

892. Which ITIL volume looks at stakeholder needs?

A) Service Design

B) Service Operations

C) Service Strategy

D) Service Transition

893. What BEST describes the purpose of an audit engagement letter?

A) Lists all relevant parties to take part in an audit

B) Documents the timeline and deliverables for the audit

C) Provides authorization to carry out an audit

D) Describes a focused exercise intended for a very specific purpose and can track change requests

894. Which phase of the Waterfall SDLC collects non-functional requirements?

A) Phase 3B

B) Phase 3A

C) Phase 1

D) Phase 2

895. When auditing BPR, which of the following areas is the auditor's primary concern?

A) That controls will not be properly created in the final solution

B) That control modifications are not properly documented

C) That key controls may be reengineered out of a business process

D) That a resulting risk analysis is not performed on the final solution

896. What is the BEST description of reputation?

A) True and credible

B) Unbiased, unprejudiced and impartial

C) Highly regarded in terms of source or context

D) Correct and reliable

897. Which of the following is the BEST description of an authentication header?

A) Data added to the header when using IPSec in tunnel mode

B) An IPSec session attribute that dictates various configuration options

C) The encrypted payload when using ESP

D) An IPSec mode that encrypts both the payload and header

898. When auditing EDI, which of the following is NOT an area that should be considered?

A) Edit checks identify erroneous, unusual or invalid transactions

B) The sender should include segment count totals into the header

C) Encryption is used

D) Each inbound transaction is logged on receipt

899. Which of the following biometric terms best describes hand topography?

A) The shape, length and width of hand and fingers

B) A complete record of ridges and valley on a finger

C) Certain features of a fingerprint

D) A side camera captures the contour of the palm and fingers

900. Which of the following BEST describes ISO/IEC 38500 Corporate governance of information technology?

A) A German collection of documents useful for detecting and addressing security weaknesses in an IT environment

B) A specification for service management that is aligned with ITIL

C) Targeted for those at the highest level of an organization and provides guiding principles on the acceptable use of IT from a legal and ethical point of view

D) Created in the UK and provides a very hands-on and detailed framework on implementing GEIT

901. Which of the following BEST describes ISO 20000?

A) A specification for service management that is aligned with ITIL

B) A process-based security model for IT

C) Targeted for those at the highest level of an organization and provides guiding principles on the acceptable use of IT from a legal and ethical point of view

D) A series of standards that help an organization implement and maintain an information security program, and is the standard to which most companies are certified against

902. What type of application follows the software development life cycle and attempts to collect, store and share information with users on a need-to-know basis?

A) User-acceptable applications

B) Business-focused applications

C) Organization-centric applications

D) End-user-centric applications

903. What is the proper order of an APT life cycle?

A) Initial compromise, internal reconnaissance, establish foothold, escalate privileges, move laterally, maintain presence, complete the mission

B) Initial compromise, establish foothold, escalate privileges, internal reconnaissance, move laterally, maintain presence, complete the mission

C) Initial compromise, escalate privileges, establish foothold, internal reconnaissance, maintain presence, move laterally, complete the mission

D) Initial compromise, internal reconnaissance, establish foothold, move laterally, escalate privileges, maintain presence, complete the mission

904. Which of the following security planning roles BEST describes a managers?

A) Oversees the incident response capability

B) Provides assistance based on subject matter expertise

C) Manages individual incidents

D) Acts as the liaison to business process owners

905. When starting a project, which of the following is NOT a recognized opportunity to communicate to team members?

A) One-on-on-one meetings

B) Project wiki standup

C) Project start workshops

D) Kick-off meetings

906. Which of the following non-removable disk-based solutions BEST describes a host-based replication?

A) A solution that looks like a tape library but really uses a disk array for storage

B) Taking an image of a system, restoring onto a second system, and backing up this secondary environment

C) Software living on a server that replicates changes to another server invisibly

D) Similar to host-based replication, but it is carried out at the disk array level instead of software installed on the OS

907. Which of the following is NOT an area of audit concern when reviewing ATMs?

A) Review the ability to generate exception reports from an audit trail

B) Review encryption key change management procedures

C) Examine the ATM card slot, key pad and enclosure to prevent skimming of card data and capture of PIN during entry

D) Examine the physical perimeter to ensure a well-lit area

908. Which of the following BEST describes token passing?

A) Permission to communicate is handed to each computer in-turn

B) Used primarily in mainframe environments where a primary station gives permission to each computer to speak

C) A computer attempts to speak and backs off if a collision is detected

D) All transmissions contain sufficient redundancy to reconstitute the original data if a collision occurs

909. Which of the following BEST describes the end user role?

A) Tasked with managing data and the data architecture

B) Responsible for daily operations related to business services

C) The actual user of data, including both internal and external users

D) Answers technical questions and solve problems faced by internal employees

910. Which BEST describes capacity management?

A) Documenting future needs and translating into purchasing decisions

B) Ensuring that funding levels are available for required hardware purchases

C) Watching computing and network resources so that levels match business plans

D) Bringing strategy, goals and execution into alignment by setting capacity levels

911. Which is the BEST definition of a crisis incident?

A) An incident that can have a serious material impact on the continued functioning of the business and is often proportional to the length of the incident

B) An incident that results in a negative material impact on business processes and may affect other systems, departments of customers

C) An incident that produces no negative material or financial impact

D) An incident that causes no significant damage

912. What is NOT a basic element when reviewing the BCP?

A) Review the business continuity terms

B) Review business infrastructure

C) Review the document

D) Plan testing

913. Which of the following BEST describes a migration screenplay?

A) Identifying affected modules and data entities during a data migration project

B) Provides adapters to connect to both the legacy and new repositories

C) Provides translation services between two repositories

D) A list of tasks needed to deploy legacy data to production

914. Which of the following statements is NOT true regarding a digital signature?

A) The signature can be reused

B) The signature cannot be forged

C) The signed message cannot be altered because it will render the signature invalid

D) The signature is authentic and encrypted

915. Which type of audit examines controls and how well they deliver CIA?

    A) Specialized

    B) Compliance

    C) IS

    D) Financial

916. Which of the following is the BEST description of a digital envelope?

    A) An IPSec mode that only encrypts the IP payload

    B) Used to secure IP communication between two endpoints

    C) The combination of an encrypted message and the secret key

    D) How IPSec manages keys

917. Which of the following is NOT a disadvantage of CSA?

    A) The overhead of CSA can become just another item to get done

    B) If the company does not act on employee suggestions morale will suffer

    C) It can provide a false security of remaining in compliance

    D) If successful, the company might mistake CSA for a real audit

918. Which is greatest source of man-made threats?

    A) Employees

    B) Mistakes

    C) An advanced persistent threat, or APT

    D) External attackers

919. Which of the following BEST describes how data flows from a LAN to a WAN?

    A) LAN > (magic happens here) > WAN

    B) LAN > switch > DSU > CSU > switch > WAN

    C) LAN > switch > CSU > DSU > switch > WAN

    D) LAN > switch > DCE > DTE > switch > WAN

920. What is the most important aspect of choosing a risk assessment approach?

    A) It is acceptable to all stake-holders

    B) It is based on well-known standards

    C) It is used consistently throughout the audit

    D) It reports in the same manner as other approaches used within the audit

921. Which of the following is NOT an advantage of outsourcing?

    A) Liabilities are often mitigated

    B) Achieving economies of scale by reusing component software

    C) Better requirements and specifications

    D) Greater experience with a specific area than in-house staff

922. Which of the following are valid concerns when using VoIP?

    A) Vendors tend to be less reputable due to the low barrier of entry

    B) It is less reliable than traditional telephony

    C) Some countries ban the use of VoIP

    D) Security concerns increase because we have to deal with voice and data

923. What is NOT true about employee bonding?

    A) It is a control used during the hiring process

    B) It protects against losses due to theft, neglect or mistakes

    C) It is not legal in some countries

    D) It is used only within non-federal organizations

924. Which of the following statements is NOT true regarding UAT?

A) The accepted version must be version-controlled

B) If production data is to be used, confidential data must be scrubbed before use

C) The data used should represent production data as close as possible

D) The test environment should not be alterable during testing, except for changes made by the vendor

925. Which of the following BEST describes a 4GL query and report generator?

A) A 4GL that generates 3GL code such as COBOL or C

B) A proprietary language also running inside of a database but on an enterprise-scale server

C) A specialized language that can extract data and produce reports

D) A language that can run inside of a database on embedded devices

926. Which of the following BEST describes a key value NoSQL database?

A) All values are stored with an attribute name

B) Based on graph theory

C) Values are retrieved by specifying the column

D) Entire documents are stored as ether XML or JSON

927. Which value estimates the amount of time required to getting a compromised facility back to an acceptable level of operation?

A) MTO

B) RTO

C) RPO

D) AIW

928. Which of the Waterfall SLDC phases do we encounter first when purchasing software?

A) Phase 3B

B) Phase 3A

C) Phase 4B

D) Phase 4A

929. Which of the following BEST describes a logic bomb attack?

A) An attack executed across the Internet against web applications

B) Software that waits for a specific condition to be reached and then launches an internal attack

C) A DoS attack meant to bring down a service by overwhelming it with a huge amount of traffic

D) Denying consumers the use of a service or server

930. You are auditing a business and need to ensure information systems are well-documented. What audit technique is BEST suited?

A) Observing Processes and Employee Performance

B) Reviewing IS Policies and Procedures

C) Interviewing Appropriate Personnel

D) Reviewing IS Documentation

931. Which of the following is the BEST definition of an influence project organization?

A) The project manager does not have official authority to manage the project

B) The project manager does have official authority over the project

C) Project authority is shared between the project manager and department heads

D) Multiple project managers share authority over the project

932. When auditing a lights-out operation, which of the following is NOT something an auditor to validate?

A) Remote access to the master console in case of a software failure is secured

B) Routine access is properly logged

C) Contingency plans allow for the proper identification of a disaster in the unattended facility

D) Tests of the software are performed on a periodic basis, especially after changes or updates have been applied

933. What are the five rights that access rules commonly provide?

A) Create, copy, update, delete and execute

B) Create, move, update, delete and execute

C) Create, copy, move, delete and execute

D) Create, read, update, delete and execute

934. Which of the following definitions BEST describes a mixed environment?

A) Security is completely under the control of IS management

B) Security is under the direction of individuals, but the overall responsibility remains with IS management

C) Security is under the direction of IS management, with IS management staff maintaining a close relationship with users

D) Security is under the direction of individuals, but adheres to the guidelines established by IS management

935. Which of the following is NOT an item an auditor would look for when reviewing environmental controls?

A) The testing interval for fire suppression systems

B) The most recent test dates for UPS and generators

C) The most recent version of the DRP is available

D) Power supply to water and smoke detectors

936. Which of the following BEST describes a ring topology?

A) All nodes are connected directly to a central device

B) All nodes are connected directly to each other

C) A single cable runs the entire length of the network, with nodes all connected directly to this backbone

D) All nodes are physically connected in a ring

937. What is an emerging threat?

A) A hint that something is going on based on mounting evidence

B) A threat based on new technology

C) A threat which has struck only a handful of organizations

D) A forewarning from vendors based on anecdotal evidence from their customers

938. What is the BEST description of an emergency release?

A) A release that contains small enhancements and fixes

B) A release that contains significant changes to existing functionality or the addition of new features

C) A release that prevents significant downtime or impact to the customer

D) A release that addresses a small list of customer complaints

939. Which of the following BEST describes a script kiddie?

A) A skilled person who is interested in proving how smart they are by breaking into systems

B) Someone who is not a skilled individual, but simply uses tools created by others to break into systems

C) A person who happens upon unprotected information and decides to take advantage of the situation

D) A party having an increased access but does not possess any loyalty that an employee might have

940. Which of the following descriptions BEST describes bottom-up estimating?

A) Estimates the cost of each activity in the current project, and sums the results

B) Looks at previous estimates of employee hours, materials cost and technology, and uses statistics to extrapolate those estimates to our current project

C) The quickest estimation technique, and uses estimates from prior projects

D) Looks at the raw costs in a previous project and extrapolates to the current project

941. Which of the following BEST describes availability?

A) Provides users with continuous, reliable and secure services

B) Occurs when we can connect networks using different technologies or operating at different speeds

C) Allows a network to scale up or to support new services

D) Means an organization can support a mixed network that delivers highly-integrated solutions

942. Which of the following BEST describes the reconnaissance method of a browsing attack?

A) An attack that studies the communication patterns on a network to deduce information

B) A methodical approach to identify the software and hardware running in the target's network

C) An attack in which the names, directories, privileges, shares and policies are listed

D) An attack performed by a manual search in software, OSs or add-on utilities

943. What is the term describing when a vulnerability is taken advantage of by an attacker?

A) Control

B) Exploit

C) Impact

D) Threat

944. When dealing with sampling, which term BEST describes the average value of all samples?

A) Level of risk

B) Sample mean

C) Tolerable error rate

D) Expected error rate

945. Which definition BEST describes a hybrid model?

A) The solution is privately hosted but connects across the public Internet into another application

B) The solution is entirely hosted inside of a company's intranet and is not accessible externally

C) The solution is privately hosted, but a select few other companies are allowed to access it

D) The solution is hosted across the Internet and is publicly accessible

946. Which of the following is NOT a goal for application controls?

A) Data is maintained and not lost

B) Only complete, accurate and valid data is accepted

C) Processing results meet the expected outcome

D) Background processes execute on-time

947. Which of the following BEST represents the grandfather-father-son rotation scheme?

A) Son is the last backup, father is the every 7th backup, and grandfather is every 30th backup

B) Son is the daily backup, father is the last backup of the week, and grandfather is the last backup of the month

C) Son is the weekly backup, father is the last backup of the month, and grandfather is the last backup of the year

D) Son is the weekly backup, father is the monthly backup, and grandfather is the annual backup

948. Which of the following statements is false?

A) CRM is the process of tracking and managing relationships with customers

B) Analytical CRM does not require operational CRM data

C) Operational CRM captures data about the interaction between the customer and employees

D) Operational CRM focuses on the customer's experience

949. Which of the following BEST describes data-in-motion?

A) Applications deployed to log onto each system and look through the various data stores

B) Any information persisted to storage such as hard drives, USB drives, tape backups or in live databases

C) Information that is being manipulated by end users at their workstation

D) Any information moving around a network or being transferred between two processes

950. Which of the following is NOT a valid authorization control?

A) Online access controls

B) A hash total

C) A unique password

D) A physical signature

951. Which BEST describes polymorphic virus?

A) Malicious software that does not cause damage other than silently listening and collecting sensitive information to send back to the attacker

B) Malicious software that can self-replicate across a network by copying itself from computer to connected computer

C) Malicious software that can alter its appearance to outwit malware scanners

D) Malicious software that usually tries to get itself appended to the end of legitimate programs on a computer

952. Which of the following is NOT an IDS algorithm?

A) Neural network

B) Fourier transformation

C) Signature

D) Statistical

953. What does an XML schema provide?

A) Identifies the source of the XML payload

B) A description of the accompanying XML payload

C) Retransmission requirements

D) Encryption/decryption parameters

954. Which BEST describes a bot herder?

A) A collection of previously compromised computers

B) A compromised computer

C) Uses compromised computers to carry out a distributed attack

D) A denial attack that is launched from many compromised computers

955. Which BEST describes the difference between computer crime and computer abuse?

A) Abuse calls a law into question but does not clearly violate it

B) The jurisdiction and the court sentence

C) The geographical location

D) And abuse becomes a crime when the activity is prosecuted

956. What is the best definition of resource leveling?

A) Obtaining additional resources to offset task durations that tend to spike

B) Attempting to hire team members of the same height

C) Smoothing out resource peaks and valleys

D) Assigning resources well in-advance of the project kick-off

957. Which control category warns of attempted or successful violations of a security policy?

A) Detective

B) Compensating

C) Preventative

D) Corrective

958. Which of the following BEST describes the presentation access layer of BI?

A) Where the results of data preparation are stored

B) The point at which end-users interact with the system

C) Contains the bulk of interesting data, and is usually a relational database

D) Contains the logic necessary to prepare data from the warehouse

959. Which of the following statements does NOT represent an area in which an auditor will need to focus?

A) Review all OS configuration folders and files used to grant special privileges

B) Look for an active capacity management function

C) Examining problem reports and error logs to ensure they are addressed in a timely manner

D) Evaluate help desk activity to see which areas receive the most reports

960. Which is the BEST definition of change management?

A) Managing change to a system so integrity is maintained

B) Managing change to a system so reliability and security is maintained

C) Managing change to software that may impact end-users

D) Managing change to electronic documents

961. Which of the following statements is NOT true regarding synchronous communication?

A) Both devices must agree on a start time

B) It is not as reliable as asynchronous

C) It requires a very stable connection that may be used by more than two devices

D) It is ideal for high-volume transmissions

962. Which of the following BEST describes a surge protector?

A) Mitigates short-term interruptions such as sags, spikes and surges

B) Measures the incoming electrical current and either increase or decrease the charge to ensure a consistent current

C) An increase in voltage

D) Caused by electrical storms or nearby noisy electrical equipment such as motors, fluorescent lighting or radio transmitters

963. Which of the following statements about logical access is NOT true?

A) Centralized management results in controls being monitored more frequently

B) Decentralized management speeds up the resolution of issues

C) Decentralized management allows each location to manage their own security

D) Centralized management implements the same rules and standards across the entire company

964. What is the BEST definition of elasticity?

A) Resources can rapidly scale up or down

B) Storage capabilities can increase as-needed

C) Bandwidth can be gradually increased in response to traffic

D) The billing model can change according to real-time use

965. Which of the following BEST represents one or more attributes belonging to one entity that map to another entity's primary key?

    A) A relational key

    B) A primary key

    C) A foreign key

    D) A key

966. Which of the following BEST describes WPA2?

    A) The first real security for wireless traffic

    B) Marginally better than its predecessor

    C) Only have to know the SSID and authenticate using an extremely weak protocol

    D) Claimed to provide protection equivalent to unsecured traffic traveling over a physical Ethernet cable

967. Which term refers to eavesdropping on telecommunications lines?

    A) Wiresniffing

    B) Landsniffing

    C) Wiretapping

    D) Data inference

968. When auditing network infrastructure, which of the following is NOT a primary goal?

    A) Ensure the proper controls are being used

    B) Ensure standards are being used for the design

    C) Ensure standards are being used for selecting a network architecture

    D) Check that costs for procuring and operating a network do not exceed the benefits

969. An employee is voluntarily leaving the company on good terms. Which of the following is not required under best practices?

    A) Arrangement of final paychecks so the employee is removed from the active payroll

    B) Review of the termination interview to gather insight from the employee's perception of management

    C) Deletion or revocation of all assigned logon IDs and passwords

    D) Notification to appropriate staff and security personnel about the employee's status being changed to 'terminated'

970. Which of the following BEST describes non-operational in the data source layer of BI?

    A) Data provided by systems external to the BI system

    B) Data easily collected but has not yet been processed

    C) Data collected during normal business operations and normally held in easy-to-access databases

    D) Data needed by end users but is not currently in an accessible format

971. Which of the following is NOT true regarding RFID?

    A) The microchip always contains a unique identifier

    B) A tag consists of both a microchip and antenna

    C) An active tag has the same communication distance as a passive tag but is more reliable

    D) A passive tag draws power from radiation sent from the reader

972. Which TOGAF ADM phase identifies the gap between as-is and to-be?

    A) Migration planning phase

    B) Implementation governance phase

    C) Business architecture phase

    D) Opportunities and solutions phase

973. When dealing with sampling, which term BEST describes looking at certain attributes that match some type of criteria?

A) Proportional sampling

B) Attribute sampling

C) Stop-or-go sampling

D) Discovery sampling

974. Which FEA reference model describes how to build services?

A) Business Reference Model

B) Service Component Reference Model

C) Technical Reference Model

D) Data Reference Model

975. Which statement is true regarding short-term and long-term plans?

A) Long-term goals address strategic changes in the business' IT environment

B) Long-term goals should be revisited at least every two years

C) Short-term plans cover audit goals to be covered within the next two years

D) The business should decide on a short-term or a long-term approach, but having both will simply confuse the situation

976. Which of the following BEST describes an airlock entrance?

A) An unauthorized person following an authorized person through a secured entry

B) A control that uses two doors, in which the person entering must close the first door before the second door may be opened

C) Requires that all visitors be escorted by a responsible employee

D) A control used by all incoming personnel and normally monitored by a receptionist

977. Which of the following is NOT a recommended way to mitigate risks when using virtualization?

A) Any changes to a host must go through stringent change management processes

B) A HIDS (Host IDS) should be installed on each VM as well as the hypervisor

C) Strong physical and logical access controls to the host and its management console must be applied

D) VMs should be segregated in the network just like a physical machine would be

978. Which of the following is NOT a primary goal for portfolio management?

A) Focus on internal resources only

B) Prioritize and schedule projects

C) Optimize the results of the portfolio, but not the individual projects

D) Ensure knowledge transfer across projects

979. Which of the following is NOT a required component for an EDI system?

A) Communications software

B) A shared standard

C) Translation software

D) A partner profile

980. Which framework is geared specifically to IT?

A) FEA

B) Balanced Scorecard, or BSC

C) Capability Maturity Model Integration, or CMMI

D) COBIT 5

981. What is the BEST reason an auditor should use sampling?

A) Sampling provides the best balance between accuracy and precision

B) There is not enough time to look at every transaction or data point

C) A sampling approach requires fewer authorizations

D) Many laws and regulations require this approach

982. When auditing digital signature capabilities, which of the following is NOT an attribute to look for?

A) The signature can be verified

B) The mechanism for generating and assigning the signature is under the sole control of the person using it

C) The digital signature has not expired

D) The digital signature is unique to the person using it

983. Which of the following terms does not apply to having to provide both a password and a token?

A) Strong authentication

B) 2-factor authentication

C) Multifactor authentication

D) Bi-direction authentication

984. Which of the following is NOT a step in the BIA process?

A) Gather assessment material

B) Gather final approval and record signatures

C) Analyze the information

D) Document the results and present recommendations

985. What type of risk deals with material errors going unnoticed by the auditor?

A) Control risk

B) Audit risk

C) Inherent risk

D) Detection risk

986. In relation to an expert system, which BEST describes facts?

A) Facts expressed in one of several models

B) Data that comes in from a sensor or system that is being monitored

C) Artificial intelligence to infer relationships and arrive at a decision

D) Components within a system yet to be loaded with facts or rules

987. Which of the following descriptions BEST describes IS management?

A) Ensures CIA, or confidentiality, integrity and availability

B) Makes sure that processes run smoothly

C) Coordinates alignment between IT execution and corporate strategy

D) Manages resources

988. Which federal law sets the minimum amount of capital for financial organizations based on the level of risk each face?

A) GDPR

B) Basel Accords

C) SOX

D) HIPAA

989. Which of the following is NOT a valid way to reduce outsourcing risk?

A) Use short-term contracts

B) Ensure the vendor sub-contracts the most sensitive functions

C) Leverage escrows when dealing with source code

D) Contract with multiple suppliers

990. Which of the following BEST describes the operations manager role?

A) Responsible for maintaining multi-user computer systems including the network connecting them together

B) Defines and maintains the structure of a corporate database, and is the custodian of the company's data

C) Is normally separate from the IT department and reports up through the CISO

D) Responsible for running the data center, including managing staff

991. Which of the following BEST describes a proxy server?

A) A server that stores data and acts as a repository for information

B) A server that is dedicated to a single function and normally is not capable of being extended

C) A server that hosts the software programs that networked consumers utilize

D) A server that sits between an end-user and a resource, and makes requests to the resource on the user's behalf

992. Which of the following is NOT true of ATM?

A) It is a switching technology but uses cells instead of packets

B) It is a great choice for audio and video transmission and provides QoS

C) It does not use virtual circuits so guaranteed bandwidth is not possible

D) It can be very cost-efficient because companies are billed based on the bandwidth used

993. Which of the following BEST describes a stand-alone WLAN?

A) A wireless network in which the AP is also connected to another network

B) A wireless network in which both computers are connected to an access point instead of each other

C) A frequency range within wireless traffic

D) A wireless network made up of two computers talking to each other over wireless cards

994. Which of the following BEST describes echo checking?

A) Validates that all data sent to a host is returned with no lost data

B) Operates at the data link or network level and often recommend possible solutions to issues

C) Provides a real time display of network nodes and status

D) Monitors packets flowing along a link and produces network usage reports

995. Which of the following is NOT a key capability that a full-fledged DLP must provide?

A) The ability to control network appliance to prevent sensitive data form leaving the network

B) Integration with directory services allowing the DLP to map a network address to a specific user

C) A backup and restore feature to preserve policies and settings

D) Some type of a workflow management capacity so that we can configure how incidents are handled

996. Which of the following depend on the size and complexity of a PBX?

A) The number of auditors required

B) The final reports needed

C) Types of skills needed

D) How long the audit will take

997. Which BEST describes the difference between compliance and substantive testing?

A) Compliance testing proves our controls match corresponding procedures, while substantive testing ensures the controls fulfill everything within the procedure

B) Compliance testing proves we can monitor controls, while substantive testing proves we can test controls

C) Compliance testing proves controls are compliant, while substantive testing proves that controls can provide CIA

D) Compliance testing proves we have controls to carry out procedures, while substantive testing proves that those controls are working

998. What is the BEST definition for non-objective?

A) A result not directly tied to the business success, but must be achieved for ancillary reasons

B) Results that are out of scope for the project and are not expected to be delivered

C) A result not directly tied to the business success, but may contribute to project success

D) The primary reason for a project and can always be tied directly to business success

999. Which statement is true regarding materiality?

A) Materiality is a measure of the level of risk associated with a specific control

B) Material error can often be a simple oversight

C) A material error does not fundamentally change how something is seen

D) As materiality increases, the impact increases

1000. Which of the following BEST describes the information system security engineer role?

A) Reviews results and deliverables for each phase to confirm compliance with the stated requirements

B) Acts as subject matter experts for the development team

C) Carries out the tasks that will inform the security officer of how well the system implements proper security measures

D) Ensures the deliverable provides an appropriate level of protection

1001. What is NOT a typical source for APTs?

A) Activist groups

B) Corporate espionage

C) Armed forces

D) Intelligence agencies

1002. Which of the following BEST describes physical topology?

A) How computers are arranged relative to each other within a network

B) How the cables are laid out and how they are connected to each computer

C) How computers use various protocols to communicate with each other

D) How the computers communicate over the physical cabling

1003. Which term identifies the automated evaluation technique that tags transactions with a unique identifier?

A) Integrated test facility

B) Snapshot

C) Audit hook

D) SCARF/EAM

1004. Which BEST describes malicious code?

A) Malware that disguises itself as useful program such as a utility, OS patch or game

B) Bits of software code left by a programmer to allow them back in at a later date

C) Capturing a message in-transit, and modifying, delaying or deleting it

D) Software installed onto a target computer to steal information or cause further harm

1005. Which of the following BEST describes manual logging?

A) A control that uses two doors, in which the person entering must close the first door before the second door may be opened

B) Video cameras that capture local activity around a facility

C) The act of a person signing into and out of a physical log

D) Automate logging by electronic and biometric locks

1006. Which of the following is NOT a primary driver for continuous auditing?

A) The use of software to ensure financial controls are working

B) Detection of segregation of duties controls

C) Real-time financial monitoring

D) Prevention of fraud scandals

1007. Which of the following BEST describes a sag?

A) A decrease in voltage

B) An increase in voltage

C) A total failure with a complete loss of power

D) A severely reduced voltage due to the failure of a power company to supply power within an acceptable range

1008. Which of the following BEST describes gaining access by using packet replay?

A) Capturing legitimate packets passing by on a network, and then sending them back

B) An attack executed across the Internet against web applications

C) Guessing passwords to gain access to a system by simply rotating through all possible values until the system grants access

D) Exploiting a small window of time between the time that a security control is applied and the time that a service is used

1009. Which of the following is NOT a recognized hiring risk?

A) Reference checks may not be carried out

B) Contract or third-party staff may go-around the HR policies

C) An employee lack of awareness on confidentiality requirements may lead to unintentional leaks

D) RACI matrices may not be filled out properly

1010. Which BEST describes the relationship between a goal and a strategy?

A) Strategy is the plan to reach a goal

B) A goal dictates the strategy

C) Strategy is carried out through goals

D) Goals and strategy are defined in parallel

1011. What is executed when we detect mistakes or intentional failures in following procedures?

A) Audit trail

B) Independent review

C) Exception reporting

D) Supervisory review

1012. Which definition BEST describes a private cloud?

A) The solution is privately hosted but connects across the public Internet into another application

B) The solution is hosted across the Internet and is publicly accessible

C) The solution is privately hosted, but a select few other companies are allowed to access it

D) The solution is entirely hosted inside of a company's intranet and is not accessible externally

1013. Which of the following BEST represents the hierarchy in portfolio management?

A) Portfolio > program > project

B) Portfolio > project > plan

C) Portfolio > plan > project

D) Portfolio > project > program

1014. Which of the following BEST describes a bus topology?

A) All nodes are connected directly to each other

B) A single cable runs the entire length of the network, with nodes all connected directly to this backbone

C) All nodes are connected directly to a central device

D) All nodes are physically connected in a ring

1015. Which of the following is NOT a risk when dealing with end-user computing?

A) The solution will more than likely not encrypt data

B) There may be no secure mechanism to require authentication

C) It could easily increase unexpected training costs as the software is not budgeted

D) There may be no authorization implemented

1016. Which of the following statements regarding incidents is NOT true?

A) A reasonable approach is to assign any new incident a major classification until more information can be obtained

B) A crisis incident should never be assigned to an outage lasting less than 30 minutes

C) Negligible incidents do not have to be documented

D) A major incident can turn into a crisis based on the length of the outage

1017. Which control category makes up for a weakness in another control?

A) Deterrent

B) Corrective

C) Compensating

D) Detective

1018. Which of the following BEST describes a cookie?

A) A marker or address that identifies a document or a specific place in a document

B) The connection between Internet users and the Internet service provider

C) A file that a browser stores on the local computer's hard drive

D) Computers that do not use any type of address translation

1019. Which COBIT 5 intrinsic quality measures how highly regarded the source of a value is?

A) Accuracy

B) Objectivity

C) Reputation

D) Believability

1020. Which BEST describes message modification?

A) Malware that disguises itself as useful program such as a utility, OS patch or game

B) Software installed onto a target computer to steal information or cause further harm

C) Capturing a message in-transit, and modifying, delaying or deleting it

D) Bits of software code left by a programmer to allow them back in at a later date

1021. Which of the following is NOT a risk when dealing with social media?

A) It may increase customer expectations regarding levels of customer service

B) An employee may use a personal account to communicate work-related information

C) It could cache information on the local computer that is deemed to be private

D) Copyrighted material may be posted

1022. Which of the following BEST describes a passive data dictionary?

A) Dictates attributes to be indexed

B) Can be viewed or printed only

C) Provides the capability to validate and format the contents

D) Describes each field's use and characteristics

1023. Which of the following is NOT a valid control for offsite libraries?

A) Backup media must be physically locked up

B) Do not store backups for too long of a period

C) Backups should be encrypted

D) Multiple copies of backups must be maintained

1024. Which is the BEST description of relay-baton?

A) Two equally-qualified people split identical duties and slowly transition one to another position

B) Small portions of knowledge and responsibilities are transferred in phases

C) Two people swap duties in increasing frequency until each is performing the other's job

D) A person watches what another does and asks questions, with a final hand-off on a specific date

1025. Which of the following security planning roles BEST describes a security specialists?

A) Oversees the incident response capability

B) Communicates to other departments such as legal, human resources, and public relations

C) Detects, investigates, contains and recovers from incidents

D) Manages individual incidents

1026. You are auditing and want to make sure that employees are executing their duties in the right manner. What audit technique is BEST suited?

A) Reviewing IS Documentation

B) Reviewing IS Policies and Procedures

C) Review of IS Organization Structures

D) Reviewing IS Standards

1027. It has been 6 months since you delivered a final audit report for a customer, and partner of that customer has asked for a copy of the report to validate compliance. What is the BEST course of action?

A) Decline to provide a copy and refer them to the customer

B) Get approval from the customer's senior management before providing a copy

C) Provide a copy if you prefer, because as the auditor you own all rights to the information

D) Agree to provide a high-level summary of the findings, but refer them to the company if they wish further details

1028. Which is the BEST definition of patch management?

A) Managing change to electronic documents

B) Managing change to a system so reliability and security is maintained

C) Managing change to a system so integrity is maintained

D) Managing change to software that may impact end-users

1029. Which of the following is a valid reason for an OS to isolate two processes?

A) A process should not be able to execute an instruction at the same time as another process

B) A process should not be able to communicate with other processes

C) A process should not be able to access functionality unless it has been explicitly granted authorization

D) A process should not have access to the same memory chip that the OS has access to

1030. Which of the following is an example of 'something you have?

A) A token device

B) A password

C) A fingerprint

D) A voice print

1031. Which is the BEST definition of an SLA?

A) A non-binding contract between two parties that expresses the optimal level of service both are striving for

B) A legally-binding contract between an external provider and the internal department focused on liability mitigation

C) An agreement between a service provider and a service consumer describing responsibilities for each

D) An agreement between an IT organization and the customer detailing the service to be provided

1032. Which COBIT 5 contextual quality measures how up-to-date a value is?

A) Relevancy

B) Currency

C) Interpretability

D) Understandability

1033. When an auditor walks through each process to assess compliance and note any deviations, which control type benefits the most?

A) Procedural

B) Administrative

C) Technical

D) Physical

1034. Which of the following items is NOT a main component of the motherboard?

A) CPU

B) RAM

C) Power Supply

D) ROM

1035. When auditing change management, which of the following areas is NOT an auditor's major concern?

A) Access to program libraries is restricted

B) Coding standards were followed with each change

C) Change requests are approved and documented

D) Supervisory reviews are conducted

1036. Which of the following BEST describes a metropolitan area network?

A) Covers a limited are such as a home, office or even a campus with multiple buildings

B) A network limited to a city or region, but normally offers higher data transfer rates than larger networks

C) Covers broad areas such as a city, region, nation or even an international link

D) A specialized version of a LAN dedicated to storing large amounts of data

1037. Which ISO 27000 role provides an independent assurance to management on the effectiveness of security controls?

A) The auditor

B) Security advisor group

C) Information security administrator

D) Information security steering committee

1038. Which of the following BEST describes in-process client?

A) Runs within containers hosted on another computer

B) A component requiring some type of a host to start and execute

C) An application that exposes parts of itself to be used by other software

D) A service that runs across the network on a dedicated server

1039. Which of the following are NOT a common control to mitigate DSS risk?

A) Meet user needs and embed the DSS process into the company's culture

B) Focus on technical infrastructure as opposed to developing a fan-base

C) Keep the overall solution simple

D) Divide the project into multiple, manageable pieces

1040. Which of the following BEST describes interoperability?

A) Provides users with continuous, reliable and secure services

B) Means an organization can support a mixed network that delivers highly-integrated solutions

C) Occurs when we can connect networks using different technologies or operating at different speeds

D) Allows a network to scale up or to support new services

1041. Which of the following is NOT a type of damage resulting from computer crime?

A) A loss of asset availability

B) Sabotage

C) Blackmail, industrial espionage and organized crime

D) Legal repercussions

1042. Which BEST describes system testing?

A) Exercises the entire solution across multiple systems

B) Exercises a single system

C) Exercises an individual program or module

D) Carries out exercises to ensure that two or more components communicate properly with each other

1043. Which of the following BEST describes the core data warehouse layer of BI?

A) Copies and transforms data into and out of the warehouse format and assures quality control

B) Provides access to the various data sources while at the same time hiding how that data is stored

C) Provides access to operational, external and non-operational data

D) Contains the bulk of interesting data, and is usually a relational database

1044. Which of the following is NOT an area an auditor would focus on when reviewing access paths?

A) The original location of data and who can access it

B) If the data owner has authorized in writing access to data

C) How input data from a user is validated

D) How operating systems within the path are maintained

1045. Which of the following biometric terms best describes a retina scan?

A) Fingerprint and the creases, ridges and grooves of the palm

B) Blood-vessel patterns on the back of an eyeball

C) Bone structure, nose ridge, eye widths, forehead size and chin shape

D) The colored portion surrounding the pupil

1046. Which is the best way to ensure control monitoring is taking place?

A) Review processes with management to ensure all monitoring aspects are covered

B) Observe employees going about their daily routine

C) Make sure the output of logs and audit hooks are in place and being validated

D) Look for documentation that proves the correct processes are in-place

1047. Which BEST describes an unambiguous list of steps required to accomplish a task?

A) Standard

B) Procedure

C) Guideline

D) Policy

1048. Which of the following is NOT a group involved in the creation of a BCP?

A) Support services

B) Business operations

C) Help desk

D) Information processing support

1049. Which of the following BEST describes the systems development manager role?

A) Acts as a liaison between end users and the IT team

B) A manager or director responsible for information used to run a business

C) Plans and executes IS projects, manages the associated budget and reports progress to the appropriate management

D) Responsible for programmers and analysts who implement and maintain systems

1050. Which BEST describes a trap door?

A) Capturing a message in-transit, and modifying, delaying or deleting it

B) Bits of software code left by a programmer to allow them back in at a later date

C) Malware that disguises itself as useful program such as a utility, OS patch or game

D) Software installed onto a target computer to steal information or cause further harm

1051. Which of the following is NOT a metric collected when testing a recovery plan?

A) The number of people required to bring the system up to full capacity

B) The accuracy of data entry and processing cycles at the recovery site vs. normal accuracy

C) The elapsed time for completion of each major component of the test

D) The amount of work performed at the backup site by people and by information systems

1052. Which of the following BEST describes SSH?

A) A third party that provides individuals and enterprises with access to the Internet

B) A network protocol using cryptography to secure command line communication between two networked computers

C) A protocol used to transfer files over a TCP/IP network

D) The standard email protocol on the Internet.

1053. Which of the following is NOT a valid category of debugging tools?

A) Log parsing

B) Memory dump

C) Output analyzer

D) Logic path monitor

1054. Which is NOT an example of an application control?

A) A process that calculates totals for reporting every 30 minutes

B) A service that runs each hour and checks database records to ensure they align with acceptable patterns

C) Validation logic in a web form that prevents a user from submitting the form

D) A backend server process checking incoming EDI feeds

1055. Which framework focuses on SLAs between IT and customers?

A) The Open Group Architecture Framework, or TOGAF

B) Information Technology Infrastructure Library, or ITIL

C) ISO 27000 Series

D) Risk IT Framework

1056. Which of the following is NOT a checkpoint where plan testing should be carried out?

A) At least once per year

B) According to industry standards

C) After key changes in personnel, technology or the business environment

D) After major revisions

1057. Which ISO 27000 role drives security policies, guidelines and procedures?

A) The auditor

B) Information security steering committee

C) Security advisor group

D) Information security administrator

1058. What BEST describes why a Gantt chart is unique over other project presentations?

A) It provides a visual graph of all tasks showing start and end dates, and tracks resources

B) It alone provides the ability for crashing, relaxing and resource leveling

C) It is spelled with two Ts

D) It requires an advanced software package

1059. Which of the following BEST describes white box testing?

A) Rerunning previous tests to ensure recent changes have not broken something that used to work

B) Testing an application with full knowledge of the inner workings

C) Testing that answers the question 'Are we building the right product?'

D) Testing two versions of the same application

1060. Which of the following BEST describes valuable papers and records insurance?

A) Insurance that legally protects a business in case it commits an act, error or omission that results in a loss

B) Insurance that reimburses lost profit as a result of an IT malfunction or security incident that causes the loss of computing resources

C) Insurance that covers the actual cash value of information assets that have been disclosed, or physically damaged or lost

D) Insurance that covers loss from dishonest or fraudulent acts by employees and is most commonly carried by financial institutions

1061. Which of the following BEST describes a compiler?

A) Translates human-readable languages into binary code

B) One-step above binary code

C) Instructions that a computer can understand

D) The intermediate product of changing human-readable language into binary code

1062. Which of the following is NOT an area of risk for image processing?

A) Selecting the incorrect scanners

B) Insufficient storage capacity

C) The lack of proper planning in selecting the right system

D) A redesign of workflows may not be carried out

1063. Which BEST describes the actions to be taken if a CISA-certified auditor does not follow ISACA's Code of Professional Ethics?

A) An investigation may be launched into the certification holder's conduct and potentially disciplinary measures

B) A panel of peer CISA holders may be convened to assess the situation and recommend disciplinary actions

C) A formal statement may be issued requesting that organizations no longer work with the auditor

D) The CISA certification may be revoked

1064. Which of the following statements BEST describes DSS?

A) A framework providing steps to reduce the possible decisions to a point at which each possibility can undergo an extensive analysis

B) An interactive system that helps in making decisions by providing decision models and data

C) A system designed to provide the top few decisions likely to result in achieving business goals by analyzing past performance

D) A series of processes that predict likely future events based on a combination of big data analysis and trends in the organization's industry

1065. Which of the following is the BEST description of ISAKMP?

A) An IPSec mode that only encrypts the IP payload

B) Used to secure IP communication between two endpoints

C) How IPSec manages keys

D) The combination of an encrypted message and the secret key

1066. When auditing IS operations and observing employees, which of the following is NOT something the auditor should note?

A) A work schedule has been established and is followed

B) That controls exist to promote efficiency and to adhere to established standards and policies

C) That adequate supervision is present

D) That controls have been implemented for IS management review, data integrity and security

1067. Which of the following BEST describes gaining access by using brute force?

A) An attack executed across the Internet against web applications

B) Exploiting a small window of time between the time that a security control is applied and the time that a service is used

C) Guessing passwords to gain access to a system by simply rotating through all possible values until the system grants access

D) Capturing legitimate packets passing by on a network, and then sending them back

1068. Which of the following standards is NOT based on XML?

A) XWrap

B) XML encryption

C) XQuery

D) XSL

1069. What COBIT 5 tool is used to capture both the current and future states?

A) Process Assessment Model, or PAM

B) Goals cascade

C) Intrinsic Qualities

D) Process Reference Model

1070. Which definition BEST describes a community cloud?

A) The solution is hosted across the Internet and is publicly accessible

B) The solution is entirely hosted inside of a company's intranet and is not accessible externally

C) The solution is privately hosted, but a select few other companies are allowed to access it

D) The solution is privately hosted but connects across the public Internet into another application

1071. Which of the following is NOT an advantage virtualization can provide?

A) We can easily clone that virtual machine by spinning up multiple copies, all running at the same time

B) We can run different OSs or versions of an OS at the same time on the same host

C) We can share the same physical memory addresses across multiple virtual machines

D) We can easily backup a virtual machine by taking a snapshot, or image

1072. At which OSI layer do we find TCP ports?

A) The Session layer

B) The Transport layer

C) The Presentation layer

D) The Network layer

1073. Which of the following BEST describes a crawler?

A) Information that is being manipulated by end users at their workstation

B) Any information persisted to storage such as hard drives, USB drives, tape backups or in live databases

C) Any information moving around a network or being transferred between two processes

D) Applications deployed to log onto each system and look through the various data stores

1074. Which of the following is the BEST description of tunnel mode?

A) The encrypted payload when using ESP

B) Data added to the header when using IPSec in tunnel mode

C) An IPSec mode that encrypts both the payload and header

D) An IPSec session attribute that dictates various configuration options

1075. What is a common function NOT supported by GAS?

A) Data selection

B) File reorganization

C) Parallel processing

D) Statistical functions

1076. Which TOGAF architecture domain provides a blueprint for systems?

A) Applications

B) Business

C) Technical

D) Data

1077. What is a major disadvantage of a BIA?

A) It is seldom completed due to complexity

B) Assessments tend to be worst-case

C) Some laws prevent its use

D) It almost always requires an outside party

1078. When discussing paths of logical access, which of the following BEST describes a remote access?

A) Enacted by both front-end and back-end systems

B) Represented by physical proximity to a computer

C) Carried out using a local network and can be accomplished even though the user is on a different floor or even a different physical building

D) Carried out across a network, but the user is generally sitting in a location that has not been physically secured and is normally in a different city

1079. Which of the following is NOT a General ISAAS standard?

A) Maintain professional education and skills

B) Exercise due professional care

C) Ensure proper communication with management

D) Remain independent and objective

1080. Which of the following BEST describes a honeypot?

A) A real environment that can be attacked

B) A weaponized IDS capable of aggressively defeating attacks

C) A software application that pretends to be a server vulnerable to attack

D) Appears to be a normal environment

1081. Which approach to risk analysis is BEST used when we need to interject some objectivity without requiring accuracy?

A) Quantitative

B) Qualitative

C) Semi-quantitative

D) Semi-qualitative

1082. In relation to an expert system, which BEST describes a knowledge interface?

A) A list of questions to ask a user until a conclusion is reached

B) A graph of nodes and arcs between those nodes

C) Used to load facts into the knowledge base without requiring a programmer

D) A series of 'if...then' relationships

1083. Which of the following are the five types of anti-malware technology solutions?

A) Switchers, active monitors, cyclic checkers, behavior blockers and destroyers

B) Scanners, passive monitors, CRC checkers, behavior blockers and destroyers

C) Switchers, passive monitors, cyclic checkers, active blockers and immunizers

D) Scanners, active monitors, CRC checkers, behavior blockers and immunizers

1084. What is a predisposing condition?

A) Risks that an insurance company will not cover

B) A scenario which may lead to rapid emergence of new vulnerabilities

C) An existing risk which a business accepts rather than undergo mitigation

D) Risks that are inherent in the industry within which a business lives

1085. What is the BEST contrast between continuous monitoring and continuous auditing?

A) Continuous monitoring an IT function, while continuous auditing is an accounting function

B) Continuous monitoring requires significant hooks to be placed into software, while continuous auditing does not directly deal with software

C) Continuous monitoring is carried out by automated IT processes, while continuous auditing requires a human to make decisions

D) Continuous monitoring creates alerts, while continuous auditing reacts to alerts

1086. Which BEST describes masquerading?

A) Occurs when the attacker waits around while a valid user or machine authenticates itself, and then assumes the authenticated identity

B) The act of sniffing network packets as they pass by

C) Occurs when a computer sends packets that appear to be coming from another IP address

D) The act of modifying data without anyone noticing

1087. Which of the following BEST describes the media management role?

A) Controls industrial machinery spread out over large areas

B) The process of entering information into a system manually, using a batch process or online

C) Controls all information stored on removable media

D) Collects and converts incoming information and ensures the proper distribution to the user community

1088. Which of the following BEST describes the data access layer of BI?

A) Contains the bulk of interesting data, and is usually a relational database

B) Provides access to operational, external and non-operational data

C) Provides access to the various data sources while at the same time hiding how that data is stored

D) Copies and transforms data into and out of the warehouse format and assures quality control

1089. Which of the following BEST describes errors and omissions insurance?

A) Insurance that reimburses the business for expenses incurred in maintaining operations at a facility that experiences damage

B) Insurance that covers the actual cash value of papers and records that have been disclosed, or physically damaged or lost

C) Insurance that legally protects a business in case it commits an act, error or omission that results in a loss

D) Insurance that covers loss from dishonest or fraudulent acts by employees and is most commonly carried by financial institutions

1090. Which type of audit looks at how multiple controls logically function together?

A) Operational

B) Forensic

C) Administrative

D) Integrated

1091. Which of the following definitions BEST describes a distributed environment?

A) Security is under the control of individuals

B) Security is under the direction of IS management, with IS management staff maintaining a close relationship with users

C) Security is under the direction of individuals, but adheres to the guidelines established by IS management

D) Security is under the direction of individuals, but the overall responsibility remains with IS management

1092. According to ISO 25010, which attribute measures a stated level of performance over time?

A) Efficiency

B) Portability

C) Functionality

D) Reliability

1093. Which is NOT something that will impact control strength?

A) If it proactive or reactive

B) If it is preventative or detective

C) If it is manual or automated

D) If it has formal or ad-hoc

1094. Which of the following BEST describes re-engineering?

A) Developing a single system that combines all previous features or multiple systems, but delivered in a more efficient manner

B) The process of updating an existing system by extracting and reusing design and program components

C) Replacing an existing system by starting over from the original specifications

D) Deconstructing two different systems and recreating a single system that provides only the required previous features

1095. What are the phases of a penetration test?

A) planning, reconnaissance, attack and reporting

B) Reconnaissance, planning, discovery, attack and reporting

C) planning, discovery, probing, execution and reporting

D) Planning, discovery, attack and reporting

1096. What are three valid approaches to risk management?

A) OCTAVE, NIST SP 800-30 and Zachman Framework

B) PDCA, CMMI and COBIT 5's Risk Management Process

C) Risk IT framework, NIST SP 800-30 and COBIT 5's Risk Management Process

D) FEA, Risk IT framework and NIST SP 800-30

1097. What BEST describes the two things does testing do for us?

A) Provides proof for stakeholders that changes were implemented correctly and allows us to track changes as they are made

B) Validates that functions work properly and allows us to track changes as they are made

C) Provides proof for stakeholders that changes were implemented correctly and tells us if a change has negatively impacted other areas

D) Validates that functions work properly and tells us if a change has negatively impacted other areas

1098. Which BEST describes a back door?

A) Software installed onto a target computer to steal information or cause further harm

B) Malware that disguises itself as useful program such as a utility, OS patch or game

C) Capturing a message in-transit, and modifying, delaying or deleting it

D) Bits of software code left by a programmer to allow them back in at a later date

1099. What term represents how close two measurements are to each other?

A) Confidence level

B) Precision

C) Population

D) Accuracy

1100. Which of the following BEST describes a deadman door?

A) A control that uses two doors, in which the person entering must close the first door before the second door may be opened

B) Automate logging by electronic and biometric locks

C) The act of a person signing into and out of a physical log

D) Video cameras that capture local activity around a facility

1101. What does PaaS stand for?

    A) Platform as a Service

    B) Presentation as a Service

    C) Product as a Service

    D) Policy as a Service

1102. Which of the following statements concerning WBS is NOT true?

    A) Each WP should not exceed 10 days

    B) All WBS data is housed in the CMDB

    C) Each WP must be unique within a WBS

    D) All WPs must be detailed at the same level within a WBS

1103. You are working on a project which produces many non-tangible results such as increasing certain skillsets in employees. Which project approach to define objectives will work best and why?

    A) WBS, since it is able to schedule the project

    B) OBS, since it simply tracks project components with relationships

    C) WBS, since it simply tracks project components with relationships

    D) OBS, since it is able to schedule the project

1104. Which of the following BEST describes a biometric door lock?

    A) A lock that uses a numeric key pad or dial

    B) A control that uses two doors, in which the person entering must close the first door before the second door may be opened

    C) A lock that uses human characteristics to identify an individual attempting to unlock a door

    D) A lock containing a sensor that requires a magnetic card key, or a chipped card key or token to be placed against it

1105. Which of the following BEST describes a servlet?

    A) A traffic concentration spot

    B) A Java applet or small program that runs within a web server environment

    C) A program written in a portable, platform-independent computer language

    D) An executable, machine-independent software program running on a web server

1106. Which of the following items is NOT something you would expect to find in an information security policy?

    A) How risk will be assessed and managed.

    B) Employee responsibilities for managing security information

    C) The importance in enabling information sharing.

    D) A base list of controls to be implemented by IT

1107. Which of the following is NOT a primary method to improve email security?

    A) Educate employees on the dangers of social media attacks

    B) Properly maintain the email server

    C) Use encryption technologies

    D) Ensure the server meets security policies and guidelines

1108. To ensure that each phase of the SDLC is properly documented, the auditor should look for several types of documentation. Which of the following is NOT one of those types?

    A) An economic breakdown showing actual vs. forecast expenses

    B) A project schedule with highlighted dates for the completion of key deliverables

    C) Goals describing what is to be accomplished during each phase

    D) Key deliverables by phases with individuals assigned direct responsibilities for each

1109. Which of the following BEST describes a help desk report?

A) Checks for data transmission accuracy and errors

B) Tracks the availability of telecommunication lines and circuits

C) Identifies the time necessary for a command entered by a user at a terminal to be answered by the host system

D) Provides a history of problems and their resolution

1110. Which of the following changes would NOT directly impact privacy?

A) A change in the CPO role

B) Updates to the change management process

C) A change in third-parties the company does business with

D) New programs or changes in existing programs

1111. When auditing a life cycle, which of the following is NOT an advantage of a V-model over an agile approach?

A) The auditor's effectiveness is much greater when there are formal procedures and guidelines identifying each phase

B) The auditor has greater capability to help the team to course correct during each sprint

C) The auditor can become involved in the technical aspects of the project based on his skills and abilities

D) The auditor can examine all phases of the project and report directly to management on how well the progress is proceeding

1112. When working with sampling, which one of the following statements is true?

A) If the value of all data points is relatively close, then we can expect less precision, and the larger the sample size will need to be

B) The less confident we need to be in the result, the larger the sample size can get

C) The more confident we want to be in the result, the more we will need to decrease the sample size

D) The more variable the data is, the less precision we can expect, and we therefore need to increase the sample size to get a good result

1113. Which of the following BEST describes a relational database 4GL?

A) A proprietary language also running inside of a database but on an enterprise-scale server

B) A 4GL that generates 3GL code such as COBOL or C

C) A specialized language that can extract data and produce reports

D) A language that can run inside of a database on embedded devices

1114. Which of the following is NOT true concerning site acceptance testing?

A) It uses real data

B) The site is not publicly accessible during this time

C) It executes the same tests as UAT

D) Is happens in the production environment

1115. Which type of audit focused on the discovery, disclosure and subsequent follow-up of fraud and crimes?

A) IS

B) Specialized

C) Compliance

D) Forensic

1116. Which of the following BEST describes the reconnaissance method of resource enumeration and browsing?

A) An attack in which the names, directories, privileges, shares and policies are listed

B) An attack performed by a manual search in software, OSs or add-on utilities

C) An attack that studies the communication patterns on a network to deduce information

D) A methodical approach to identify the software and hardware running in the target's network

1117. Which of the following functions below does the project steering committee NOT perform?

A) Provides qualified representatives who participate in all requirements definition, acceptance and training activities

B) Reviews project progress and holds emergency meetings if required

C) Coordinates and advises

D) Takes corrective action regarding personnel changes, budgets or schedules, changes in project objectives, and the need for redesign

1118. Which of the following BEST describes access rules?

A) An access method in which the user can delegate rights as-needed

B) An access method which gives the user no ability to change the level of access granted to others

C) Data that dictates the rights a user has to specific assets

D) A matrix of users and assets with the permission residing at the intersections

1119. Which of the following BEST describes ISM3?

A) Created in the UK and provides a very hands-on and detailed framework on implementing GEIT

B) A specification for service management that is aligned with ITIL

C) A series of standards that help an organization implement and maintain an information security program, and is the standard to which most companies are certified against

D) A process-based security model for IT

1120. In relation to an expert system, which BEST describes a knowledge base?

A) Data that comes in from a sensor or system that is being monitored

B) Components within a system yet to be loaded with facts or rules

C) Artificial intelligence to infer relationships and arrive at a decision

D) Facts expressed in one of several models

1121. Which is the BEST description of PPP?

A) It encapsulates dissimilar protocols so that two different networks can communicate

B) Achieves higher rates because it uses all available frequencies on a UTP line

C) The first truly digital connection for the masses to travel over copper phone lines

D) A newer technology, it is a switching technology but uses cells instead of packets

1122. What is the most important first step to take to get a handle on asset management?

A) Conduct a visual inspection of the facilities to look for weaknesses

B) Create an inventory list of existing assets

C) Immediately start labeling every new asset with a unique identifier

D) Establish checkpoints to control assets leaving and entering the facility

1123. Which of the following BEST describes a double blind test?

A) Carried out with the full knowledge of staff, and the pen testing team is given information about the network design

B) Executed from within the network perimeter and is designed to reveal risks from ether an internal user, or an external user that managed to get through the network perimeter

C) Requires the pen testing team to execute the simulated attack without any knowledge of the internal system, but internal staff are aware that it is happening

D) Requires the pen testing team to execute the simulated attack without any knowledge of the internal system, and internal staff are not aware that a simulated attack is being carried out

1124. Which of the following statements concerning OOSD is NOT true?

A) It builds a solution by grouping data with procedures

B) An object's data is called an attribute

C) OOSD can be used with most SDLC methodologies

D) An object's functionality is called a method

1125. Which of the following is NOT true of ISDN?

A) It uses circuit-switching

B) It began appearing in the late 1990s

C) It was the first truly digital connection for the masses to travel over copper phone lines

D) The standard has 2 types of channels – a B channel running a C Channel

1126. When dealing with sampling, which term BEST describes the maximum percentage of errors our sample is allowed to have before we call it a mis-fire and do it over?

A) Sample mean

B) Level of risk

C) Expected error rate

D) Tolerable error rate

1127. Which framework BEST helps an organization make improvements in an incremental and standard manner?

A) Balanced Scorecard, or BSC

B) Capability Maturity Model Integration, or CMMI

C) COBIT 5

D) FEA

1128. Which of the following tools is the BEST for managing a portfolio?

A) CMMI

B) BSC

C) PAM

D) COBIT 5's EDM02

1129. Which of the following is NOT a core characteristic of DSS?

A) It concentrates more on efficiency and less on effectiveness

B) It solves problems that are ambiguous and unstructured

C) It emphasizes flexibility and adaptability as the preferred method

D) It combines models and analytics with traditional databases

1130. What is the BEST description of understandability?

A) If it is presented in the same format

B) How easily it is comprehended

C) If it is in the correct language and units and is clear

D) How compactly it is presented

1131. Which BEST describes a deadlock TOC/TOU attack?

A) Occurs when two trusted processes get in each other's way, effectively locking them both up

B) Occurs when an untrusted and a trusted process attempt to access the same physical memory

C) Occurs when the OS and a trusted process attempt to access the same resource

D) Occurs when an untrusted process manages to insert itself in between TOC and TOU

1132. Which of the following is the MOST important aspect of handling incidents?

A) Being able to handle multiple incidents simultaneously

B) Prioritizing incidents to optimize limited resources

C) Being able to quantify the impact of a given incident

D) Having good guidance on how to escalate unresolved incidents

1133. When auditing outsourcing, which of the following should the auditor be familiar with?

A) Management assertions and how well each address the services being provided by the service provider

B) FEA

C) How to obtain the report, review it and present results to management for further action

D) SSAE 16 reports including SOC 1, SOC 2 and SOC 3

1134. Which of the following is NOT a valid inbound transmission control?

A) Use receipt totals to verify the number and value of transactions

B) Use encryption

C) Perform edit checks prior to updating an application.

D) Manage change control for procedures

1135. Which of the following is the BEST description of AES?

A) The most common modern symmetric system

B) Using one key for encryption and a different key for decryption

C) A one-way encryption that results in the same length of ciphertext regardless of the plain text

D) The most common outdated symmetric system

1136. What is the BEST definition of opportunity cost?

A) The cost associated with a failed attempt to invest in a new area due to a lack of in-house expertise

B) The cost of taking advantage of an opportunity that is not within the current growth plan

C) The potential cost of missing an opportunity due to it being outside of the organization's core expertise

D) The cost of not being able to take advantage of an opportunity due to a lack of available resources

1137. Which of the following definitions BEST describes a centralized environment?

A) Security is under the direction of individuals, but the overall responsibility remains with IS management

B) Security is completely under the control of IS management

C) Security is under the direction of IS management, with IS management staff maintaining a close relationship with users

D) Security is under the direction of individuals, but adheres to the guidelines established by IS management

1138. Which of the following BEST describes a data director?

A) Provides translation services between two repositories

B) Provides adapters to connect to both the legacy and new repositories

C) Identifying affected modules and data entities during a data migration project

D) A list of tasks needed to deploy legacy data to production

1139. Which BEST describes compliance?

A) Filing the proper paperwork and credentials to ensure licenses are properly managed

B) Ensuring that applicable industrial standards are adhered to

C) Monitoring and enforcing employee behavior such that it aligns with business goals

D) Measuring policies, procedures and controls to ensure they are being enacted and effective

1140. In OOSD, which of the following statements BEST describes inheritance?

A) Extending a class through another class

B) Duplicating an object

C) The ability of a child instance to do something different than a parent instance would do

D) Extending the ability of one object my combining it with another

1141. Which of the following BEST describes CCTV?

A) The act of a person signing into and out of a physical log

B) Video cameras that capture local activity around a facility

C) Automate logging by electronic and biometric locks

D) A control that uses two doors, in which the person entering must close the first door before the second door may be opened

1142. Which of the following BEST describes a high-interaction honeypot?

A) A weaponized IDS capable of aggressively defeating attacks

B) A real environment that can be attacked

C) Appears to be a normal environment

D) A software application that pretends to be a server vulnerable to attack

1143. Which of the following security planning roles BEST describes a coordinator?

A) Oversees the incident response capability

B) Manages individual incidents

C) Detects, investigates, contains and recovers from incidents

D) Acts as the liaison to business process owners

1144. Which of the following BEST describes cybersecurity insurance?

A) Insurance that protects a business from losses experienced as a result of third-party claims

B) Insurance that covers losses incurred as a result of a network-based attack

C) Insurance that reimburses lost profit as a result of an IT malfunction or security incident that causes the loss of computing resources

D) Insurance that covers loss from dishonest or fraudulent acts by employees

1145. Which of the following BEST describes the security officer role?

A) Ensures the deliverable provides an appropriate level of protection

B) Reviews results and deliverables for each phase to confirm compliance with the stated requirements

C) Acts as subject matter experts for the development team

D) Carries out the tasks that will inform the security officer of how well the system implements proper security measures

1146. What is the best definition of a forward pass?

A) Throwing of the ball in the direction that the offensive team is trying to move

B) Going through each task sequentially until we arrive at the shortest possible time to complete the project

C) Evaluating each task duration to arrive at a final project length

D) Giving the project schedule to the team to finalize

1147. Which of the following is the BEST description of security association?

A) An IPSec mode that encrypts both the payload and header

B) The encrypted payload when using ESP

C) Data added to the header when using IPSec in tunnel mode

D) An IPSec session attribute that dictates various configuration options

1148. What of the following areas of a computer is NOT targeted by malware?

A) The file directory system

B) In-memory page files

C) Boot and system areas

D) Executable program files

1149. Which of the following is NOT a risk when dealing with P2P software?

A) It increases the danger of the business being held liable for copyrighted files

B) It makes the computer's address well-known

C) P2P software often reaches into sensitive folders and leaks information

D) It increases the propagation of malware

1150. Which term identifies the automated evaluation technique that raises red flags when an error or irregularity is encountered?

A) Continuous and intermittent simulation

B) Audit hook

C) Snapshot

D) SCARF/EAM

1151. At which OSI layer do protocols such as UDP and ICMP operate?

A) Layer 4

B) Layer 3

C) Layer 2

D) Layer 5

1152. Which of the following is NOT true regarding testing response and recovery plans?

A) The test should be executed to the point immediately prior to declaring a disaster

B) When a plan appears to be 100% successful, the interval between periodic testing may be increased

C) If a plan is not tested it leaves the business with a false sense of security that it will not fail

D) A third-party should be present to monitor and evaluate the test

1153. Which of the following is the BEST definition of a matrix project organization?

A) Multiple project managers share authority over the project

B) The project manager does not have official authority to manage the project

C) Project authority is shared between the project manager and department heads

D) The project manager does have official authority over the project

1154. Which electronic payment method requires the user to be online?

A) Electronic deposit

B) Electronic money

C) Electronic check

D) Electronic transfer

1155. Which of the following is NOT an item that should be included with an external party contract?

A) Ownership of intellectual property, including works that are created in collaboration with the vendor

B) How disputes will be resolved and under what legal jurisdiction the process will follow

C) Assignability of the contract should be stated

D) If the vendor is allowed to subcontract work on behalf of the organization

1156. Which of the following items is NOT something that should be included in an outsourcing contract when specifying the right to audit?

A) The ability of the provider to sub-contract covered operations

B) What SLAs are in-place to handle incident response, and if they are documented and communicated to all involved parties

C) How auditing is allowed to be carried out

D) The visibility the auditor will have into the provider's internal controls that carry out CIA and preventative, detective and corrective duties

1157. When carrying out a risk analysis using a qualitative or semi-quantitative method, what are represented by the X and Y axis?

A) Impact and Likelihood

B) Impact and criticality

C) Business value and criticality

D) Business value and Likelihood

1158. Which of the following is NOT a reason that BI is becoming more common place?

A) Increasing hardware capacity have brought BI capabilities into the mainstream

B) Organizations are increasing in size and complexity such that massive amounts of data hide the needed answers

C) The drive to find new ways to beat the competition is increasing

D) To meet legal and regulatory compliance

1159. Which of the following is NOT a step an auditor will need to carry out when reviewing software licensing?

A) Review all software contracts

B) Scan the entire network and produce a list of all installed software

C) Become familiar with the list of all standard, user and licensed software in-use

D) Correlate workstation activity with actual users

1160. Which of the following statements is NOT true when discussing biometric system failures?

A) CER is expressed as a unitless number

B) A type 1 error rejects an authorized individual

C) The crossover error rate is the point at which FRR equals FAR

D) A type 2 error accepts an unauthorized individual

1161. Which of the following BEST describes an application server?

A) A server that is dedicated to a single function and normally is not capable of being extended

B) A server that sits between an end-user and a resource, and makes requests to the resource on the user's behalf

C) A server that hosts the software programs that networked consumers utilize

D) A server that stores data and acts as a repository for information

1162. At which OSI layer do we find HTTP browser traffic?

A) The Application layer

B) The Transport layer

C) The Session layer

D) The Presentation layer

1163. When evaluating an alternative processing facility, which of the following actions are NOT recommended?

A) Obtain a copy of the contract with the alternative processing facility's vendor

B) Ensure the contracted level of power and telecommunication capabilities are present

C) Check the vendor's references

D) Review any contract to ensure that all verbal promises are in writing

1164. Which of the following descriptions BEST describes drilling up and drilling down ?

A) Filtering data matching one or more attributes, and then presenting a summary of that data

B) Summarizing data at a high level, and then drilling down into the detail as-needed

C) Looking back in time to see statistics as they used to be within a given time period

D) Cross-matching a single attribute, and then sorting based on time

1165. Which statement below BEST describes the 'man month' dilemma?

A) Subtracting more people does not provide an equivalent reduction in the project timeline

B) Adding more people does not provide an equivalent boost in productivity

C) Subtracting more people does not provide an equivalent reduction in costs

D) Adding more people does not add an equivalent increase in the project timeline

1166. What is the BEST description of interpretability?

A) If it is presented in the same format

B) If it is in the correct language and units and is clear

C) How compactly it is presented

D) How easily it is comprehended

1167. Which TOGAF ADM phase creates the strategy to go from as-is to to-be?

A) Business architecture phase

B) Migration planning phase

C) Implementation governance phase

D) Opportunities and solutions phase

1168. When dealing with network security, which is the most important area an auditor should be concerned with?

A) If the security policies align with the business strategy

B) If a SEIM is in-place

C) Activity logs

D) The ability to examine traffic in real-time

1169. Which of the following BEST describes a blind test?

A) Requires the pen testing team to execute the simulated attack without any knowledge of the internal system, and internal staff are not aware that a simulated attack is being carried out

B) Executed from outside of the network's perimeter and represents an external attacker with no prior knowledge of the network

C) Carried out with the full knowledge of staff, and the pen testing team is given information about the network design

D) Requires the pen testing team to execute the simulated attack without any knowledge of the internal system, but internal staff are aware that it is happening

1170. Which is the BEST source for auditing criteria?

A) As defined by the audit scope

B) Standards internal to the business

C) Well-known standards

D) Standards a specified by ISAAS

1171. What IT risk management level are we operating at when considering if we are complying with laws and regulations?

A) Project

B) Procedural

C) Operational

D) Strategic

1172. Which of the following BEST describes a partial mesh topology?

A) Any combination of token ring, bus or star topologies

B) All nodes are connected directly to a central device

C) All nodes are connected directly to each other

D) A single cable runs the entire length of the network, with nodes all connected directly to this backbone

1173. What is the term for any unauthorized activity interfering with normal processing?

A) Invalid actions

B) System exposure

C) Rogue activities

D) Technical exposure

1174. Which of the following statements BEST describes a data mart?

A) Data distributed to subsets based on time of collection

B) The entire data collection prepared and indexed for real-time filtering

C) A subset of the warehouse carved off to meet a specific need

D) The results of exploring large amounts of data to find patterns and trends

1175. Which BEST describes a trojan horse?

A) Capturing a message in-transit, and modifying, delaying or deleting it

B) Bits of software code left by a programmer to allow them back in at a later date

C) Software installed onto a target computer to steal information or cause further harm

D) Software installed onto a target computer to steal information or cause further harm

1176. Which BEST describes unit testing?

A) Carries out exercises to ensure that two or more components communicate properly with each other

B) Exercises a single system

C) Exercises an individual program or module

D) Exercises the entire solution across multiple systems

1177. In which phase of the Waterfall SDLC do we identify stakeholders?

A) Phase 1

B) Phase 2

C) Phase 3B

D) Phase 3A

1178. Which OSI layer(s)does the TCP Application layer map to?

A) Layers 6 through 4

B) Layers 2 and 1

C) Layer 3 and 4

D) Layers 7 through 5

1179. Which of the following BEST describes piggybacking?

A) A control that uses two doors, in which the person entering must close the first door before the second door may be opened

B) A control used by all incoming personnel and normally monitored by a receptionist

C) Requires that all visitors be escorted by a responsible employee

D) An unauthorized person following an authorized person through a secured entry

1180. Which of the following is the BEST description of CPS?

A) Confirms that an entity is the real owner of a public key

B) Something that tells us how a CA validates authenticity

C) A list of invalid certificates

D) Confirms that you are a real person or company

1181. Which of the following subjects is an auditor NOT expected to understand when auditing information systems?

A) File-layouts

B) Database specifications

C) Object orientation

D) Various encryption algorithms

1182. Which ITIL volume aligns IT with the organization?

A) Service Transition

B) Service Design

C) Service Operations

D) Service Strategy

1183. Which of the following is NOT a recognized benefit of carrying out a BIA?

A) It increases the understanding around loss of a particular function

B) It raises the level of awareness for response management

C) It forces the documentation of the functions analyzed

D) It prioritizes restoration activities

1184. Which BEST describes the purpose of SCM?

A) To spotlight customer relationship concerns in order to increase growth

B) To solve supply management issues by automating routing

C) To allow all links in a chain to communicate in real-time and move to a JIT model

D) To provide a key metric in determining the optimum model for CRM

1185. When dealing with sampling, which term BEST describes is the percentage of samples that may be in error?

A) Expected error rate

B) Sample mean

C) Level of risk

D) Tolerable error rate

1186. Which definition BEST describes a public cloud?

A) The solution is entirely hosted inside of a company's intranet and is not accessible externally

B) The solution is privately hosted but connects across the public Internet into another application

C) The solution is privately hosted, but a select few other companies are allowed to access it

D) The solution is hosted across the Internet and is publicly accessible

1187. Which of the following statements BEST describes spear phishing?

A) The use of an email to trick a specific group of people with highly-targeted content into giving away valuable information

B) The use of an email to trick a person into giving away valuable information

C) Calling someone over a phone and convincing them to give away their password

D) An email appears to come from an authoritative email address but in reality, was sent from an attacker

1188. Which of the following BEST describes a screened-host firewall?

A) A computer that is physically connected to only two private networks

B) An application firewall that uses a proxy server for each protocol

C) A computer that is physically connected to two or more different private networks by multiple network interfaces

D) An application firewall that uses only one proxy server for all traffic

1189. When a computer crime is being carried out, which of the following descriptions BEST describes a target?

A) The computer launching an attack when one computer attacks another

B) The computer being attacked when one computer attacks another

C) A computer used to trick a person into giving away confidential information

D) A computer being used to attack a non-computer

1190. Which of the following BEST describes an internal test?

A) Executed from outside of the network's perimeter and represents an external attacker with no prior knowledge of the network

B) Requires the pen testing team to execute the simulated attack without any knowledge of the internal system, but internal staff are aware that it is happening

C) Executed from within the network perimeter and is designed to reveal risks from ether an internal user, or an external user that managed to get through the network perimeter

D) Requires the pen testing team to execute the simulated attack without any knowledge of the internal system, and internal staff are not aware that a simulated attack is being carried out

1191. Which of the following BEST describes a NIDS?

A) Monitors all network traffic

B) Is installed on a computer and monitors traffic coming into and out of the computer

C) Looks at passing traffic to see if it can detect any attach patterns or unauthorized usage

D) Is installed on a computer and monitors all local traffic as well as network traffic

1192. Which BEST describes the G. Gorry-M.S. Morton framework?

A) A framework that looks at how structured a process is and the level of management that watches over the process

B) A framework that employs a 2-dimensional matrix of maturity and perspectives

C) A framework that focuses on generating family trees

D) A framework that uses prototypes to evolve through each new iteration

1193. Which of the following is NOT an advantage of SSO?

A) It increases security for each application taking part

B) Multiple passwords are no longer required

C) The time it takes to log into multiple applications is greatly reduced

D) Resetting forgotten passwords becomes much easier

1194. Before choosing an audit methodology, what must first be completed?

A) A signed SOW

B) Identification of third-party contributors

C) The definition of scope and goals

D) Preaudit Planning

1195. Which of the following is NOT a recommended step to mitigate crash/restart vulnerabilities?

A) Use a PBX firewall

B) Alter modules to remove embedded passwords if found

C) Carry out crash/restart vulnerability tests

D) Adjust restart procedures so they eliminate the vulnerability

1196. Which of the following BEST describes the steps of computer forensics?

A) Protect data, acquire data, image, extract, interrogate, ingest and normalize, report

B) Protect data, image, acquire data, extract, ingest and normalize, interrogate, report

C) Acquire data, protect data, image, extract, interrogate, ingest and normalize, report

D) Acquire data, protect data, image, extract, ingest and normalize, interrogate, report

1197. What BEST describes overall audit risk?

A) Audit risk = inherent risk + control risk - detection risk

B) Audit risk = detection risk + inherent risk - control risk

C) Audit risk = control risk + detection risk - inherent risk

D) Audit risk = inherent risk + control risk + detection risk

1198. Which of the following BEST describes FTP?

A) A protocol used to transfer files over a TCP/IP network

B) The standard email protocol on the Internet.

C) A standard terminal emulation protocol used for remote terminal connections

D) A third party that provides individuals and enterprises with access to the Internet

1199. Which of the following BEST describes the end user support manager role?

A) Acts as a liaison between end users and the IT team

B) A manager or director responsible for information used to run a business

C) Responsible for programmers and analysts who implement and maintain systems

D) Plans and executes IS projects, manages the associated budget and reports progress to the appropriate management

1200. Which electronic payment method is the easiest to understand and implement?

A) Electronic transfer

B) Electronic deposit

C) Electronic check

D) Electronic money

1201. Which of the following is NOT true regarding awareness training?

A) It starts as soon as new hires have completed the onboarding process

B) Posters, newsletters and screensavers are usually used to reinforce security training

C) Training materials are often administered online

D) It extends to all third-party entities who have any level of involvement with the organization's internal processes

1202. Which of the following BEST describes FM-200?

A) Automated systems are only allowed in dark facilities where no people are present

B) A gas that reduces the amount of oxygen available for a fire to use

C) Releases pressurized gas that removes oxygen from the air, but was discontinued in the 1990s

D) A gas that extinguishes a fire by lowering the temperature of the components

1203. Which of the following BEST describes the security architect role?

A) Designs systems based on user needs

B) Develops and maintains applications that eventually run in a production capacity

C) Evaluates potential security technologies, and establishes security policies and procedures

D) Implements the designs created by a security architect

1204. A control matrix is used to do identify what?

A) A weak level of controls

B) Strong controls

C) The area containing the greatest number of controls

D) Compensating controls

1205. A small company prioritizes cost above all else. Which type of recovery site is the BEST choice?

A) Cold site

B) Duplicate site

C) Warm site

D) Mobile site

1206. What is the BEST description of a major release?

A) A release that addresses a small list of customer complaints

B) A release that contains small enhancements and fixes

C) A release that contains significant changes to existing functionality or the addition of new features

D) A release that prevents significant downtime or impact to the customer

1207. Which BEST describes business process re-engineering?

A) Replacing an existing process by starting over from the original requirements

B) Deconstructing two different processes and recreating a single process that provides only the required previous capabilities

C) A thorough analysis and significant redesign of a business process or management system

D) Developing a single process that combines all previous capabilities or multiple processes, but executed in a more efficient manner

1208. Which of the following is NOT a processing control?

A) Limit checks on amount

B) Duplicate check

C) Run-to-run totals

D) Programmed

1209. What is NOT one of the three things an auditor should do when using an ISAAS guideline?

A) Use it to justify a reduction of scope

B) If departing from a standard, justify it

C) Use it to implement a standard

D) Use professional judgement when applying it to a specific audit

1210. Which BEST describes the difference between certification and accreditation?

A) Certification is carried out by an external party, while accreditation is an internal approval

B) Accreditation confirms acceptability, while certification is the acceptance of the accreditation

C) Accreditation is carried out by an external party, while certification is an internal approval

D) Certification confirms acceptability, while accreditation is the acceptance of the certification

1211. You are purchasing a rather expensive software product for a vendor and want to protect yourself form risk in case the vendor goes out of business. Which of the following is the BEST course of action to take?

A) Ensure language in the purchase contract includes obligations that cover such a scenario

B) Source from two different vendors

C) Put the source code in escrow

D) Require the vendor to provide a copy of the source code at the time of purchase

1212. In case of a disaster, a company needs to be up and running in a backup facility within hours but operates in an area with no close recovery facilities. Which type of recovery site is the BEST choice?

A) Warm site

B) Mirror site

C) Hot site

D) Mobile site

1213. Which of the following BEST represents the steps involved in project management?

A) Initiate, prepare, execute, close

B) Initiate, prepare, execute, monitor, close

C) Initiate, plan, execute, control

D) Initiate, plan, execute, control, close

1214. Which of the following BEST describes a network analyzer?

A) Monitors packets flowing along a link and produces network usage reports

B) Validates that all data sent to a host is returned with no lost data

C) Operates at the data link or network level and often recommend possible solutions to issues

D) Provides a real time display of network nodes and status

1215. Which type of audit is targeted for outsourced services?

A) Specialized

B) Forensic

C) Administrative

D) Financial

1216. What type of segregation of duty control restricts the ability of users to enter data along specific paths?

A) Transaction authorization

B) Principle of least privilege

C) Custody of assets

D) Access to data

1217. When visiting current users of a vendor's product under consideration for purchase, what is NOT an area that is a top priority?

A) Is the vendor responsive to problems with its products, and do they deliver on-time?

B) Does the vendor have reliable 24x7 support?

C) What is the level of customer satisfaction regarding the vendor's commitment to provide training, support and documentation?

D) Is the vendor's deliverable dependable?

1218. Which of the following BEST describes a network protocol analyzer?

A) Validates that all data sent to a host is returned with no lost data

B) A TCP/IP-based protocol that monitors and controls different variables throughout the network

C) Monitors packets flowing along a link and produces network usage reports

D) Provides a real time display of network nodes and status

1219. Which is the BEST description of ATM?

A) The first truly digital connection for the masses to travel over copper phone lines

B) An older technology, it was designed to compensate by adding error checking and correcting as well as fault tolerance, resulting in a high overhead

C) An older technology, it allowed more than one party to share in a single dedicated line across a WAN

D) A newer technology, it is a switching technology but uses cells instead of packets

1220. Which of the following BEST describes audit reduction tool?

A) Looks for a specific sequence of events known to indicate an attack

B) Looks for anomalies in user or system behavior

C) Captures audit trails or logs and performs a real-time analysis on the incoming data

D) Takes raw data and prepares it for a manual review by trimming out records that have no security significance

1221. What term describes the prevention of unauthorized disclosure of information?

A) Confidentiality

B) Integrity

C) Availability

D) Authentication

1222. What term describes the activities a person should accomplish?

A) Informed

B) Role

C) Skill

D) Responsibility

1223. What is the best definition of crashing?

A) Negotiating with stakeholders to alter scope in an effort to reduce the project delivery date

B) Shortening tasks by paying a premium

C) An event that will increase auto insurance premiums

D) An event occurring when two competing tasks consume the same resources simultaneously

1224. Which of the following BEST describes the SMTP protocol?

A) An incoming email protocol with no security and that supports only a single client

B) An incoming email protocol that provides security and supports multiple clients

C) An incoming email protocol designed to work with Outlook

D) An outgoing email protocol

1225. Which configuration provides the best protection?

A) A combination of the signature and statistical models

B) A combination of the neural, statistical and signature models

C) A combination of the neural and signature models

D) A combination of the neural and statistical models

1226. Which of the following BEST describes a DMZ?

A) Uses a packet-filtering firewall and a proxy server

B) Uses two packet-filtering firewalls and an application firewall

C) A public facing server that has been hardened against external attacks.

D) Creates a private self-contained network between the two packet-filtering firewalls

1227. Which of the following security planning roles BEST describes a director?

A) Oversees the incident response capability

B) Communicates to other departments such as legal, human resources, and public relations

C) Manage individual incidents

D) Detects, investigates, contains and recovers from incidents

1228. Which process is BEST used to update an existing process to reduce costs?

A) Root Cause Analysis

B) Benchmarking

C) Business Process Reengineering

D) Balanced Scorecard

1229. Which of the following BEST describes the POP protocol?

A) An incoming email protocol designed to work with Outlook

B) An incoming email protocol that provides security and supports multiple clients

C) An incoming email protocol with no security and that supports only a single client

D) An outgoing email protocol

1230. When dealing with AI systems, which of the following is NOT an area an auditor should be concerned with?

A) Ensure that the proper level of expertise was used in developing the basic assumptions and formulas

B) Review source code management to ensure rule changes have been authorized

C) Review the decision logic built into the system to ensure that the expert knowledge or intelligence in the system is sound and accurate

D) Review security access over the system, specifically the knowledgebase

1231. Which value defines the minimum level of capability that must be restored before normal operations can resume?

A) RPO

B) SDO

C) MTO

D) MTD

1232. Which is NOT a COBIT 5 quality subdimension?

A) Contextual

B) Comprehensive

C) Security or accessibility

D) Intrinsic

1233. When dealing with sampling, which term BEST describes the standard deviation of the entire data set?

A) Stratified mean per unit

B) Unstratified mean per unit

C) Population standard deviation

D) Sample standard deviation

1234. Which statement BEST describes image reputation damage?

A) Protecting a company's public-facing image by suppressing any knowledge of an event

B) Repairing a portrait of the company's founder

C) The prevention of reputation erosion due to market conditions

D) Dealing with an event that will likely cause a loss of trust

1235. Which of the following is the BEST definition of a time context?

A) The method in which a project's value is shared to stakeholders

B) A project's unique communication paths relative to the organization and other parallel projects

C) The intervals between components in which work is not executed

D) The overall project calendar that includes 'pre' and 'post' activities

1236. Which of the following BEST describes a stand-alone client?

A) A service that runs across the network

B) A component requiring some type of a host to start and execute

C) Runs within containers hosted on another computer

D) An application that exposes parts of itself to be used by other software

1237. Which phase of the Waterfall SDLC produces an impact analysis?

A) Phase 2

B) Phase 3A

C) Phase 3B

D) Phase 1

1238. Which of the following is NOT a type of paid licensing?

A) Per seat

B) Per CPU

C) Concurrent users

D) Active users

1239. When auditing a client-server application, which of the following areas is the LEAST important for an auditor?

A) Application controls cannot be bypassed

B) If traffic is encrypted

C) Access to configuration or initialization files is kept to a minimum, and are audited

D) Passwords are always encrypted

1240. What is the primary advantage of using the V-Model SDLC?

A) Development s split into two separate functions – testing and user acceptance

B) As development proceeds testing becomes less granular

C) As development proceeds testing becomes more granular

D) Development is split into two separate functions – testing and validation

1241. Which of the following components does NOT represent mobile code?

A) COM

B) ActiveX

C) VBScript

D) JavaBeans

1242. Which of the following is NOT a valid risk when using RFID?

A) Externality risk

B) Privacy risk

C) Integrity risk

D) Business process risk

1243. Which BEST describes interface testing?

A) Exercises an individual program or module

B) Exercises the entire solution across multiple systems

C) Carries out exercises to ensure that two or more components communicate properly with each other

D) Exercises a single system

1244. Which of the following BEST describes the system administrator role?

A) Defines and maintains the structure of a corporate database, and is the custodian of the company's data

B) Is normally separate from the IT department and reports up through the CISO

C) Responsible for maintaining multi-user computer systems including the network connecting them together

D) Responsible for running the data center, including managing staff

1245. Which BEST describes security testing?

A) Incrementally increasing the size of the database until the application fails

B) Increasing the number of active users until the system fails

C) Looking for a proper level of access controls

D) Simulating a heavy amount of traffic during peak areas

1246. Which of the following BEST describes the purpose of mandatory leave?

A) To determine if a job function is actually required for continued business purposes

B) To detect if the employee on leave has been involved in improper or illegal activities

C) To ensure HR leave policies are being implemented

D) To assess how well an employee has been performing his or her job

1247. Your company's IT function is not very involved with the overall business strategy. What is the BEST solution for this problem?

A) Add the CIO or CTO to the IT strategy committee

B) Request that the board of directors provide a top-down direction to integrate the two

C) Create an IT steering committee chaired by a member of the board of directors who understands IT

D) Bring in an outside party to explore options

1248. In OOSD, which of the following statements BEST describes an object?

A) A parent class

B) Extending a class through another class

C) The ability of a child instance to do something different than a parent instance would do

D) The instantiation of a class

1249. Which of the following BEST describes the MAPI protocol?

A) An outgoing email protocol

B) An incoming email protocol with no security and that supports only a single client

C) An incoming email protocol designed to work with Outlook

D) An incoming email protocol that provides security and supports multiple clients

1250. Which of the following is true?

A) A general control will be more effective than a countermeasure

B) A countermeasure will be more efficient than a general control

C) A countermeasure will be more effective than a general control

D) A countermeasure will be less effective than a general control

1251. When dealing with network continuity, which statement BEST describes alternative routing?

A) Routing information through an alternate medium such as copper cable or fiber optics

B) Providing fail-over systems automatically

C) Subscribing to two or more network service providers at the same time

D) Routing traffic through split or duplicate cables

1252. Which of the following is not a recommended security control for ATMs?

A) A reconciliation of all general ledger accounts should be executed

B) Access to a customer's account after a number of unsuccessful attempts should be implemented

C) Systems should be confirmed to not stored PINs

D) Procedures for PIN issuance and protection should exist, including delivery of PINs

1253. Which of the following is NOT a valid method for multiplexing data?

A) PPP

B) TDM

C) FDM

D) ATDM

1254. Which is normally implemented as file logging?

A) Reconciliation

B) Exception reporting

C) Transaction logs

D) Audit trail

1255. Which best describes decompiling?

A) The process of studying an application or component to see how it works, and then using that information to create a similar product

B) Observing how a system responds to various inputs, and then documenting that behavior

C) Tearing down a system into its original source code and documenting how it works

D) Ensuring a system that has been re-engineered performs properly

1256. Which of the following BEST describes an external schema?

A) How the data is physically stored

B) How the database looks from an external viewpoint

C) How the files are arranged on a single disk

D) How the database sees data being stored

1257. What does a countermeasure do?

A) Provides multiple layers of defense

B) Tracks the value that a control provides

C) Enumerates the number of times a control stops an attack

D) Targets a specific threat

1258. Which of the following statements about auditing the information security policy is NOT true?

A) It should be reviewed when significant changes to the enterprise or risk levels are encountered

B) It should be reviewed at least once per year

C) It should have a defined owner responsible for evaluation

D) The review is performed by executives

1259. Which best describes reverse engineering?

A) Tearing down a system into its original source code and documenting how it works

B) Observing how a system responds to various inputs, and then documenting that behavior

C) The process of studying an application or component to see how it works, and then using that information to create a similar product

D) Ensuring a system that has been re-engineered performs properly

1260. What term describes the inability to deny having sent a message?

A) Confidentiality

B) Nonrepudiation

C) Authentication

D) Availability

1261. Which of the following BEST describes extra expense insurance?

A) Insurance that reimburses lost profit as a result of an IT malfunction or security incident that causes the loss of computing resources

B) Insurance that protects a business from losses experienced as a result of third-party claims

C) Insurance that reimburses the business for expenses incurred in maintaining operations at a facility that experiences damage

D) Insurance that covers the actual cash value of papers and records that have been disclosed, or physically damaged or lost

1262. Which of the following BEST describes in-process server?

A) An application that exposes parts of itself to be used by other software

B) Runs within containers hosted on another computer

C) A component requiring some type of a host to start and execute

D) A service that runs across the network

Random Answers

1. A	2. D
3. D	4. C
5. A	6. D
7. A	8. C
9. D	10. B
11. B	12. A
13. A	14. C
15. B	16. A
17. A (The transfer of physical to electronic currency has been going on for decades)	18. A (The UAT specifications should be thorough and complete)
19. A	20. C
21. B	22. B
23. D	24. A
25. C	26. D
27. C	28. A
29. A	30. C
31. C	32. B
33. C	34. D
35. D	36. D
37. B	38. C
39. C (Rollback steps should ALWAYS be designed in regardless of the expected risk)	40. A
41. D	42. B
43. D	44. D
45. A	46. C
47. B (The fourth component is an administration console)	48. A (The point is not to prove that documentation exists, but documentation could be used to prove the other three)
49. A	50. B
51. A	52. A
53. D	54. D
55. A	56. B
57. B	58. D
59. D	60. B
61. D	62. D
63. C	64. A
65. D (Hard drives should never be stored with any packing material that can cause static, such as Styrofoam)	66. A
67. C	68. D
69. C	70. C
71. A	72. D
73. D	74. B
75. B	76. A
77. C	78. C (While the auditor needs to make sure the right criteria was used in making the decision, the final decision is normally not up for debate unless the process was invalid)
79. C	80. A (An analysis of the selection reasoning should be present, but a detailed analysis is required only for the selected alternative, not those rejected – for those a quick summary should suffice)
81. C	82. B
83. D	84. D
85. C	86. A
87. D	88. D
89. A	90. D
91. B	92. D
93. A	94. B

95. C	96. C
97. A	98. D
99. C	100. A (Since banks forget who sent an electronic payment, no interest can be awarded)
101. D	102. C
103. C (4th generation languages on-procedural and often object-oriented, and while they do offer higher-level functions than binary and assembly, they don't completely replace the need for those languages (and binary code is arguably NOT a language))	104. A
105. B	106. D
107. D	108. A
109. B	110. A (Traditional EDI historically allows more than one partner to participate using a VAN)
111. A	112. C
113. D	114. D
115. A	116. B
117. D	118. A
119. B	120. A
121. B	122. A
123. C	124. D
125. B	126. D
127. A	128. C
129. A	130. B
131. B	132. B
133. D	134. C
135. A (Changes to the application should be reflected in stored CASE product data as well)	136. B
137. C (USB 4.0 does not exist at the time of this writing)	138. B (Each user within an external party must have unique identifiers such as user IDs and passwords must be used)
139. A	140. D
141. C (Basic rate interface, primary rate interface and broadband ISDN are the three base implementations)	142. D
143. D	144. D
145. A	146. A
147. B	148. D
149. C	150. D
151. A	152. C (Change and release management should be aligned and respect each other, but should remain apart as processes to ensure proper SoD)
153. B	154. A
155. B	156. D (ERDs are covered inn Phase 3B)
157. A	158. D
159. A	160. A
161. A	162. A
163. C	164. D
165. B (Under some circumstances, a digital certificate can be redeemed more than once)	166. D
167. A	168. A
169. D	170. A
171. C	172. A
173. D	174. C
175. A	176. C
177. A	178. D
179. B	180. D
181. A	182. A
183. A	184. D

185. C	186. C
187. C	188. B
189. A (Users will be unable to specify the purpose or usage patterns in advance – that is why the prototype model is so important)	190. A
191. D	192. D
193. A (Waterfall requires all requirements up-front, RAD does not produce a reliable deliverable cadence and OOSD is not a development methodology. Scrum is the only viable alternative listed.)	194. A
195. C	196. B
197. A	198. C
199. B (All security patches should be tested before deployment)	200. C
201. C	202. C
203. C	204. B (It uses all available frequencies on a UTP line)
205. D	206. C
207. A	208. B
209. C	210. A
211. B	212. C
213. D	214. C
215. C	216. B
217. B	218. A
219. A	220. C
221. C	222. D
223. C	224. C
225. A	226. B
227. D	228. D
229. A	230. A
231. C	232. D
233. A	234. D
235. B	236. D (There is usually some custom coding required even for purchased software)
237. A	238. A
239. C	240. B
241. A	242. A
243. A	244. A
245. C	246. D
247. C (While a common feature of DBMSs, this capability is not provided by DD/DS)	248. B
249. C	250. C
251. D (The other items should be required non-IT resources and estimated cost)	252. C
253. C	254. B
255. B	256. A
257. B	258. A (A computer-based anti-malware solution is preferred, as network traffic is only one entry point for malware)
259. B	260. A
261. B	262. A
263. A	264. A
265. B (Optical disks are the preferred medium for data banks)	266. A
267. A (The exact opposite is true: If we find ourselves spending too much time handling incidents, then we should look at problem management)	268. A
269. A	270. B

271. D	272. C (This happens in the post-implementation review)
273. B	274. D (SIRS doesn't exist)
275. D	276. C
277. A	278. D
279. C (B2B is the other model)	280. C
281. C	282. B (While an OS does have such a capability as a result of a core protection mechanism, shutting down peripherals is not core function)
283. A	284. D
285. C	286. B
287. D	288. A
289. A	290. D
291. B	292. C
293. D	294. B
295. D	296. D
297. C	298. D (By logging to a separate server, the attacker must own both servers to cover their tracks)
299. A	300. D
301. B	302. C
303. A (While this may indeed impact capacity needs, it is something that will visibly become apparent whereas the remaining metrics can remain hidden if not proactively monitored)	304. B
305. A	306. D
307. A	308. D
309. C	310. D
311. A	312. C (3rd generation languages require input parameters, while many object-oriented 4th generation languages support object properties (or attributes) instead)
313. B	314. A
315. B	316. A
317. B	318. B
319. D (This is a focus for phase 4B, not 3B)	320. D
321. A (Identify personally identifiable information, or PII, that the business processes)	322. D
323. A	324. B
325. B	326. B
327. D	328. D
329. D	330. D
331. C	332. D
333. C (The remaining two are those that assist in faster program development and those that improve operational efficiency)	334. A
335. C	336. A (Input data is fed into an encryption system but is not part of one)
337. D	338. B
339. C	340. D (Employee social media use is a privacy concern and could negatively impact a business, but this is a topic covered under other audit areas)
341. D	342. A (It will have more than two trunk lines that terminate at the PBX; a single trunk line can carry multiple phone lines)
343. D	344. D
345. D	346. A
347. B	348. B
349. C	350. B
351. B	352. A

353. B	354. C (While scope-creep often results in unnecessary features, features that were never asked for by the customer is seldom a problem)
355. A	356. C
357. A	358. B
359. A	360. A (Securing separate and dedicated administrative ports is recommended over disabling)
361. D	362. A
363. B	364. D
365. A	366. C
367. B	368. C
369. A	370. C
371. B (While longer keys provide more security, asymmetric algorithms have no limit on the key length)	372. C
373. B	374. B
375. B	376. B
377. D	378. D
379. C (SLAs operate based on verifiable metrics, and a 'confidence level' is not particularly helpful)	380. D
381. C	382. B (Workstation ID and online access controls are authorization controls, and transaction logs is an input control)
383. A	384. C
385. D	386. B
387. A	388. B
389. D	390. D
391. D	392. C (Although not technically enforced, banks try to 'forget' who created a digital certificate)
393. A (While CPR may revive a human, it is little use to computers)	394. D
395. B	396. A
397. B	398. D
399. D	400. B
401. D	402. C
403. B	404. C
405. B	406. D
407. A	408. B (A utilization report is part of hardware monitoring, but it focuses on resource utilization, not performance metrics. The difference may seem like semantics, but the accepted name of the report is 'utilization report')
409. C	410. B
411. D (The other risks are mistranslated requirements, from within the organization and form the external environment)	412. A
413. B	414. D
415. B	416. A
417. B	418. C
419. C	420. B
421. C	422. D (Business continuity processing is the other important type of insurance)
423. D	424. A
425. C	426. A (Because SSO becomes a single point of failure, reliability is actually decreased)
427. A	428. A
429. B	430. B
431. B	432. B
433. D (The implementation phase follows the testing phase, so it is impossible to verify the final implementation at this point)	434. A

435. B	436. A
437. D (Secure key exchange is a function of PKI, not basic encryption)	438. C
439. C (Key users of the system should be interviewed to determine their understanding of how the system will operate and to assess their level of input into the design of screen formats and output reports)	440. C
441. B	442. C
443. C	444. A
445. B	446. C
447. A	448. B (Firewalls are a network technology and not specific to client-server)
449. A	450. D
451. C	452. A
453. B	454. A (It implements both encapsulation AND framing)
455. B	456. A
457. B	458. D
459. A	460. A
461. C	462. B
463. A	464. C
465. B	466. D (IPX is a network protocol, not a component of PPP)
467. C	468. C
469. B	470. D
471. C	472. A
473. C	474. A
475. A	476. D
477. A	478. D
479. D	480. C
481. A (While the auditor should consume any documentation, the point of this audit is not to force staff to create additional documentation)	482. B
483. A	484. C
485. B	486. D
487. A	488. B
489. B	490. A
491. C	492. C (While this might work with the most secure military facility, it is hardly a feasible step for the average organization)
493. B	494. D
495. A	496. B
497. D	498. A
499. C (It can provide authentication but only by using encryption)	500. A
501. A	502. A
503. C	504. A
505. D	506. B
507. A	508. A
509. B (A BIA is crucial but an IMS does not necessarily warrant a dedicated analysis)	510. C
511. D	512. A
513. C	514. A
515. A	516. C
517. A	518. A
519. C	520. B
521. A	522. A
523. C	524. A
525. B	526. A

527. A	528. C
529. C (QAT normally completes before UAT is authorized to start)	530. B
531. B	532. C
533. C	534. D
535. A (There are two policies recommended – the second is to implement a rule set covering who can access the Internet from within a company's network, what information should be exposed outside of the intranet, and define which networks are trusted and untrusted)	536. C
537. C	538. C
539. B	540. D (The steps are: review the current state, design the future state, write requirements, select vendors, finalize requirements, and create the POC)
541. C	542. B
543. B	544. A
545. A	546. B
547. B	548. D
549. B	550. A (The SDLC methodology does not indicate failure or success, but the company's familiarity and past success with the chosen SDLC will be a good indicator)
551. A	552. B
553. D	554. B
555. C	556. A
557. D	558. A
559. C	560. D
561. A	562. A
563. C	564. A
565. C	566. C
567. B	568. A (Because PERT uses three estimates per task – optimistic, most likely and worst-case – it is the best choice to use when known durations are a risk)
569. B	570. C
571. D	572. D (Only the top-level WBS may represent the final deliverable)
573. C	574. D
575. B	576. C
577. C	578. C (While true, hard-to-understand decompiler results is not an area an auditor needs to be concerned with)
579. A	580. C
581. A	582. A
583. C	584. C
585. D	586. B (Although this is a wise precaution, especially given recent news with Target, this is not a common area an auditor will look into)
587. C (While it is technically possible to send data over a voice line, it would be fairly difficult to execute and slow)	588. B
589. C	590. D
591. A	592. A
593. A (Traditional often EDI does not use any type of credentialed authentication)	594. C (Water detectors in the computer room should be placed under raised floors and near drain holes)
595. D	596. D
597. C	598. A
599. A	600. A
601. B (The best location is on the middle floors of a multi-story building)	602. C
603. C	604. B
605. B	606. D

607. C	608. A
609. C	610. D
611. B	612. C
613. A	614. B
615. A	616. B
617. C	618. A
619. B (It cannot detect sensitive information in graphics files)	620. D
621. D (Parity checking is a data file control)	622. A
623. B	624. A
625. A	626. D
627. B	628. A
629. A	630. C (Neither type is more reliable than the other or provides a different throughput – the difference is the type of data that can be transmitted at the same time)
631. D	632. A
633. D	634. D
635. C	636. C
637. D	638. A
639. D	640. C
641. B	642. A
643. C	644. C
645. D	646. B
647. B	648. C
649. C	650. A
651. A	652. A
653. D	654. B
655. C	656. B (It is actually less reliable than traditional telephony due to latency and bandwidth fluctuation)
657. A	658. D (While job dependencies cannot be removed simply by automating jobs, they can be modeled so secondary jobs are not executed if the primary job fails, reducing errors)
659. D	660. C
661. D (The phases are definition of requirements and service levels, bidding, selection, acceptance, maintenance and compliance)	662. A
663. C	664. D
665. C (The CSU/DSU is a WAN technology)	666. D
667. D (Many companies will outsource the actual evidence gathering and will therefore have no need to maintain this type of equipment)	668. C
669. B	670. B
671. B (While network credentials are used with remote access, their creation falls under more general logical access management)	672. A
673. B (Data corruption is more common when unplugging flash drives, but it is not a factor when using as a long-term storage device)	674. D
675. A	676. C
677. A	678. D
679. A	680. B
681. C	682. A
683. D	684. A
685. B	686. B (The other item to include is who is sponsoring the project)
687. C	688. C
689. C	690. C

691. D	692. C
693. C	694. B
695. B	696. A
697. C	698. D
699. D	700. B
701. C	702. C
703. A	704. D
705. C	706. B
707. B	708. B
709. B	710. C
711. A (The auditor would check to see if the existing privacy policy is compliant, but would not update it)	712. C
713. D (It is one of the older protocols and is not in-use much these days)	714. A
715. C	716. C (Some penetration tests are not considered to be valid unless internal employees remain unaware)
717. B (While it can reduce the number of bugs, it does not eliminate them)	718. B
719. A	720. A
721. D	722. D (Timebox management is an iterative approach that favors early delivery over complete delivery, which allows the scope of each delivery to fluctuate when time and resources are set)
723. B	724. D
725. B	726. D
727. C	728. A
729. C	730. C
731. C (An n-tiered architecture contains 3 or more tiers, so a 3-tier architecture is also called an n-tier architecture)	732. D (Use check digits on control fields is an inbound control)
733. D (Quality is the missing CSF)	734. C (Activity IS heavily logged AND alerts network administrators to the activity)
735. C	736. A
737. C	738. C (They should be inspected at least once per year)
739. B	740. C (While this is true, appliance firewalls have been hardened against such attacks and this risk is minimal)
741. C	742. C
743. C	744. A
745. C	746. B
747. D	748. D (It is a physical layer device)
749. B	750. C
751. C	752. A
753. C	754. A
755. A	756. D
757. C	758. D
759. D	760. A
761. A	762. C
763. D	764. C
765. C	766. C
767. B	768. A
769. A	770. D
771. C	772. C
773. B	774. B
775. C	776. D
777. B	778. C (Source lines of code (SLOC) and function point analysis (FPA) are the two most common)
779. B	780. B
781. C	782. A

783. B	784. D
785. C	786. A
787. D	788. B
789. C	790. B
791. A	792. B
793. B (Any path having slack time cannot be a critical path)	794. A
795. D	796. D (Appliances are less capable than software implementations)
797. B	798. C
799. B	800. D
801. A	802. A
803. C	804. A (The criteria are turnaround time, response time, system reaction time, throughput, workload or capacity, compatibility and utilization)
805. D	806. C
807. C	808. C
809. B	810. C
811. B	812. B
813. D	814. D
815. B	816. C
817. D	818. B
819. B (Optical fiber is smaller and lighter than metallic cables of the same capacity)	820. B
821. B	822. B
823. D	824. D
825. A (Normalization reduces data duplication, while denormalization can increase duplication)	826. D (If no activity in an active session has been detected, the session should be automatically locked or logged off)
827. A	828. B
829. B	830. A (An exception report check is a processing control)
831. A (This is carried out during the post-implementation review)	832. A
833. A	834. D (A legitimate feature is never a backdoor, which bypasses all known security and is intended to be hidden by all but the programmer)
835. D	836. B
837. D	838. B
839. C	840. A
841. D	842. B
843. A	844. A
845. C (The other valid option is use software through the cloud, using a software as a service (SaaS) model)	846. C
847. D	848. B
849. A	850. C
851. C	852. C
853. A	854. C
855. A	856. A
857. D	858. A
859. B	860. D
861. C	862. D
863. B	864. C
865. B	866. D
867. C	868. B
869. C	870. C
871. B	872. A
873. C	874. C
875. C	876. D
877. B	878. B

879. A	880. D
881. D	882. B
883. C	884. D
885. B	886. C
887. C (IM traffic is very light-weight compared to other traffic)	888. C (A source document is an authorization control)
889. B	890. A
891. D	892. A
893. D	894. D
895. C	896. C
897. A	898. B (Segment counts should be in the trailer, while batch and transaction count totals are in the header)
899. D	900. C
901. A	902. C
903. B	904. C
905. B	906. C
907. D (The physical area outside of the ATM hardware is not within of the auditor's ATM responsibilities)	908. A
909. B	910. C
911. A	912. B ('Review the applications covered by the plan' is the missing element)
913. D	914. A
915. C	916. C
917. C	918. A
919. B	920. C
921. A	922. A (There is little evidence that this statement is true)
923. D	924. D (Any change must be explicitly approved regardless of the source)
925. C	926. A
927. B	928. D
929. B	930. D
931. A	932. B
933. D	934. B
935. C (Documents such as an emergency evacuation plans should be available, but a DRP is examined at a higher level than when reviewing environmental controls)	936. D
937. A	938. C
939. B	940. A
941. A	942. D
943. B	944. B
945. A	946. D
947. B	948. B
949. D	950. B (A hash total is a batch control)
951. C	952. B (Fourier transformation is a mathematical concept, not an IDS algorithm)
953. B	954. C
955. B	956. C
957. A	958. B
959. D	960. A
961. C	962. A
963. A	964. A
965. C	966. A
967. C	968. A (While the proper use of controls is covered in this area, it is not a primary goal)
969. C	970. D
971. C (An active tag has a greater communication distance but costs more)	972. C

973. A	974. C
975. A	976. B
977. B	978. A (Portfolio management focuses on BOTH internal and external resources)
979. D (While a partner profile is often required before data may be transmitted, it is not one of the three listed requirements for the EDI system itself)	980. D
981. B	982. C
983. D	984. B
985. D	986. B
987. D	988. B
989. B	990. D
991. D	992. C (It uses virtual circuits so that guaranteed bandwidth is possible)
993. B	994. A
995. A	996. B
997. D	998. B
999. D	1000. C
1001. B	1002. B
1003. B	1004. D
1005. C	1006. B
1007. A	1008. A
1009. D	1010. A
1011. B	1012. D
1013. A	1014. B
1015. C	1016. B
1017. C	1018. C
1019. C	1020. C
1021. C (Social media applications will normally only cache information already publicly available)	1022. B
1023. D	1024. B
1025. C	1026. B
1027. B	1028. B
1029. C (Process must be able to communicate to other processes, accessing memory shared on the same chip is a very common thing as long as physical memory addresses are not shared, and parallel execution is a common feature of modern OSs.)	1030. A
1031. D	1032. B
1033. D	1034. C
1035. B (Coding standards should be followed, but this is not a major concern when auditing change management)	1036. B
1037. A	1038. B
1039. B (Develop a satisfactory support base in both technical infrastructure as well as a fan-base – people who are promoters of the DSS approach)	1040. C
1041. A	1042. A (While it may not make much sense, testing a single system is covered under integration or interface testing)
1043. D	1044. B
1045. B	1046. C
1047. B	1048. C
1049. D	1050. B
1051. A	1052. B
1053. A	1054. A
1055. B	1056. B
1057. B	1058. A
1059. B	1060. C

1061. A	1062. B
1063. A	1064. B
1065. C	1066. A
1067. C	1068. A (XWrap does not exist)
1069. A	1070. C
1071. C	1072. B
1073. D	1074. C
1075. B	1076. A
1077. B	1078. D
1079. C	1080. C
1081. C	1082. C
1083. D	1084. B
1085. C	1086. A
1087. C	1088. C
1089. C	1090. A
1091. C	1092. A
1093. A	1094. B
1095. D	1096. C
1097. D	1098. D
1099. B	1100. A
1101. A	1102. D (Some WPs can be lightly detailed while others can be heavily detailed as long each defines the required work, duration and cost)
1103. B	1104. C
1105. B	1106. D
1107. A (While educating employees is important, it does not directly protect email security – it simply decrease the fallout after security is defeated)	1108. A (An economic forecast is valid, but actual costs is not expected to be available at this point)
1109. D	1110. A
1111. B (The V-model does not have sprints)	1112. D
1113. A	1114. B (Unless this is a brand-new rollout, the site will almost always be live during this activity)
1115. D	1116. A
1117. A (This is a function of user management)	1118. C
1119. D	1120. D
1121. A	1122. B
1123. D	1124. C (Since OOSD is simply a programming technique, it can be used with ALL SDLC methodologies)
1125. D (The standard has 2 types of channels – a B channel running a D Channel)	1126. D
1127. B	1128. D
1129. A	1130. B
1131. A	1132. B
1133. B (FEA is a framework and is not specific to outsourcing)	1134. D (Manage change control for procedures is an outbound control)
1135. A	1136. D
1137. C	1138. B
1139. D	1140. A
1141. B	1142. B
1143. D	1144. B
1145. A	1146. B
1147. D	1148. B
1149. C (P2P itself software is generally trustworthy, but the software a person downloads using the software is not)	1150. B
1151. B	1152. B
1153. C	1154. D (Both electronic money and checks are carried out using digital certificates which can be used offline)

1155. C (Non-assignability of the contract should be stated)	1156. A
1157. A	1158. A (While it is true that hardware has enabled BI, it is not a reason that businesses are adopting it)
1159. D	1160. A (CER is expressed as a percentage)
1161. C	1162. A
1163. B	1164. B
1165. B	1166. B
1167. D	1168. C
1169. D	1170. C
1171. C	1172. A
1173. D	1174. C
1175. D	1176. C
1177. B	1178. D
1179. D	1180. B
1181. D	1182. D
1183. C	1184. C
1185. A	1186. D
1187. A	1188. A
1189. B	1190. C
1191. A	1192. A
1193. A (Individual application security is not impacted)	1194. C
1195. B (If embedded passwords are found, patch the load module to replace them. Authorized manufacturer personnel can be given the new password, if needed.)	1196. A
1197. D	1198. A
1199. A	1200. A
1201. A (It starts with the onboarding process, not after)	1202. D
1203. C	1204. A
1205. A	1206. C
1207. C	1208. B (A duplicate check is an input control)
1209. A	1210. D
1211. C	1212. D
1213. D	1214. C
1215. A	1216. A
1217. B	1218. C
1219. D	1220. D
1221. A	1222. D
1223. B	1224. D
1225. A	1226. B
1227. A	1228. C
1229. C	1230. B (While reviewing source code management does fall within an auditor's description, it is not specific to AI)
1231. B	1232. B
1233. C	1234. D
1235. D	1236. D
1237. D	1238. D (Per workstation, named users and enterprise are the remaining paid license types)
1239. B	1240. B
1241. C (VBScript is a scripting language that runs inside of a browser sandbox, whereas the other options install and execute directly)	1242. C (Confidentiality and availability may be at risk, but risk of integrity of data is very limited as the data is relatively difficult to alter)
1243. C	1244. C
1245. C	1246. B
1247. C	1248. D
1249. C	1250. C
1251. A	1252. C (Systems should not be allowed to store PINs in an unencrypted fashion)

1253. A (PPP is a protocol, not a multiplexing method)	1254. D
1255. C	1256. B
1257. D	1258. D (The review is performed by management)
1259. C	1260. B
1261. C	1262. B